Constructing "Data" in Religious Studies

NAASR Working Papers

Series Editor: Brad Stoddard, McDaniel College in Westminster, Maryland.

NAASR Working Papers provides a venue for publishing the latest research carried out by scholars who understand religion to be an historical element of human cognition, practice, and organization. Whether monographs or multi-authored collections, the volumes published in this series all reflect timely, cutting edge work that takes seriously both the need for developing bold theories as well as rigorous testing and debate concerning the scope of our tools and the implications of our studies. NAASR Working Papers therefore assess the current state-of-the-art while charting new ways forward in the academic study of religion.

Published:
Method Today: Redescribing Approaches to the Study of Religion
Edited by Brad Stoddard

"Religion" in Theory and Practice: Demystifying the Field for Burgeoning Academics
Russell T. McCutcheon

Forthcoming:
Hijacked: A Critical Treatment of the Public Rhetoric of Good and Bad Religion
Edited by Leslie Dorrough Smith, Steffen Führding and Adrian Hermann

Jesus and Addiction to Origins: Toward an Anthropocentric Study of Religion
Willi Braun (edited by Russell T. McCutcheon)

Key Categories in the Study of Religion: Contexts and Critiques
Edited by Rebekka King

Remembering J. Z. Smith
Edited by Russell T. McCutcheon and Emily D. Crews

Constructing "Data" in Religious Studies

Examining the Architecture of the Academy

Edited by
Leslie Dorrough Smith

SHEFFIELD UK   BRISTOL CT

Published by Equinox Publishing Ltd.

UK: Office 415, The Workstation, 15 Paternoster Row, Sheffield, South Yorkshire S1 2BX

USA: ISD, 70 Enterprise Drive, Bristol, CT 06010

www.equinoxpub.com

First published 2019

© Leslie Dorrough Smith and contributors 2019

All rights reserved. No part of this publication may be reproduced or transmitted in any form or by any means, electronic or mechanical, including photocopying, recording or any information storage or retrieval system, without prior permission in writing from the publishers.

ISBN-13 978 1 78179 675 7 (hardback)
978 1 78179 676 4 (paperback)
978 1 78179 677 1 (ePDF)

British Library Cataloguing-in-Publication Data
A catalogue record for this book is available from the British Library.

Library of Congress Cataloging-in-Publication Data
Names: Smith, Leslie Dorrough, 1975– editor.
Title: Constructing "data" in religious studies : examining the architecture of the academy / edited by Leslie Dorrough Smith.
Description: Bristol: Equinox Publishing Ltd., 2019. | Series: NAASR working papers | Includes bibliographical references and index.
Identifiers: LCCN 2018032330 (print) | LCCN 2018053601 (ebook) | ISBN 9781781796771 (ePDF) | ISBN 9781781796757 (hb) | ISBN 9781781796764 (pb)
Subjects: LCSH: Religion—Methodology. | Religion—Study and teaching.
Classification: LCC BL41 (ebook) | LCC BL41 .C588 2019 (print) | DDC 200.72—dc23
LC record available at https://lccn.loc.gov/2018032330

Typeset by JS Typesetting Ltd, Mid Glamorgan

Dedicated to the memory of Jonathan Z. Smith
(1938–2017)

Contents

Introduction   1
"If I Had a Nickel for Every Time ...": Thinking Critically about "Data"
Leslie Dorrough Smith

Part I: Subjects

1. Partitioning "Religion" and its Prehistories: Reflections on Categories, Narratives, and the Practice of Religious Studies   9
   Annette Yoshiko Reed
   RESPONSES
2. A More Subtle Violence: The Footnoting of "the Aboriginal Principle of Witnessing" by the Truth and Reconciliation Commission of Canada   27
   Adam Stewart
3. Categorization and its Discontents   38
   M Adryael Tong
4. Categorizing Contrariety: Narrative and Taxonomy in the Construction of Sikhism   48
   John Soboslai
5. Interrogating Categories with Ethnography: On the "Five Pillars" of Islam   61
   Jennifer A. Selby

Part II: Objects

6. Objects and Objections: Methodological Reflections on the Data for Religious Studies   73
   Matthew C. Baldwin
   RESPONSES
7. The Red Hot Iron: Religion, Nonreligion, and the Material   101
   Petra Klug
8. Surprised by History: Encountering Data in Religious Studies   114
   Holly White
9. Governance and Public Policy as Critical Objects of Investigation in the Study of Religion   127
   Peggy Schmeiser
10. *Negative Dialektik* and the Question Concerning the Relation between Objects and Concepts   136
    Lucas Wright

Part III: Scholars

11 "The Thing Itself always Steals Away": Scholars and the Constitution of their Objects of Study 151
Craig Martin
RESPONSES
12 Scholars and the Framing of Objects 175
Vaia Touna
13 Serial Killers and Scholars of Religion 183
Martha Smith Roberts
14 Caffeinated and Half-baked Realities: Religion as the Opium of the Scholar 192
Jason W. M. Ellsworth
15 On the Seminal Adventure of the Trace 202
Joel Harrison

Part IV: Institutions

LABOR
16 Finding the Devil in Indiana Jones: Mythologies of Work and the State of Academic Labor 221
James Dennis LoRusso
TEACHING
17 Teaching in the Ideological State of Religious Studies: Notes towards a Pedagogical Future 235
Richard Newton
DEPARTMENTS
18 Competencies and Curricula: The Role of Academic Departments in Shaping the Study of Religion 246
Rebekka King
RESEARCH
19 Religious Studies Research in an Era of Neoliberalization 256
Gregory D. Alles

Epilogue

The Gatekeeping Rhetoric of Collegiality in the Study of Religion 267
Aaron W. Hughes and Russell T. McCutcheon

Index 293

Introduction

"If I Had a Nickel for Every Time ...": Thinking Critically about "Data"

Leslie Dorrough Smith

When I was a Ph.D. student in religious studies, I remember contacting a scholar who I thought would be excited about a potential research project that I had in mind. I was toying around with the idea that a certain controversial and politically engaged religious group wasn't as unusual or even as distinctive as scholars often argued. More specifically, while I was willing to acknowledge that the group's emotionally charged, persuasive rhetoric made it influential, I was not so sure that this made it particularly *unusual*—after all, many high-profile groups have these qualities. Yet scholars up to that point had spoken about the group as if it represented an altogether unique beast on some religious landscape.

I was hoping that this scholar would give me some guidance on how I might proceed with my idea (an idea that, as it turns out, would turn into my dissertation, and which would, in different form, eventually become my first book). But when I presented this idea to him, his response was less than enthusiastic. He told me kindly, if rather directly, that what I wanted to study wasn't interesting enough to warrant my attention; it wasn't actual data. If I were to paraphrase him today in the words of my own students, he might have told me that what I wanted to study "wasn't a thing."

Undeterred, I pressed on, committed to the project, and as I have mentioned, it became something much larger. The finished book proposed a new theoretical model to explain why that particular religious group was able to glean tremendous social power. The final chapter—intended to be the "surprise!" moment—featured the culminating argument, which was that this group was not at all unusual when compared to other cultural groups trying to do the same thing, even if they were more successful at achieving their goals. That chapter thus became an analysis not so much of the group itself, but about why the *scholars* who studied the group might have an interest in portraying their data as something so very different, so bizarre, and often, so aberrant. The reason, I stated, was that the group embodied a partisan stance that diverged sharply from the political sentiments of many scholars, and thus I argued that scholars were, under the guise of objective analysis, exercising their own political muscle.

I knew in advance that the thesis had the potential to be unpopular, and I was warned by advisors and colleagues alike that, professionally speaking, I was walking a bit of a tightrope. But as the (largely positive) reviews rolled in, something odd happened: no one seemed to notice the last chapter. As if a major portion of the book had been printed in invisible ink, one review after another spoke about how interesting my rhetorical model was and how well it explained the success of this very persuasive and dangerous (their words) group, and yet there was nary a word about the overarching argument (or the "punchline," as I saw it). The more that other scholars ignored the heart of my argument while highlighting other portions with which they were more comfortable, the more it became apparent to me that they, too, were part of the larger scholarly trend about which I had written. The issue, simply put, was a disagreement over what constitutes legitimate data.

If the classroom often acts as a sort of microcosm of the types of issues that dominate our larger field of academic study, then what its exchanges reveal about the word "data" are quite telling in their relative brevity. This is not to say that such conversations do not happen, but that they often transpire at the level of lip service. We very commonly teach our students about major theories of religion, taking our time to talk about the futility of arriving at any single definition or model. But we often present these models as lenses through which we interpret our data, and in so doing avoid the much harder conversation about what criteria we used to label them as data in the first place.

In a sense, this trajectory is almost inevitable since certain notions of data are embedded in our institutional structures: many of us are hired based on a "tradition" that is our specialty; departments dispense their educational wares through widely accepted terms and conceptualizations of what religion is; and most graduate students know that their success in getting admitted to a particular program (and securing funding) is predicated on presenting a research agenda that their potential professors can recognize as meaningful or intelligible, by which I mean proposals that invoke the aforementioned traditions, movements, or historical phenomena the "religiosity" of which is already taken for granted.

Foundational presumptions such as these have been the analytical focus of the North American Association for the Study of Religion's (NAASR) annual conference for the past several years. In 2015 and 2016, NAASR conference panelists examined how we treat the categories "theory" and "method" (respectively) in the academic study of religion, not just by describing how their many iterations are deployed and function, but more to the point, the politics that inspire this deployment. The 2017 program, which is the basis for this book, continued this line of inquiry by examining "data"—that is, the element that we often take for granted as the central building block of the academy. By considering the mechanisms through which we define and domesticate our data, this volume will examine how such data comes into being, is rendered intelligible in scholarly circles, and reflects the politics of the institutions that make our work possible.

As with NAASR's earlier conferences devoted to "theory" (2015) and "method" (2016), the conversations at the 2017 conference recognized that, when it comes to thinking through the category "data," there is a peculiarly large amount of scholarly conversation in the academy for an unusually small amount of critical application. In fact, Aaron Hughes's choice of title for the book that came from NAASR's 2015 conference proceedings (*Theory in a Time of Excess: Beyond Reflection and Explanation in Religious Studies Scholarship*) indicates the sheer volume of conversations about theory that circulate today and that, yet, are strangely absent in any depth in the things we read and teach. Theory, method, and data, it seems, are words that get engaged in the field with great frequency, but which, for many, do very little to alter the way that scholarship is constructed and used.

Why? While are any number of reasons, I suspect that this ambivalence reveals our discomfort with the fact that scholarship is inherently and thoroughly political. Perhaps this is why the questions we ask in a 100-level undergraduate course are much the same ones with which senior scholars wrestle; there are not answers that do not come without high political stakes, both from the general public and within scholarly circles (as the epilogue will fully elaborate), nor is there a way to discuss the work of religious studies without engaging these very issues. They include: When we say that we study religion, are we studying essences or constructed things? Is there a reality "out there" before we choose to name it? Are religious people's claims fundamentally different than those made outside of a religious context? Should insider interpretations receive special privilege as a matter of respect to those very participants? Is the academy merely the venue through which we conduct our work, or do its principles and structures pre-select what counts as data?

The excess of conversation about the nature of data paired with a paucity of serious application also reveals the discomforts, the shakiness, the instability of the act of scholarship—an admission of our own creative license that many, I suspect, would prefer to otherwise ignore. In his landmark text *Tropics of Discourse*, historian and literary critic Hayden White argued that we have a way of deferring to certain hermeneutical patterns when we conduct our analysis in a way that our data often becomes like a self-fulfilling prophecy. Our anticipation that things happen in such-and-such a way or our presumption that a particular explanatory schema is the "logical" and "obvious" path forward to discuss an event or thing is itself an interpretive process (White 1978: 2), for the very sense that something is noteworthy, causal, or related to something else is often predicated on preconceived assumptions that, themselves, constitute the act of scholarship.

This is why, in White's words, "the data always resist the coherency of the image which we are trying to fashion of them" (White 1978: 1). The things we have selected to study may not "come quietly" (as they say on police shows) in part because they may not represent the cohesiveness or quality that we believe they should. Perhaps we would do well, then, to understand this problem of "excess" as an act of domestication, for one could argue that such excesses reveal an acknowledgement of a particular critical vantage point at the same time that they recoil against its political implications. The middle ground—plenty of talk, little application—seems safest.

For religious studies scholars, one sign of this excess lies in a peculiar rite of passage in scholarship that appears to display a critical awareness of the flexibility of the term "data" at the same time that it indicates the very absence of such a thing. This ritual of which I speak involves engaging, at various points, the words "there is no data for religion," that famous line from none other than the late Jonathan Z. Smith. It is not too much to say that Smith's mark on the field of religious studies has been not only indelible but ground-breaking insomuch as his work represents a significant shift away from a long-established tradition wherein religion was understood as a relatively self-evident phenomenon, the criterion for which was its supposedly sacred character.

This theologically oriented perspective was roundly rejected by Smith, who, as a thinker far more interested in think*ing*—that is, in pondering how scholars think, frame, and conceptualize their objects of study—was one of the first in the field to argue that the scholarly process is, in many ways, an imaginative, inventive act of fabrication, even if for a particular purpose and/or useful function. This oft-repeated excerpt is from Smith's book *Imagining Religion: From Babylon to Jonestown*, and it reads as follows:

> while there is a staggering amount of data, of phenomena, of human experiences and expressions that might be characterized in one culture or another, by one criterion or another, as religious—*there is no data for religion*. Religion is solely the creation of the scholar's study. It is created for the scholar's analytic purposes by his [sic] imaginative acts of comparison and generalization. Religion has no independent existence apart from the academy. For this reason, the student of religion, and most particularly, the historian of religion, must be relentlessly self-conscious. Indeed, this self-consciousness constitutes his [sic] primary expertise, his [sic] foremost object of study ... For the self-conscious student of religion, no datum possesses intrinsic interest. It is of value only insofar as it can serve as exempli gratia of some fundamental issue in the imagination of religion. (Smith 1982: xi)

Smith uttered this phrase in the context of a larger conversation, well known to many, about how the scholar of religion's central task is to both de-familiarize that which is often considered mundane, ordinary, or familiar for the sake of the critical discoveries such a technique allows and, simultaneously, to find points of similarity and commonality in phenomena often thought to be odd, radical, or marginal. But at all points, just as White suggested, Smith is using the observation to signal that, in the sentence, "What do we study?," the object "we" is more important than the subject "what." Put differently, it is we scholars—political, contingent, culturally bound agents—who choose what we deem worthy of our attention. The world is filled with all sorts of random, miscellaneous phenomena, and we are the ones who pick out some of it and put our focus there.

Thus the entire point of Smith's utterance, if one also takes seriously its last few sentences, is to produce a certain self-consciousness in the scholar about the way in which s/he produces scholarship that reveals, at least to some degree, the artificiality of the act. When the reader finds those words mentioned in this present volume, it is my hope that they reflect not just the self-consciousness of which Smith speaks, but also the depth that is so often lacking in these conversations. Indeed, Smith himself once mused about how often this quotation is uttered with relatively little regard for its impact:

If I had a nickel for every time that sentence has been quoted I could have retired forty years ago. But I have to say that sometimes the way the quote is used is de-familiar to me! I wasn't saying we should abolish the term ["religion"], for example. I didn't think I was saying anything very significant when I wrote that. I thought it was a self-evident proposition and I just went on. (Braun and McCutcheon 2018: 71)

If what was quite radical has been domesticated, it is also the intent of this volume to not just reinvigorate that radical edge, but to ask about the forces that continue to motivate the movement away from it. Smith once described his choice of the verb "imagine" in the title *Imagining Religion* as one that involves "an ambivalence as to the status of the endeavor with respect to the fictive and the actual" (McCutcheon 2018: 7). As Russell McCutcheon notes, statements such as these are often subjected to the domestication process by scholars who wish to turn this ambivalence into a certainty by calling something a "cultural construction" even as they treat it as an instance of cultural mediation. Mediation, he notes, is a concept that allows some concept of a "core" to exist, one that is merely altered by different cultural conditions even as it presumes a thing that underlies the altering (ibid.: 10). Acknowledging construction, on the other hand, echoes this critical ambivalence of which Smith speaks: it recognizes a phenomenon at the same time that it also concedes that the act of recognition (and from it, intelligibility, description, explanation, value, etc.) is a selective, contingent one.

This present volume's aim, then, is to resist allowing this conversation about data to continue to hover at the surface. While each contributor addresses these issues through a variety of different topical applications and points of expertise, what they provide as a collection is twofold: first, a reflection on the problems, strategies, and political structures through which scholars identify (and therefore create) data; and second, an examination of the institutions, extensions, and applications of that data.

To accomplish this aim, the volume is organized into four different parts, each of which describes a central aspect of data identification and formation: "Subjects," "Objects," "Scholars," and "Institutions." These first three divisions are spearheaded by a key essay and followed by four responses, all of which consider how the politics of the academy determine the very nature of the things we purport to study. Part IV ("Institutions") examines what these concepts look like as they are applied to and further institutionalized in college and university structures. It, in turn, includes four essays that grapple with how data is conceptualized and deployed in our teaching, departments, research, and labor.

The volume closes with an epilogue by Aaron W. Hughes and Russell T. McCutcheon, who together consider the topic of collegiality and the very real stakes involved in thinking critically about data. The concept of collegiality seems to be an individual, if not interpersonal, matter, and yet Hughes and McCutcheon demonstrate that it is a highly flexible trope that can be deployed at will to sanction scholars and their work when their critical conceptualizations of data (and scholarship, more broadly) infringe upon the prevailing attitudes and orthodoxies among scholars of religion.

Finally, I would be remiss if I did not mention that those oft-uttered words of J. Z. Smith mentioned earlier seem ever more poignant as he died a little over a month after these papers were first presented. While there have been many recollections, tributes, and other sorts of memorials to a person with such a tremendous legacy, many members of NAASR have been deeply impacted by his call for a rigorous self-consciousness. This book is dedicated to his memory.

Leslie Dorrough Smith is Associate Professor of Religious Studies and Director of the Women's and Gender Studies program at Avila University. She is the author of *Righteous Rhetoric: Sex, Speech, and the Politics of Concerned Women for America* (Oxford University Press, 2014) and *Compromising Positions: Sex Scandals, Politics, and American Christianity* (Oxford University Press, forthcoming).

References

Braun, Willi and Russell T. McCutcheon (2018). *Reading J. Z. Smith: Interviews and Essay.* New York: Oxford University Press.

Hughes, Aaron W. (ed.). 2017. *Theory in a Time of Excess: Beyond Reflection and Explanation in Religious Studies Scholarship.* London: Equinox.

McCutcheon, Russell T. 2018. *Fabricating Religion: Fanfare for the Common e.g.* Berlin: W. de Gruyter.

Smith, Jonathan Z. 1982. *Imagining Religion: From Babylon to Jonestown.* Chicago, IL: University of Chicago Press.

White, Hayden. 1978. *Tropics of Discourse: Essays in Cultural Criticism.* Baltimore, MD: Johns Hopkins University Press.

Part I
Subjects

Chapter 1

Partitioning "Religion" and its Prehistories: Reflections on Categories, Narratives, and the Practice of Religious Studies

Annette Yoshiko Reed

Perhaps nothing has more unified the discipline of religious studies in the past fifty years than the practice of historicizing, interrogating, de-bunking, de-naturalizing, relativizing, and otherwise unsettling its very subject. Since the appearance of W. C. Smith's *Meaning and End of Religion* in 1962, the anachronism of the concept and category of "religion" has been revealed and re-revealed repeatedly (Smith 1963).[1] In the 1990s alone, its contingent and culturally bound "origins" were critically exposed in influential works by Talal Asad (1993), Russell McCutcheon (1997), Daniel Dubuisson (1998), and J. Z. Smith (1998). Nor have these celebrated, much-cited, and prominent acts of unveiling sufficed to abate the trend. Recent examples include Brent Nongbri's *Before Religion: A History of a Modern Concept*, published in 2013, and Carlin Barton and Daniel Boyarin's co-authored *Imagine No Religion: How Modern Abstractions Hide Ancient Realities* from 2016.[2]

Each scholar, of course, adds his/her own points of insight, not least because these and other studies on the topic bear different points of emphasis. Some appeal foremost to etymology and genealogy to unmask "religion" as an anachronistic term for periods prior to the Protestant Reformation and European colonialism (e.g., Smith 1963). Others focus more on contextualizing, historicizing, or analyzing the determinative modern settings of its "invention" and institutionalization (e.g., Asad 1993). Still others focus on the task of countering the still-common recourse to its conventionalized usage as if a timeless or natural notion (e.g., Dubuisson 1998), especially for the study of antiquity (e.g., Nongbri 2013; Barton and Boyarin 2016).

Yet the repetition remains notable nonetheless—seemingly akin, at times, to an act of necromancy, whereby the much-vanquished assumption of a neutral, natural, or universal notion of "religion" becomes a specter raised again and again, in part for the sake of being slain again. In this exploratory essay, I take this repetition as an invitation to look more closely at what studies assume and occlude. I am not concerned here with the accuracy or even efficacy of such arguments, nor even with the questions of where the explanatory power of the second-order category "religion" ends and when scholars should turn instead to "native terminology."[3] My concern, rather, is with "religion" as a particularly potent example of what categories can *do*.

Precisely because of the highly reiterative character of the scholarly debate, the category of "religion" provides an especially apt focus for reflecting on the power and limits of categorization as a scholarly *practice*. Notwithstanding the iconoclastic rhetoric of demystification that marks many of the books proclaiming the anachronism of "religion," after all, this very questioning is almost as old as the discipline of religious studies itself (at least in the forms that it is currently institutionalized in North America).[4] Furthermore, the practice of critiquing the category is now quite central to the disciplinary boundary-marking that distinguishes religious studies. That "religion" is *not* a neutral, natural, essential, or universal classificatory rubric is one rare point of consensus connecting specialists from otherwise far-flung subfields and corners of religious studies.[5] And this contention also serves as one of the clearest markers distinguishing those scholars trained in religious studies from those scholars trained in theology, classics, history, South Asian studies, Jewish studies, and so on. No less than the past creation of a taxonomy of "world religions" (on which see Masuzawa 2005), the current critical discourse surrounding "religion" points to the power of the practice of categorization—as constituted, in this case, both by the use of abstractions to order and organize knowledge (and the resultant construction of experts and expertise) and by the localized and particularistic contestation of such abstractions (and the resultant construction of experts and expertise).

The books by Nongbri (2013) and Barton and Boyarin (2016) exemplify the specific role that scholars of the ancient Mediterranean world have taken up within this broader discipline-uniting discourse—that is, the task of culling Jewish, Christian, and Greco-Roman pasts for hints of the prehistory of the modern "invention" of "religion(s)." As with the broader discussion, this task has been pursued largely through a focus on words and their histories, with special attention to the first-known attestations of Greek and Latin terms corresponding to familiar English terms for "religion" and religions. Scholars of antiquity have debated possible precedents for the category and concept of "religion," and they have also debated the precise moments in history when such terms came to mean something akin to what we now call "religion(s)" (e.g., Boyarin 2003, 2004; Rives 2007: 1–53, 202–210; Schott 2008; cf. Boyarin 2018). And so too with identity-labels now commonly understood as denoting specific religious identities, such as "Jew," "Christian," "pagan," and so forth.[6]

These debates have been highly productive. In the process of bringing the specialized study of ancient Judaism and Christianity further into conversation with the rest of the discipline of religious studies, they have helped to shed new light on the changes wrought in and by the Christianization of the Roman Empire in Late Antiquity—as Boyarin (2003), Jeremy Schott (2008), James Rives (2007: 1–53, 202–210), and others have so richly shown. In what follows, however, I would like to approach the issue from a different direction. Rather than looking to specific words that may or may not serve as precedents for the category of "religion" as we now know it in the West today, I would like to reflect on the power and limits of the practice of categorization in relation to other modern and premodern practices of ordering knowledge.

In attending to the practice of creating and contesting categories *as practice*, my interest is ultimately in opening the way for exploring what is "before religion" from a somewhat less teleological perspective. Accordingly, the first part of this essay will reflect on the creation and contestation of "religion" in relation to the power and limits of practices of categorization, and the second part will then turn to consider these same issues through the lens of two specific premodern examples of other practices for organizing those varied types of knowledge that we now study in terms of "religious identity," "religious change," and "religious difference"; for the latter, I shall focus in particular on the practice of creating narratives that remap synchronic diversity onto chronological time, thinking with the contrast between the Pseudo-Clementine *Homilies* and Epiphanius's *Panarion*. Even as I look to specific examples that speak to "Judaism," "Christianity," and "Jewish Christianity," my broader aim will be to draw attention to the current overdependence on word-studies and to signal some of the problems in pursuing such studies in atomized isolation,[7] including but not limited to a myopic focus on those words and approaches that seem most to presage our own understanding of "religion" and the dominant practices in scholarship on it. It may be tempting to look to the past to answer the question of *when* notions familiar to us today came to arise and become prominent; to do so, however, may skew our understanding of past and present alike (Reed 2018: 389–438). Although this essay is preliminary and experimental, I hope at the very least to make a case for attending to the diversity of premodern modes of theorizing, not least as a reminder of the limits of words and practices of categorization to produce "religion(s)."

To the degree that these reflections shall have some practical horizon, it shall be especially in relation to the question of what we can or should *do* when we encounter data that does not fit into our taxonomies of "religion" and definitions of "religions"—such as those materials that fall between the cracks of disciplines because they resist tidy sorting along a bifurcated line of "religion" and "science," for instance, or those tropes or texts that have inspired seemingly endless scholarly debates about their "Jewish" or "Christian" points of origination or influence, or those materials that scholars have shoehorned into clumsily hyphenated "hybrids" like "Jewish-Christianity." Due to the constraints of space, I shall focus here especially on the last. But my suggestion—meant more broadly—is that sometimes the problem may not be either with the material, or even with the anachronism of the category, but rather with the expectations that *we* as scholars habitually bring to the very practice of categorization.

When our data do not fit the taxonomies of our current concepts of "religion(s)," the usual scholarly habit has been to dismiss them as idiosyncratic or marginal, either omitting them from our narratives about the developments of "a religion" or relegating them to footnotes therein. But what happens when we take such cases, instead, as a warning against our scholarly habit of overestimating the power of classification to explain? And what if we also take such cases as an invitation to look to the past with an eye to a broader range of strategies for explaining difference and mapping continuity?

Categorization and the "Invention" of "Religion"

Recent studies of "religion" largely concur that the task of the expert in religious studies is in part—in Nongbri's words—to unsettle the popular "assumption that religion is a universal human experience, a part of the 'natural' human experience that is essentially the same across cultures and throughout histories" (Nongbri 2013: 1). For him, as for Smith (1963) and others before him, the interrogation of the prehistory and history of the word "religion" is central to this task of conceptual correction, foremost because of the problem of its anachronism: it is "common to see even scholars using the word 'religion' as if it were a universal concept native to all human cultures," even though "no ancient language has a term that really corresponds to what modern people mean when they say 'religion'" (Nongbri 2013: 7, 13).[8] Accordingly, the proposed antidote is the illustration "that 'religion' [i.e., as a word and concept] does indeed have a *history*" (ibid.: 7, 154). Just as Nongbri's telling of this history is largely synthetic, so his inquiry is characteristic in its intended result—namely, "the distinction between ancient worlds (in which the notions of religion and being religious did not exist) and modern worlds (in which the ideas of religion produced from the sixteenth to nineteenth century have come to structure everyday life in many parts of the world)" (ibid.: 154).[9] Nongbri's 2013 book is thus characteristic of the broader scholarly discourse noted above, wherein—beginning already with Smith (1963)—the problems in universalizing the concept and category of "religion" are articulated through the tracing of the development of the meaning of the word as we know it today and the identification of those periods before which no such corresponding word existed.[10]

In their 2016 book, Barton and Boyarin make some of the same points. Yet their choice of foci also serves to unsettle one of the main assumptions of the earlier scholarly discourse—that is, the notion that specialists in antiquity contribute to the broader disciplinary discussion of "religion(s)" by using their knowledge of ancient languages and cultures to identify those periods in which the concept was *not yet* present, and/or to pinpoint those moments (e.g., Babylonian Exile; Maccabean Revolt; origins of Christianity; Christianization of the Roman Empire) at which changes took place that would eventually lead to the notion of "religion" as we now know it. What Barton and Boyarin show, however, is that even those Greek and Latin terms that most seem to serve as ancient precedents for our modern notion of "religion"—such as Greek *thrēskeia* and *eusebeia*, and Latin *religio*—elude such interpretation when considered fully within the contexts of the specific corpora in which they occur. Accordingly, their study shifts the discussion so as to reframe the problem of the anachronism of the word "religion" for the study of antiquity, less as an ontological problem (i.e., what is and is not "out there") and more as an opportunity for a perspectival shift—that is, as a push for us, as scholars, to ask "what is possible to *see* when we cease to *look*" for what we expect of "religion(s)" from the common modern notions thereof (Barton and Boyarin 2016: 1).[11]

What Barton and Boyarin (2016) thus resist, in the process, is the temptation to atomize ancient sources in which related words occur and to plot them as a series of points in the line of what is thereby constructed as the story of the development of the concept and category of "religion" as we know it today. And, significantly for our purposes, they do so with an explicit sense of self-consciousness about the particularity of the modern scholarly proclivity for categories:

> ... while *all* language relies on categories and abstractions, in certain complex cultures, particular prestige and faith is put not only in language over direct experience of the world, but particularly in the reification of deductively drawn abstracts even over generalizations derived from observation of particulars. (Barton and Boyarin 2016: 3)[12]

Our own trust in the explanatory power of categorization reflects something of our own culture's concepts of what constitutes knowledge, explanation, and the exercise of expertise. Such concerns may not be universal, but neither are they peculiar to modernity. Rather, one finds something similar—as Barton and Boyarin remind us—also for some elites in the Roman Empire. Accordingly, it is important to take seriously these and other past practices and products of categorization on their own terms, resisting the temptation to read them merely as precedents for our own categories or to plot them as if simply nodes in some univalently teleological trajectory to our present.

Whether or not Jews, Christians, and/or "pagans" in the Roman Empire had any word or concept akin to our notion of "religion," it remains that some of them did share an interest in creating abstract categories and/or totalizing systems of taxonomic distinction to organize and explain their encounters with differences in beliefs about the divine and cultic rites, sites, and structures.[13] In the field of Classics, the intensification of elite Roman practices of classification has been much discussed in relation to imperial power (e.g., Murphy 2004; König and Whitmarsh 2007; Woolf 2011), and among scholars of Patristics and Late Antiquity, their Christian appropriation has also been richly analyzed, especially in relation to the development of heresiology (e.g., Schott 2007; Berzon 2016). In the process, such studies have helped to highlight some of the cultural work that categories and categorization can *do*, making visible what the *longue durée* success of some efforts (at the expense of others) has rendered invisible.[14]

This point perhaps proves particularly pressing for specialists in ancient Judaism and Christianity, for whom the task of categorizing and contesting categories is often taken for granted as if an act of necessary if not sufficient explanation. No end of articles, for instance, have been written about whether this or that text can be labeled with this or that term ("Jewish," "Christian," "apocalyptic," "sapiential," and so on). And no end of articles have been written also debating the anachronism of these very labels—typically with no explicit explanation of what is at stake either in the labeling of texts or in the rejection of certain labels.

In a recent article on "Categorization, Collection, and the Construction of Continuity," I thus attempted to experiment with exploring some alternative approaches (Reed 2017). There, I looked to the outsized place of abstract categories like "apocalypticism" and "mysticism" in scholarly debates about the continuities between Second Temple Judaism, early Christianity, and late antique Judaism. Scholars often note the problems with these categories in relation to the degree to which abstractions and/or anachronisms can shape and narrow our modern perspectives on the past. But something may be missed—I there suggested—when we redress the scholarly habit of categorizing ancient materials into modern categories only by critiquing specific modern categories, tracing their ancient prehistories, and pinpointing the moments of their "invention."

Instead, we might do well to step back and reflect on what we expect categories to *do*—not just for the analysis of this or that ancient text but also for us as scholars. In the case of "apocalypticism" and "mysticism" at least, much of their function has been to naturalize and emphasize some connections and trajectories within and between "religions," and to downplay or efface others. Accordingly, I there asked what might be gained by experimenting instead with alternate analytical foci that highlight different elements of premodern and modern continuity-construction. In particular, I pointed to the practice of anthologizing as one alternate analytical focus, which can serve to redirect our attention to the rich data attesting the many different ways in which continuity and connections have been drawn and re-drawn around what we now label as "apocalyptic" and "mystical" texts, between and beyond "religions," in shifting configurations from Late Antiquity to the present.

Whereas the imposition of modern categories like "apocalyptic(ism)" and "mysticism" highlights some dynamics and naturalizes some connections between texts, a consideration of ancient, medieval, and modern acts of anthologizing shows how these connections are only some of the ways in which continuities were constructed around these same texts during their long histories of transmission. Some of these ways may correspond to what we might expect, looking back from a presentist purview; others, however, frustrate the division of "Judaism" and "Christianity" in what we now take for granted as the distinction between "religions"—and in some cases precisely because they also jar with current expectations concerning the distinctions between "religion," "science," and "magic."

In what follows, I would like to extend this experiment with an eye to the consequences for the power and limits of categorizing "religion(s)." To do so, I shall experiment with yet another alternate analytical focus, which highlights yet another type of continuity-constructing and knowledge-ordering practice—namely, what we might call narrativization, or the practice of ordering knowledge along the axis of time and articulating claims of continuity through the organizational principle of chronology. Like categorization, this is a practice that is common *both* in the ancient materials that we now study as "religions" *and* in how we as scholars now study "religion." As such, it might be an interesting point of juxtaposition, helping to bring our expectations of categories and categorizations into further relief, while also enabling us to reflect more fully on our own practices in relation to a fuller sense of the past.

If Nongbri (2013: 13) is correct that the "universality of religion" still remains "a basic assumption of most work in the Humanities," it is perhaps in part because of the very category has come to be naturalized (at least in North America) by conventionalized rhetoric and common reading habits, but also in part because the very practice of categorizing "religions" has informed the construction of expertise within certain disciplinary domains and institutional structures, especially but not only in academe. In this sense, it stands as a "parade example" of the practices studied by sociologists of knowledge such as Eviatar Zerubavel (1999: 67), whereby such acts of "actively 'sculpting' islands of meaning" come to be perceived as if acts of "simply identifying already-existing natural ones." To assess the current scholarly discourse about "religion(s)," thus, it may be useful to move beyond assessing the word, the classificatory practices surrounding it, and the presumptions thereby smuggled into scholarly analysis. At this point, it may be useful further to ask what is achieved and elided by the very scholarly acts of repeatedly recounting a word's "origins" and recurrently debating the precise moment of its "invention"—or, in other words, by our own acts of creating narratives to try to neutralize and naturalize the particularity of our own scholarly practices.

As noted above, studies from Smith (1963) to Nongbri (2013) have considered "religion" in part to distinguish a premodern past "before religion" from a modern situation in which it is presumed that the term can be applied accurately and descriptively. Whether or not we are persuaded by this or that argument about the precise moment of this "invention," the debate provides another interesting example of the continuity-constructing and knowledge-ordering practices that now naturalize "religion"—akin, in this case, to what Zerubavel (1999: 85) describes as the "social partitioning of the past" through periodization, selective retelling of events, and the bracketing off of "prehistory." As in the case of anthologizing, I would suggest that awareness of our own practices should not serve simply as an end in itself, nor as a self-critique in service of maintaining some mirage of scholarly practice as disembodied or de-historicized objectivity. Perhaps more productive, in my view, is to take such insights instead as an invitation for further analysis of the past and present alike.

As with the practice and products of categorization, the practice and products of narrativization are often taken for granted in relation to what they naturalize about "religion(s)." Something might be learned when we set aside the task of exploring the prehistory and genealogy of "religion" by searching antiquity for the first known attestations of words that so happen to resemble our sense of "religion," and investigate some examples of premodern practices of narrating prehistory and genealogy—including those that dovetail with our modern narratives about the "origins" of "religions" or the "invention" of "religion," but also those that do not.

Narrativization and the Partitioning of Prehistories of "Religions"

Much of my own reflection on problems of "religion" and categorization has been spurred by my work on the Pseudo-Clementine *Homilies*—one of the late antique texts that most infamously resists categorization into any taxonomy of distinct "religions" with mutually exclusive identities and separate lines of historical development. This fourth-century Greek novel, written in Syria in the name of Clement of Rome, claims to preserve teachings of the apostle Peter.[15] The apostle is here made directly to counter many of those contentions that scholars commonly adduce as marking the differentiation of "Christianity" from "Judaism" (see further Reed 2018: 175–254). Here, for instance, Gentiles are not exempt from observing Torah laws such as menstrual separation, ritual purification after intercourse, restrictions on meat-eating, and so on.[16] And, far from arguing that the Gentile Church has supplanted the chosenness of the Jewish people, the Jewish apostle Peter is here used to reveal that the coming of Jesus opened a path for the salvation for Gentiles that is already and still open by Moses and the Torah for the Jews. Those "pagans" who heed what Peter here preaches, thus, are not presented as those who "convert" between "religions" as much as impure people who are purified and return to primordial piety. And, significantly for our purposes, they are never here called "Christians," but rather mostly "God-fearers" and sometimes "Jews."[17]

The Pseudo-Clementine *Homilies* thus blur or resist what are typically treated as the major distinctions between "Judaism" and "Christianity" as drawn through identity-labels and ritual practices in those Christian writings most often used by scholars to define what does and does not count as sources for "the history of Christianity" and as opposed to sources for "the history of Judaism."[18] And so too with history as represented within the Pseudo-Clementine *Homilies* itself, wherein claims of commonality and continuity are positively drawn, not just from Jesus to Peter to bishops, but also from and between them to Moses, Pharisees, and other Jews (Reed 2018: 175–216).

In modern times, the challenges of categorizing the Pseudo-Clementines has been answered mostly through the construction of a clumsy hybrid category, "Jewish-Christianity"—the contents of which are commonly treated as marginal to the histories of both "Christianity" and "Judaism" (i.e., at best a curious late survival of Christianity's originary Jewishness but almost always also an exception to the rule of the development of both "religions" along paths of increasing distinction) (Carleton Paget 1999). It was, in fact, partly to account for this very text that the category of "Jewish-Christianity" was even invented (Reed 2018: 255–294). Not only did the first printing of one of its Greek manuscripts help to catalyze the initial conceptualization of "Jewish-Christianity" by the Deist controversalist John Toland in the eighteenth century, but the rediscovery and critical edition of a second manuscript in the mid-nineteenth century spurred the subfield of modern scholarship on "Jewish-Christianity," as cultivated in the crucible of the Tübingen school (Reed 2018: 264–269, 361–371). And, at least since F. C. Baur (1831), the Pseudo-Clementines have been the main source with which this subfield has grappled when seeking to defuse the seeming paradox of its combination of these two purportedly conflicting "religious identities." Significantly, for our purposes, scholars have largely done so through a historiographical sleight of hand enabled by the rational magic of source-criticism—speculating about hypothetical sources so as to project these late antique texts back into the dialectically Jewish "origins" of Christianity—back into the undifferentiated prehistory, as it were, of "Christianity" as "religion," back when "*all* Christians were Jewish Christians." However the valuation of this connection to prehistory has been configured, moreover, the function has been the same, namely, to bracket these sources as irrelevant for the study of the very period from which they actually derive (Reed 2018: 15–56).

And this pattern continues even today. In the last decade or so, the Pseudo-Clementines have been increasingly re-read in their own fourth-century contexts. Nevertheless, as in the past, these sources remain bracketed off, as if fossils or relics, rendered irrelevant by developments in what are deemed the defining historical developments in Late Antiquity. This defining narrative is no longer one about triumph of "orthodoxy," but rather the story of the fourth century as a seminal moment in the prehistory of the modern "invention" of "religion," as well as *the* decisive era for the separation of "Judaism" and "Christianity" as "religions." Yet the narrative remains told from the same sources, omitting or bracketing the same other sources, with the labeling of some sources as "Jewish Christian" especially enabling such omission.

The problem with scholarly patterns of selectivity with respect to "Judaism" and "Christianity" is an issue that I have elsewhere discussed in some detail (Becker and Reed 2003; Boustan and Reed 2008; Reed 2018). My interest, here, is in the work done by prehistory—both in the current scholarly debate about the category of "religion" (wherein punctilinear narratives of modern "invention" produce a sense of "*before*" "religion") and in the premodern sources that have and have not been used to study it.

Whereas debates about the category, definition, and heurism of "Jewish-Christianity" have run in circles for decades upon decades now without any sense of resolution, a focus on the representation of prehistory, and the narrativization of ritual and doctrinal difference, might be useful as a fresh entry-point into the Pseudo-Clementines as well as serving as an interesting focus for reflecting self-consciously on how critiqued categories can still shape analyses in practice. As is common in a number of late antique sources, the Pseudo-Clementine *Homilies* evoke the image of an undifferentiated past, which is defined as the primordial unity prior to historical time, but also as the common *telos* of all individuals thereafter. In a narrative framed as a series of public sermons to crowds of "pagans" in Tripolis in particular (*Hom.* 8–11), the apostle Peter seeks to persuade his listeners to reject their polytheism, idolatry, and animal sacrifice by appealing to this undifferentiated past and by describing the progression of historical time, by contrast, as a process of ritual and doctrinal differentiation, leading to the multiplicity that now seems so natural to them.

The account includes a number of features common in ancient and late antique narratives about the origins of civilization. For our purposes, the parallels with the reference to prehistory in Epiphanius's *Panarion* prove most useful.[19] Both the Pseudo-Clementines and Epiphanius evoke the beginning of human history as an era before any error, and both trace the beginning of improper commerce with the otherworldly and the resultant spread of sin to the period right before the Flood. And, in both cases, the corruption of differentiation awaits the period after the Flood and especially after the death of Noah. The figure variously called Nebrod and Nimrod, whom both equate with Zoroaster, is central to the development of differences in the ways that humankind worshipped in both as well: for Epiphanius, his reign marks the spread of "every transgression," and the idolatry central to "Hellenism" in particular is here traced to Serug. The Pseudo-Clementines make the same point but in more specific terms, explaining that Zoroaster was killed by lightening, which lead his people to build a temple in his memory and to worship the fire sparked by lightening—whereby, in turn, Persian fire rituals spread also to other peoples, inspiring the development of sacrifice among Babylonians and Egyptians. In the Pseudo-Clementines, moreover, the example of Zoroaster is further presented as exemplary of the lived cycles of memory and forgetting that led, with the passing of time, to the multiplication of deities: here and elsewhere, great men who died are said to be monumentalized, only to have the meanings of their monuments forgotten, and their memorialization drifting over time into the forgetting of the men themselves and their worship as gods—not least because of the exploitation of such moments of weakness and forgetting by self-interested idol-makers and magicians.

For our purposes, these parallels prove interesting for multiple reasons. First, they help to highlight the shared ideas and practices that shaped the Pseudo-Clementine *Homilies* and Epiphanius's *Panarion*—two late antique texts that consolidate a similar set of earlier traditions about the prehistory of what we might call the "history of religion(s)." Both outline a genealogical narrative charting out different stages and processes of differentiation whereby the ritual and doctrinal differences in their present are presented as having emerged from a primordial unity of piety and proper practice, which each then presents as the ideal to which to strive to return, even as they explain how the diversity known to their readers came to be. In sum, points of what we might call "religious difference" are thus mapped along an axis of historical time, such that similarities and differences between the practices of Persians, Egyptians, Babylonians, and Greeks become part of one story, with distinctions plotted out and explained through pinning their points of differentiation from and along the same line. In some senses, then, the practice of narrativizing their similarities and differences might be likened to some of the practices that what we now call "the history of religion(s)" as well.

The two are not alone in this, of course. But what makes this particular pairing especially poignant, for our purposes, are contrasts with respect to categorization. For Epiphanius, the task of categorizing difference is primary, and these moments in the development of early human worship are cited in the process of sorting and labeling different deviating Christian groups and with explicit taxonomic concern for organizing knowledge into abstract categories even for pre-Christian phenomena ("Barbarism," "Hellenism," and so on). The narrative of chronology, in other words, is subordinated to an ultimately synchronic, largely atemporal, and totalizing task of classification. The Pseudo-Clementine *Homilies*, by contrast, outlines its parallel account as a narrative put in the mouth of Peter as an explanation for the present condition of "pagans," grounding his call for their baptism, purification, and embrace of the One God of Israel (Reed 2018: 117–142). Much the same knowledge is here organized, but categorization is notably absent—and may even be actively resisted.

The parallels in content between the Pseudo-Clementines and Epiphanius also prove notable in light of their contrasting modern reception, which has been marked by habits of scholarly selectivity whereby the highly classificatory work of Epiphanius has been used as if a neutral frame to categorize, sort, and analyze texts like the Pseudo-Clementines (and, as a result, to subordinate the first-hand witness of these particular texts themselves to his second-hand reports about the "Ebionites" in particular; *Pan.* 30). When we dismiss this somewhat counterintuitive scholarly habit, however, their parallels also enable comparisons that bring the differences between the two into sharper relief, perhaps also with respect to the limits of those late antique practices of categorization exemplified by Epiphanius.

The mid-fourth-century date of the Pseudo-Clementine *Homilies* puts it well after the "invention" of the category of "Christianity" by Ignatius (esp. *Magn.* 10.1–3), for instance, and well after Tertullian's rereading of "Judaism" as if a commensurate "religion-like" category—and also well into the process of what might otherwise seem to be a dominant sense of "Jewish" and "Christian" as mutual exclusive if not conflicting labels of identity. Yet the Pseudo-Clementines does not describe those Gentile converts made by Peter as "Christian," and no reference is made to "Christianity"; Peter himself self-identifies here as a "Jew," and Clement similarly self-describes as a Gentile who has come to embrace the "law and God of the Jews" (Reed 2018: 117–142). The only time that a possible distinction is raised that is akin to what we might separate as "Judaism" and "Christianity," in fact, it is only to reveal the true unity behind the appearance of difference: the teachings of Moses and the teachings of Jesus are here revealed to be actually the same, and the secret of their soteriological equality is explained to be unknown to some only because of a divine act of occlusion.[20] Rather than producing expertise and claiming authority by claiming knowledge of the taxonomic systems of order that make sense of differences among human beliefs, practices, and so on, the Pseudo-Clementines does the converse, producing expertise and claiming authority by deconstructing divisions to reveal the true unity behind them.

Even here, however, the emphasis falls less on categories *per se* and more on claimed continuities extending along the axis of time. What appears to be different, but is shown to be the same, is the lineage of learning and practice connecting Moses with the Pharisees and the lineage of learning and practice connecting Jesus with his Jewish apostles and their Gentile followers. And, in the process, what we might call "Jewish" and "Christian" difference is left out of its narrativization of differentiation, gathered together instead into the primordial unity of truth.

The Pseudo-Clementines thus resists our "religion"-based taxonomies both in its content and in its own theorization of difference. The latter, however, is perhaps no less telling for its departures from those heresiological modes of classification exemplified by Epiphanius and often heralded as precursors to the modern making of "religion." Both within and beyond the Pseudo-Clementine's narratives about the prehistory, history, and present state of human worship, what is emphasized instead is a set of overlapping binaries. These binaries, in turn, resonate with other modes and examples of categorization before and beyond "religions"—which are perhaps no less widespread, even if not as teleologically tethered to our particular moment in modernity. In the Pseudo-Clementines, for instance, "Jew" and "Greek" remains a defining contrast, albeit redefined so that all those who observe the Law given to them are in some sense "Jews" (Reed 2018: 76–77, 117–142). And this division corresponds to that between ritual purity and ritual impurity, on the one hand, and Israel and the nations, on the other—the former in ways that draw on the levitical laws of the Torah, and the latter in ways that recall what Ishay Rosen-Zvi and Adi Ophir (2011, 2015; also Rosen-Zvi 2016) have recently posited as an early Rabbinic development in the construction of a unified singular sense of "the *goy*."

That the Pseudo-Clementine *Homilies* theorizes the various received binaries that it synthesizes is explicit in its model of true and false prophecy, and especially in the resultant revelation of the common origins of all these contrast—that is, in the contrast of demonic and divine, whereby demons are the inspiration of false prophets, the inventors of Greek *paideia*, and those who are the source of all the ritual and doctrinal error that has proliferated upon the earth since the descent of the fallen angels and the birth of their monstrous sons, whose spirits still enter all those "pagan" bodies who consume of those sacrifices offered to idols in particular. And, for this too, there is ample precedent. Justin Martyr, for instance, similarly tells a genealogy of error in terms of the contrast of demonic and divine knowledge (Reed 2004). And so too with Tatian, in that case mapping the demonic similarly onto Greekness as well (*Oratio ad Graecos* 31, 35, 42).

Seen from one perspective, then, the omission of the Pseudo-Clementines from our narratives about the history of "Judaism," the history of "Christianity," and the prehistory of "religion" serves as a reminder of our habits of privileging those sources that most resemble our own modern scholarly practices. This pattern has often been noted for the longstanding scholarly habit of using Hellenistic-style histories, such as those of Josephus and Eusebius, to create the structuring narratives into which other sources are slotted. And it has similarly been noted for the tendency to downplay those sources that explain the workings of history and the cosmos with primary appeal to demons.[21] To these patterns, we might also wish to add our scholarly habit of using those particular sources that fit best with the categories, concerns, and reading practice naturalized by the modern notions of "religion" and "religions."

Before and beyond "Religion(s)"?

Much attention has been granted, especially recently, to those sources most concerned with categorization between "Jew" and "Christian," and among "Christians," and these are often used as the basis from which to label, sort, and analyze other sources which are either less explicitly classificatory in character or which are classificatory in ways that just do not so happen to map so neatly onto our own desire to find evidence of premodern peoples sorting themselves and others into distinct "religious" identities (i.e., such as in the case of the Mishnah and other early Rabbinic literature, which richly abound in many modes of classification but not in a manner that marks "Christians," for instance, as distinct).[22] In this sense, it is perhaps telling that the same decades that have seen increased concern for questioning categories and subcategories of "religion" have also seen a growth of new interest in heresiology, in general, and especially in those heresiologists, like Epiphanius, who theorize and organize difference through categories, taxonomies, and totalizing attempts at classification.[23] Much has been learned in the process, but it might be worth attending to what texts, trends, and practices are thereby further marginalized.

To attend to the past with an eye to a broader range of knowledge-ordering practices, beyond categories and classification, may perhaps also prove useful for rethinking our own current conversations about the category of "religion"—here too: by looking to what they privilege and to what they efface. Like other narratives that plot difference along the axis of time, our scholarly narratives about the modern "invention" of "religion" create their own sense of an undifferentiated domain of prehistory. In the process, they naturalize our privileging of *some* sources, *some* continuities, and *some* trajectories over others.

Seen from this perspective, when we reflect on what is "before religion" with Nongbri, the term that is perhaps most in need of more interrogating may actually not be "religion" at all, but rather "before." Together with the rhetoric of anachronism, this sense of "before" distracts from the fact that one need not build a time machine to encounter cultures in which this demarcation of "religions" is not primary or meaningful. One need only buy a plane ticket. The narrative, in other words, unintentionally reinscribes a sense of time that is not just problematically linear, but massively and myopically Eurocentric. And this problem too may be one for which we might benefit by relativizing of our own practices of organizing knowledge, not just with an eye to the past but also to the present as well.

Annette Yoshiko Reed is Associate Professor in the Skirball Department of Hebrew and Judaic Studies and Department of Religious Studies at New York University. Her research explores identity and difference among Jews and Christians, especially in Late Antiquity.

Acknowledgments

Earlier forms of this essay were presented at Bowdoin College and Indiana University Bloomington. Special thanks to Shaul Magid, Matthew Chalmers, Jae Han, Jillian Stinchcomb, Aaron Hughes, and Jeremy Schott for feedback and critiques.

Notes

1   The repetition that marks this discourse is also noted by Hughes (2006: 128–129). For other examples see also McCutcheon (2015).

2   To be sure, both Nongbri (2013) and Barton and Boyarin (2016) explicitly acknowledge these and other predecessors.
3   On "native terminology" and its limits see Smith (2004: 134). For some interesting examples in practice, however, see also Campany (2003); Becker (2009).
4   When answering Dubuisson, for instance, Aaron Hughes (2006: 129) observes that that "the theoretical study of religion at least as it has existed within certain quarters in the North American Academy over the past ten to fifteen years ... is highly, one could almost say obsessively, self-critical. Every term or category that our predecessors held dear—for example, ritual and sacred—has undergone interrogation at the most fundamental of levels ... It is precisely this questioning of the tropes, terms, metaphors and genealogies that the discipline has bequeathed to us that is at the heart of the contemporary study of religion. This questioning has been responsible for the shift in the history of religions from the global to the local. One no longer sees monographs devoted to 'patterns' of religion. Instead, one frequently finds studies of a particular text, a set of texts or a particular community, including certain conclusions that may be of use to others working with different data but with similar problematics. The result is that we are slowly calling into question the autonomy of 'religion.'"
5   This is most readily seen in the parallel practice of resisting, relativizing, and/or historicizing the constraint of various non-Christian traditions into the rubric of "religions" (see, e.g., Jensen 1998; King 1999; Girardot 1999; Boyarin 2004; Batnitzky 2011; Josephson 2012).
6   The latter has been pursued most intensely for the words "Jew" and "Judaism" (esp. Greek *Ioudaios, Ioudaismos*—see, e.g., Mason 2007; Baker 2016; Boyarin 2018; cf. Schwartz 2011; Reed 2018: 474–488). See also the 2014 Marginalia forum on *Jew and Judean: A Forum on Politics and Historiography in the Translation of Ancient Texts*. On "Hellenism," "paganism," and "Christianity" as well, see also Boin (2014) and sources cited there, as well as Anidjar (2015) and Reed (2018: 57–84, 117–142, 384–438).
7   David Lambert (2016) makes a parallel point for word-studies in general within Biblical Studies. Following James Barr in noting the degree to which word-studies can smuggle in theological and ideological presumptions under the guise of neutral philology, Lambert extends Sheldon Pollack's call that for "a double historicization ... that of the philologist—and we philologists historicize ourselves as rarely as physicians heal themselves—no less than that of the text," positing the need for "a dialogic engagement that acknowledges current frameworks, while still holding out the possibility for finding meaningful difference (i.e., alternatives to dominant conceptions) in and through ancient texts." My suspicion is that the traditional model of word-studies in biblical studies has invisibly exerted some influence on the current discussion of "religion" as well, not least in naturalizing a largely Protestant approach to history that places the modern scholar in the position of using knowledge of words in ancient languages to unmask error in the present and/or to reveal an authentic or original past.
8   By this modern sense, Nongbri (2013: 7) also means its treatment as if a self-evidently discrete, timeless, and universal "sphere of life ideally separated from politics, economics, and science." And this separation too is here framed—again, characteristically—in terms of a development in time: "the act of distinguishing between 'religious' and 'secular' is a *recent* development" (ibid.: 2–3).
9   I should stress that my aim is not to single out this particular study for any critique, but rather to treat it as characteristic of the broader discourse that it brilliantly summarizes and synthesizes.

10 Notably, Nongbri (2013: 15-24) leaves open the possibility that the term "religion" can be used in study of ancient periods but just stresses that it must be done with self-consciousness that such analysis is redescriptive rather than descriptive for those periods prior the development of the word and concept "religion."

11 Nongbri (2013: 64) also moves in this direction, especially at the end of his chapter on "Some (Premature) Births of Religion" and in the book's concluding comments calls for "descriptive accounts to "what we have been called 'ancient religions' … to be disaggregated and rearranged in ways that correspond better to ancient peoples' own organizational schemes" (ibid.: p. 159). See also now Boyarin (2018).

12 So too with other elites in other settings, even if this proclivity cannot be presumed to be universal *per se*. For this point for China, for instance, see Campany (2003).

13 The potential value of shifting our attention away from the category of "religion" to the very practice of categorization is suggested from parallel moves in the scholarly discourse surrounding other categories common across religious studies. The late twentieth-century critique of the category of "heresy," for instance, has enabled the emergence in recent years of a new concern for heresiology; see now Berzon (2016). My suggestion here is that "religion" might be ripe for some similar reorientations.

14 See further Zerubavel (1999: 67)—there stressing that "when we draw lines and make distinctions, we do so not only as human beings or as individuals, but also as social beings."

15 The Pseudo-Clementine *Homilies* are commonly dated ca. 300-320 CE; this work is extant in the original Greek and probably of Syrian provenance. There is also a second major version of the Pseudo-Clementine romance of recognitions, the *Recognitions*, which is commonly dated ca. 360-380 CE; this version was also originally written in Greek, but now extant in full only in Rufinus's Latin translation (ca. 407 CE). See further now Jones (2012) and Reed (2018).

16 E.g., Pseudo-Clementine *Homilies* 7.8.1-3: "And this is the service he (i.e., God) has appointed: to worship Him only; and to trust only in the Prophet of Truth (i.e., Moses and/or Jesus); and to be baptized for the remission of sins and thus by this pure baptism to be born again unto God by saving water; not to partake of the table of demons—that is, from food offered to idols, dead carcasses, strangled (animals), those caught by wild beasts, blood; not to live impurely; to wash after intercourse with women; for them also to keep menstrual purity; for all, to be sober-minded; to act well; not to do injustice, looking for eternal life from the all-powerful God and asking with prayer and continual supplication that they may win it." See also 11.28-30; 13.4, 9, 19.

17 Clement of Rome, for instance, is here described not as a "pagan" convert to Christianity but rather as one "seduced by a certain barbarian called Peter to speak and act after the manner of the Jews" (*Hom.* 4.7.2)—an assessment with which then agrees, proclaiming the wickedness of the ancestral customs that he chose to abandon (4.8.1, 3, 6; cf. 4.11.1-2) and asserting that "the doctrine of the 'barbarian Jews,' as you call them, is most pious, introducing One as the Father and Creator of all this world, by nature good and just" (4.13.3).

18 For the contrast with John Chrysostom see Côté (2012); for the contrast with Eusebius, see Reed (2018: 175-216).

19 For other points of parallel and contrast with Epiphanius, see Reed (2015; 2018: 143-174).

20 Esp. Pseudo-Clementine *Homilies* 8.6-7: "… Jesus is concealed from the Hebrews who have taken Moses as their teacher and Moses is hidden from those who have believed Jesus. For, since there is a single teaching by both, God accepts one who has believed

either of these. To believe a teacher is for the sake of doing the things spoken by God. And our lord himself says that this is so: 'I thank you, Father of heaven and earth, because you have concealed these things from the wise and prudent, and you have revealed them to sucking babes' (Mt 11:25/Lk 10:21). Thus God Himself has concealed a teacher from some (i.e., Jews), who foreknew what they should do, and He has revealed [him] to others (i.e., Gentiles), who are ignorant about what they should do. Neither, therefore, are the Hebrews condemned on account of their ignorance of Jesus, by reason of Him who has concealed him, if, doing the things commanded by Moses, they do not hate him whom they do not know. Neither are those from among the Gentiles condemned, who know not Moses on account of Him who hath concealed him, provided that these also, doing the things spoken by Jesus, do not hate him whom they do not know."

21 Bruce Lincoln (2012: 31) nicely makes the point for demonology: "it was—and remains—a major part of many religions and cultures ... [but] the topic has received less scholarly attention than one might expect. The bases of demonological discourse having been discredited during the Enlightenment, it would seem the topic has been drained of all save antiquarian interest. With few exceptions, most studies are condescending in tone and superficial in their engagement, as if reflecting residual anxiety that such foolishness might be contagious or—a less magical construction of the same dynamic—that evincing too much interest can damage one's reputation."

22 For this point on Rabbinic literature, see references and discussion in Reed (2018: 57–84, 389–438).

23 Esp. Berzon (2016); Kim (2015); Jacobs (2016). Notably, as Matthew Chalmers has noted, Epiphanius has attracted much attention recently, even to the neglect of those writers like Origen who loom so large in earlier studies of heresiology like A. Le Boulluec (1985).

References

Anidjar, Gil. 2015. "Christianity, Christianities, Christian." *Journal of Religious and Political Practice* 1: 39–46. https://doi.org/10.1080/20566093.2015.1047687

Asad, Talal. 1993. *Genealogies of Religion*. Baltimore, MD: Johns Hopkins University Press.

Baker, Cynthia M. 2016. *Jew*. Key Words in Jewish Studies. New Brunswick, NJ: Rutgers University Press. Barton, C. and D. Boyarin. 2016. *Imagine No Religion: How Modern Abstractions Hide Ancient Realities*. New York: Fordham University Press. https://doi.org/10.2307/j.ctt1dfnt8f

Batnitzky, Leora. 2011. *How Judaism became a Religion*. Princeton, NJ: Princeton University Press. https://doi.org/10.1515/9781400839711

Baur, Ferdinand Christian. 1831. "Die Christuspartei in der korinthischen Gemeide, der Gegensatz des petrinischen und paulischen Christentums in der alten Kirche, der Apostel Petrus in Rom." *Tübinger Zeitschrift fur Theologie* 4: 61–206.

Becker, Adam H. 2009. "Martyrdom, Religious Difference, and 'Fear' as a Category of Piety in the Sasanian Empire." *Journal of Late Antiquity* 2(2): 300–336. https://doi.org/10.1353/jla.0.0045

Becker, Adam H., and Annette Y. Reed (eds.). 2003. *The Ways that Never Parted: Jews and Christians in Late Antiquity and the Early Middle Ages*. Texts and Studies in Ancient Judaism 95. Tübingen: Mohr Siebeck.

Berzon, T. 2016. *Classifying Christians: Ethnography, Heresiology and the Limits of Knowledge in Late Antiquity*. Berkeley, CA: University of California Press. https://doi.org/10.1525/california/9780520284265.001.0001

Boin, Douglas. 2014. "Hellenistic 'Judaism' and the Social Origins of the 'Pagan-Christian' Debate." *Journal of Early Christian Studies* 22: 167–196. https://doi.org/10.1353/earl.2014.0017

Boustan, Ra'anan S., and Annette Y. Reed, 2008. "Blood and Atonement in the Pseudo-Clementines and *The Story of the Ten Martyrs*: The Problem of Selectivity in the Study of Judaism and Christianity." *Henoch* 30(2): 111–142.

Boyarin, Daniel. 2003. "Semantic Differences; Or, 'Judaism/Christianity.'" In A. H. Becker and A. Y. Reed (eds.), *The Ways that Never Parted*, 65–85. Texts and Studies in Ancient Judaism 95. Tübingen: Mohr Siebeck.

Boyarin, Daniel. 2004. *Border Lines*. Divinations. Philadelphia, PA: University of Pennsylvania Press.

Boyarin, Daniel. 2018. *Judaism*. Key Words in Jewish Studies. New Brunswick, NJ: Rutgers University Press.

Campany, R. F. 2003. "On the Very Idea of Religions (In the Modern West and in Early Medieval China)." *History of Religions* 42: 287–319. https://doi.org/10.1086/378757

Carleton Paget, J. 1999. "Jewish Christianity." In William Horbury, W. D. Davies, and John Sturdy (eds.), *The Cambridge History of Judaism*, vol. 3: *The Early Roman Period*, 733–742. Cambridge: Cambridge University Press.

Côté, D. 2012. "Le problème de l'identité religieuse dans la Syrie du IVe siècle: Le cas des Pseudo-Clémentines et de l'Adversus Judaeos de S. Jean Chrysostome." In Simon Claude Mimouni and Bernard Pouderon (eds.), *La croisée des chemins revisitée: Quand l'Église et la Synagogue se sont-elles distinguées?*, 339–370. Paris: Cerf.

Dubuisson, Daniel. 1998. *L'Occident et la religion: Mythes, science et idéologie*. Brussels: Editiones Complexe.

Girardot, N. J. 1999. "Finding the Way: James Legge and the Victorian Invention of Taoism." *Religion* 29: 107–121. https://doi.org/10.1006/reli.1999.0187

Hughes, Aaron W. 2006. "Haven't We Been Here Before? Rehabilitating 'Religion' in Light of Dubuisson's Critique." *Religion* 36: 127–131.

Jacobs, Andrew S. 2016. *Epiphanius of Cyprus: A Cultural Biography of Late Antiquity*. Christianity in Late Antiquity Series. Berkeley, CA: University of California Press. https://doi.org/10.1525/california/9780520291126.001.0001

Jensen, L. M. 1998. *Manufacturing Confucianism: Chinese Traditions and Universal Civilization*. Durham, NC: Duke University Press.

Jones, F. Stanley. 2012. *Pseudoclementina Elchasaiticaque inter Judaeochristiana: Collected Studies*. Leuven: Peeters.

Josephson, J. A. 2012. *The Invention of Religion in Japan*. Chicago, IL: University of Chicago Press. https://doi.org/10.7208/chicago/9780226412351.001.0001

Kim, Young. 2015. *Epiphanius of Cyprus: Imagining an Orthodox World*. Ann Arbor, MI: University of Michigan Press. https://doi.org/10.3998/mpub.7588638

King, R. 1999. "Orientalism and the Modern Myth of Hinduism." *Numen* 46: 146–186. https://doi.org/10.1163/1568527991517950

König J. and T. Whitmarsh (eds.). 2007. *Ordering Knowledge in the Roman Empire*. Cambridge: Cambridge University Press. https://doi.org/10.1017/CBO9780511551062

Lambert, David. 2016. "Refreshing Philology: James Barr, Supersessionism, and the State of Biblical Words." *Biblical Interpretation* 24: 332–356. https://doi.org/10.1163/15685152-00243p03

Le Boulluec, Alain. 1985. *La notion d'hérésie dans la literature grecque IIe-IIIe siècles*. 2 volumes. Paris: Études augustiniennes.

Lincoln, Bruce. 2012. *Gods and Demons, Priests and Scholars: Critical Explorations in the History of Religions*. Chicago, IL: University of Chicago Press. https://doi.org/10.7208/chicago/9780226035161.001.0001

Mason, Steve. 2007. "Jews, Judaeans, Judaizing, Judaism: Problems of Categorization in Ancient History." *Journal for the Study of Judaism* 38: 457–512. https://doi.org/10.1163/156851507X193108

Masuzawa, Tomoko. 2005. *The Invention of World Religions: Or, How European. Universalism Was Preserved in the Language of Pluralism.* Chicago, IL: University of Chicago. https://doi.org/10.7208/chicago/9780226922621.001.0001

McCutcheon, Russell T. 1997. *Manufacturing Religion*. New York: Oxford University Press.

McCutcheon, Russell T. 2015. "The Category 'Religion' in Recent Publications: Twenty Years Later." *Numen* 62: 119–141. https://doi.org/10.1163/15685276-12341358

Murphy, T. 2004. *Pliny the Elder's Natural History: The Empire in the Encyclopedia.* Oxford: Oxford University Press.

Nongbri, Brent. 2013. *Before Religion: A History of a Modern Concept.* New Haven, CT: Yale University Press. https://doi.org/10.12987/yale/9780300154160.001.0001

Reed, Annette Yoshiko. 2004. "The Trickery of the Fallen Angels and the Demonic Mimesis of the Divine." *Journal of Early Christian Studies* 12: 141–171. https://doi.org/10.1353/earl.2004.0027

Reed, Annette Yoshiko. 2015. "Retelling Biblical Retellings: Epiphanius, the Pseudo-Clementines, and the Reception History of the Book of Jubilees." In M. Kister, H. Newman, M. Segal, and R. Clements (eds.), *Tradition, Transmission, and Transformation, from Second Temple Literature through Judaism and Christianity in Late Antiquity*, 304–321. Leiden: Brill. https://doi.org/10.1163/9789004299139_013

Reed, Annette Yoshiko. 2017. "Categorization, Collection, and the Construction of Continuity." *MTSR* 29(3): 268–311. https://doi.org/10.1163/15700682-12341391

Reed, Annette Yoshiko. 2018. *Jewish Christianity and the History of Judaism: Collected Studies.* Tübingen: Mohr Siebeck. https://doi.org/10.1628/978-3-16-156060-6

Rives, James B. 2007. *Religion in the Roman Empire.* Malden, MA: Blackwell.

Rosen-Zvi, I. 2016. "What if We Got Rid of the Goy? Rereading Ancient Jewish Distinctions." *Journal for the Study of Judaism* 47: 1–34. https://doi.org/10.1163/15700631-12340458

Rosen-Zvi, I. and A. Ophir. 2011. "Goy: Toward a Genealogy." *Dine Israel* 28: 69–11.

Rosen-Zvi, I. and A. Ophir. 2015. "Paul and the Invention of the Gentiles." *Jewish Quarterly Review* 105: 1–41. https://doi.org/10.1353/jqr.2015.0001

Schott, Jeremy. 2007. "Heresiology as Universal History in Epiphanius's *Panarion*." *Zeitschrift für Antikes Christentum* 10: 546–563. https://doi.org/10.1515/ZAC.2006.037

Schott, Jeremy. 2008. *Christianity, Empire, and the Making of Religion in Late Antiquity.* Philadelphia, PA: University of Pennsylvania Press. https://doi.org/10.9783/9780812203462

Schwartz, Seth. 2011. "How Many Judaisms Were There?" *Journal of Ancient Judaism* 2: 208–238. https://doi.org/10.13109/jaju.2011.2.2.208

Smith, Jonathan Z. 1998. "Religion, Religions, Religious." In Mark C. Taylor (ed.), *Critical Terms for Religious Studies*, 269–284. Chicago, IL: University of Chicago Press.

Smith, Jonathan Z. 2004. "Manna, Mana Everywhere, and /ʊ/ʊ/." In Jonathan Z. Smith, *Relating Religion: Essays in the Study of Religion*, 117–144. Chicago, IL: University of Chicago Press.

Smith, W. C. 1963. *The Meaning and End of Religion.* New York: Macmillan.

Woolf, G. 2011. *Tales of the Barbarians: Ethnography and Empire in the Roman West.* Malden, MA: Wiley-Blackwell. https://doi.org/10.1002/9781444390810

Zerubavel, E. 1999. *Social Mindscapes.* Cambridge, MA: Harvard University Press.

Chapter 2

A More Subtle Violence: The Footnoting of "the Aboriginal Principle of Witnessing" by the Truth and Reconciliation Commission of Canada

Adam Stewart

Annette Yoshiko Reed (Chapter 1, this volume) writes:

> When our data do not fit the taxonomies of our current concepts of "religion(s)," the usual scholarly habit has been to dismiss them as idiosyncratic or marginal, either omitting them from our narratives about the developments of "a religion" or relegating them to footnotes therein.

She continues:

> But what happens when we take such cases, instead, as a warning against our scholarly habit of overestimating the power of classification to explain? And what if we also take such cases as an invitation to look to the past with an eye to a broader range of strategies for explaining difference and mapping continuity?

One very public example of the quite literal marginalization of religious data that failed to fit the taxonomies of current concepts of religion, was the footnoting of "the Aboriginal principle of witnessing" by the Truth and Reconciliation Commission of Canada (hereafter TRC). The TRC was one of the six main components of the Indian Residential Schools Settlement Agreement (hereafter IRSSA), which was signed in May of 2006 and directed the spending of what has amounted to more than $6 billion worth of initiatives to date, intended to redress the violence done to Indigenous Canadians through the federally funded and Christian-operated Indian residential school system (Indian Residential Schools Settlement Agreement 2006b).[1] Although its purpose was to contribute to the decolonization of Indigenous-Settler relations in Canada—and, admittedly, it did contribute to this objective—I argue that the work of the TRC was, nonetheless, guided by an essentialist taxonomy of Indigenous religion that perpetuated, rather than ameliorated, a longstanding colonial practice of homogenizing inconvenient Indigenous differences in order to more easily manage the colonized and expedite the interests of the Government of Canada.

In order to both substantiate this claim and to suggest a way forward for those studying similarly complex religious data, I do four things. First, I clarify the nature and mandate of the TRC as one of several components of the much larger

IRSSA. Second, I explain the origin and development of the TRC's specific definition of "the Aboriginal principle of witnessing." Third, I describe the utility of this definition in helping to expedite the work of the TRC as well as the violence caused by its strategic essentialization of Canadian Indigenous practices of witnessing. Finally, I recommend Reed's method of narrativization as an alternative strategy for scholars of religion—or, as in the case of the TRC, bureaucrats or politicians developing or implementing public policy involving religious data—to consider when studying practices that likewise fail to neatly fit into existing scholarly taxonomies of religion. The application of this methodology to Indigenous practices of witnessing might have resulted in an understanding of these practices that more accurately reflected reality, grafted onto existing Indigenous Canadian historiographies, and resisted repeating the colonial violence of homogenization. I also propose that narrativization could help others avoid making the same kinds of totalizing mistakes in their own domains of professional practice.

The Indian Residential Schools Settlement Agreement

In May 2006, representatives of Indian residential school survivors, the Government of Canada (which provided the primary financial support for the operation of Indian residential schools), and some of the Christian organizations that directly operated these schools (the Anglican Church of Canada, the Presbyterian Church of Canada, the United Church of Canada, and several Roman Catholic entities), signed the IRSSA (Indian Residential Schools Settlement Agreement 2006b: 1). This agreement was the product of a complex and lengthy negotiated settlement between the above mentioned parties in response to several lawsuits filed on behalf of survivors seeking both public recognition of, and financial compensation for, the violence done to the approximately 150,000 Indigenous children who attended one of the 139 Indian residential schools funded and recognized by the Government of Canada between 1831 and 1996 whose purpose was to assimilate these children into Settler society as part of much larger political, social, and religious nation building efforts (Indigenous and Northern Affairs Canada 2015b, 2016; Legacy of Hope Foundation 2014: 6).

Many survivors were, of course, interested in receiving financial rewards as compensation for the violence that was done to them. My conversations with survivors—and the many hours that I have spent listening to and reading the accounts of many more—lead me to conclude that, for most survivors, pecuniary concerns were secondary to the primary desire for legitimating their shared suffering as a pathway to healing from the violence perpetrated against them and their communities by Indian residential schools (Dewar, Favell, and Stewart 2015; Wesley-Esquimaux and Smolewski 2004). In fact, several survivors that I have spoken with gave away their usually meagre settlement awards—when contrasted to the suffering that they endured—to support the work of survivor societies and research centers, or to help defray the costs of post-secondary education for their children, grandchildren, great-grandchildren, or other relatives.[2] Although the authors of the IRSSA were careful to address survivors' desire for the public recognition of their suffering by noting, for instance, their shared concerns for "a fair, comprehensive and lasting resolution of the legacy of Indian Residential Schools" as well as "the promotion of healing, education, truth and reconciliation and commemoration," the predominant rhetoric—and more importantly, structure and outcome—of the agreement, was liability amelioration through the mechanism of financial reparation, or what David Gaertner aptly describes as an, "'ideology of economy'" (Gaertner 2016: 136). This fact is, perhaps, best illustrated by comparing the $5,225,382,698 spent to date on implementing the IRSSA's reparative components through the Common Experience Payment and the Independent Assessment Process, with the significantly lower amount of $737,638,909 spent to date on the IRSSA's public recognition and healing components through the Personal Credits for educational services derived from the remaining balance of the Common Experience Payment fund, the TRC, the Commemoration Fund, the Aboriginal Healing Foundation, and the Health Support Component (Aboriginal Healing Foundation 2017; Indigenous and Northern Affairs Canada 2015a, 2017a, 2017b; Truth and Reconciliation Commission of Canada undated a).[3]

Despite its guiding reparative rationale, the IRSSA did direct significant resources to public recognition and healing, the most prominent example—largely due to the necessarily public and self-disseminating nature of its work—being the TRC. The mandate of the TRC was articulated in Schedule N of the IRSSA, and hinged on three overarching objectives: (1) uncovering and publicizing the truth about the violence caused by Indian residential schools, (2) facilitating healing for Indigenous Canadians who were the objects of this violence, and (3) promoting reconciliation between Indigenous and Settler Canadians. The TRC was further directed to put these three broad objectives into concrete action through the implementation of seven more specific goals, one of the better known being its charge to provide the Government of Canada with recommendations for addressing the ongoing legacy of Indian residential schools. These recommendations were released in 2015 as *Truth and Reconciliation Commission of Canada: Calls to Action* and—despite the fact that only seven of the TRC's ninety-four recommendations have been implemented at the time of this writing—represent the most significant political outcome of the IRSSA (Indian Residential Schools Settlement Agreement 2006a: 1–2; Mosby 2017; Truth and Reconciliation Commission of Canada 2015).

The goal, however, that received the most sustained public attention was the TRC's charge to "Witness, support, promote and facilitate truth and reconciliation events at both the national and community levels" (Indian Residential Schools Settlement Agreement 2006a: 2). The TRC accomplished this goal through the gathering of nearly 7,000 written and audio and video recorded statements from survivors, intergenerational survivors, Indian residential school staff, those with special knowledge of the Indian residential school system, and prominent Canadian public figures, largely during hundreds of national, regional, and community events held across the country. These statements joined the more than five million documents gathered and generated by the TRC that also documented the violence caused by Indian residential schools across Canada (National Centre for Truth and Reconciliation undated a, b). The defining feature of not only the

TRC, but each of the various Truth and Reconciliation Commissions that have been established around the world over the last approximately two decades, is the deliberate space given to both victims and perpetrators of historical violence to communicate, or give witness to, their direct experiences of these events, which is believed to contribute to reconciliation between these two groups (Gaertner 2014: 446). Given the centrality of the practice of witnessing to the fulfillment of the TRC's mandate, it stands to reason that the either success or failure of the TRC hinged on the definition of witnessing that it employed.

The Footnoting of "the Aboriginal Principle of Witnessing"

Interestingly, attached to the word "witness" within the IRSSA's description of this most public outcome of the work of the TRC, is an eight-word footnote that reads: "This refers to the Aboriginal principle of 'witnessing'" (Indian Residential Schools Settlement Agreement 2006a: 2). What makes this footnote interesting is that, unlike what is explicitly being argued by the use of the singular words "the" and "principle" in the phrase "the Aboriginal principle of 'witnessing,'" there does not exist a single, pan-Indigenous principle of witnessing held in common by all Indigenous people throughout Canada that can be summarized by just eight, tidy words. The existence of 617 First Nations, fifty-three Inuit communities, as well as a number of regional Métis communities across Canada, each possessing distinct cultural and linguistic characteristics, means that the term "witnessing" will necessarily carry different meanings among Indigenous Canadians. The inevitable questions that arose regarding the unrepresentative nature of the IRSSA's understanding of Indigenous practices of witnessing, prompted the TRC to release a slightly expanded definition in 2009 that read, "The term witness is in reference to the Aboriginal principle of witnessing, which varies among First Nations, Métis and Inuit peoples. Generally speaking, witnesses are called to be the keepers of history when an event of historic significance occurs. Partly because of the oral traditions of Aboriginal peoples, but also to recognize the importance of conducting business, building and maintaining relationships in person and face to face" (Gaertner 2016: 137; Truth and Reconciliation Commission of Canada undated b).

It was at this juncture that the TRC had the opportunity to restate the IRSSA's reductive definition of witnessing—to de-marginalize the practice by moving it from a footnote to a substantive part of its work—but, instead, the TRC persisted in its use of the singular words "the" and "principle" in its definition. For a moment it looked like, if it would not restate its definition of witnessing, it might at the very least expand it, when the TRC acknowledged that witnessing "varies among First Nations, Métis and Inuit peoples." The TRC, however, negated whatever value this statement may have had when, in the very next sentence, it used the phrase "generally speaking" to further signal the TRC's commitment to an essentialist understanding of a single, pan-Indigenous practice of witnessing common to all Indigenous people in Canada. Although the TRC's expanded definition offered an interesting challenge to the western legal tradition that understands witnesses as those who *possess and authenticate* historical knowledge, by arguing that witnesses are instead those who *receive and disseminate* historical knowledge, it, nonetheless, failed to recognize the diversity—or, in the case of some Indigenous traditions, lack—of opinions regarding the practice of witnessing found within the hundreds of different Indigenous communities across Canada (Gaertner 2014).

David Gaertner's forensic analysis of the genealogy of the TRC's expanded definition of "the Aboriginal principle of witnessing" has conclusively demonstrated that it derives from the Coast Salish and Interior Salish peoples of the Pacific Northwest (Gaertner 2016: 139–142). In 2009, the Vancouver Organizing Committee for the 2010 Olympic and Paralympic Winter Games developed a definition of witnessing deeply rooted in Coast Salish and Interior Salish traditions in an effort to engage and include the members of these local Indigenous communities into the games. Gaertner shows that the TRC's expanded definition was not simply based on the Vancouver Organizing Committee's definition, but appropriated some of the exact phrases used in a witnessing ceremony organized by the Vancouver Organizing Committee just three months before the release of the TRC's expanded definition. The TRC's dependency on the Vancouver Organizing Committee's definition of witnessing, Gaertner rightly argues, "raises questions about the TRC's relationship and responsibility to communicate beyond the Salish Sea" and "risks normalizing a geographically specific tradition that may or may not apply across all communities (ibid.: 141, 142). Furthermore, the TRC's expanded definition was intended to clarify the brief and vague definition of "the Aboriginal principle of witnessing" originally outlined in the IRSSA, but, in the end, it only served to further obfuscate the meaning of the concept. This was perhaps best illustrated in 2010 when Chief Commissioner of the TRC Murray Sinclair and Commissioners Wilton Littlechild and Marie Wilson were asked to explain what the phrase "the Aboriginal principle of witnessing" meant. The Commissioners indicated that they were not sure what the phrase meant, with Sinclair even going so far as to admit that the meaning of the phrase was debatable (Angel 2010).

The pan-Indigenous definition of "the Aboriginal principle of witnessing" first employed by the IRSSA and subsequently adopted by the TRC, reveals the influence of the world religions paradigm—that is, the social construction of broad types of religion (e.g., Hinduism, Christianity, Islam) under which more specific types of religion (e.g., Shaivism, Pentecostalism, Sufism) can be neatly categorized—that continues to dominate both the academic study of religion and the public understanding of religion more generally. The main critique of the world religions paradigm is that, in artificially forcing what are often very different religious traditions to fit into a single shared category, it accentuates (and sometimes invents) similarities and diminishes (and sometimes ignores) differences between religious traditions, resulting in the invention of homogeneous concepts of religion that do not exist in reality (Masuzawa 2005; Smith 1998). When the world religions paradigm is applied to Indigenous religion, Bjørn Ola Tafjord calls this definitional strategy the "'Indigenous religion(s)' as a class of religions" language game or taxonomy. He notes that this taxonomy is most commonly used to delimit Indigenous religion for pragmatic reasons in education, publishing, employment, and library science (Tafjord 2017: 27-28, 30 n.3). I suggest that this taxonomy is also used by bureaucrats and politicians because of its particular effectiveness in minimizing Indigenous differences in order to expedite public policy development and implementation relating to diverse populations of Indigenous people. In other words, adopting the IRSSA's definition of "the Aboriginal principle of witnessing" that was, I argue, influenced by the Indigenous religion(s) as a class of religions taxonomy, allowed the TRC to ignore and subsume any competing narratives regarding Canadian Indigenous practices of witnessing under a convenient, single pan-Indigenous definition.

The Colonial Violence of Homogenizing Indigenous Differences

If, then, the TRC's definition of "the Aboriginal principle of witnessing" was not only unrepresentative of Indigenous people across Canada, but also so elusive as to not even be understood by the TRC's Commissioners themselves, why did the TRC remain so committed to this definition? What purpose or function did this definition serve? Two explanations are immediately apparent. First, quite simply, a pan-Indigenous definition of "the Aboriginal principle of witnessing" would have significantly simplified the work of the TRC as a bureaucratic entity. The recognition that there existed different, competing, and, in some instances, the absence of, Canadian Indigenous practices of witnessing, would have significantly complicated the TRC's collection of survivor statements and the fulfillment of its mandate. It is important to remember that the TRC was a component of a massive settlement agreement intended to resolve the largest class action lawsuit in Canadian history to date, in which the principally responsible respondent was one of the most bureaucratically sophisticated and wealthiest nations in the world. It is hardly cynical to claim that the Government of Canada's primary interest regarding the implementation of the IRSSA—which certainly would have been known to the TRC—was not the promotion of truth, healing, and reconciliation between Indigenous and Settler Canadians, but, rather, the resolution of the terms of the IRSSA as quickly and efficiently as possible. It seems reasonable to assume, then, that the TRC would have strenuously avoided substantively tinkering with the language of the IRSSA, not only because this would have conflicted with the interests of the Government of Canada, but because it is the very nature of a settlement agreement as a particular type of legal instrument to avoid any type of ambiguity that might risk its timely resolution.

Second, despite the many weaknesses of its pan-Indigenous definition of "the Aboriginal principle of witnessing," the TRC would have been motivated to sustain this definition because it empowered the TRC to, as Gaertner writes, "mobilize as a politically cohesive unit against the Goliath of settler colonialism" (Gaertner 2016: 139). Indigenous Canadians and their many "allies" had been advocating for the type of public recognition of the violence caused by the Indian residential school system for decades, beginning most concertedly with the commencement in 1991 of the Royal Commission on Aboriginal Peoples (Royal Commission on Aboriginal Peoples 1996). To disrupt this long-awaited event due to something as seemingly trivial as a definition was simply not a politically realistic option for the TRC. By intentionally avoiding the critical, historical, and scientific study of Indigenous practices of witnessing, the TRC instead adopted the critical caretaker methodology advocated by scholars like Atalia Omer, which confuses the critic and caretaker modes of practice,[4] but which, in this case, was especially effective at allowing the TRC to adopt an activist framework that expedited its mandate to promote truth, healing, and reconciliation—rather ironically—at the cost of ignoring the truth about Indigenous practices of witnessing (Stewart 2018).

Some might ask, who cares? Indian residential schools caused significant harm, and, even admitting that their definition of witnessing was less than representative, the TRC still brought some measure of closure to the legacy of Indian residential schools. What is the problem with that? Moreover, some may also query, the TRC Commissioners—one a journalist and the other two lawyers—were bureaucrats, so can we really hold them to the same standards as we do scholars of religion? In response to these questions, I would say, first, by marginalizing Indigenous practices of witnessing that did not coalesce with Coast Salish and Interior Salish traditions, the TRC perpetuated the longstanding colonial practice of homogenizing Indigenous differences in an attempt to more easily manage the colonized. This aspect of the TRC's effort to "work towards a stronger and healthier future" by ameliorating risk for the Government of Canada and those settlers that it represents, can be seen as a continuation of the violence caused by Indian residential schools, whose primary reason for existing was to homogenize Indigenous difference in order to provide a better future for Canada's largely westward and northward migrating settlers and industries (Miller 1996; Milloy 2017). Second, I do not think that—when developing or implementing public policy involving religious data—we should hold bureaucrats or politicians to a lesser standard than we do our colleagues. To argue that governments should not be expected to consult appropriately credentialed scholars of religion when working with religious data is tantamount to claiming that they should similarly be excused from consulting, for instance, appropriately credentialed engineers when planning and building a bridge. If anything has been learned from the history and legacy of Indian residential schools, it is that misinformed public policy regarding culture and religion can cause just as much—in fact, much greater—harm than can an improperly built bridge.

Annette Yoshiko Reed's Method of Narrativization

What framework other than classification could the TRC have used to understand Indigenous practices of witnessing differently, thereby helping them to avoid participating in Canada's colonial legacy? What "other practices," as Reed puts it, can we as scholars of religion use "when we encounter data that does not fit into our taxonomies of 'religion' and definitions of 'religions'" so that we might avoid making the same kinds of totalizing mistakes (Chapter 1, this volume)? In such circumstances, Reed recommends experimenting with two alternative strategies that she calls anthologizing and narrativization. Rather than omitting or footnoting inconvenient differences, anthologizing involves carefully investigating these differences in order to look for a broader range of possible continuities. Of special interest to those who study Indigenous religion, however, might be Reed's practice of narrativization, which she defines as "the practice of ordering knowledge along the axis of time and articulating claims of continuity through the organizational principle of chronology" so that "similarities and differences between the practices ... become part of one story" (ibid.). Assuming that religious practices are compared with sensitivity to the historical record, linguistic dexterity, and theoretical sophistication, the organizing principle of chronology proposed by Reed, I believe, would significantly help to mitigate the risks that similarities become exaggerated or differences are disregarded, resulting, instead, in a more complete and interesting narrative that avoids simple homogenization (Hughes 2017: 112).

It is not difficult to imagine how the practice of narrativization might have been especially useful for explaining the differences and continuities that exist within the diversity of Indigenous Canadian practices of witnessing. Instead of lazily adopting the definition of witnessing used in one very specific geographical context as the basis for a single, pan-Indigenous principle of witnessing, the TRC could have certainly used some of its $60 million budget to have investigated these diverse traditions with the goal of generating a narrative that explained—rather than marginalized—differences, and mapped—rather than extrapolated—continuities. This is, of course, the way that many Indigenous Canadians already explain an assortment of differences and continuities that exist between their different traditions such as language, myth, ritual, and territory. The resulting narrative could have been used to generate a definition and protocol—or more likely, an assortment of definitions and protocols—that would have more accurately reflected reality, grafted onto existing Indigenous Canadian historiographies, and resisted repeating the colonial violence of homogenization. Laden by a definition of "the Aboriginal principle of witnessing" that was rooted in an essentialist taxonomy of Indigenous religion, the TRC, instead, culled from its consideration any divergent narratives regarding Indigenous Canadian practices of witnessing that did not fit its colonial, homogeneous construction of these practices. It is difficult to imagine a field of inquiry within the discipline of religious studies in which the narrativization of religious practice would not be equally as helpful. Reed originally developed this method within the milieu of early Christian studies, and I recommend its use in the study of contemporary Indigenous religion, but, since all forms of religious practice have a chronological—no matter how brief—component, it possesses a broad range of possible applications that are limited only by the willingness of scholars, bureaucrats, and politicians to experiment with what is both a more scientifically rigorous and ethically responsible methodology than is uncritical taxonomic classification.

Adam Stewart is an Associate Professor of Sociology at Crandall University, Moncton, New Brunswick, Canada.

Notes

1. The other five main components of the IRSSA were the Common Experience Payment, the Independent Assessment Process, the Commemoration Fund, an endowment given to the Aboriginal Healing Foundation to fund healing programs that addressed the legacy of the Indian residential school system, and the Health Support Component that provided emotional and mental health services to survivors, intergenerational survivors, and participants of TRC events.
2. The IRSSA made allowance for two distinct types of claims. Any survivor who could prove their attendance at an Indian residential school recognized by the Government of Canada could submit a Common Experience Payment claim. The average award for all 79,309 Common Experience Payment claims approved as of March 31, 2016, was $20,457 amounting to a total of $1,622,422,106. Survivors who could additionally prove that they experienced sexual or what was defined as "serious" physical abuse at an Indian residential school recognized by the Government of Canada could submit an Independent Assessment Process claim. The average award (not including legal costs) for all 30,557 Independent Assessment Process claims approved as of June 30, 2017, was $102,530 amounting to a total of $3,133,009,210. It is important to note that in addition to the compensation—equal to 15 percent of a client's Independent Assessment Process award—automatically paid to a claimant's lawyer by the Government of Canada, lawyers could also apply for supplementary legal fees totaling as much as 15 percent of their client's award. These additional legal fees were not paid by the Government of Canada, but, rather, were deducted directly from claimant's awards, meaning that the average Independent Assessment Process award actually received by claimants was less than $102,530 (Indian Residential Schools Adjudication Secretariat 2015: 47–48; Indian Residential Schools Settlement Agreement 2006b: 43–53; Indigenous and Northern Affairs Canada 2017b).
3. These figures do not include all of the associated costs assumed by the Government of Canada for administering these programs.
4. On the one hand, the critic caretaker binary, perhaps most clearly explicated by Russell T. McCutcheon (1997a, 1997b, 1998, 2001, 2012), argues that scholars of religion carry out their work in either one of two mutually exclusive modes of practice: as a critic of cultural practices, or a caretaker of religious tradition, but not as both. On the other hand, the critical caretaker binary, advocated by Atalia Omer (2011, 2012, 2013a, 2013b), argues that, in addition to the two modes of practice described by McCutcheon, a third mode of practice, that she calls critical caretaker, is possible, which allows scholars of religion to combine the roles of critic and caretaker when they encounter conflict or social injustice (see Stewart 2018).

References

Aboriginal Healing Foundation. 2017. "What is the Aboriginal Healing Foundation?" Retrieved from www.ahf.ca/faqs.

Angel, Naomi. 2010. "IRS TRC and an Aboriginal Principle of Witnessing." Tracing Memory (blog), May 8. Retrieved from https://tracingmemory.wordpress.com/2010/05/08/irs-trc-and-an-aboriginal-principle-of-witnessing.

Dewar, Jonathan, Rosalie Favell, and Adam Stewart. 2015. "Celebrating Resilience." Exhibited at the Closing Ceremonies of the Truth and Reconciliation Commission of Canada, Ottawa, Ontario, May 31–June 3. Funded by the Aboriginal Heritage Component, Museums Assistance Program, Department of Canadian Heritage, Government of Canada.

Gaertner, David. 2014. "20 October 2008: Translating Reconciliation." In Kathy Mezei, Sherry Simon, and Luise von Ftotow (eds.), *Translation Effects: The Shaping of Modern Canadian Culture*, 444–458. Montreal: McGill-Queen's University Press.

Gaertner, David. 2016. "'Aboriginal Principles of Witnessing' and the Truth and Reconciliation Commission of Canada." In Dylan Robinson and Keavy Martin (eds.), *Arts of Engagement: Taking Aesthetic Action In and Beyond the Truth and Reconciliation Commission of Canada*, 135–156. Waterloo: Wilfrid Laurier University Press.

Hughes, Aaron. W. 2017. *Comparison: A Critical Primer*. Sheffield: Equinox.

Indian Residential Schools Adjudication Secretariat. 2015. *Desk Guide for Legal Counsel Practicing in the IAP*. Ottawa: Indian Residential Schools Adjudication Secretariat.

Indian Residential Schools Settlement Agreement. 2006a. "Schedule 'N': Mandate for the Truth and Reconciliation Commission." Retrieved from www.residentialschoolsettlement.ca/SCHEDULE_N.pdf

Indian Residential Schools Settlement Agreement. 2006b. "Settlement Agreement." Retrieved from www.residentialschoolsettlement.ca/IRS%20Settlement%20Agreement-%20ENGLISH.pdf.

Indigenous and Northern Affairs Canada. 2015a. "Commemoration Partners." Retrieved from www.aadnc-aandc.gc.ca/eng/1338475691486/1338475747252.

Indigenous and Northern Affairs Canada. 2015b. "Recognized Indian Residential Schools." Retrieved from www.aadnc-aandc.gc.ca/eng/1100100015606/1100100015611.

Indigenous and Northern Affairs Canada. 2016. "Indian Residential Schools." Retrieved from www.aadnc-aandc.gc.ca/eng/1100100015576/1100100015577.

Indigenous and Northern Affairs Canada. 2017a. "Indian Residential Schools Settlement Agreement—Health Support Component." Retrieved from www.aadnc-aandc.gc.ca/eng/1483562394651/1483562419241.

Indigenous and Northern Affairs Canada. 2017b. "Statistics on the Implementation of the Indian Residential Schools Settlement Agreement." Retrieved from www.aadncaandc.gc.ca/eng/1315320 539682/1315320692192.

Legacy of Hope Foundation. 2014. *100 Years of Loss: The Residential School System in Canada*, 2nd edition. Ottawa: Legacy of Hope Foundation.

Masuzawa, Tomoko. 2005. *The Invention of World Religions: Or, How European Universalism Was Preserved in the Language of Pluralism*. Chicago, IL: University of Chicago Press. https://doi.org/10.7208/chicago/9780226922621.001.0001

McCutcheon, Russell T. 1997a. "A Default of Critical Intelligence? The Scholar of Religion as Public Intellectual." *Journal of the American Academy of Religion* 65(2): 443–468. https://doi.org/10.1093/jaarel/65.2.443

McCutcheon, Russell T. 1997b. *Manufacturing Religion: The Discourse of Sui Generis Religion and the Politics of Nostalgia*. New York: Oxford University Press.

McCutcheon, Russell T. 1998. "Talking Past Each Other—Public Intellectuals Revisited: Rejoinder to Paul J. Griffiths and June O'Connor." *Journal of the American Academy of Religion* 66(4): 911–917. https://doi.org/10.1093/jaarel/66.4.911

McCutcheon, Russell T. 2001. *Critics Not Caretakers: Redescribing the Public Study of Religion*. Albany, NY: SUNY Press.

McCutcheon, Russell T. 2012. "A Direct Question Deserves a Direct Answer: A Response to Atalia Omer's 'Can a Critic Be a Caretaker Too?'" *Journal of the American Academy of Religion* 80(4): 1077–1082. https://doi.org/10.1093/jaarel/lfs071

Miller, J. R. 1996. *Shingwauk's Vision: A History of Native Residential Schools.* Toronto: University of Toronto Press.

Milloy, John S. 2017. *A National Crime: The Canadian Government and the Residential School System*, 2nd edition. Winnipeg: University of Manitoba Press.

Mosby, Ian. 2017. *Unreserved*. Radio interview by Rosanna Deerchild. CBC Radio One, October 22, 2017.

National Centre for Truth and Reconciliation. Undated a. "Accessing the Collection." Retrieved from http://nctr.ca/archives-pages.php#statements (accessed October 28, 2017).

National Centre for Truth and Reconciliation. Undated b. "Statements and Videos." Retrieved from http://nctr.ca/archives-pages.php#statements (accessed October 28, 2017).

Omer, Atalia. 2011. "Can a Critic Be a Caretaker too? Religion, Conflict, and Conflict Transformation." *Journal of the American Academy of Religion* 79(2): 459–96. https://doi.org/10.1093/jaarel/lfq076

Omer, Atalia. 2012. "On Professor McCutcheon's (Un)critical Caretaking." *Journal of the American Academy of Religion* 80(4): 1083–1097. https://doi.org/10.1093/jaarel/lfs079

Omer, Atalia. 2013a. "In the Critic vs. Caretaker Dichotomy A Magic Dwells: Parroting McCutcheon, Policing 'Religion' (A Rejoinder to Merinda Simmons)." *Method and Theory in the Study of Religion* 25(4-5): 382–402. https://doi.org/10.1163/15700682-12341301

Omer, Atalia. 2013b. *When Peace Is Not Enough: How the Israeli Peace Camp Thinks about Religion, Nationalism, and Justice*. Chicago, IL: University of Chicago Press. https://doi.org/10.7208/chicago/9780226008240.001.0001

Royal Commission on Aboriginal Peoples. 1996. *Report of the Royal Commission on Aboriginal Peoples*. 5 vols. Ottawa: Supply and Services Canada.

Smith, Jonathan. Z. 1998. "Religion, Religions, Religious." In Mark C. Taylor (ed.), *Critical Terms for Religious Studies*, 269–284. Chicago, IL: University of Chicago Press.

Stewart, Adam. 2018. "A Logico-Indigenous Critique of Atalia Omer's Critical Caretaker Binary." *Religious Studies and Theology* 37(1): 66–78. https://doi.org/10.1558/rsth.34745

Tafjord, Bjørn Ola. 2017. "Towards a Typology of Academic Uses of 'Indigenous Religion(s)', or Eight (or Nine) Language Games that Scholars Play with this Phrase." In Greg Johnson and Siv Ellen Kraft (eds), *Handbook of Indigenous Religion(s)*, 25–51. Leiden: Brill. https://doi.org/10.1163/9789004346710_003

Truth and Reconciliation Commission of Canada. Undated a. "About Us." Retrieved from www.trc.ca/websites/trcinstitution/index.php?p=4 (accessed October 27, 2017).

Truth and Reconciliation Commission of Canada. Undated b. "Honorary Witness." Retrieved from www.trc.ca/websites/reconciliation/index.php?p=331 (accessed October 27, 2017).

Truth and Reconciliation Commission of Canada. 2015. *Truth and Reconciliation Commission of Canada: Calls to Action*. Winnipeg: Truth and Reconciliation Commission of Canada.

Wesley-Esquimaux, Cynthia C., and Magdalena Smolewski. 2004. *Historic Trauma and Aboriginal Healing*. Ottawa: Aboriginal Healing Foundation.

Chapter 3

Categorization and its Discontents

M Adryael Tong

In her chapter, Annette Yoshiko Reed sets out to "reflect on the power and limits of the *practice* of categorization in relation to *other* modern and premodern practices of ordering knowledge" (Chapter 1, this volume;, emphasis in the original). She notices that our assumptions about what categorization should *do* lead us to "naturalize our privileging of *some* sources, *some* continuities, and *some* trajectories over others" (ibid.; emphasis in the original). In my response, I analyze Reed's paper as a philosophical critique of the current scholarly practices of categorization within the study of religion in late antiquity. I believe that Reed diagnoses two unconscious desires that drive these practices. The first is the human desire to understand the totality of all knowledge. The second is the desire to recognize oneself in the past. From there I build on Reed's analysis of the dangers of a practice of categorization beholden to these desires, and offer four possibilities for further scholarly engagement that could mitigate some of their dangers.

Categories and Their Relation to the Unconscious

The first of the desires that drives our scholarly practice of categorization is the desire to understand the world—to taxonomize the totality of human knowledge into universally recognizable buckets to which we can always meaningfully refer. However, this desire is frustrated "when we encounter data that does not fit into our taxonomies" (Reed, Chapter 1, this volume). When confronted with an infinitely diverse reality, our first instinct is repression—to stick our heads in the sand. As Reed notes, "When our data do not fit the taxonomies of our current concepts, the usual scholarly habit has been to dismiss them from our narratives" (ibid.). When repression proves unsatisfying, our second instinct is then to revise our categories—to retool them so that we might again get back to our task of taxonomizing. This repetition of desire and frustration drives an unending cycle of construction and contestation. As Reed describes it, the practice of categorization is "constituted, in this case, *both* by the use of abstraction to order and organize knowledge (and the resultant construction of experts and expertise) *and* by the localized and particularistic contestation of such abstractions (and the resultant construction of experts and expertise)" (ibid.; emphasis in the original). Thus, religious studies resembles the now-clichéd quote from *The Six Million Dollar Man*: "We can rebuild him. We have the technology. We can make him better than he was. Better, stronger, faster." Yet this process of constant improvement is never completed both because of the complexity and diversity endemic to any reality—historical or present—coupled with the distorting effects on our perception of the archive as a result of the second desire.

This second desire is a desire to find recognition of ourselves in the past. By this I mean the desire to recognize ourselves in our historically reconstructed narratives. We want to believe that we are not so different from those people in the past, and that there is some commonality or continuity between them and us. Unfortunately, as Reed demonstrates, this desire has a tendency to "skew our understanding of the past and present alike" (Chapter 1, this volume) by privileging certain historical narratives over others. This in turn undermines our first desire to understand all knowledge. Reed points out two forms in which this desire reveals itself in the study of religion in late antiquity. The first is in the privileging of those ancient methodologies that most resemble our own. For example, Reed compares the scholarly reception of Epiphanius's *Panarion* to that of the Pseudo-Clementine *Homilies*. She notes that, although both texts narrativize a kind of "fall from grace" of humankind (ibid.), *Panarion*, with its goal of "an ultimately synchronic, largely atemporal, and totalizing task of classification," (ibid.) bears more resemblance to modern scholarly practice than the Pseudo-Clementine *Homilies*, which resist an impulse towards categorization. Since *Panarion*'s method of categorization most closely mirrors modern scholarly practices, we more readily find recognition, and perhaps more importantly, authorization of our own practices in the past. This form of confirmation bias leads to the privileging of *Panarion* within the study of religion in late antiquity, while the Pseudo-Clementine *Homilies*, are "shoehorned into clumsily hyphenated 'hybrids' like 'Jewish-Christian'" (ibid.). Our categorization practices thus fail to account fully for the diversity within the historical archive. In turn, such "shoehorning" attempts frustrate our first desire for a fully taxonomized world, neatly organized without remainder, and often leads us to again re-tool our categories—"better, stronger, faster."

The second form of this desire for self-recognition in the past occurs as a result of the first. Upon finding elements in the past that resemble our methods and assumptions, we then attempt to organize the archive according to how we expect the past "should" look. At the same time, because historical data is necessarily diverse, we then develop methods that allow us to naturalize those expectations. The logic is circular and works according to these steps:

1. We recognize an ancient system of categorization that most resembles our own.
2. We then adopt its logics to develop "objective" scholarly tools—such as lexical definitions, etc.
3. We then apply those tools back on the raw historical data.

In the case of the study of religion in late antiquity, this desire most often reveals itself in what Reed diagnoses as "the current overdependence on word-studies" and "myopic focus on those words and approaches that seem most to presage our own understanding of 'religion' and the dominant practices in scholarship on it" (Chapter 1, this volume). As Reed notes, what is so devious about the popularity of word-studies is that they "can smuggle in theological and ideological presumptions under the guise of neutral philology" (ibid.). In other words, we "discover" exactly what the tools were made to discover, and still act surprised.

Beyond the Categorization Principle

If Reed offers the diagnosis—the revelation and demystification of the two impossible desires driving our neurotic compulsion to repeat an endlessly disappointing process of construction and deconstruction—are there any therapeutic practices that might lead us out of the "problematically linear, massively and myopically Eurocentric" (Chapter 1, this volume) narrative of the "history of religion(s)" and provide grist for the publishing mill that keeps us all employed? Here, I propose four main trajectories that Reed's work, both explicitly and implicitly, invites us to consider for further research: native methodologies, historical periodization, complexifying difference, and ethics and philosophy. As my research focuses on much of the same work as Reed (i.e., Judaism and Christianity in late antiquity), my examples are drawn from our shared archive and scholarly community. However, I believe that all of these areas could find ready analogues in the study of other historical periods and religious traditions.

Native Methodologies

Reed explicitly encourages us to experiment with "alternate analytical foci that highlight different elements of premodern and modern continuity-construction" (Chapter 1, this volume), such as anthologizing and narrativization. Her analysis of the Pseudo-Clementine's theory of history suggests that our way of doing history is but only *one* way among many. Just as scholars today use different methodologies to study history, we should not be so surprised that our historical predecessors did as well. By emphasizing methodological differences—in addition to ideological differences—among historical texts, we resist overly-simplistic narratives and allow ourselves to encounter the archive on its own terms. Furthermore, we allow for the creation of new—but not exclusive—systems of categorization. For example, Christine Hayes's recent monograph, *What's Divine About Divine Law?*, examines the conceptions of Mosaic Law among Second Temple Jewish, Pauline, and Rabbinic texts in light of a Greco-Roman legal theory that opposed divine/natural law to human law. By organizing these texts according to the way they theorize the *relationship* between Mosaic Law and divine/natural law, rather than whether the texts portray the Mosaic law positively or negatively, Hayes presents a new way of categorizing ancient Jewish legal material. For example, Hayes shows that although Paul and Philo agree with the Greco-Roman dichotomization of divine/natural law and human law, they disagree on whether Mosaic law shares any characteristics with the former category (Hayes 2015: 7).

Creating categories based on the *how* the text "thinks" rather than *what* it "says" allows us to see new similarities and differences occluded by other forms of categorization, and thus provides a kind of "check" on hegemonic categorization practices within the field.

While I think this kind of work that categorizes based on meta-level questions, such as methodology, could be an enormously rich area for future exploration,[1] I also have two (somewhat related) caveats. The first is that this kind of work requires a certain level of comfort within a field (or subfield) with the idea of having a variety of categorization practices. This could be tolerable as long as the field maintains one standard categorization practice for heuristic purposes, or as long as the number of alternative categorization schemes remain relatively small. I worry that the proliferation of numerous practices of categorization might exacerbate the problem of increasingly narrow intellectual silos already present within the guild—but, perhaps not. I could just as easily imagine different categorization practices facilitating collaborative projects across established subfields and scholarly communities. A multiplication of categories and categorization practices also poses a pedagogical challenge, especially in courses where instructors are expected to cover a wide range of material. For example, I teach a class on Judaism that covers texts from the Hebrew Bible to contemporary Israeli literature, and have often found it difficult to strike a balance between complicating historical narratives, and not confusing students.

The second caveat I would offer those interested in developing new categorization practices is that working with identity categories—especially identity categories in which real people are deeply invested—is a fraught enterprise. While it might be relatively safe to shuffle religious texts—and perhaps even religious practices, or lived religious phenomena—among various categories and categorization schemes, playing around with identity can have serious consequences. Categories such as race, gender, ethnicity—even religion—are not merely heuristic devices to be interrogated, demystified, and deconstructed as if they were disconnected from the real world. These categories constitute lived social realities. So, while it may be one thing to classify the Pseudo-Clementine *Homilies* as a Jewish-Christian hybrid text (Chapter 1, this volume), it is perhaps something else entirely to suggest that such hybridity persists into our contemporary era. Although Reed does not emphasize the role modern religious convictions play in scholarly practices of categorization—except in a footnote (ibid.)—an awareness of both the effects of religion on scholarship, and of scholarship on contemporary religious communities, would be beneficial to scholars of religion.[2]

The *Hypatia* controversy in 2017, which occurred after the feminist philosophy journal *Hypatia* published Rebecca Tuvel's article "In Defense of Transracialism" (2017) should serve as a warning to those who would play carelessly with categories. Although Tuvel sought to raise "theoretical and philosophical questions... that merit our reflection" (quoted in Weinberg 2017) in arguing that "since we should accept transgender individuals' decisions to change sexes, we should also accept transracial individuals' decisions to change races" (Tuvel 2017: 264), her article was not received as mere speculation. One scholar wrote that Tuvel, "enacts violence and perpetuates harm in numerous ways throughout her essay" (Berenstain 2017), and an "Open Letter to Hypatia" accuses the article of "fail[ing] to seek out and sufficiently engage with scholarly work by those who are most vulnerable to the intersection of racial and gender oppressions" (quoted in Weinberg 2017). In response to the controversy, *Hypatia*'s associate editors posted an apology to Facebook stating that "Clearly, the article should not have been published" (April 20, 2017). This was then disavowed in a Board of Directors' Statement, which clarified that the apology had been issued on behalf of the associate editors alone (May 18, 2017). A news article reporting on the controversy wrote that the article had "provoked a schism in philosophy" and that "the rifts are deepening" (McKenzie et al. 2017). Regardless of one's views on the controversy, it is clear that questions about categories and categorization cannot be isolated from larger questions about politics, personhood, and power.

Historical Periodization

Another potential avenue for further study I take from the provocative ending of Reed's article, which suggests that "the term that is perhaps most in need of more interrogating may actually not be 'religion' at all, but rather '*before*'" (Chapter 1, this volume). Here, Reed refers directly to Brent Nongbri's 2013 monograph, *Before Religion: A History of a Modern Concept*, but I interpret her as including in her critique the larger trend within religious studies that seeks "to unmask 'religion' as an anachronistic term" (ibid.). What makes Reed's paper so sharp is that she critiques not only the limited and limiting reconstructions of history that these studies present (ibid.), but also their presumption of the scholar of religion and the field of religious studies as centralized around Western civilization (ibid.). Her critique, perhaps most importantly, reveals the way this historical scholarship has structured our *relationship* to time. This is because to posit a time "before religion" performs the double fossilization not only of the past, *but of our time as well*. After all, to say that there is a time "before religion" necessarily implies that whatever is meant by "religion" must be something that exists now, thus freezing a singular moment in the past as a moment without difference—while simultaneously enacting the same procedure in the present. However, as Reed points out, "one need not build a time machine to encounter cultures in which this demarcation of 'religions' is not primary or meaningful. One need only buy a plane ticket" (ibid.). In other words, we should not be surprised when the "before religion" model fails to capture the complexity of the historical archive when it does not even accurately represent the present.

Reed's critique also opens up a challenge not only to our use of categories but also our conceptualization of time. Beyond a re-evaluation of our practices of categorization, perhaps we might also take a second look at our practices of periodization. For example, Matthew Chalmers, in an article with *The Public Medievalist*, suggests that a kind of strategic anachronism (à la Gayatri Spivak's "strategic essentialism") could be a productive tool for historians. Spivak developed the idea of "strategic essentialism" as a means of counteracting what her critics saw as an abject pessimism in her work. In one interview, she says, "I think we have to choose again strategically, not universal discourse but essentialist discourse ... I must say I am an essentialist from time to time" (see Spivak 1984–1985: 183, also Spivak 1987: 281). Her point is that sometimes it is politically expedient—perhaps even necessary—to adopt essentialist language in order to effect one's political goals. In his article, Chalmers argues that using the term "anti-Semitism" to describe pre-modern anti-Judaism is beneficial despite its anachronism: "By making the process of concept-formation visible, we see more clearly what affects our own assumptions—and the behaviours helpful to us in making sure we write our histories, rather than letting our inherited assumptions speak for us" (Chalmers 2017). This deliberate deployment of a historian's *faux pas* thus becomes a way of revealing the potentially pernicious ideologies that accusations of "anachronism" often occlude.

Another interesting opportunity for further research on the relationship between scholarship and time would be to examine the differences between periodization practices across subfields. Within the field of Jewish Studies, for example, it is not unusual to find monographs that cover vast expanses of time. Hayes's book covers material from Plato to the Babylonian Talmud (roughly fourth century BCE to fifth century CE). Shaye Cohen's *Why Aren't Jewish Women Circumcised?* goes from Genesis to "1843 and Beyond" (2005: 208). Conversely, it is not uncommon to find books or articles on early Christianity that focus on a single century—for example, Einar Thomassen's "Orthodoxy and Heresy in Second-Century Rome" (2004); Joseph Trigg's *Origen: The Bible and Philosophy in the Third-Century Church* (1983); or Peter W. L. Walker's *Holy City Holy Places: Christian Attitudes to Jerusalem and the Holy Land in the Fourth Century* (1990). This is not to say that early Christian studies does not produce monographs on longer historical periods, for example, Peter Brown's *The Rise of Western Christendom: Triumph and Diversity, AD 200–1000* (2013). Nor is Jewish studies devoid of period-specific material either, for example, Jacob Neusner's book chapter, "Constantine, Shapur II and the Jewish-Christian Confrontation in Fourth Century Iran" (1987). Nevertheless, the general contours of the fields certainly seem to have quite different attitudes towards time—and how much time is appropriate to cover in a historical project. I imagine there is the potential for some interesting interdisciplinary work on this subject that could lead to a deeper understanding of how the ways in which scholars and subfields understand time shapes those scholars and subfields' scholarship.

Complexifying Difference

In framing her paper as a reflection on categorization as a *practice*, Reed also invites us to pay attention to our practices and processes of ordering knowledge overall. She writes that when it comes to categories in religious studies, "much of their function has been to naturalize and emphasize some connections and trajectories within and between 'religions,' and to downplay and efface others" (Chapter 1, this volume). Categories thus create relationships and orientations between and among things. Specifically, categories set up the twin assumptions that all the items within a category are similar in some way and that all of the items outside of the category are different from the items inside the category in some way. But, what exactly do we mean when we designate things as "similar" or "different"? In the *Order of Things*, Michel Foucault asks, "How, at the end of the sixteenth century, and even in the early seventeenth century, was similitude conceived?" He then goes on to describe the rich semantic web of resemblance, listing numerous "notions" of similarity: "*Amicitia, Aequalitas (contractus, consensus, matrimonium, societas, pax, et similia), Consonantia, Concertus, Continuum, Paritas, Proportio, Similitudo, Conjunctio, Copula*," (Foucault 1971: 17) with the four essential similarities of convenience, emulation, analogy, and sympathy. Foucault offers only *one* notion of difference—antipathy—which, as its name implies, is conceptualized in *opposition* to sympathy. As he writes, "antipathy maintains the isolation of things and prevents their assimilation; it encloses every species within its impenetrable difference" (ibid.: 24).

In the section referenced above, Foucault limits his interests only to the sixteenth century. However, I think his elaborate description of similarity in comparison to his more sparse description of difference gets at something that may be true about all forms of categorization: namely, that while scholars may use well-developed vocabularies for talking about the relationships between elements within a group, we seem to have a more difficult time conceptualizing the relationship between an element within a group and an element outside that same group, *unless* the relationship is oppositional and thus, *antipathetic*. In other words, one of the reasons I have had so much trouble tackling the idea of Jewish-Christian difference in my own work (without the introduction of a third term, like "Greco-Roman") is because it is so difficult to talk about the relationship between those two categories in a way that does not characterize that relationship as oppositional. When we think of the categories of Judaism and Christianity together, similitude feels threatening. It is as if too much similarity would cause the categories to collapse into each other. J. Z. Smith theorized that the antipathetic nature of the categories "Judaism" and "Christianity" was due to their nature as "proximate other" to one another. As Smith explains, "While the 'other' may be perceived as being either LIKE-US or NOT-LIKE-US, he is, in fact, most problematic when he is TOO-MUCH-LIKE-US, or when he claims to BE-US. It is here that the real urgency of a 'theory of other' emerges" (Smith 1985: 47). However, as scholars such as Reed have shown, when we situate the study of Jews and Christians *within the Roman Empire*, the relationship between "Judaism" and "Christianity" (not to mention "Roman-ness") becomes far more complicated (Reed and Dohrmann 2013). If, as Hayim Lapin (2012) suggests, we understand the rabbis as Romans, and we take seriously the simultaneous Christianization of the Roman Empire with the Romanization of Christianity, what might we learn anew about the relationship between Judaism and Christianity? Is there a way to complicate a "theory of the other," despite proximity to—and perhaps even mutual participation in—a third category? Might there be difference without antipathy?

Ethics and Philosophy

My final suggestion for further (renewed?) scholarly interest is a subject Reed never articulates directly, but which I believe suffuses her entire paper—a serious engagement with ethics and philosophy. Throughout this response, I have attempted to show that Reed's critique of a particular scholarly practice in the historical study of religion is relevant not only to the field of professionalized knowledge production—academia—but also drives to the heart of some of humanity's most profound and important questions. To think about categorization does not only mean to think about history, but also about real human relationships.

As Audre Lorde explains in her essay, "Age, Race, Class, and Sex: Redefining Difference," the division of humans into categories—especially by the intellectual elite—is not a neutral act, but rather one with an exceptionally painful and violent history. She writes, "much of Western European history, conditions us to see human difference in simplistic opposition to each other: dominant/subordinate, good/bad, up/down, superior/inferior" (Lorde 1984: 114). The problem with this dichotomization, she argues, is that "we pour the energy needed for recognizing and exploring difference into pretending those differences are insurmountable barriers, or that they do not exist at all. This results in voluntary isolation, or false treacherous connections" (ibid.: 115). The desires that drive the scholarly practice of categorization—to grasp the totality of human knowledge and to recognize our own resemblance in the past—are dangerously elitist. These desires cause us to privilege our ways of knowing over methodologies and epistemologies that seem foreign, and relegate those texts and traditions that confound our expectations to the margins. In so doing, we not only run the risk of erasing a history that holds profound significance to real, living humans today, but we also prioritize our desire for wholeness—for a world we understand and in which we feel comfortable—over multiplicity and messiness.

Lorde's accusation that "we do not develop the tools for using human difference as a springboard for creative change within our lives. We speak not of human difference, but of human deviance" (ibid.: 115-116) is a warning to those who deploy categories without an awareness of the ways practices of categorization encode ideologies. At the same time, it also emphasizes the potential for categorization to enact "creative change." How could the historical study of religion work towards developing intellectual resources for that goal, rather than reinscribing inherited structures of oppression? What would it take, as Lorde suggests, for humans to "recognize[e] and explor[e] difference, [rather] than pretending those differences are insurmountable barriers, or that they do not exist" (ibid.)? How can we imagine relationship between categories that refuses both "voluntary isolation" and "false treacherous connections"? Can we imagine difference *differently*? Reed's critique gives us an opening—a launching pad—to embark on work that could potentially transform not only the way we do history, but also how we think about the world in which we live.

M Adryael Tong is an Assistant Professor of New Testament at the Interdenominational Theological Center in Atlanta, Georgia. Engaging with contemporary theory and continental philosophy, her work focuses on how early Christian and rabbinic Jewish discourses on circumcision shaped the cultural narrative of "The Parting of the Ways."

Notes

1. For example, in his forthcoming dissertation, "Writing the Early History of Judaism and Christianity: A New Proposal," Princeton Ph.D. candidate Ari Lamm argues that instead of categorizing ancient texts along an axis of Christian or Jewish, we ought to group texts based upon the procedural norms under which they operate.
2. Reed has written more extensively on the relationship between theology and scholarship elsewhere (see Reed and Becker 2007: 4–16).

References

Berenstain, Nora. 2017. "Nora Berenstain on Rebecca Tuvel and Hypatia." Facebook (April 29). Archived on GenderTrender. Retrieved from https://gendertrender.wordpress.com/nora-berenstain-on-rebecca-tuvel-and-hypatia (accessed May 15, 2018).

Brown, Peter. 2013. *The Rise of Western Christendom: Triumph and Diversity, AD 200–1000*, 10th anniversary edition. Malden, MA: Wiley-Blackwell.

Chalmers, Matthew. 2017. "'Anti-Semitism' before 'Semites': The Risks and Rewards of Anachronism." *Public Medievalist* (13 July). Retrieved from www.publicmedievalist.com/anti-semitism-before-semites (accessed May 5, 2018).

Cohen, Shaye J. D. 2005. *Why Aren't Jewish Women Circumcised? Gender and Covenant in Judaism*. Berkeley, CA: University of California Press. https://doi.org/10.1525/california/9780520212503.001.0001

Foucault, Michel. 1971. *The Order of Things*. New York: Pantheon Books (reprinted 1994, New York: Vintage Books).

Hayes, Christine. 2015. *What's Divine About Divine Law? Early Perspectives*. Princeton, NJ: Princeton University Press. https://doi.org/10.23943/princeton/9780691165196.001.0001

Lapin, Hayim. 2012. *Rabbis as Romans: The Rabbinic Movement in Palestine, 100–400 CE*. Oxford: Oxford University Press. https://doi.org/10.1093/acprof:oso/9780195179309.001.0001

Lorde, Audre. 1984. "Age, Race, Class, and Sex: Redefining Difference." In Audre Lorde, *Sister Outsider: Essays and Speeches*, 114–123. Freedom, CA: Crossing Press.

McKenzie, Lindsay, Harris, Adam, and Zamudio-Suaréz. 2017. "A Journal Article Provoked a Schism in Philosophy. Now the Rifts are Deepening." *Chronicle of Higher Education* (May 6). Retrieved from www.chronicle.com/article/A-Journal-Article-Provoked-a/240021 (accessed May 15, 2018).

Neusner, Jacob. 1987. "Constantine, Shapur II and the Jewish-Christian Confrontation in Fourth Century Iran." In Jacob Neusner (ed.), *Religion, Literature, and Society in Ancient Israel, Formative Christianity and Judaism, Vol. I: Formative Judaism*, 131–152. Lanham, MD: University Press of America.

Reed, Annette Yoshiko, and Adam H. Becker. 2007. "Introduction." In Adam H. Becker and Annette Yoshiko Reed (eds.), *The Ways That Never Parted*, 1–34. Minneapolis, MN: Fortress Press.

Reed, Annette Yoshiko, and Natalie B. Dohrmann. 2013. "Introduction: Rethinking Romans, Provincializing Christendom." In Natalie B. Dorhmann and Annette Yoshiko Reed (eds.), *Jews, Christians, and the Roman Empire: The Poetics of Power in Late Antiquity*, 1–22. Philadelphia, PA: University of Pennsylvania Press. https://doi.org/10.9783/9780812208573.1

Smith, J. Z. 1985. "What a Difference a Difference Makes." In Jacob Neusner et al. (eds.), *"To See Ourselves as Others See Us": Jews, Christians, "Others" in Late Antiquity*, 1–48. Chico, CA: Scholars Press.

Spivak, Gayatri. 1984–1985. "Criticism, Feminism and Institution." Interview with Elizabeth Gross. *Thesis Eleven* 10/11 (November/March): 175–187.

Spivak, Gayatri. 1987. *In Other Worlds*. New York: Methuen (reprinted 2006, New York: Routledge). https://doi.org/10.1177/072551368501000113

Thomassen, Einar. 2004. "Orthodoxy and Heresy in Second-Century Rome." *Harvard Theological Review* 97(3): 241–256. https://doi.org/10.1017/S0017816004000690

Trigg, Joseph. 1983. *Origen: The Bible and Philosophy in the Third-Century Church*. Atlanta: John Knox Press.

Tuvel, Rebecca. 2017. "In Defense of Transracialism." *Hypatia* 32.2 (Spring 2017): 263–278. https://doi.org/10.1111/hypa.12327

Walker, Peter W. L. 1990. *Holy City Holy Places: Christian Attitudes to Jerusalem and the Holy Land in the Fourth Century*. Oxford: Clarendon Press.

Weinberg, Justin. 2017. "Philosopher's Article On Transracialism Sparks Controversy (Updated with response from the author)." *Daily Nous* (May 1). Retrieved from http://dailynous.com/2017/05/01/philosophers-article-transracialism-sparks-controversy (accessed May 15, 2018).

Chapter 4

Categorizing Contrariety: Narrative and Taxonomy in the Construction of Sikhism

John Soboslai

In a fascinating essay from Annette Yoshiko Reed (Chapter 1, this volume), we are presented not only with a promising new dynamic through which to approach studies of what we call "religion," but also an analysis that drove home some of the most salient points of concern when it comes to seeking the "religion" of premodern and nonwestern peoples. Her analysis recaptured ways of ordering knowledge outside of the taxonomic drive that characterizes modern scientific and social scientific efforts. As we have disposed of "religion" as a universal, transtemporal and transcultural category, Reed encourages us to question the ways categories in general are anything more than strategies aiming towards normative goals. At the same time, her piece touches upon the ways scholars of religion use the issue of categorization as a practice of self-signaling, noting how the eschewing of any essence of religion is a "rare moment of consensus" in academic circles (ibid.). After inquiring into the foundation of this consensus and analyzing some ways to conceptualize our scholarly categorization praxis, I will explore a variant application of Reed's model. In complement to her focus on the unity espoused by Pseudo-Clementine, I will consider how taxonomic considerations were employed in Sikh attempts toward constructing disunity in the early and mid-twentieth century.

Philosophical Frames of Categorization

Processes of ordering knowledge have long been seen as a necessary step in human understanding, giving them an aura of objectivity and neutrality that Reed plays her part in striking down. Often, I would argue, we approach the question of the category of "religion" by setting up a Kantian foil: after exposing the assumptions of treating religion as an *a priori* category and then proceeding to demonstrate the various ways religion is constructed in particular places and times, we proudly reflect on our analytical insights. It is in part the pride that comes from such a perception that perpetuates the self-signaling act of explicitly recognizing the "much-vanquished assumption of a neutral, natural, or universal notion of 'religion'" (Chapter 1, this volume). Of course, while Kant argued that a certain faith in a Highest Good was appropriate on account of that Good being "an *a priori* necessary object of our will and inseparably bound up with the moral law," his rational approach to religion through morality did not attend directly to modern scholarly concerns (Kant 1996 [1788]: 5:114). When it came to the rational bases for the belief in God, Kant pointed to what Clifford Geertz might have called a general framework of existence (Geertz 1973); if we accept that there are indeed moral obligations incumbent upon us, then we must accept that there is a structure to reality where a divine being intentionally ensured that benefits follow from moral action. For Kant, we are justified in believing in moral rightness only if we accept that the universe does in fact have an order that makes moral goodness both necessary and sufficient for true happiness.

While his discussions around religion remained focused on issues of reason and morality, resulting in his assertion that religion's moral exemplars serve as its *raison d'être*, his process and conceptual structure seem to linger at the edges of our anthropological investigations.[1] Apart from the examples of "religious" institutions that would challenge Kantian metaphysics, our inability to determine such institutions as "religious" relies on the assignment of particular characteristics as more or less in line with idiosyncratic ideas of what constitutes "religion." As has been repeatedly shown, even the attempt to distinguish discretely "religious" properties from other spheres of experience is complicated by an awareness of how power structures seek to establish what intrinsic properties can be ascribed to the sphere of religion. Modern religious studies scholarship shows the porousness of religion's conceptual boundaries by demonstrating how the category itself is the result of reflection following cross-cultural contact, and few if any attempt to recapture an impossible *a priori* ground of the category religion, no matter how often our arguments seem to take such a starting point as given.

Reed's work offers a provocative new method through which to trace how *a posteriori* categorizations of religion coalesce, diverge, and dissolve in particular places in time. Wearied and unconvinced by attempts to garner insight about the category of religion and its precursors through studies that seek to trace the lineage of the word itself—and thereby draw conclusions about the concepts and practices it has referenced—she turns our attention to the practice of categorization itself, and its role for both scholars and practitioners. We might say that Reed has done her part in encouraging us to think about how to trace a kind of nominalist, Humean development of religion by insisting that our cultural categories are not only *a posteriori*, but that the very methods by which such designations are established vary with time and culture.

Prior to Kant's articulation of conceptualism, David Hume's nominalism held that general ideas are nothing more than terms used to reference a group of particular ideas, which themselves are a result of our direct impressions. He saw those associations drawn through a number of key relations, such as resemblance; after deriving an idea of "religion" through our direct impressions, we go on to use the term for anything that resembles those initial impressions (Hume 1874: 1.1.7). Resemblance, however, is not identity, and Hume recognized that resemblances did not require "having any common circumstance the same," (ibid.: 1.1.7 n. 2) a statement that resonates with Ludwig Wittgenstein's analysis of "language games" in his *Philosophical Investigations*. Wittgenstein held that seeking a consistent, essential core meaning in all uses of a word misconstrues how language works. He argued the sentence, rather than the word, was the base unit of meaning, insisting that usage in context anchors understanding rather than any inherent and independent definitions.

In 2000, Benson Saler and Don Wiebe publicly debated the various benefits and drawbacks of using Wittgensteinian family resemblances as a way out of the "essentializing" trap in defining or conceptualizing religion, and their direction links with this means of drawing up a series of particulars under a common label.[2] Rather than approaching religion as having intrinsic qualities that qualify something as "religious," we need to attend instead to how practices and beliefs become "religious" through extrinsic relationships to other forms of life.

The manner in which Hume sees our ideas being formed can also be useful in considering how we construct the subject matter of religious studies. Not only are our general ideas a result of particular ideas which bear a resemblance to each other, but they are also derived from our sense impressions. We develop an idea of "religious" based upon those impressions we had when we first encountered something called religion, be it the smell of incense at a church service, the sound of the *azan* calling us to prayer, or even the sight of sacred symbols we see and connect to what we are told is "religion." The solipsism inherent in such ideas is part of what modern religious studies rebels against, since if our idea of religion is based on a smell of incense, we might be hesitant to identify services that do not employ incense as "really religious." The specificity that spawns general ideas leads to an inevitable parochialism in applying such labels to beliefs and practices developed outside our context. Moreover, if our idea of religion is drawn from impressions of individualized spiritual practices that have become distinct from practices of politics or public morality, those forms of practice that engage the spiritual and political simultaneously will naturally be excluded, as Talal Asad showed (Asad 1993). In looking to resemblance as a basis for categorization, we must remain alert to how common characteristics are themselves merely a product of the driving impressions that gave rise to the concept of religion itself.

Narrativization and Contiguity

What Reed encourages us to do in part is to consider another of Hume's modes of relations, contiguity. Though Hume's focus regarding contiguity revolves around our experience of causation, contiguous relationships can be another lens through which to perceive the ways we group concepts under the label "religion." Particularly considering Reed's central focus—the construction of "Christianity," "Judaism" and perhaps "Jewish-Christianity"—contiguity is an essential consideration. The covenant established between Abraham and the God that would provide him a great nation is at issue for both Jewish and Christian (and Muslim) communities, and it is of great importance for groups to demonstrate that they are the true inheritors of that agreement. Narrative construction is the central means through which that contiguity was established, making Reed's focus on "the practice of creating narratives that remap synchronic diversity onto chronological time" particularly apt (Chapter 1, this volume). As opposed to the means by which we form impressions according to Hume—namely direct sense perception—narrative provides a means of *constructing* impressions. Highlighting certain aspects of a tradition and downplaying others can create a greater or lesser sense of continuity, and therefore a greater or lesser sense of sameness. The question becomes at what point do contiguous traditions become severed, and what means are used to make such judgments? This change in perspective can enhance our awareness of how perceived relations themselves come about as the result of strategic attempts towards inclusion and exclusion. Focusing too much on the specter of religion's *a priority* can mean missing the creative means of categorization that is mobilized towards assertions of continuity, and condemnations of deviance.

So instead of tracing the genealogy of our concept of religion through word-origin studies, Reed encourages us to investigate the construction (or deconstruction) of religious identity and difference in specific places and times, which she terms narrativization. Just as Asad encouraged us to move beyond thinking of a religious sphere where questions of power are excluded, Reed asks us to look at how religious groups themselves do things to history towards creating socio-religious divisions. Whether or not a group is seen as appropriately continuing a tradition is the question of the accepted contours of that tradition, something not given but created, and often created in multiple forms simultaneously.

Her essay offered insight into a few strategies employed by premodern Jewish and Christian groups in such pursuits. Analyzing the dynamics of narrativization (along with passing mentions of anthologizing which she more fully examined in her recent MTSR article),[3] Reed showed how inclusion and exclusion come about through a variety of discursive efforts toward boundary-marking as well as boundary-removal. While reflecting on this program, I was reminded of that central pedagogical text in the academic study of religion, Jonathan Z. Smith's "Religion, Religions, Religious" (Smith 2004). In reflecting on the transitions of the term "religion" over history, Smith found "the most common form of classifying religions, found in both native categories and scholarly literature, is dualistic and can be reduced, regardless of what differentium is employed, to 'theirs' and 'ours'" (ibid.: 187–188). This insight can trigger a student's perspective in a radical way, bringing to light the complexities involved in that which they had until that moment taken for granted. For scholars, tracing the ways in which that most primary of religious dualities—"ours" and "theirs"—was created and defended through rhetorical strategies sheds light on both the spiritual contours of communities, and the means by which people seek to establish appropriate carriers of tradition.

Reed's expert focus on the relationship and co-construction of ancient Judaism and early Christianity was a useful one to examine these concerns. Those who have claimed to be the chosen people of Abraham's covenant have a ready need for showing continuity and unity, since a divinely preferred status was at issue. In both the stories of the Tanakh and the Christian New Testament, narrative is the central way that this essential connection is derived, and Reed is surely right that scholarly practices of categorization rely on the same method of drawing communities of practice together. Seeking clarity, individuals and institutions tell stories to firm up dividing lines and encourage association with "our way" as opposed to "their way." In doing so, as Reed notes, they "naturalize and emphasize some connections and trajectories ... and downplay others" (Chapter 1, this volume).

While this is surely a necessary habit in the practice of categorizing, questioning the routine use of narrative as a central means of drawing distinctions can be useful in inquiring into the goals of categorizing itself. It can also shed insight into whether narrativization serves as a means of explaining changes in practice, or if a change in practice follows a narrative of continuity. In looking to myth as the determinant of what creates a sense of likeness, are scholars more likely to fall into the kinds of rhetorical traps used by parties with a vested interest in showing continuity? What kinds of changes would we see if we were to look at other forms of continuity, say enduring ritual practices, as the distinguishing factor? Would it result in a taxonomy that was more or less useful to the scholar? (Since, if we accept that "religion" is the creation of the scholar employed towards certain analytical ends, utility would appear as the most fundamental metric with which to measure such methodological concerns.)

Still, narrative has long been essential to affirmations of identity. Where one comes from, how they became who they are, and the relation of current groups to past ones are all a matter of story. Scholars with whom Reed engages, like Daniel Boyarin and Brent Nongbri, looked at how such stories in the service to categorization can blind later researchers to the messy and nuanced situation on the ground in West Asia at the dawn of the Common Era. Hyphenated terms like "Jewish-Christianity" promised to highlight how the firm divisions we associate with religious categories were misleading. Categories are generally read as absolutes—the signifier "Christian" is employed to signify a group that was "not-Jewish"—but the messiness of life is rarely so neat. Methodologically, using a hyphen to join two labels would appear to be the inverse of the now common use of plurals to avoid suggesting a unified and monolithic religion (or idea of religion); where William Arnal and Russell McCutcheon are right to point to the ways plurals "leave unexamined just what it is about the plural... that makes them all members of a single genus" (Arnal and McCutcheon 2013: 11), hyphenated labels suggest a group cohered around a set of characteristics shared by both groups. However, the suggestion of a discrete, self-identifying group with established boundaries still lingers. Attending primarily to the construction of social boundaries implicitly accepts that such boundaries are, so to speak, real and accurate reflections of life on the ground. Where such plurals were not employed by the groups they are used in reference to, Reed brings us to consider the means through which those on the ground sought to create the divisions themselves.

From Continuity to Discontinuity

Though contiguity is an important concept, I want to continue Reed's experiment using another of Hume's relational forms: contrariety. Hume distinguishes contrariety in different ways, but we can distinguish between a logical and empirical form of contrariety, where the former has to do with rational paradoxes (something cannot both be and not-be simultaneously) while the latter is concerned with observations of difference. The contours of contrariety have troubled scholars of Hume, but there is relative consensus that its core revolves around relations of dissimilarity.[4] Dissimilarity is a product of experience and perception, and one that can be a result of intentional acts of construction just as much as continuity. Looking at practices of creating "abstract categories and totalizing systems of taxonomic distinction to organize and explain" differences in beliefs and practices can help us understand attempts towards establishing difference as well as sameness (Chapter 1, this volume). Therefore, however much energy we put into demonstrating how sameness is developed, we should spend equal energy considering the way groups intentionally create dissimilarity.

Transnational Sikh groups of the early twentieth century present such an opportunity. The colonial rule of the British Raj led Sikhs to create perceptions of discontinuity as a means of seeking recognition as a "religion" in the eyes of their contemporary political institutions. This case allows for inquiry into the same dual concerns of Reed's work; first, the relationship between two coexisting sets of spiritual, moral, and political practices was at issue, one that developed out of the other. While Christians were aiming to remain connected to the divine covenant that defined Judaism, Sikhs were seeking to demonstrate their difference from the panoply of practices grouped under the label "Hinduism."[5] The landscape of "a religion" constructed at a particular historical and cultural moment is the second line of analysis, since the need to explicitly adapt to the colonizer's conception of a discrete religion was at issue.

In the early 1900s, Sikhs were angling for greater representation in the British imperial government, and as Indian independence crept closer, they sought a substantial voice in the anticipated administration (see Soboslai 2018). Doing so meant concretizing "Sikhism" as a self-contained tradition separate from its "Hindu" heritage. In doing so not only did Sikhs contend with the colonial imported category of "religion," but also with a power structure that simultaneously allowed religious practices while condemning political activity seen to pose a threat to British rule (Murphy 2013). The temporal and spiritual rule labeled *miri-piri* by the Tenth Guru Gobind Singh was a concern, since it transgressed that assumed boundary separating political from "religious" concerns. Its disruption of the colonial distinction of "religion" and "not-religion" is reflected in the Tibetan *Ganden Phodrang* form of government which ascribed both political and spiritual authority to the Dalai Lamas, and the Communist Chinese Party's response to its perceived seditious nature is reflected in the British concerns for their subjects' indigenous practices.

The Hinduism that Sikhs sought to distinguish themselves from was itself a product of such forces. The term's origin is generally traced back to the root *Sindhu*, which was a Sanskrit term that referred simply to the group of people living near the Indus Valley. The term began with more of a "secular" referent than a "religious" one. Muslim rulers would later name the Indian subcontinent

Hindustan, and in the seventeenth and eighteenth centuries British forces would employ it to distinguish the indigenous cultural practices of that area, widely based in Vedic texts, from "religions" like Islam and Christianity. As European interest in Asian cultures flourished in the eighteenth century with significant political repercussions, the term "Hindoo" was used to conflate the diversity of practices set up in opposition to the religions they were more comfortable with; Hinduism as a religious label began as a designation of what was not-Christian and not-Muslim.

At the turn of the twentieth century, many in South Asia—including significant numbers of Sikhs themselves—saw Sikhs as practitioners of a marginal kind of Hinduism, the abstract "religion" which had long included guru traditions. Just as Reed notes that the Jewish-Christianity analyzed by Barton and Boyarin has been treated as a marginal practice in the ancient world, Harjot Oberoi has discussed at length the Sanatan Sikh tradition that existed side-by-side with the dominant Singh strand of Sikhism, but has been treated as peripheral when treated at all (Oberoi 1994: ch. 2; Reed 2018: 11). The designation Sanatan connects with the *sanatana dharma,* the "eternal tradition," which was used to designate the lineage of practice based in Vedic texts which became known as "Hinduism."[6] A taxonomic and narrative battle where purity and right practice is at issue is already evident.

When imperial rule came to an end following the First and Second World Wars—where Sikhs had served in disproportionately high numbers—the Indian subcontinent was divided into the sibling states Pakistan and India; the former was created as a home for the area's Muslim population, while the latter was defined by the common cultural institutions of Hinduism. While religion was one factor considered among others like language and population, a program was sparked to demonstrate Sikhism not as one Hindu practice among others, but as its own religion, and therefore deserving of its own representation. Such a goal was prefigured by the conception of *miri-piri* mentioned above, which was ritually professed by the cry "*Raj Karega Khalsa*"—"the Khalsa shall rule"—an affirmation of sovereignty recited at the close of every Sikh religious service.

The degree of success in Sikh self-categorizing therefore had potentially huge political ramifications. Some political forces during the struggle for Indian independence encouraged Sikhs to be seen as part of an undifferentiated Hinduism, just as Reed saw at stake in the Pseudo-Clementine writing. Many Sikhs, on the other hand, demanded recognition of their difference. That tactic required a twofold effort: first, the contours of Sikh traditions had to be defined in relation to British expectations about what constitutes (and does not constitute) religion, and second, those contours had to be shown to be distinct from "Hinduism." While Reed's reading of the *Homilies* shows how narratives could encourage unity by recalling an undifferentiated past, the same strategies were employed to sever Sikhism into its own fruit of the world religion's tree. "A religious practice" shifted to "*the* Sikh religion."

Separating Sikhism

Such a distinction was far from clear when the twentieth century began. Many Sikhs did not appear to believe a nonporous identity separate from Hinduism was necessary or even preferred. Prior to 1905, Hindu statues were in residence in the Golden Temple in Amritsar, the heart of the Sikh world, and Hindu rites were routinely practiced by those who identified as Sikh. In the words of Oberoi, "the either/or dichotomy is not to be taken for granted, for the religious life of people, particularly in the pre-colonial period, was characterized by a continuum. There was much interpenetration and overlapping of communal identities" between Hindus, Sikhs, and even Muslims (Oberoi 1994: 12; see also Barrier 1979). Richard Fox relates how the confusion was evident in the 1891 census:

> [O]ver a third of the people who referred to themselves as Sikhs claimed they belonged to the Hindu religion and were Sikh only by sect. Of these, the great majority were Sajdharis ("Hindu Nanakpanthi" or "Hindu Sikh"), but fifteen percent were Singhs (Hindu "Gobind Singhi"). Two-thirds of the Sikhs believed they constituted a separate religion, and among these, not only were there the expected Singhs but also there was a large Sajdhari minority, comprising nearly forty percent of them. The Sikh population was almost evenly divided between Singhs and Sajdharis. Later censuses showed less of this variation, in part because the British stopped publishing data on sects and in part because Singh reformism led the former Sajdharis to report themselves either as Hindus or Singhs. (Fox 1985: 112)

No consensus existed around either of the questions driving this inquiry. We could classify Sikhs in this period as Hindu-Sikh, mirroring the move by scholars like Daniel Boyarin, but in this case it would serve as taking an ideological side. Hindu Nanakpanthi (referencing the traditions laid down by Guru Nanak, to whom all varieties of Sikhs trace their origin) is a native identity, but that fact complicates our ability to use Hindu-Sikh as a practical, analytical label. The hyphenated pairing would obfuscate and predetermine precisely what was at stake in their attempts at categorization.

The isolation of Sikhism from Hinduism was not a necessary, natural evolution, but a product of "categorizing and contesting categories," and constructing *discontinuities* along the axis of time (Chapter 1, this volume). That process revolved heavily around political concerns. J. S. Grewal argues "the 'sectarian' differences between the various groups within the Sikh community were not really sectarian. They differed not on the basis of doctrine so much as in their basic attitude towards the state" (Grewal 1979: 37). Narratives highlighting oppression and persecution by both the Muslim Mughal Empire and Hindu communities were told by the popular Akali Dal movement, which further pressed for a distinct Sikh *panth* to be considered alongside Hinduism and Islam (Axel 2001: 84). Moreover, the Shiromani Gurdwara Parbandhak Committee (SGPC) led the charge to reform the administration of gurdwaras, which served as ritual centers of Sikh life as well as the connective tissue of the global Sikh community. The SGPC took issue with the *mahants*, British appointed managers of gurdwaras who allowed Hindu practices to continue within Sikh places of worship and who were seen as colonial puppets (Fox 1985: 82–89, 110). Many *mahants* were from the Udasi sect, who saw Sikhism as a branch of Hinduism and therefore provided a reference point for both the religious and political issues at stake.

Interestingly, different groups seeking Sikh autonomy used different tactics vis-à-vis religion. The SPGC, facing a fierce British opposition to any organizations of a political bent, stressed their religious nature while recognizing the potential confusion stemming from their nationalist language. In one communication they stressed that "though essentially religious in spirit and objectives, it is thoroughly national in outlook … the movement is purely religious and has no secular object or intention. The SPGC is a purely religious body and has no desire for the establishment of Sikh Raj" (Singh 1965: 57). While the collective body of Sikhs was referred to by the term *quam*—nation—it was essential that colonial agents recognized that such a label did not equate to efforts towards sovereignty.[7]

At the same time, the radical Ghadr Party, which sought to spark revolution in India during the First World War from their centers in North America, shunned religious identity outright. Though its ranks were mostly filled with Sikhs it eschewed any religious considerations for its membership, preferring to pursue their goals through a pan-Indian approach. They blatantly sought independence from the British Empire, and ensured those they tried to convince that they did not seek a religious state, driving it home by rhetorically attacking obedience to clerical authority and over-attachment to sites of worship. This overt opposition to religion has understandably led many scholars to characterize the Ghadr Party as inherently secular (see for example Fox 1985: 116–119; Juergensmeyer 1979: 173–190). The convoluted questions around the concept of religion in the period, however, has led Parmbir Singh Gill to eloquently argue that we are better served seeing a new form of religiosity at issue, one that showed "neither a rejection of 'religion as such' *nor* an aversion to the 'political use of religion', but an abjuration of those aspects of religiosity which ran contrary to the imperatives of anticolonial resistance" (Gill 2014: 29). Gill notes how political concerns drove the conceptual understanding of religion at the time, and that contest has consequences for scholars today concerned with analyzing the practical forms of that historical moment.

Further demonstrating the interplay of taxonomic concerns around religions and religion is the colonial support of the Singh form of Sikhism. Singhs, or *amritdhari* Sikhs, are those who have been baptized in the *Amrit Sanchar* rite, which employs sacred water and military symbolism to initiate individuals into the Khalsa set up by Guru Gobind Singh. Singhs are known for displaying the "five K's" that include the *kesh*—uncut hair—and the *kirpan*—the sword, and are expected to work towards establishing the sovereign Sikh polity of the Khalsa Raj. Ironically, thanks to the military nature of this form of Sikhism combined with the service of Sikhs during the World Wars and their identification as a "martial race," the British government embraced and validated Singh Sikhs as the only true practitioners of Sikhism.[8] The same mindset that sought self-government would ultimately serve the Raj, much to the chagrin and shame of later communities. The near hegemony of *amritdhari* representations today is a consequence of the very kinds of knowledge-organization that Reed discussed, both by Sikhs and British officials. Moreover, the Udasi sect's opposition to the increasing dominance of Sikhism offers an example of how local and particular narratives of difference, continuity, and change can affect our own scholarly perceptions, along with the political consequences of such endeavors.

Early twentieth-century Sikh "practice[s] of creating narratives that remap synchronic diversity onto chronological time" was accompanied by an assertion of difference, which Sikhs established through reference to components that their Western colonizers expected from "religions" (Chapter 1, this volume). These included a textual canon along with a focus on textual passages espousing religious peculiarity, recognizing a distinct "lineage of learning and practice" coming from the ten human Gurus (ibid.), a common core of spiritual tenets linking Punjabi and diaspora Sikhs into a single community, and created connections to a sacred language and homeland. Anne Murphy, whose analyses of Sikhism in this period ably attend to these complexities, noted how the writings of prominent Sikh reformer Bhai Vir Singh "produced a particular vision of the transcendent as Sikh 'theology' modeled upon European understandings of the transcendent" (Murphy 2015: 153). While Sikh communities sought to determine their own character in light of colonial expectations, Murphy reminds us that the delicate balance between religion and politics was repeatedly (and unintentionally) disturbed by the government. In recognizing the validity of the Gurdwara Reform Movement on the basis of gurdwaras representing the corporate body of all Sikhs, the British colonial government "politically recognized a religious body to act in the public sphere, to represent religious sites and through them the interests of a religious community in political terms, even as it decried the mixing of religion and politics" (Murphy 2013: 58). Multiple agents act in an ever-shifting context to produce an understanding of the concept "religion" while concurrently attempting to employ that category towards diverse ends. The consequences of such contests extend beyond their socio-cultural and political context and continue to inform the work of scholars today.

The normative procedure of "naturaliz[ing] and emphasiz[ing] some connections and trajectories ... and effac[ing] others" does not happen in a vacuum (Chapter 1, this volume). When we seek to understand how particular groups go about organizing knowledge and concepts, we must look also at the socio-political forces prompting and guiding such a pursuit alongside intrinsic ideological demands. The unity insisted upon by Christian theology should certainly not be a base assumption of all such attempts. Just as Hume recognized a broad number of relationships at work in forming our ideas, the same associations can broaden our awareness of how we construct the boundaries of specific religions as well as the concept itself. Understanding the "why" of organizing knowledge alongside the "how" is necessary to understand why certain aspects of traditions are championed over others.

While Reed's focus was on premodern theorizing, her approach can inform modern contexts engaging the category religion, and to what extent particularly situated attempts at establishing such categories serve a variety of goals. How the creation of religion as a category commits us to certain constellations of "religions" alters not only the academic, but social and political landscapes. One of the most significant things I took away from her essay was her insight into how we as scholars tend to privilege sources and discourses that align with our own taxonomic expectations. Such a partiality can lead us to accept certain voices as "proper" representation for the traditions that concern us, based on merely their own alignment with our classificatory syntax. It further raises the question of whether we are still relying on created expectations of what religion is—a constructed essence—that we seek, find, and repeat in dealing with other systems of classification.

John Soboslai is an Assistant Professor in the Department of Religion at Montclair State University. He holds an MA in the history of religion from Columbia University, and a Ph.D. in religious studies from the University of California, Santa Barbara. Specializing in martyrdom and global religious violence, he was named Sherman Emerging Scholar of 2016, and in 2015 University of California Press published his co-authored book *God in the Tumult of the Global Square*.

Notes

1. For Kant's central discussion of religion, see his *Religion Within the Limits of Reason Alone* (Kant 1960 [1793]).
2. See Saler (1999) and Wiebe (2000).
3. See Reed (2017).
4. See for example Hawkins (1976). The dichotomy of logical and empirical contrariety was inspired by Cohen (1978).
5. Of course, concerns about differentiation were active for Christian groups at varying points.
6. A work that provides both a useful background for the development of the term "Hinduism" along with an inquiry into the relative appropriateness of using Hinduism or sanatana dharma as an appropriate label for the body of practices based in Vedic texts is Ian Levy's posthumous "Is the term 'Sanatana Dharma' More Appropriate than the Term 'Hinduism' to Describe the Vedic Tradition?" (Levy 2016).
7. See ch. 1 of Axel (2001) for a good discussion of the relative terms used in reference to the collective bodies of Sikhs.
8. As Richard Fox puts it, Singh Sikhs "imposed the same definition on the Sikh religious community that the colonial authorities espoused: the only true Sikh as a Singh" (Fox 1985: 114).

References

Arnal, William E., and Russell T. McCutcheon. 2013. *The Sacred is the Profane: The Political Nature of "Religion."* New York: Oxford University Press. https://doi.org/10.1093/acprof:oso/9780199757114.001.0001

Asad, Talal. 1993. *Genealogies of Religion: Discipline and Reasons of Power in Christianity and Islam*. Baltimore, MD: Johns Hopkins Press.

Axel, Brian Keith. 2001. *The Nation's Tortured Body: Violence, Representation, and the Formation of a Sikh Diaspora*. Durham, NC: Duke University Press.

Barrier, N. Gerald. 1979. "The Role of Ideology and Institution Building in Modern Sikhism." In Mark Juergensmeyer and N. Gerald Barrier (eds.), *Sikh Studies: Comparative Perspectives on a Changing Tradition*, 41–51. Berkeley, CA: University of California Press.

Cohen, Benjamin. 1978. "Contrariety and Causality in Hume." *Hume Studies* 4(1) (April): 29–39. https://doi.org/10.1353/hms.2011.0561

Fox, Richard G. 1985. *Lions of the Punjab: Culture in the Making*. Berkeley, CA: University of California Press.

Geertz, Clifford. 1973. *Interpretations of Culture*. New York: Basic Books.

Gill, Parmbir Singh. 2014. "A Different Kind of Dissidence: The Ghadar Party, Sikh History and the Politics of Anticolonial Mobilization." *Sikh Formations* 10(1): 23–41. https://doi.org/10.1080/17448727.2014.890800

Grewal, J. S. 1979. "A Perspective on Early Sikh History." In Mark Juergensmeyer and N. Gerald Barrier (eds.), *Sikh Studies: Comparative Perspectives on a Changing Tradition*, 33–39. Berkeley, CA: University of California Press.

Hawkins, R. J. 1976. "Simplicity, Resemblance and Contrariety in Hume's Treatise." *The Philosophical Quarterly* 26(102) (January): 24–38. https://doi.org/10.2307/2218802

Hume, David. 1874. *A Treatise of Human Nature*. London: Longmans, Green and Co.

Juergensmeyer, Mark. 1979. "The Ghadar Syndrome: Immigrant Sikhs and Nationalist Pride." In Mark Juergensmeyer and N. Gerald Barrier (eds.), *Sikh Studies: Comparative Perspectives on a Changing Tradition*, 173–190. Berkeley, CA: University of California Press.

Kant, Immanuel. 1996 [1788]. *Critique of Practical Reason*, trans. Werner Pluhar. New York: Hackett Publishing. https://doi.org/10.1017/CBO9780511809576

Kant, Immanuel. 1960 [1793]. *Religion Within the Limits of Reason Alone*, trans. Theodore Greene. New York: HarperOne.

Levy, Ian. 2016. "Is the Term 'Sanatana Dharma' More Appropriate than the Term 'Hinduism' to Describe the Vedic Tradition?" *Transpersonal Psychology Review* 18(2) (Fall): 58–69.

Murphy, Anne. 2013. "Defining the Religious and the Political: The Administration of Sikh Religious Sites in Colonial India and the Making of a Public Sphere." *Sikh Formations* 9(1): 51–62. https://doi.org/10.1080/17448727.2013.774706

Murphy, Anne. 2015. "The Formation of the Ethical Sikh Subject in the era of British Colonial Reform." *Sikh Formations* 11(1–2): 149–159. https://doi.org/10.1080/17448727.2015.1024033

Oberoi, Harjot. 1994. *The Construction of Religious Boundaries*. New York: Oxford University Press.

Reed, Annette Yoshiko. 2017. "Categorization, Collection, and the Construction of Continuity: 1 Enoch and 3 Enoch in and Beyond 'Apocalypticism' and 'Mysticism'." *Method and Theory in the Study of Religion* 29: 268–311. https://doi.org/10.1163/15700682-12341391

Saler, Bensons. 1999. "Family Resemblance and the Definition of Religion." *Historical Reflections/Réflexions Historiques* 25(3): 391–404.

Singh, Ganda. 1965. *Some Confidential Papers of the Alkali Movement*. Amritsar: Shiromani Gurwara Pargandhak Committee, Sikh Itihas Research Board.

Smith, Jonathan Z. 2004. "Religion, Religions, Religious." In Jonathan Z. Smith, *Relating Religion: Essays in the Study of Religion*, 179–197. Chicago, IL: Chicago University Press.

Soboslai, John. 2018. "Sikh Self-Sacrifice and Religious Representation during World War I." *Religions* 9(2): 1–18. https://doi.org/10.3390/rel9020055

Wiebe, Don. 2000. "Problems with the Family Resemblance Approach to Conceptualizing Religion." *Method & Theory in the Study of Religion* 12(14): 314–322. https://doi.org/10.1163/157006800X00229

Chapter 5

Interrogating Categories with Ethnography: On the "Five Pillars" of Islam

Jennifer A. Selby

Introduction

Annette Yoshiko Reed's chapter sophisticatedly interrogates how religious studies scholars employ categories, with attention to what they *do* and how they are often taken for granted in scholarly work. Categorization is a perennial task for scholars who reference diverse data and, as Reed shows, scholars of religion may be particularly attuned to delimiting their objects of study (Chapter 1, this volume). They often do so to argue that the foci of their studies are neither universal nor neutral. In her paper, Reed references her work on Epiphanius's *Panarion* and the Pseudo-Clementine *Homilies* to attend to the power and limits of categorizing these texts as falling within "Judaism," "Christianity," and/or "Jewish-Christianity." In this short response, I consider some of Reed's warnings and clarifications about categories, including "much-noted problems of anachronism, abstraction, and reification" (ibid.), and how they inform interrogation of my own entirely different research context and methodological approach to this "thing" called religion that our scholarship has in common.

In her engagement with fourth century texts typically attributed to Judeo-Christianity and variations thereof, Reed shows how categorization is inherently historical and political. Someone (in a place of authority) determines what is in and what is out. To be clear, in our discussion at the 2017 NAASR meetings in Boston, neither Reed, myself, nor her other respondents suggested that we do away with categories. We employ them because they are useful: they reduce unwieldy data, they offer guidance to the most accepted and widely used matters, whether or not, in the Aristotelian sense, they are based on natural taxonomies. They offer, to borrow from J. Z. Smith (1982), a "focusing lens." In this short response, I seek to briefly consider what categories *do* in determining what is in and what is out, and why this matters, in relation to my own recent research.

More concretely, I ask: what is privileged and/or effaced when, within a social scientific perspective, we move away from a dominant framework for categorizing beliefs and practice in Islam: the "five pillars" [*arkan al-Islam*]? These pillars, the reader will recall, include a declaration of faith, daily prayer, almsgiving, fasting in the month of Ramadan and *hajj*, or pilgrimage to Mecca. To interrogate this five-part framework, I draw on two strands of data: first, qualitative interviews conducted in 2012–2013 with Muslims in Montreal and St. John's, Canada,[1] to which I will return in a moment, and second, a recently compiled bibliography of scholarship on Islam and Muslims in Canada.[2] Given that "Islam(s) and Muslims in/of Canada" is a relatively nascent field, it has been possible to assemble most scholarly production to date, located in a number of disciplines, including anthropology, gender studies, law, political science, religious studies, and sociology, and to a lesser extent in community health, cultural studies, history, and terrorist studies. When we look at the corpus of English- and French-language scholarly knowledge production—which presently constitutes 21 single-spaced pages—it becomes clear that most has been published since 2001 and has expanded exponentially since 2008, dovetailing with Canadian debates on the presence of Islam in the public sphere. Qualitative-based approaches and discourse analysis are the most common methodologies. My own work in this corpus has been primarily qualitative and ethnographic. As always, there are politics in these approaches. In relation to Islamic and Muslim Studies, these politics include a common reaction against a longstanding Orientalist philological approach in Islamic Studies (well critiqued by Said 1978; Abu-Lughod 1989; Deeb and Winegar 2015) and an older style of anthropology that treated its subjects as primitive and un-modern.

Discussion

Rather than rehearsing these politics or considering theological discussions on the underpinnings of the pillars, I briefly reflect on what the "five pillars" categorization, often taken for granted in this qualitative-based work, does in delimiting and codifying Muslimness in the Canadian scholarly context. Even if not overtly delimited within a single *sura* (chapter) in the Qur'an (Hughes 2013: 210), the notion of five pillars has theological and historical purchase. Fourteen centuries after a seventh-century *hadith* (the sayings attributed to the Prophet) in which the Prophet Muhammad is said to have described the foundations of Islam as having been "built upon five,"[3] the pillars remain central to Introduction to Islam textbooks, posters in mosque basements for visitors, and in the descriptions of religious life by many of our interlocutors in Montreal, Quebec and St. John's, Newfoundland and Labrador. Robert Hefner (1998: 92) explains the saliency of the categorization collapse of heterogeneity in Islam into five pillars: they reflect a "world-religions-based" approach, which he sees as responding to "demands for a unitary profession of faith." In order to broadly compare traditions, distillation is useful. Other trends also appear. For instance, on the one hand, a scholarly privileging in the field of Islamic Studies on the fixedness of its central revealed text arguably extends to the encouragement of the five-pillars framework. On the other hand, an emphasis more generally in the study of religion on the visual and ritual components of religiosity may also privilege the reliance on the pillars as tantamount to Muslim practice and belief (and not other creeds or guiding principles).

There have been proposals for alternative frameworks to conceptualize and categorize Muslim practice and belief, even if not to move away specifically from the five pillars as a point of reference. Let us briefly consider two of these other models. Based on his qualitative research among Muslim volunteers in charitable organizations in Western Europe whose religiosity is evident in all parts of their lives, William Barylo (2018) argues for the academic examination of Islam not through the current social scientific more functionalist emphasis on ritual (akin to the pillars), but as though it were a "matrix" that shifts depending on context. Nadia Fadil (2006: 72) has similarly noted, in relation to her ethnographic work in Antwerp, how her interlocutors' experiences of religiosity and citizenship show how "religion is not practiced, but lived," or that religionists embody their Muslim perspectives in social and political realms so that approaching practice with a rigid framework does not adequately reflect what people do. Part of the arithmetic in this anti-categorization is a "lived religion" approach, currently in vogue in qualitative work on Islam.[4] In part, the "lived religion" approach aims to respond to a trend in the early 2000s that focused on piety and Islamic "Revivalist" movements.[5] But, it can also be a useful approach to move away from pre-set, too-narrow categories, to more organic narratives. But here we must tread carefully, as the notion of "lived religion" has also been used as an authenticity marker (lived religion = real religion). As many method and theory scholars have asked (i.e., Ramey 2015; on problematizing the notion of the everyday, see Fadil and Fernando 2015), what religion is there but "lived"?

To return to my departing question, what happens if we purposefully disentangle the "five pillar" categorization in our interview schedules with self-defined Muslims? What does the omission *do* to what we know about Muslim life, and eventually to the disseminated scholarly contents? In 2012–2013, Lori G. Beaman, Amélie Barras and I conducted interviews with 90 self-identified Muslims in St. John's, NL and Montreal, QC about "everyday/everynight" Muslimness (Selby, Barras, and Beaman 2018). One of our hypotheses was that if we moved our interview schedule away from asking about and assuming a pillar understanding of Islam we would uncover different data on Islam(s) in Canada from what has been published to date. Part of the rationale for the exclusion of the category was our reading of the academic literature on Muslims in Western contexts since the early 2000s, which we felt tends to focus on visibility and difference, whether on prayer, visible religious signs, and related Islamophobia and anti-Muslim racisms. We wondered whether this pervasive lens might also work to produce data on a "problematic" Islam as constitutive of the Muslim Canadian experience. In other words, we questioned what would happen if we chronicled how Islam—as one of several points of identity in our participants' lives—emerged in our interlocutors' everyday interactions.

Referencing Kim Knott's (2005, 2009) work on the centrality of space in shaping the lived experience of religiosity, Barras, Beaman, and I therefore deliberately directed our interview schedule to reflect upon our interlocutors' social interactions of religiosity in different places, such as at restaurants, in buses, in mosques, at work, in grocery stores, at the dinner table of friends, at public pools, at community events, and so on. We hoped that such precision and spatiality would bring us closer to how Islam is lived through individual lenses rather than responses to a pillar checkbox on prayer, fasting, modest dress, halal foods, and so on.

The approach produced a number of other effects. For one, these everyday moments beyond the pillar categorization allowed us to decenter the notion that there is one Islamic orthodoxy or truth and move away from categories that reinforce this idea. Even if some of our respondents articulate their religiosity related to the five pillars, they frame Islam in a certain way. In this way, we took a moderate constructionist approach (following Beckford 2003; Taira 2013) that aimed to question a "proper" or normative Islam and that acknowledged that power, privilege and status are "legitimated by the religious traditions that are socially defined as authentic" (McGuire 2008: 190). More concretely, Fadil (2011: 93) notes, from an Asadian approach that sees Islam as a discursive tradition, we saw that "Islamic piety" does not necessarily refer to rigid or conservative viewpoints, but to a set of multiple epistemological procedures, discourses and practices that are considered authoritative and are thus given a prescriptive legitimacy (see also Schielke and Debevec 2012: 6). This aim of moving away from strict categories may not seem to be particularly original. And yet, despite the recognition that Muslims live out their practice in myriad ways and come from Sunni, Shi'ia, Sufi, and other backgrounds, branches and sects, we have noted with the scholarly work published to date in Canada, that this observation has rarely been translated into scholarship. Among others, we therefore sought to recognize that, as with any religious group, Muslims practice in innumerable ways.

Our aim was not to delineate a "proper" object of study. We did not overtly seek to promote "moderate Muslims" or that practice is necessarily more complex or more worthy of study than text. Rather, we suggested that in relying on the five pillars, much of the social scientific scholarship published in Canada in the socio-political post-9/11 climate, when these individuals often experience heightened surveillance, could unintentionally affirm a homogeneous pious Muslim archetype. Differences based on lived experience are flattened. One aspect we did not anticipate in conceiving of our interview schedule was the difficulty of moving away from these categories. Despite our methodological and theoretical attention to this point, when we began analyzing our 90 transcripts, we noted—admittedly, embarrassingly—that our own work at times inadvertently invoked them, and arguably reproduced and mobilized a "five-pillar Muslim". Two examples from our study in Canada reveal the subtle but significant ways these categories are difficult to navigate (for more, see ch. 1 in Selby et al. 2018).

"Siddra", 50, lives with her three daughters and two sons at home in a suburb of St. John's, Newfoundland and Labrador, on the east coast of Canada. She self-identifies as Muslim, is of Pakistani origin and lived in Saudi Arabia and Dubai before relocating with her oil-industry-working husband and their children to North America's most easterly city. When our conversation lulled on a November morning in her bright living room, we prompted her about her religious practices by drawing on the pillars. Tellingly, in response, she twice noted her lack of formal training in Islamic theology and voiced concern that she was not providing the right answers. Siddra inferred that the "right answers" would better reflect interpretations of the traditions of Islam within the pillars framework. In other words, in referencing the pillars as a reflex to prompt conversation, we may have unintentionally shamed her. Later in the interview, when we asked a standard concluding question about how the state might address concerns or issues that affect her, she became animated, stating, "I want my children to [be able to] walk to the [public] library. If they can walk to McDonald's, they can walk to the library!" Based on her animated tone and willingness to speak at length on the subject of public library access, while wearing a hijab and engaged in everyday prayer and halal-framed dietary practices, these facets of her identity were not among Siddra's primary concerns. Enthusiasm emerged for Siddra when she spoke about a lack of municipal services close to her home. If our interview schedule had only focused on the most politicized elements of her practice, her concerns about getting her children active in her community—which she understands vis-à-vis Islam—would have been missed.

A second inference to the five-pillars-understood framework of practice relates to impromptu questioning in our interview with "Caroline," a 35-year-old Montreal-based convert. When we asked her about whether she chose a daycare for her son because its menu was *halal*, we assumed that this dietary restriction was important for her:

> Interviewer: Your son, is he at daycare? And did you choose a daycare where they offer halal meals?
> Caroline: So [*Fait que*], we took—we decided to let him eat meat even if it's not halal ... while asking Allah to forgive us because we are lazy and [uneasy laughter] that's it.

As we coded transcribed interviews, it became clear that the way in which we framed our unscripted follow-up question foregrounded religiosity in how she chose childcare for her son. Caroline noted that halal daycares in her area of the city are rare, and that to place her son in one of these facilities would have involved a long commute, which she did not have the "courage" to do. Like Siddra, she apologetically explained her choices. She appeared uncomfortable in "admitting" the non-religiously framed reasons for which she enrolled her son at this childcare facility. Our impromptu question appeared to make her feel uneasy, as though we were judging her. In sum, we unintentionally framed her daycare choice in such a way that given the circumstances she was unable to follow "correct" Islam. For her, in this instance, the financial question outweighed a religiously based rationale.

Conclusion

Upon first glance, these miscommunications may appear negligible. We did not catch them until we read and reread our transcripts. My point is that researchers, myself included, may inadvertently contribute to a pressure toward conservatism or orthodoxy in the questions we pose and categories we employ, whether consciously or not. Together these frameworks that emphasize codified practices and belief as if they were emblematic of religiosity may not actually reflect what people tell us or what they do in their everyday lives.

A reflex to return to the pillars, as I have thought about in this short intervention, has a number of noteworthy consequences, of which I consider three. First, the flexibility and contradictions within Muslim life are more easily obscured. Even if our interview schedule aimed to move away from the categorization, in prompting participants with the pillars, we may inadvertently encourage our interviewees to describe religious practice statically, reflecting an Orientalist-influenced predisposition to view Islam by reference to texts and their demands upon the believer. Scholars then can reproduce this kind of data in their findings and do not acknowledge a more "matrix" or "lived religion" perspective.

Second, this unintentional emphasis on "five-pillars Islam" in our own interviews may have acted as a subtle form of shaming that serves to underpin essentialized characterizations of the "good" or "pious" Muslim, exacerbating a tendency among participants to identity with more conservative versions in an interview (cf. Mamdani 2004; Jeldtoft 2011: 1144). Siddra and Carolyn responded with worry that they were not "Muslim enough" and apologized for not fully practicing the pillars. Our aim was not to codify our participants on a scale from atheist to non-practicing to moderate to conservative, but we did hope they would share their experiences sincerely.

And third, the pillar focus saturates individual Muslims with an exclusive "Muslimness" that can be seen as analogue to widespread myopathy on race (e.g. as natural, self-evident, unyielding). As I show in some of my other work, this saturation positions Muslim minorities to all-too-familiar dynamics of state regulation and racialized politics (Selby 2012). In this political moment, problematizing this category collapse matters. In sum, with attention to the potential (even if unintentional) liberalizing effects of moving away from the pillars (Hughes 2015 captures a broader trend of scholarship rendering Islam liberal), I wonder whether the categorization may erase difference and flatten lived experience in ways that do not reflect the breadth of contemporary Muslim Canadian life.

On this point, I return to Reed, who usefully asks, "what can or should we *do* when we encounter data that does not fit into our taxonomies of "religion" and definitions of "religion"""? (Chapter 1, this volume). Obviously, our methods—here, research questions and interview schedules—largely determine the data we collect and the data we discard in the final scholarly product. These categorizations are clearly influenced by our understanding of "Islam." What could happen to Reed's analysis if "Jew" or "Christian" were entirely absent from her analysis? Could their absenteeism unintentionally reify these categories? In this vein, when considering our findings, should we keep the taxonomies in question as referents or attempt to move away from them altogether? In considering Siddra and Caroline's narratives, I conclude that—while they self-identify as Muslim, their religiosity is a central part of their identity and they are familiar with the notion of the pillars in describing their religious practice—there are other factors and politics that, in some instances, can be more important for them. Asking beyond the five pillars captures some of these experiences, which, arguably, can be found more organically through ethnography, where one is not only confined by an interview schedule. The pillars thus remain a fruitful categorization from which to depart to gauge why and what is left in and out of the data we produce.

Jennifer A. Selby is Associate Professor of Religious Studies and affiliate member of Gender Studies at Memorial University of Newfoundland, Canada. Her research, teaching, and supervision broadly consider Muslim life in contemporary France and Canada and the delineations of secularism. She is the author of *Questioning French Secularism: Gender Politics and Islam in a Parisian Suburb* (Palgrave Macmillan, 2012) and co-editor of *Debating Sharia: Islam, Gender Politics, and Family Law Arbitration* (University of Toronto Press, 2012).

Notes

1. I gratefully acknowledge the participation of our anonymized interlocutors in St. John's and Montreal, support from the Social Sciences and Humanities Research Council, and the research assistance of Caitlin Downie and Jennifer Williams. Beaman and I conducted interviews in St. John's and Barras in Montreal. The passage from the interview with "Caroline" has been translated by us from French to English.
2. This bibliography is a work in progress in so far as it is regularly updated (www.mun. ca/relstudies/more/producingislams/biblio.php). It was compiled with contributions from scholars of Islam and Muslims in Canada, including those who attended a workshop on knowledge production on Islam in Canada at Carleton University in September 2017. As described on the website, while more unwieldy, we chose not to categorize the citations by date or theme.
3. This website (https://honeyfortheheart.wordpress.com/40-hadith/hadith-03-islam-is-built-on-5-pillars) claims the hadith can be attributed to one of the "rightly guided" Caliphs, Abdullah ibn Umar al-Khattabf. Four of the pillars are mentioned in the Qur'an, in 2:177 and the pilgrimage (*hajj*) in 22:27. The categorization is said to have been systematized by Abu 'Abd al-Qahir al-Baghdadi in "On the Roots of Religion" in the early eleventh century (Knott 2016: 2).
4. Social scientists have long been interested in considering lived realities, both through the lenses of what has been called "the everyday" (following Goffman 1956; de Certeau 1984; McGuire 2008; Smith 1987) and through recent social scientific research on Muslim realities (Schielke 2009a, 2009b; Deeb 2015; Brown 2016).
5. I (Selby 2016) note the academic trend since 2005 (and the significance of Mahmood's 2005 book on a female piety movement in Cairo) to turn to the terms "Islamic piety," "revolution," and/or "revival" in describing Muslim practice.

References

Abu-Lughod, Lila. 1989. "Zones of Theory in the Anthropology of the Arab World." *Annual Review of Anthropology* 18: 267–306. https://doi.org/10.1146/annurev.an.18.100189.001411

Barylo, William. 2018. "Appropriating Islam as Matrix: Young Muslim Volunteers Blurring the Lines between Sacred and Profane." *Method and Theory in the Study of Religion* 29: 181– 204. https://doi.org/10.1163/15700682-12341383

Beckford, James A. 2003. *Social Theory and Religion*. Cambridge: Cambridge University Press. https://doi.org/10.1017/CBO9780511520754

Brown, Rachel. 2016. "How Gelatin Becomes an Essential Symbol of Muslim Identity: Food Practice as a Lens into the Study of Religion and Migration." *Religious Studies and Theology* 35(2): 89–113. https://doi.org/10.1558/rsth.32558

De Certeau, Michel. 1984. *The Practice of Everyday Life*, trans. Steven F. Rendall. Berkeley, CA: University of California Press.

Deeb, Lara. 2015. "Thinking Piety and the Everyday Together: A Response to Fadil and Fernando." *HAU: Journal of Ethnographic Theory* 5(2): 93–96. https://doi.org/10.14318/hau5.2.007

Deeb, Lara, and Jessica Winegar. 2015. *Anthropology's Politics: Disciplining the Middle East*. Stanford, CA: Stanford University Press.

Fadil, Nadia. 2006. "'We Should Be Walking Qurans': The Making of an Islamic Political Subject." In Gerdien Jonker and Valérie Amiraux (eds.), *Politics of Visibility: Young Muslims in European Public Spaces*, 53–78. Bielefeld: Transcript-Verlag.

Fadil, Nadia. 2011. "On Not-/Unveiling as an Ethical Practice." *Feminist Review* 98: 83–109. https://doi.org/10.1057/fr.2011.12

Fadil, Nadia, and Mayanthi L. Fernando. 2015. "Rediscovering the 'Everyday' Muslim: Notes on an Anthropological Divide." *HAU: Journal of Ethnographic Theory* 5(2): 59–88. https://doi.org/10.14318/hau5.2.005

Goffman, Erving. 1956. *The Presentation of the Self in Everyday Life*. New York: Random House.

Hefner, Robert W. 1998. "Multiple Modernities: Christianity, Islam, and Hinduism in a Globalizing Age." *Annual Review of Anthropology* 27(1998): 83–104. https://doi.org/10.1146/annurev.anthro.27.1.83

Hughes, Aaron W. 2013. *Muslim Identities: An Introduction to Islam*. New York: Columbia University Press.

Hughes, Aaron W. 2015. *Islam and the Tyranny of Authenticity: An Inquiry into Disciplinary Apologetics and Self-Deception*. Sheffield: Equinox.

Jeldtoft, Nadia. 2011. "Lived Islam: Religious Identity With 'Nonorganized' Muslim Minorities." *Ethnic and Racial Studies* 34(7): 1134–1151. https://doi.org/10.1080/01419870.2010.528441

Knott, Kim. 2005. "Researching Local and National Pluralism: Britain's New Religious Landscape." In Martin Bauman and Samuel M. Behloul (eds.), *Religiöser Pluralismus empirische Studien und analytische Perspektiven*, 45–68. Bielefeld: Transcript Verlag.

Knott, Kim. 2009. "From Locality to Location and Back Again: A Spatial Journey of the Study of Religion." *Religion* 39(2): 154–160. https://doi.org/10.1016/j.religion.2009.01.003

Knott, Kim. 2016. *Islam: The Five Pillars*. Retrieved from https://crestresearch.ac.uk/resources/five-pillars-guide

Mahmood, Saba. 2005. *The Politics of Piety: The Islamic Revival and the Feminist Subject*. Princeton, NJ: Princeton University Press.

Mamdani, Mahmood. 2004. *Good Muslim, Bad Muslim: America, the Cold War, and the Roots of Terror*. New York: Three Leaves Press.

McGuire, Meredith. 2008. *Lived Religion: Faith and Practice in Everyday Life*. New York: Oxford University Press.

Ramey, Steven. 2015. "When Acceptance Reflects Disrespect: The Methodological Contradictions of Accepting Participant Statements." *Method and Theory in the Study of Religion* 27: 59–81. https://doi.org/10.1163/15700682-12341324

Said, Edward, 1978. *Orientalism*. New York: Pantheon Books.

Schielke, Samuli. 2009a. "Ambivalent Commitments: Troubles of Morality, Religiosity and Aspiration Among Young Egyptians." *Journal of Religion in Africa* 39(2): 158–185. https://doi.org/10.1163/157006609X427814

Schielke, Samuli. 2009b. "Being Good in Ramadan: Ambivalence, Fragmentation and the Moral Self in the Lives of Young Egyptians." *Journal of the Royal Anthropological Institute* 15(1): 24–40. https://doi.org/10.1111/j.1467-9655.2009.01540.x

Schielke, Samuli and Liza Debevec. 2012. "Introduction." In Samuli Schielke and Liza Debevec (eds.), *Ordinary Lives and Grand Schemes: An Anthropology of Everyday Religion*, 1–16. New York: Berghahn.

Selby, Jennifer A. 2012. *Questioning French Secularism: Gender Politics and Islam in a Parisian Suburb*. Anthropology of Religion Series. New York: Palgrave Macmillan.

Selby, Jennifer A. 2016. "Muslimness and Multiplicity in Qualitative Research and in Government Reports in Canada." *Critical Research on Religion* 4(1) (April): 72–89. https://doi.org/10.1177/2050303216630298

Selby, Jennifer A., Amélie Barras, and Lori G. Beaman. 2018. *Beyond Accommodation: Everyday Narratives of Muslim Canadians*. Vancouver: University of British Columbia Press.

Smith, Dorothy E. 1987. *The Everyday World as Problematic: A Feminist Sociology*. Boston, MA: North Eastern University Press.

Smith, Jonathan Z. 1982. *Imagining Religion: From Babylonia to Jonestown*. Chicago, IL: University of Chicago Press.

Taira, Teemu. 2013. "The Category of 'Invented Religion': A New Opportunity for Studying Discourses on 'Religion'." *Culture and Religion: An Interdisciplinary Journal* 14(4): 477–493. https://doi.org/10.1080/14755610.2013.838799

Part II
Objects

Chapter 6

Objects and Objections: Methodological Reflections on the Data for Religious Studies

Matthew C. Baldwin

The Data for Religious Studies

[S]ome of us stand clustered with the like-minded off to one corner of our big tent, where we whisper—and sometimes intemperately announce—our objections. I don't object to objections. Far from it. They're inevitable, and good for this organization. (Tweed 2016: 289)

[D]ata is a function of theory and different theories make different things into data. (McCutcheon 2014: 68)

I placed a jar in Tennessee, / And round it was, upon a hill. (Stevens 1923)

A datum is a thing considered as "given"—as evident—but who or what presents it, who accepts the given as evidence, and as evidence of what? Russell McCutcheon seems right to suggest that the theories we hold (be they explicit or implicit, grand or miniature) generate the data we find. In asserting this, McCutcheon is at least in part referring to definitions. He has written that our "definitions are theories in miniature," describing them as "actively stipulative and not merely passively descriptive" (McCutcheon 2015: 120 n. 2). The things presented as "givens" in research reveal, first and foremost, the theoretical perspectives of the researcher. We do not start from randomly observed "facts," only to decide later that some of the observations we have recorded happen to illuminate a matter of professional significance. We are already in motion before we begin. We set out from particular places with particular questions, carrying our assumptions as cargo and tools, in the company of colleagues, knowing beforehand what will count as significant, how to look for it, and where to find it. We should, therefore, exercise all due self-reflective caution in our expeditions. After all, Columbus found a way to his India, with lasting consequences for the world.

In scholarship, we present data as data, assuming that our claims about the world will be accepted as given things, by using methods such as careful record keeping, description, and reporting, meticulous documentation and citation of sources, *et cetera*. All of these practices assume the possibility or even the inevitability of disagreement. They acknowledge that one researcher's proposed givens may wind up as another's contested matters. For this reason it seems good that Thomas Tweed signaled in his 2015 Presidential Address to the American Academy of Religion that he does not to object to objections. Objecting to objections would involve the scholar in an unfortunate self-contradiction. We can presume, therefore, that Tweed spoke from a place of good humor. And yet, one might well object to his characterization of some objections as "intemperate," or to his implication that the objections he has noticed all originate with "like minded" (read "closed-minded") cliques gathered in a "corner" away from the vital center of the "tent." We might also wonder about his claim that objections are "good for the organization;" this appears to presume a pragmatic account of progress in the human sciences, not to mention assuming in advance that "the organization" will always be the most important institutional space in which such progress takes place. Neither progress nor the organization seem inevitable. Yet it does seem right to recognize that objections, as such, are. Can we all begin, then, by agreeing to this? There is disagreement. Disagreement is a thing. This is my proposed initial datum, my jar placed in Tennessee.

Religious Studies as a Social Formation

To borrow a term from Bruce Lincoln, I take it as a given that "religious studies" is an "ethnonym," that is, a name for what may be metaphorically described as a tribe of people (Lincoln 1996: 225).[1] I would not wish to claim, as Lincoln did for "history of religions," that "religious studies" may be termed a "disciplinary ethnonym." After all, the members of our loosely governed academic tribe practice many different disciplines, leading some to describe religious studies as "interdisciplinary" (e.g., Coward 2006). (I myself would prefer the label "multidisciplinary," since field practitioners usually practice their different disciplines in parallel rather than in concert.) In any case, true disciplinary unity is lacking, and so the term "field of study" works better than "discipline" for conceptualizing the academic practice of "religious studies."[2]

Our field ethnonym has several synonyms, among them: "study of religion." Again modeling my analysis on Lincoln's, I suggest that this version of the ethnonym implies that field practitioners possess an "object of study" ("religion"). But in contrast to Lincoln's analysis I would note that the designation "study of religion" commits us to no particular methodology. After all, the word "study" signals nothing at all about what technologies or ways of scholarship will be practiced. "Study" offers little beyond the vague idea of methodical "zeal" implied by the Latin root of the word, *studium*.[3]

And what provides common shelter to this eclectic tribe of *bricoleurs*? In recent years, many, including Tweed, have invoked the "Big Tent" metaphor to describe the institutional unity that accommodates our diversity. Tweed rightly notes that the "Big Tent" metaphor corresponds to "our disagreements about the scope of the academic study of religion" (Tweed 2016: 288–289 and n. 1). What precisely this image suggests about the socio-academic architecture of Religious Studies remains a matter to be debated.[4] In any case, as Tweed suggests, objections abound and they go far beyond classic conflicts between "insider" (confessional) versus "outsider" (scientific) approaches to "religion." We are at odds with one another over fundamental issues of philosophy, metaphysics, social theory and methodology.[5]

In any case, the people of this field known as "Religious Studies" are a sub-tribe of academia, united by their recognizable genealogy in professional association, and in cognate institutional practices of research and teaching, including overlapping curricula and subject areas, and other shared modes of discursive self-construction. In other words, "Religious Studies" names a "social formation," however loosely gathered its constituents may be in "society."[6]

There is Data for the Study of Religion

I take it as another given that, although one can argue, as Gary Lease did, that "there is no religion,"[7] it is not possible to claim that there is no "study of religion." Though Deans and Provosts may remain unsure, I should not have to argue this point with the membership of the North American Association for the Study of Religion (NAASR). A correlate claim is that, while one might agree in some form with Jonathan Z. Smith, that "there is no data for religion" (Smith 1982: xi) it is not possible to claim that "there is no data for Religious Studies."

I intend two senses for this claim, and neither of them are meant to refute Lease or Smith. On the one hand, one can take, as McCutcheon has chosen to do, the social and discursive facts of religious studies scholarship as one's data (McCutcheon 1997; cf. von Stuckrad 2013). As I write these words, many thousands of scholars from around North America and the world are preparing to convene in Boston for the 2017 Annual Meetings of NAASR and the American Academy of Religion (AAR) and the Society of Biblical Literature (SBL). Hundreds of publishers will also show up and fill a massive room with books representing every corner of the field (and several adjacent ones as well). These scholars come from university and college departments of "Religion," "Religious Studies," "Religion and Philosophy" (and "Theology"). Every course listed in their catalogs, every syllabus, every class period, every paper they present, each article or book they publish, or public lecture they deliver; all online and print indices or abstracts of their works; all the topical encyclopedias, guides, and manuals they produce; the subject-headings by which library scientists classify their research; the book sales and citation figures; their blogs, websites, and social media activity; any or all such things can constitute "data for religious studies," because any of it can serve as evidence of a discernible class of socio-cultural practices within the contemporary world of academia.[8]

On the other hand, the phrase "data for religious studies" is also meant to gather together all that "religious studies" scholars have put forward as their own givens, their "data," that is, the things presented, analyzed and theoretically explained in their research. Indeed, there is ample evidence that "religious studies" practitioners have trained their learned and specialized attentions on a myriad of diverse objects (events, persons, artifacts, institutions, writings, relationships, languages, culture systems, and so on) which are treated procedurally as data, that is, as material for research.[9]

Pace Gustavo Benavides (2003), the generation of all this "data" does not refute Smith's famous dictum.[10] We must look beyond Smith's emphatic "six words" and remember their context:

> while there is a staggering amount of data, of phenomena, of human experiences and expressions that might be characterized in one culture or another, by one criterion or another, as religious—*there is no data for religion*. Religion is solely the creation of the scholar's study. (Smith 1982: xi)

Smith's statement assumes that diverse and mutually distinct criteria (discourses, definitions and theories) have been operationalized in scholarship ("the scholar's study"), producing "a staggering amount of data." Practitioners in the field quite deliberately collect and assemble, curate, collate, establish, preserve, translate, publish and disseminate their "data." Consider for example the recently constructed electronic clearinghouse of Religious Studies "data," as presented by Edward Slingerland and Brenton Sullivan (2017). Very generally speaking, analysis of all such "data" and argument based on it is precisely what characterizes "Religious Studies" discourses. So there can be "data for Religious Studies," in this second sense, without necessitating the idea that "there is data for religion." In fact it is precisely all these reams of data which lead Smith to his conclusion. There has yet to appear a unified "object of study" underwriting the diversity. There are many objects construed as "religious;" but *religion itself* has not appeared as an object.

"Religion" as a Field-Organizing Category (aka "Object of Study")

Another given: the category "religion" has itself been the subject of nearly constant scrutiny, contention, and debate in the scholarship of the last five or six decades—a period which, at least in North America, corresponds to the rise of contemporary religious studies as an independent academic field represented among university departments of study. It seems inconceivable that anyone in the field would ignore or dismiss the results of this tradition of critical scholarship on "religion" as a category employed in human thought—but another given is that many of our colleagues do ignore and dismiss or minimize it. In spite of ongoing discussion and disagreement, in "religious studies" (and also in other fields of human science where "religion" putatively comes into view) the vast majority of scholars continue to employ the term "religion" as if it named an objective entity producing self-evident effects independently of what any particular human might think about it, like one of Jupiter's moons. In other words, a naive or common-sense realist point of view about "religion" unjustifiably prevails among scholars.

The results of the debate on the category "religion" ought not to be ignored. We have come a long way from Wilfred Cantwell Smith to Jonathan Z. Smith, Timothy Fitzgerald, McCutcheon, Tomoko Masuzawa, Brent Nongbri (and others). The results of this tradition of scholarship can be epitomized as follows. Scholarship on the category "religion" has emphasized the long history of the term among peoples for whom Latin has been a linguistic influence. Lexicographical analysis of both popular and elite usage of the variants of "religion" (especially in Latin, French, English, and German) shows that the referent of the term has constantly shifted. We can trace a lineage of uses of the word, from ancient Roman ones signifying ritual obligations to the state and its gods; to the dedication of medieval monastic lives; to Protestant critiques of the variety of Protestant and Catholic practices; to power struggles over ecclesiastical authority in politics (the "wars of religion," and "secularization"); to neo-Calvinist disputes over the authenticity of the subjective experience of salvation and grace; to generalizing Enlightenment-era political discussions of the inviolability of the rights of conscience and the necessity of "religious liberty"; to the explosion of universalizing discourses about "religion" which begin with the age of exploration and colonization and continue into our own time.[11]

From the nineteenth century onwards philologists and ethnographers have attempted to make sense of the bewilderingly diverse human world which was opened up to European academics as a consequence of the age of exploration and colonialism. These scholars assembled large mountains of "data for Religious Studies," applying comparative and morphological criteria to the materials of the world in assembling their givens. Benson Saler's proposal to regard "religion" as a concept based on a Western "paradigm" (Saler 1999) has at least some heuristic value for thinking about how all this data has been assembled. (This appeal to Saler should not be read as my full endorsement of Saler's constructive claim that we *ought* to think of "religion" as an unbounded, family resemblance type polythetic category which is properly rooted in its Western paradigm, but rather an observation that scholars assembling their data do seem to have operated from some sort of Western paradigm.)

Europeans began the tradition that became "religious studies" by classifying the behaviors and social formations of other peoples comparatively, using as a basis for comparison a paradigm of "religion" made up initially of conceptual components that had been extracted from Western traditions.

The paradigm includes a jumbled panoply of terms (conceptual categories) representing institutional structures, social roles and offices, postulated beings, practices, material artifacts, substances, principles, and properties. An inadequate and incomplete yet representative list of this apparatus of terms would include things like: sects, cults, assemblies, churches, communities, orders, priests and priesthoods, monks and monasteries, scribes, docents, teachers, saints, redeemers, gods, angels, demons, souls, spirits, sacrifice, offerings, devotion, ritual, magic, worship, prayer, music, scripture, meeting houses, temples, groves, grottos, altars, implements, lamps, icons, symbols, sculptures, vestments, incense, traditions, creeds, legends, myths, beliefs, theology, doctrine, salvation, purity, holiness, sanctification, sacralization, tabu, mana, *et cetera.*

The fact that "Western" (Greco-Roman, European, Christian) terminology apparently dominates the paradigm list should make evident the institutional genealogy of "religious studies." In a centuries-long dialectical process that has been directly tied to the expansion of Western economic and political power, the list has only gradually been supplemented, extended, and stretched by experience and encounter. Moreover, within the paradigm, the relative prominence of certain terms of comparison reflects the vicissitudes of Christian self-construction in the face of competitors. The dominant categories of religious studies reflect the historically emergent hegemony of Christian (and post-Christian) discourses and their implicit hierarchies of value. (Shall a given community be compared to a "church," "synagogue" or "mosque"?)

By the early twentieth century, there was an acute problem of disagreement about what could or could not be said to constitute "religion." Scholars began to seek in vain for some metatheoretical unity among the various projects of academic research into "religion." Over a century has passed since the psychologist James H. Leuba famously listed "more than fifty" definitions of religion in an appendix to his treatise *A Psychological Study of Religion: Its Origin, Function, and Future* (1912: 339–361).[12] In that time no proposed definition of "religion" has gained universal assent. Given the process by which the data accumulates, none is ever likely to do so. Under the present circumstances of the field, at best, use of a stipulated definition of "religion" authorizes the self-identified "scholar of religion" to assemble a particular field of socio-cultural data for critical analysis and explanation.[13] At worst, a definition functions to separate the authentic and inauthentic in and among particular traditions, in service of a caretaker or missionary ethos. In any case it has been argued that all definite (and even more so all indefinite) conceptions of "religion" end up positioning the researcher and student over-against the subjects of research in a field of social and interested contestation, in which ideological (and usually theological) implications are not far to seek (Arnal and McCutcheon 2013).

To my mind, it remains an always open question—not to be settled in advance for all cases—whether the term "religion," once it has been applied by a scholar (or tradition of scholarship) as a redescription of some discrete set of data drawn from a particular society or culture-group, actually does point to an underlying social or cultural "structure" unifying the selected data.[14] Such analysis runs a risk of essentialism and reification. Even more, it risks manufacturing unity where previously there had been none. It is worth pointing out here that the category "religion" itself has sometimes proven to be an "interactive kind," that is, an etic category of analysis that gets adopted into emic usage.[15] Some "non-Western" groups have indeed adopted this Western category "religion" in reference to their own social formations—in a process which has perhaps permanently transformed their conceptualization of their own societies.[16]

Although one might assume that such cases only serve to prove that the flexible and ancient Western term "religion" has isolated something widespread and "real" in human life, we might just as well argue instead that the world's stuff could always have been conceptualized differently. It is interesting to imagine an alternate world history, in which our conceptual apparatus for studying "religion" would be quite different. Mutatis mutandis, had something comparable to what we call "religious studies" emerged institutionally from South Asia, and been tied to a program of South Asian imperial and colonial expansion, we might today all be parties to a field called "dharma studies," or something similar. Indeed, "Western" self-conception of its own social formations might be dramatically different had European peoples been subjected to domination or more effective political and military opposition by South Asians or other "non-Western" civilizations.

Legitimation of Scholarship, or, the Management of Surprise

Within our enterprise as it happens to be constructed, the term "religion" is used as an instrument for the legitimation of scholarly work. After all, if you work in a religious studies program, you have to study "religion"; otherwise, why are they paying you? Luckily for us, the flexibility of this signifier means that virtually anything and everything can be included in our studies. (In this regard, the conjunction "and" is also very useful.) The term "religion" functions like a tax-stamp which permits inquiry into the dazzling variety of matters which scholars "discover" in the "wild." Thus do the constant reams of "data" generated by our competing activities of definition and theorization continuously pile up, stratifying themselves into an incoherent mountain of facts and claims. What are we to make of all this "data for religious studies"? If it is not "data for religion," then what is it?

Observing from my corner of the tent, and speaking very generally, the "data for religious studies" appear to form a record of surprise. Here I borrow the term "surprise" from J. Z. Smith.[17] I think we could just as easily speak of wonder, amazement, amusement, bemusement, shock, horror, awe, dismay, disapproval, or commendation. This term "surprise" is not meant to imply that our work is ideologically neutral, or merely playful, as if scholarly work was driven by an only too natural drive to record surprising things and share them with others. In light of the critical discovery of the ideological and political implications of the various ideas of "religion," it is clear that "religious studies" has a politico-pedagogical function within societies tied to European colonialism. It has served as an instrument of the political self-constitution of the various societies and localities which support the institutions in and through which this work takes place. By using the phrase "record of surprise," I mean to redescribe "religious studies" as a legacy of (social) self-construction via the management of encounters with difference.

The scholarly "surprise" driving religious studies is a reaction which registers across (or even manufactures) ideological and political frontiers. The management of "surprise" involves a process of translation (or redescription) which can take positive or negative forms. Positively, the "surprising" and culturally distant object can be brought near, leading to sympathetic understanding. Negatively, the scholar may comparatively defamiliarize a culturally proximate object in such a way that it becomes "surprising" and as such invites a new cycle of the process.

In any case, the resulting discourses (our comparative and classificatory efforts to appreciate, reduce, explain, or translate) form a record of the normative assumptions and unmarked categories which have defined and constructed various local conceptions of the familiar, the ordinary and the expected. Religious studies can thus be thought of as a formalized adjudication of cultural differences, concerned with the mitigation and creation of surprise, the end of which is self-construction through the organization of identity boundaries and moral hierarchies of authenticity and legitimacy.

Let me offer a sole *exempli gratia* which might grant more solidity to this claim. At the end of a substantial review of six significant works on African diaspora traditions "selected for their treatment of the material objects of Afro-Cuban religions," the reviewer argues that "[f]or scholars of material religion, [these books] offer ... ethnographic insight into the hows and wherefores of devotion which include the ritual manipulation of sacred objects," concluding:

> Material objects are often marshaled by religious practitioners to display (or at times conceal) religious devotion, to demonstrate religious expertise to members of their community and to would-be clients, to squelch the claims of rivals, and to mark the history and the boundaries of their religious practices. (Schmidt 2006: 388)[18]

At first glance this concluding sentence appears to vindicate those who claim that the categories "religion" and "religious" offer little value as analytic terms in academic research. If one removes the "r-words" from this statement, its analytical meaning appears to remain unchanged. What difference does it make here, after all, if these "practitioners," or their "devotion," "expertise," and "practices" are labeled as "religious," or not? The terms "religion" and "religious" are nowhere defined or delimited in the review, but are assumed, beginning from the third word of the essay, as self-evident labels.

Yet on second reflection, it appears that the repetition of the label "religious" does serve an important discursive function. Words operate within (and by continuously reproducing) a systematic net of conceptual differentiations that articulate ideological hierarchies and social relationships. Use of these signifiers classifies the data under consideration in a way that excludes other, less desirable or even potentially hostile (to the scholar no less than to the subjects) classifications, such as "magical," or "superstitious." Not only does this mode of discourse authorize the interest of "religious studies" scholars in these particular subjects of research ("practitioners" of "popular Catholicism, Spiritism, Santería, Palo Monte, the Abakúa society, and Pentecostalism"), but it also offers them all a protected status with political implications, prophylactically sealing off practitioners (and their objects) against deprecating and corrosive discourses that one could, realistically, expect to come into play, given the legacies of racism and colonialism, not to mention the continuing hegemony of North American Protestant assumptions about what is or is not "religion." This is the management of surprise at work.

The Material Turn in Religious Studies

> If it doesn't offer the opportunity to lick something, kiss something, eat something, or put something in your mouth, it's not a religion. (Orsi 2013)[19]

The example discussed above was not chosen randomly, but was selected to facilitate a transition from presenting what I take to be the "givens" regarding "the data for religious studies," to analysis of the popular new trend in religious studies known as "material religion" (while also touching on the closely allied approach known as "lived religion"). Because the approach to "religious studies" called "material religion" has in recent years gained enormous currency and influence within the field, the movement merits attention by anyone concerned with methodology in the study of religion. Russell McCutcheon has suggested dismissively that the "turn toward material and embodied religion sounds suspiciously like a reborn form of phenomenology of religion" (2015: 121). In this second part of this essay, I want to assess and unpack the implications of McCutcheon's critical judgment, or objection, concerning "material religion," setting it in the context of the ongoing debate on "religion" as a field-organizing category, or "object" of study.

The Phenomenological Approach Redivivus

In the humanities and social sciences the past two decades have been marked by a so-called "material turn," in which a "new materialism" has been developed alongside older, more discursive modes of modern and postmodern scholarship.[20] In an early notice of the trend, anthropologist Gosewijn van Beek described the "material turn" as a postmodern response to "the continuing debate on the epistemological status of our perception of this cultural world," but one whose direction is "perpendicular" to that of the "linguistic turn" (van Beek 1996: 5–6). Recent scholarship which explicitly invokes the "material turn" as a matter of theory has addressed a diversity of matters of interest, attempting to reorient academic approaches to literature (Grogan 2017), the body (Clever and Ruberg 2014), clothing (Suzuki 2017), garbage (Jelfs 2017), and art education (Hood and Kraehe 2017), to cite only a few illustrative examples. In "religious studies," the "material turn" manifests as a reaction against intellectualist, cognitive, and other thought- or language-oriented accounts of "religion" (both in modernist modes and in those following the postmodern "linguistic turn"). Scholars of "religion" following this turn embrace the study of what is usually termed "material culture," developing a new methodological and theoretical orientation to the work that today goes by the self-designation "material religion."

This new orientation has quickly become one of the most interesting and successful trends in our field. The journal *Material Religion: The Journal of Objects, Art, and Belief*, which commenced publication in 2005 and is now in its thirteenth volume, has positioned itself as the vanguard of the larger trend.[21] As described on the publisher Taylor & Francis's website, the journal "seeks to explore how religion happens in material culture." Glossing the "material culture" of "religion" as "images, devotional and liturgical objects, architecture and sacred space, works of arts and mass-produced artifacts," the journal intends to provide a venue for assessing "material forms," especially within "the many different practices that put them to work," including "[r]itual, communication, ceremony, instruction, meditation, propaganda, pilgrimage, display, magic, liturgy and interpretation."

All these can be described as the means "whereby religious material culture constructs the worlds of belief."[22] In a relatively short span of time, *Material Religion* has become an important forum for expert area specialists focusing on material artifacts. Many of the more than six-hundred studies (articles, reviews, and notes) which the journal has so far published so far are often sophisticated presentations of specialized inquiry into material elements ("objects") associated with particular social formations that are identified by one criterion or another as "religious."

In a ten-year retrospective article, the editors of *Material Religion* admitted that the term "'material religion' was not in common usage" when the journal began its publication. Now, they opine, "the phrase 'material religion' can be used without explanation or justification ... around the world" (Meyer et al. 2015: 105).[23] They contrast their own work with the "many studies that stress the intellectual contents, arguments, [and] doctrines of religions" or describe "'religion'" as "a set of abstract beliefs." The journal takes a special interest in the "hybrid" intersection of "bodies, practices, and things;" these are "the proper focus of religious materiality."

We may wish to concede to *Material Religion* the status of vanguard in the current "material turn" of religious studies. Its editors and authors have defined the movement's parameters and staked out this new territory with aplomb.[24] Validating the approach, *Material Religion* has been joined by various other new "centers," "institutes" and publications similarly dedicated to studying the "material culture" of "religion."[25] The "new" movement is succeeding.

And yet, something about these claims for the significance of the movement seems to be awry. "Material religion" purports to correct an imbalance in religious studies methodology, and to offer a much needed counterpoint to intellectualist approaches to "religion." But the story cannot be so simple, because, in point of fact "religious studies" has, throughout its long history, often focused on "material objects" in its investigation of "religions." For nearly a century and a half, since Müller first coined the term "Religionswissenschaft," the field has enjoyed the participation of classicists, anthropologists, archaeologists, art historians, museum curators, archivists, numismatists, epigraphers, paleographers, diplomatists, codicologists, papyrologists, collectors, and even hobbyists who have focused on the analysis and interpretation of material artifacts.[26]

Perhaps the difference is that today's "material religion" is determined not only to correct an intellectualist bias in religious studies data selection, but, at least in some of its forms, to offer a correction to theoretical conceptions of "religion" that discount the importance of "materiality," or that denigrate the material objects of "religion" as primitive atavisms when compared to the philosophical spirituality of the modern (or postmodern) world.

How Objects (Do Not) Get Theorized in "Religious Studies"

Although the word "object" appears everywhere in social scientific literature—including in the literature produced by students of "religion"—the term itself is rarely subjected to explicit theorization by the members of our field. The words "object" or "objects" occur in nearly 43 percent of articles in the 2005 second edition of the *Encyclopedia of Religion*.[27] However the *Encyclopedia* contains no general article on either term.[28] Indeed, "object" is almost never listed as a topic in the indices of significant works in religious studies.[29] Unlike many other theoretical and methodological terms of art, among scholars of religion the concept "object" is not often treated as a "subject" in its own right, worthy of exposition by theorists.[30]

Nevertheless, in the specialist literature of religious studies (including theology), the words "object" and "objects" appear quite often in titles of articles, chapters, and books.[31] In keeping with popular usage, the term as used in the literature is polyvalent. In many cases the word "object" as employed in titles registers the sense of "goal" or "focus." In numerous other cases it is used as a verb. Certain other typical usages appear with marked frequency including (allowing for variations): "object relations," "transitional objects," and other psychologically informed uses; Christian education's "object lessons;" various noetic or focal-point "object of" phrases, especially with reference to "faith," "hope," "desire," "belief," "knowledge," "cognition," "consciousness," "study," "science" or "research;" there are many papers on grammatical "objects," frequently in studies of Near Eastern philology; scores of studies of archaeologically discovered "objects" and artifacts made of "clay," "leather," "bone," "stone," "iron" etc.; plenty of articles on "physical" or "material objects;" treatments of "objects" in "museums," and as "art;" and, of course, recurrent treatments of "religious," "devotional," "liturgical," "sacred," "cult," "ceremonial," "votive" and "ritual objects." Finally of course there are the articles (mostly theological and pastoral, but also literary, epistemological, and anthropological) bearing titles that in some way juxtapose the terms "subject" and "object."[32]

The vast majority of studies of material culture in "religion" do not focus on offering theoretical or methodological reflections on "objects" per se. But there are rare exceptions, and most recently, scholars associated with "material religion" have begun to offer some more substantive reflections on "objects" and materiality in "religion."

Managing editor of *Material Religion* S. Brent Plate is one of the most visible theorists of "material religion" working in the field. Although his book, *A History of Religion in 5½ Objects* (Plate 2014), should not be objectified as the representative of the whole movement, a brief examination of it could, nevertheless, help to flag some of the ideas that are today associated with the "material religion" approach. In the subtitle of his book, Plate indicates that his purpose lies in "bringing the spiritual to its senses." Many of the studies which have been published in *Material Religion* appear to share this intention. The subtitle playfully personifies "the spiritual" as a figure in need of revival.[33] This appears to point towards a practical-theological motivation for the "material religion" project.[34] On the other hand, the book's main title is a bit misleading regarding the data considered and the methods used. Plate's "five" objects are not particular material "objects" at all, but rather classes or categories of objects: "stones," "incense," "drums," "crosses," and "bread." These are chosen because these types or kinds of objects relate to each of the five senses of the experiencing subject (the ½ object of the title). Rather than investigating the situated, temporal, interested and human uses of individual material objects approached through a careful "historical" method of contextualization (or through presenting thickly described ethnographic detail) Plate's chapters devoted to these five object-types each present a cross-cultural kaleidoscope of instances. The surveys aim to demonstrate (against an intellectualist or cognitivist account) not only that the senses are involved in "religion," but that each type of "object" has an inherent potential as a bearer of sensual, non-discursive spirituality. These nearly ubiquitous substances or figures are represented, using this quasi-phenomenological method, as practically universal manifestations of "religion"—or the sacred—in material form. It is worth noting that Plate's approach and structure of argument resembles Mircea Eliade's *Patterns in Comparative Religion* in several key ways; Eliade's argument examines "hierophanies" (manifestations of the sacred) cross-culturally, examining "the sky," "the sun," "the moon," "the waters," "the earth and woman," "vegetation," "agriculture," locative centers, and so on (Eliade 1958).

Other scholars associated with "material religion" offer similarly quasi-phenomenological theoretical moves. In a short note, Gretchen Buggeln argues that "[h]umans do things with images and objects, but objects also do things to us; because of this we need to respect their autonomy and integrity—their materiality" (Buggeln 2009: 357). Buggeln's example, a description of a contemporary white ceramic coffee mug, is meant to show how "[t]he proper place for theory is after some open-minded data collection; interpretation is built on a foundation of both connoisseurship and theory." Proposing that scholars of religion who deal with material culture should include "connoisseurship" in their approach to artifacts, Buggeln promotes a mode of appreciation which draws on curatorial expertise and "respect" for the qualities that an object manifests in the world, supposedly autonomously. This may be termed "quasi-phenomenological" because the notion of "connoisseurship" obviously calls for an epoché of epoché; the connoisseur by definition treats an object as a member of a class the characteristics of which are already known and the value of which is already appreciated. There is a self-contradiction embedded in this claim that (a) theory must come only after "open-minded" (phenomenological) collection of data, and (b) the claim that "connoisseurship" should guide that same collection. In any case *phainomena* (apparent things) do not simply "appear;" *theoria* (point of view) is essential to their "appearing."

Buggeln is not alone in making appeal to the supposed autonomy of objects as data. For example, in an affecting and compelling de-colonialist account of devotional practices in Mexico, Jennifer Scheper Hughes makes an appeal to religious studies scholars, that they ought to treat the "diverse objects of material religion" not as "inert," "silent sources of data," but rather as "practitioners" do, that is, as "sacred persons," as "'beings' not 'things'," and as "vital, dynamic, and even agentive members of the communities we study" (Hughes 2012: 20). Hughes's advice to religious studies scholars is to adopt a "horizontal" rather than "vertical" theory of "distributive agency" in which humans and objects are co-agentive beings; in this she draws on—and goes beyond—the object-oriented philosophy proposed by Jane Bennett (2010). Hughes suggests that scholars of religion should learn from their informants and sources that so-called material objects are themselves to be valued as informants and sources, co-agents affecting change within communities of practice.

I see at least two problems in Hughes's otherwise informative and politically engaged critique of the legacy of colonial oppression and marginalization which burdens the lives of her research subjects. The first is an evident tendency, in the name of emphasizing the "co-agency" of objects, actually to efface the agency of any human subjects in the research. Thus, in an account of a journey undertaken by devotees of "El Niño Jesus Doctor," Hughes slips into the passive voice, concealing the human actors who obviously carry the object. Little is said in the short account about the human agents involved in the events. We do not learn their identities, nor do we learn any details regarding the presumably human origins of the object. Hughes writes about the "image's will," but not the "will" of human participants. Such humans as are involved in the events are treated en masse only as a background to the alleged activities of a statuette. In this way the asserted co-agency of the Infant Doctor Jesus actually effaces notice of the human co-agency of the devotees, leaving only the image in the role of subject (Hughes 2012: 20). The second is that such analyses may conceal rather than reveal the play of interests which are instrumentalizing "objects" for social and material ends. For example, Hughes's analysis of the story of Christo Aparecido in Totolapan (ibid.: 18–19) offers precious little in the way of evidence for the "agency" of the Christo. Instead, the reader catches a glimpse, especially in the form of a they-said/he-said between the devotees and Padre Salvador, of an incompletely described and analyzed contest of rival human discourses. For the parties involved, the question of the Christo's alleged agency is precisely the issue at stake. Hughes' sympathy for the position of the devotees, as opposed to those of Christo's "clerical denigrators," is quite evident; it seems to lead her to take seriously only the views of the former. In effect, the folk have admirable "religion" whereas the clerics pursue contemptible "secular" ends. But rather than accepting one group's account of the Christo as an "agent" that is active in that fray—and generalizing from this to a theory of material objects as agentive—the scholar might prefer to point to the ways that a material object serves as a focal point for the contestation of political identities and economic relations, or even as an instrument useful to those who are seeking to change the material and cognitive conditions which structure their lives.

In setting up this analysis, Hughes appeals to Robert Orsi's notion of "abundant events," arguing that "religious objects" should be viewed as "abundant objects" which present "material manifestations of the sacred" which "cannot be properly comprehended, described or interpreted within a Western ontological frame." She thus regards it as proper to think of the "agency of things," and "the mystery of living matter" (the *mysterium materiae* of her article's title). The term *mysterium materiae* is a deliberate nod to Rudolf Otto's category of "the numinous," transferring to materiality itself Otto's appeal to the *mysterium tremendum et fascinans* characterizing the ineffable "numinous" object of experience that he also calls "the holy" or "sacred" (Otto 1967: 5–40).

But Wait ... There's "Something More"

A growing number of our colleagues in religious studies today openly advocate this new view of "objects," properly described, as possessing "agency" or as manifesting the "'something more' of the *fascinans*" as Otto put it (Otto 1967: 35). Examples in recent research abound, but let it serve to mention only two: in one case, we find a critic committed to the new "object-oriented ontology" whose participant-observer study of Tarot reading attributes agency (and perhaps even sentience) to the deck of cards (Gregory 2016); in another case a scholar of museum-exhibited South Asian art warns against scholars who "condescendingly" dismiss the idea of object agency, and proposing instead to ask in all seriousness, "what do Indian images really want?" (Davis 2015). This list could be easily extended.

Less poetically minded scholars should be forgiven for regarding these interesting and counterintuitive treatments of material objects—in which scholars are sometimes deliberately honoring and echoing the insider language and testimony of informants who value them, and sometimes phenomenologically describing their own encounters with objects represented as agentive—as itself the surprising data that invites investigation and explanation or reduction.[35]

In this new mystification of "materiality," data which are materially present (i.e., objects) are represented as a gateway to understanding the "origins" of "religion." Plate asserts that there is a "significance of materiality," suggesting that "students of religious life ... sometimes need to get back to the basics, back to the physical substrate upon which all religious traditions, beliefs, and practices originate" (Plate 2015: 3). Thus, in a return of the Eliadean/Ottonian category of the "hierophany," "religious objects" are sometimes described by scholars as a manifestation of "the sacred." In other cases attention to materiality in itself is proposed as a mode providing special access to "the real" that is not available to merely discursive approaches. Van Beek represents an early example of this tendency. He rightly asks whether "material culture" has "a special epistemological and phenomenological status in our understanding of culture;" he writes: "I want to have it both ways ... I want to keep the humility of objects with regard to culture as a process and at the same time award their materiality a special status (better: attribute) in the construction and perception of culture" (van Beek 1996: 9–10). Much more recently the Susan Niditch proposes that the value of attending to the "material and visceral" aspects of objects and embodied practices is that they can show where practitioners get, using a phrase borrowed from Patricia Cox Miller, "a touch of the real" (Niditch 2015: 90, 103). Interestingly, Niditch's method of looking for that "touch of the real" remains yoked to data that would be better described as discursive and literary rather than material. Two of Niditch's three "case studies" in her chapter on "Material Religion" are not studies of physical or material objects at all, but rather investigations of literary representations of physical objects which appear in the Hebrew Scriptures: the vision reports of the prophet Zechariah in Zech. 3:2-9 and 5:5-11 (Niditch 2015: 100) and the narrative describing Jeremiah's "sign acts" (also styled "performance art") in Jer. 13:1-11 and 19:1-13 (ibid.: 101–104). Of course there is no concrete evidence that these narratives offer the researcher anything more than verisimilitude; that is, a semblance (or simulacrum) of material culture as it was in ancient Judah/Yehud. In sum, the flexibility of "material religion" to incorporate into its approach data that are, strictly speaking, merely discursive representations of artifacts means that even Biblical Scholars can do this thing called "material religion" or "lived religion" while continuing to do what they have always tended to do: read texts and attribute to them "historical" (or material) referentiality.[36]

An emphasis on the study of embodied practices in "material religion" has allowed the movement to find a natural ally in the scholarly trend called "lived religion." As noted above, some scholars of "material religion" have deliberately invoked Robert Orsi's notion of the "abundant" or "the more" (Orsi 2007). Orsi, the social anthropologist of contemporary Catholicism and other traditions in New York City, has used his undeniable skills as a descriptive writer and ethnographic reporter to promote scholarship committed to accepting (or taking seriously) informants' claimed experiences of the "reality" or "presence" of what he glosses as "the gods."[37]

Repeating, in his own way, the critical deconstruction of "religion" as a category in social and scholarly discourses, Orsi's work draws attention to the ways that intellectualist accounts of "religion" are connected to the Protestant and post-Protestant critiques of the practices of Catholics and other lower status groups. Especially, he focuses on the elitism of Protestant modernity's critique of the concept of the "real presence" of Christ in the Eucharistic host, showing how it fed into intellectualist accounts of "religion," relegating the "lived religion" experienced by subaltern groups to the status of "not religion."

Orsi's entire oeuvre, taken together, can be seen as a vocal, though somewhat ironically self-contradictory objection to this trend. On the one hand, his work on "lived religion" rejects essentializing accounts of particular traditions, correctly emphasizing that all of our data comes from situated, local, material, and practical concerns of actual people (Orsi 2003). On the other hand, paradoxically, his work strikes a profoundly universalist note, as it seeks to rehabilitate Otto's perennialist account of religion as a response to "the holy," "met as the really real" (Orsi 2012). Religious studies scholars must acknowledge the presence of "the holy, the really real, the 2 + 2 = 5," or what he calls "abundant events" in the materiality of things and in lived experience.[38]

In the wake of Orsi's return to Otto, there has emerged in religious studies a trend that I would like to call "the school of the more." The characteristic discourse of this "school" employs variations of the word "more," along with other terms signaling abundance, excess, overflow, unknowability, ineffability, irreducibility, incommensurability, and so on. Examples of such rhetoric at work are readily found (e.g., Dunn 2016). Such descriptors most often serve to authorize and legitimate scholarly objections to naturalistic approaches to the study of "religion."

In certain peripheries of the school, such objections are accompanied by laments about the "passionate disbelief" of social-scientists who work on "religion" (e.g., Cantrell 2016: 390).

In place of the reductions offered by flat naturalism (let alone dreadful materialism or wicked positivism), the school of the more promotes something which resembles the tradition of Emersonian Transcendentalism. Emerson promoted an idealism of Nature as sign of the Spirit (Emerson 1849). In this new transcendentalism the very materiality of "religious" objects and embodied practices are always also an adumbration of the eternal divine and/or universal human (or both simultaneously). They are never merely particular, peculiar, local, social, economic, interested, ordinary, or otherwise mundane signs of human behavior.

Methodology in "Material Religion"

It appears to me that neither the "material religion" approach, nor the "school of the more," offer any genuinely new methodological alternatives to the study of religion. What they do offer are a new metaphysics of presence, an interpretive framework which mystifies simultaneously both materiality and subjective experience. This appears to be an effort to neutralize the epistemological problems that were posed for objectivity and subjectivity by the postmodern "linguistic turn." Some scholars in the movements offer a sort of methodological hand-waving, in which "material" and "lived religion" are problematically described as new methods of research yielding insights into the mysterious dynamics of human "religiosity." But when the chips are down, if we examine the all too ordinary genres of scholarly discourse produced in these movements we see that the methods in play are just ordinary (and even old fashioned) modes of data collection that are the common property of the human sciences; especially evident are well-worn and time-honored approaches to ethnographic and historical research.

But if there is a characteristic method at play, it may be evident in a dual refusal of the theory and methods that are favored in other corners of the tent. First, we see the refusal of the critique of the category "religion." At its best (in Orsi, for example) this first refusal is accompanied by an alternative critique of the genealogy of the category. However Orsi's sociological analysis of the power dynamic at play in the "religion/not religion" distinction does not finally lead to a categorical *Aufheben* but rather to an ironic apotheosis: in the name of protecting the particularity and value of the experience and practice of the marginalized, the critique leads back to Otto's universal account of "religion." Second, there is an evident refusal of second-order scholarly redescription and explanatory theorization. This is often accompanied by an explicit revival of the same denunciations of reductionism that have characterized religious studies scholarship since before the days of Eliade.[39] At its best, this second refusal promotes a first-order thick description of actual human behaviors and social formations, allowing for careful attention to emic discourses. But too often such a thick description does not appear, as scholars mystify rather than historicize the data. The accompanying refusals of second-order discourses also appear wedded to a barely submerged humanistic project which seeks, as Eliade proposed, to overcome the dual problem of traditional religious authority on the one hand, and pernicious secular rejection of "religion" on the other. Taken together, these two refusals of critique and theory allow for analyses which purport to privilege emic categories and self-representations, but which actually provide cover to quasi-phenomenological (or neo-Transcendental) projections of universal "real" presences and experiences (especially, of "the sacred") back onto the objects and subjects of research.

And so the manufacturing of "religion" by "religious studies" continues apace, with no end in sight. To be sure, as such it will continue to be accompanied by our "intemperate" objections.

Six Theses on Objects

I wish by way of conclusion to offer six final theoretical and methodological theses regarding the study of "objects."

1. First, that "objects" as such are always only matters before us. This claim is consistent with the results of inquiry into the origins of the English word "object." *Object* enters the language in the late 14th century through a transliteration of (that is, in a refusal or inability to translate) the substantive form of the Latin verbal adjective *objectus*. The word *objectus* comes from *obicio*, which combines *iacio*, "I throw" with *ob*, meaning "towards," "before," or "against." This word "object" cannot be defined except by tautological resort to putatively equivalent terms (especially "thing"). This reflects the word's origin in a verbal adjective. It can therefore be thought of as a substitute pronoun, or a demonstrative; it only ever stands for something else. It points and describes. Whatever is described as "object" (whether using the obsolete English adjective or the noun) will therefore inevitably bear a trace of reference to the activity of description, which is nothing other than *a someone positing a something as an object*. An object is one matter that a someone describes as standing opposed to or over against another. This is reflected in the translation of the substantive use of *objectus* in German as *Gegenstand* (the attributive use can be translated with *gegenstandig*).

2. Second, that the word "object" (like *objectus*) is only ever used by one human being speaking to or writing for another in order to describe some matter which stands in relation to them both. For this reason, I contend that "objects," properly so termed, are matters intersubjectively available (or asserted to be potentially so). In philosophy, the fraught epistemological discussion of the relationship between "object" and "subject" all too often conceals this triadic relationship, misrepresenting it in both regnant models (*intentio recta* and *intentio obliqua*) as merely diadic.[40] Objects properly so termed are object to at least two subjects. This triadic relation is embedded in

the communicative structure of language itself, making objects a fit subject for both semiology and social-cognitive approaches.[41]

3. Third, that whatever is called an "object" in discourse is always subject to and even constituted by objection. "Objection" (rather than "objectification") is the ideal term for describing the intersubjective process by which objects come to be accepted as given things (data). Speculative realist ("object-oriented") ontological approaches to objects may tend to eliminate or efface the always already present human social processes which construe things as *things for us*. Under the sign of the "democracy of objects," the agency of subjects can be concealed or forgotten. Objection is here a synecdoche for human agency. What ought to interest us more than objects, per se, is this process of *objection*, the "throwing" of matters against other matters through indexing, selection, postulation, and so on. Intersubjective communicative action establishes objects as objects (that is, as "objective"). So-called objects may through the process of objection either lose the status of object altogether, or be analyzed (broken up) into multiple different objects, or reduced to or combined with some other object. The end of objection is the assembly and disassembly of the things which constitute the human world.

4. Fourth, that not all of our "objects" are sensual or "material objects," but rather everything which we make subject to objections can still be thought of as some kind of an object. Some objects are social formations with so-called social ontologies and others are purely conceptual. Perhaps to think is itself to think up (posit or postulate) an object. This is how Locke defined "idea": the "object of understanding." And so there are also "imaginary objects" like unicorns. In that respect, in the end, all that we scholars have available for study and research are objects (even if these are also termed "subjects," interesting because of their relations to other "subjects").

5. Fifth, that in scholarship, objects must be established as objects (that is, intersubjectively available matters, or data) through methods that are best termed either scientific, genealogical, sociological, or historical. The study of an object must be grounded in a rigorous effort to communicate the process by which the posited object has been proposed as an object suitable for research. This means, practically speaking, that scholarship can never treat objects as autonomous—or as self-constituting agents—but must attend to the social, historical, and material conditions by which the object has emerged as object and become available to the research community. This involves, necessarily, the self-reflective and careful study of

genealogy and kinship, provenance, ownership, properties, contexts, economies (networks and systems—that is, social relations—involving production, reproduction, mediation, etc.), uses, influences, and finally: critical examination of the priors that result in selection and presentation by the critic in argument.

6   Sixth, that research in "religious studies," as in all branches of the human sciences, is never interested solely in theorizing the "materiality" or "presence" of objects. (In the same way we never stop once we have established the "objectivity" of an object.) This is not to say that notions of "materiality" (or "presence" or "objectivity") cannot themselves become objects for us. But especially when it comes to dealing with so-called material objects, these become objects of interest for us insofar as they have been used—as tools, instruments, and artifacts—and as such they have significance for us as primarily as evidence for the social activity and ends of human beings. And of course all "non-material" objects that interest us are also tools, instruments and artifacts! Connoisseurs, curators, and collectors all have roles to play, but in "religious studies," as in anthropology, we are ultimately interested in our fellow human beings, and the things that we make out as objects have value to our work mainly insofar as they are signs of the human. As scholars we are not here to promote mere appreciation, let alone devotion or mystification, but rather critical understanding of *what is going on*.

Matthew C. Baldwin is Professor and Coordinator of the Program in Religion and Philosophy at Mars Hill University. He teaches courses in Bible, ancient history, biblical languages, the American intellectual tradition, and method and theory in religious studies. He is the author of Whose Acts of Peter? Text and Historical Context of the Actus *Vercellenses* (Mohr-Siebeck, 2005).

Notes

1   Lincoln's first thesis reads in full: "The conjunction [*sic*] 'of' that joins the two nouns in the disciplinary ethnonym 'History of Religions' is not neutral filler. Rather, it announces a proprietary claim and a relation of encompassment: history is the method and religion the object of study" (Lincoln 1996: 225). For the record: "of" is a preposition.
2   The term "field" is often used. See, *inter alia,* titles employed by Wiebe (2009) and McCutcheon (2014). When McCutcheon has previously referred to "the discipline of religion" in a book title (McCutcheon 2003), it is to critique the field's "invention" as such (see ibid.: 54–82).
3   In his 1988 AAR Presidential Address, Robert L. Wilken (1989: 703–704) shared an anecdote of an encounter with a student of religion, in which he extolled *studium* as a methodological model for religious studies. Wilken also makes quite a fuss about the preposition "for," proposing specifically, in a way that may make the most sense to

the Christian historian of Christianity, that religious studies scholars must "care for" (McCutcheon might say "be caretakers of") the traditions they study (McCutcheon 2001).

4 In his note 1, Tweed laments the "Big Tent" concept, suggesting we need "a better metaphor, one that does not gesture playfully or dismissively toward circus images." With all due respect, I suggest that the "Big Tent" metaphor does not primarily invoke a "circus" theme. The "Big Top" of circus lore is a different signifier, after all (even if it too is a tent). In the contemporary American context where we find talk of the AAR or the field itself as a "Big Tent," the more proximate connotation of "Big Tent" is political. Over the past three decades, most often we find the "Big Tent" invoked in arguments about the scope of Republican Party politics. It appears frequently in polemics, used especially by people who find themselves being pushed out of the Republican coalition over litmus tests of various kinds, especially abortion and civil rights for LGBTQ persons (e.g., Harris 2015). Compare also Wikipedia s.v. "Big Tent." Furthermore, it is hard to resist the hypothesis that in an American context the "Big Tent" image has roots in the world of itinerant Protestant Christian revivalism. In that case, the vital center of the tent is the stage from which the preacher issues the "altar call."

5 Tweed himself names three axes of division: (a) "humanistic" versus "scientific approaches;" (b) "scholarship alone" versus "advocacy too;" and (c) "theology" versus "religious studies." The burden of his "Valuing the Study of Religion" seems to be an effort to collapse philosophically and methodologically the latter two axes (a move which doubtless causes further objections).

6 On Althusser's concept of "Social Formation," see Mack (2000) and cf. McCutcheon (2001).

7 Lease writes in full: "there cannot be a 'history of religion' for the simple reason that there is no religion: rather, such a history can only trace how and why a culture or epoch allows certain experiences to count as 'religion' while excluding others" (Lease 1994: 472).

8 McCutcheon has expressed doubts about the utility of contemporary fieldwork in "History of Religions" scholarship, but nevertheless has claimed that he considers attending academic conferences his form of fieldwork (McCutcheon 2014: 70 n. 5 and cf. 92).

9 The wild variety of terms paired with "religion," "religions," or "religious" in the Library of Congress "subject headings" list can provide sufficient evidence to establish this claim. To take only two illustrative examples, consider "Religion and state—East Asia," or "Government, Resistance to—religious aspects."

10 Benavides contends in part that Smith's dictum cannot be true because, if it were, we cannot explain the publication of Kippenberg's *Entdeckung der Religionsgeschichte* (1997). But this seems to beg the question, rather obtusely.

11 The foregoing glosses many individual points made in Saler (1987), Fitzgerald (2003), Smith (2004), Masuzawa (2005), and Nongbri (2013). Compare the essays in McCutcheon (2003).

12 Leuba distinguished three broad types of scholarly ideas of "religion": the "Intellectualistic" (1912: 339–346), involving Müller, Spencer, von Hartmann, Hegel and others; the "Affectivistic" (ibid.: 346–351), involving Schleiermacher, Tiele, Simmel, Ritschl and others; and the "Voluntaristic or Practical" (ibid.: 352–361), involving a diverse grab-bag of thinkers of idealist, positivist, and pragmatist bent, including James, Frazer, Comte, Royce, Kant, etc. In my opinion, though it is obviously dated,

Leuba's appendix ought to be required reading in Method and Theory courses (it is in public domain and freely accessible online via Google books). J. Z. Smith opines that Leuba's survey, "which lists more than fifty definitions of religion," does "not at all" mean it is impossible to give a definition of religion. "The moral of Leuba is not that religion cannot be defined, but that it can be defined, with greater or lesser success, more than fifty ways" (Smith 2004: 193).

13 This is, I think, the most significant implication of Craig Martin's argument in his valuable essay "Delimiting Religion" (Martin 2009: especially 170, 174–175).

14 Kevin Schilbrack argues that the term "religion" indexes real structures of social ontology which internally unify the various "religions" in the world (Schilbrack 2010; cf. Schilbrack 2014: ch. 4, "Do Religions Exist?").

15 Schilbrack employs this concept which is drawn from the work of Ian Hacking (see Schilbrack 2010: 1134 and cf. Schilbrack 2014: 104, 109).

16 For example, in Asia, the category "religion" was embraced in Japan during the post-colonial era (Josephson 2012). In the Indian context, there are widespread arguments and continuing disagreements (among scholars and/or between scholars and self-described "Hindus") over the origins of the idea of "Hinduism" as a distinct "religion" of India (*inter alia* see Lorenzen 1999; Bloch, Keppens, and Hegde 2010; Nicholson 2010).

17 J. Z. Smith has repeatedly used "surprise" to describe the initial impetus which leads to data selection and analysis. "The theoretical enterprise, especially modes of explanation, is called forth by surprise" (see Smith 2004: 163). Again: "The particular subject matter provides the scholar with an occasion for surprise. This becomes one point at which the outsider's view may be privileged over the insider's view. The outsider's view has a greater likelihood of being surprised" (ibid.: 208). And: "Both explanations and interpretations are occasioned by surprise. It is the particular subject matter that provides the scholar with an occasion for surprise. Surprise, whether in the natural or the human sciences, is always reduced by bringing the unknown into relations to the known. The process by which this is accomplished, in both the natural and the human sciences, is translation" (ibid.: 370–371).

Smith's "surprise" can be accompanied by a sense that a potentially humorous *aporia*, or "gap," separates the experience of the researcher from the subjects/objects of research, sparking scholarly curiosity. In an interview, student reporter Supriya Sinhababu once asked Smith, "what got you interested in the religions that you study?" Smith candidly replied, "Because they're funny. They're interesting in and of themselves. They relate to the world in which I live, but it's like a fun house mirror. Something's off. It's not quite the world I live in, yet it's recognizable. So that gap interested me" (Sinhababu 2008).

18 I wish to apologize to Schmidt for the appearance that I have appropriated elements of her article's title for my own. A friend helped me to compose my own title based on the theme of this essay, and I only became aware of Schmidt's review some months after having submitted my proposal along with its title.

19 From the video "Robert Orsi at the NYS Writers Institute in 2013"—the quote is from 37 minutes 9–16 seconds.

20 A more thorough investigation of the history of the term "material turn" is outside the scope of this project, but the phrase "material turn" began to appear in the literature a little more than twenty years ago. Early examples of its use include van Beek (1996) and Sloop (1998). ProQuest Arts and Humanities database currently lists 101 articles containing the phrase "material turn," though a number of these are merely juxtapositions of the two words (often separated by a period or comma).

21 The journal is published by Taylor & Francis. Journal information available at www.tandfonline.com/action/journalInformation?journalCode=rfmr20
22 See "Aims and Scope" on the Taylor & Francis site: www.tandfonline.com/action/journalInformation?show=aimsScope&journalCode=rfmr20
23 It is questionable whether this phrase "material religion" has as much currency outside of "religious studies" as Meyer et al. would like us to believe. The ProQuest Arts & Humanities database employs "material culture" as a subject heading, and currently lists 326 titles as belonging to that subject; among these items 17 titles are also classified in the subject "religion." "Material religion" is not a subject header in this database.
24 For example, founding editor of *Material Religion* S. Brent Plate has edited the recent handbook *Key Terms in Material Religion* (Plate 2015). Key terms include 37 alphabetically arranged single-word title articles spanning both classic topics in religious studies and more specialized concepts useful to "material culture" studies.
25 For example, Yale University now houses the "Center for the Study of Material and Visual Cultures of Religion" (http://mavcor.yale.edu) the first cycle of which began in 2008 with a diverse array of scholars as fellows. They have recently commenced publication of the on-line, open-access peer reviewed journal MAVCOR which at present has published only the first issue of its first volume. More interestingly, MAVCOR is building and maintaining an online database known as the "Material Objects Archive," which houses digital representations (pictures) of objects from a variety of traditions, along with curatorial information. The database offers advanced search capacities, and at present includes hundreds of instances. It also includes the "MAVCOR Giga Project," which is using 360º camera technology for "documenting sacred spaces."
26 To cite only one early example uniting a number of these disciplines, consider Michaelis (1885).
27 At GALE Virtual Reference Library, a "basic search" for "object or objects," limited to the publication "Encyclopedia of Religion" yields 1,442 results. The whole *Encyclopedia* (Jones 2005) contains 3,375 entries.
28 It does, however, contain articles on "Relics" (John S. Strong), "Art and Religion" (Diane Apostolos-Cappadona), "Fetishism" (Jay Geller), "Icons" (Virgil Cândea), "Museums and Religion" (Crispin Paine), "Images: Images, Icons, and Idols" (John E. Cort), "Images: Veneration of Images" (Richard H. Davis), "Visual Culture and Religion: An Overview" (David Morgan), "Iconography: Iconography as Visual Religion" (Hans Kippenberg) and other related topics.
29 At the beginning of this project I conceived the idea to compile a list of significant religious studies books which do not list "object" or "objects" in their indices, but later determined such an appendix would be too extensive. The term is usually entirely absent from indices. A near exception are occasional entries for "object relations" or "objectivity."
30 Collections of essays in method and theory, as a rule, have not treated "objects" as a topic. For example, in the influential handbook *Critical Terms for Religious Studies* (Taylor 1998), the article topics which approach closest are "Body" (William LeFleur), "Image" (Margaret R. Miles), and "Relic" (Gregory Schopen). None of the essays in the *Guide to the Study of Religion* (Braun and McCutcheon 2000) directly approach the topic. Compare their volume *Introducing Religion* (Braun and McCutcheon 2008). The topic is similarly submerged in *The Routledge Companion to the Study of Religion* (Hinnals 2010). Interestingly, even the recent *Key Terms in Material Religion* lacks a general article on

"objects" (Plate 2015). Karl-Heinz Kohl offers a very important exception to this trend (Kohl 2003). Kohl's historical and linguistic/semiotic approach to object-theory differs significantly from much work being done in the North American and British "material religion" trend. See Benavides's cautiously appreciative review (2006).

31 As of this writing the American Theological Library Association database lists 939 examples. 667 of the results date from 1819 to 2009. From 2010 to the present, we find 272 results (almost 29% of total results).

ATLA also includes the word "object" in a number of subject headings, including "Liturgical objects" (220 items), "Object (Philosophy)" (127 items), "Unidentified Flying Objects" and "Unidentified Flying Object cults" (115 items), "Devotional Objects" (129 items); cf. the frequently cross-listed subject "Material Culture" (314 results).

32 ATLA lists 37 examples.

33 What could "the spiritual" refer to here other than persons who identify as such? The idea that "the spiritual" must be brought to its senses suggests a critique of religious practice or spirituality that is overly noetic and interiorized, or insufficiently embodied and sensual.

34 I admit here to some informed speculation, but it seems to me that the publisher Beacon Press of Boston, which is operated by the Unitarian Universalist Association, may have regarded this book as a welcome addition to its suite of practical theological resources for its ministers and churches, supporting those who seek enhancement of their "spiritual" practices through more "materiality" in "religion." As the book's description on the UUA Bookstore website puts it: "*A History of Religion in 5½ Objects* is a celebration of the materiality of religious life. Plate moves our understanding of religion away from the current obsessions with God, fundamentalism, and science— and toward the rich depths of this world, this body, these things. Religion, it turns out, has as much to do with our bodies as our beliefs. Maybe even more." (See www.uuabookstore.org/A-History-of-Religion-in-5-12-Objects-P17911.aspx)

35 Regarding the widespread attribution of agency to objects (including by Religious Studies scholars, apparently), several explanatory models might contend for our attention. From the "cognitive science of religion" the concept of "hyperactive agency detection" is frequently invoked, along with related discussions of "theory of mind" (see, e.g., van Elk et al. 2016). Furthermore, old-school psychoanalytic "object relations" theory may have some promise here, especially Donald Winnicott's concept of the "transitional object," so familiar from observing play in childhood. These concepts have often been invoked in "Religious Studies" and Theology, though Winnicott's theories appear to have fallen out of fashion with the current generation (one of the most recent examples I could find of Winnicottian theorizing of object relations was LaMothe 1998).

36 Even Niditch's case study on the figural drawings found in the burial site at Khirbet Beit Lei (Niditch 2015: 92–99) treats them (necessarily) as representational communicative acts; hence these examples of "material religion" could, if one were in pursuit of different theoretical aims, just as easily be classified as evidence of the discursive nature of the data. The same is obviously true of the words (of uncertain provenance) found scratched on the tomb's walls. But this discursive approach to describing and interpreting the drawings is accompanied by a quasi-phenomenological method used for describing the tomb itself, which Niditch has apparently visited in person. In a speculative passage, she tries to enter empathetically into what an ancient visitor might "felt" entering into the tomb (ibid.: 94). She asks a series of questions which, if we are to be fully honest about the limits of our data, could never be answered by a

contemporary researcher. "Did one feel as if one were entering an adumbration of the underworld?" Perhaps not. A persuasive argument in answer to such a question (not supplied in the essay) would likely need to look to comparative discursive data drawn from ancient informants' discourses about entering tombs.

37 For Orsi, "the gods" is "a synecdoche for all the special suprahuman beings with whom humans have been in relationship in different times and places" (Orsi 2016: 4). It may be worth suggesting that Orsi's idea of "the gods" would bear comparison to Otto's notion of "the numen."

38 According to Orsi, "Abundant events are characterized by aspects of the human imagination that cannot be completely accounted for by social and cultural codes, that go beyond authorized limits; by the 'more' in William James's word (which got him into so much trouble with positivist psychologists); by the 'unthought known,' a cultural experience of déjà vu or uncanny awareness of something outside us and independent of us, yet still familiar to us. Abundant events are saturated by memory, desire, need, fear, terror, hope or denial, or some inchoate combination of these." Abundant events are characterized, he says, by five traits. They "present themselves as sui generis," (or "out of the ordinary"); they "are real to those who experience them"; they "arise at the intersection of the conscious and unconscious"; and "at the intersection of the past/present/future"; and "they are intersubjective (though this intersubjectivity may include the dead, for instance, or saints)." In regards to this last point, it should be emphasized that, given present methods of observation and data collection, no scholar can legitimately confirm the claims of research subjects to have had "intersubjective" experiences with "the gods." Honesty about the nature of data suggests we should at most say that subjects make claims about their experiences.

39 I am thinking about the overt denunciations of reductionism found in Eliade (1961).

40 Adorno attempts to overcome the internal contradiction of the *intentio obliqua* (and to move past the naive realism of the *intentio recta*) through his notion of "the primacy of objects" (Adorno 2005). But note that "the primacy of objects" does not point the way to the flat ontology of "object-oriented" speculative realism, but rather to a sublation of subject and object resulting in critical theory: "critique of society is critique of knowledge and vice versa" (Adorno 2005: 250). Thus Adorno also speaks of "primacy of the species, of society" (ibid.: 258), a notion I find congenial to my proposal to regard objects properly so called as *intersubjectively available matters*.

41 In his "manifesto," Kevin Schilbrack (2014) promotes promising new approaches to material culture (or objects) viewed as "cognitive prosthetics" extending human capacities for thought and action. Such approaches acknowledge old school semiotic approaches to the communicative symbolism of objects (e.g., Baudrillard 1996), but deepen the analysis by studying material artifacts as scaffolds to human cognition, providing a (socially distributed) apparatus for aiding development, problem solving, and similar cognitive processes (Schilbrack 2014: 40–47).

References

Adorno, Theodor W. 2005. "On Subject and Object." In Theodor W. Adorno, *Critical Models: Interventions and Catchwords*, trans. Henry W. Pickford, pp. 245–258. New York: Columbia University Press.

Arnal, William E., and Russell T. McCutcheon. 2013. *The Sacred is the Profane: The Political Nature of "Religion."* New York: Oxford University Press. https://doi.org/10.1093/acprof:oso/9780199757114.001.0001

Baudrillard, Jean. 1996. *The System of Objects*, trans. James Benedict. London: Verso. Originally published as *Le système des objets*, Éditions Gallimard, 1968.
Benavides, Gustavo. 2003. "There is Data for Religion." *Journal of the American Academy of Religion* 74(4): 895–903. https://doi.org/10.1093/jaarel/lfg105
Benavides, Gustavo. 2006. Review of *Die Macht der Dinge: Geschichte und Theorie sakraler Objekte* by Karl-Heinz Kohl. *Numen* 53(1): 120–124.
Bennett, Jane. 2010. *Vital Matter: A Political Ecology of Things*. Durham, NC: Duke University Press. https://doi.org/10.1215/9780822391623-007
Bloch, Esther, Marianne Keppens, and Rajaram Hegde (eds.). 2010. *Rethinking Religion in India: The Colonial Construction of Hinduism*. Routledge South Asian Religion Series. New York: Routledge.
Braun, Willi, and Russell T. McCutcheon (eds.). 2000. *Guide to the Study of Religion*. New York: Cassell.
Braun, Willi, and Russell T. McCutcheon (eds.). 2008. *Introducing Religion*. London: Equinox.
Buggeln, Gretchen. 2009. "A Word on Behalf of the Object." *Material Religion* 5(3): 357–358. https://doi.org/10.2752/175183409X12550007730066
Cantrell, Michael A. 2016. "Must a Scholar of Religion be Methodologically Atheistic or Agnostic?" *Journal of the American Academy of Religion* 84(2): 373–400. https://doi.org/10.1093/jaarel/lfv066
Clever, Iris, and Willemijn Ruberg. 2014. "Beyond Cultural History? The Material Turn, Praxiography, and Body History." *Humanities* 3(4): 546–566. https://doi.org/10.3390/h3040546
Coward, Harold G. 2006. "Taking its Interdisciplinary Heritage Seriously: the Future of Religious Studies in Canada." *Studies in Religion* 35(3): 403–412. https://doi.org/10.1177/000842980603500303
Davis, Richard H. 2015. "What do Indian Images Really Want? A Biographical Approach." In Bruce M. Sullivan (ed.), *Sacred Objects in Secular Spaces: Exhibiting Asian Religions in Museums*, 9–25. London: Bloomsbury.
Dunn, Mary. 2016. "What Really Happened: Radical Empiricism and the Historian of Religion." *Journal of the American Academy of Religion* 84(4): 881–902. https://doi.org/10.1093/jaarel/lfw011
Eliade, Mircea. 1958. *Patterns in Comparative Religion*, trans. Rosemary Sheed. Lincoln, NE: University of Nebraska Press. Reprinted 1996.
Eliade, Mircea. 1961. "History of Religions and a New Humanism." *History of Religions* 1(1): 1–8. https://doi.org/10.1086/462437
Emerson, Ralph Waldo. 1849. *Nature*. Boston, MA: James Munroe & Co.
Fitzgerald, Timothy. 2003. *The Ideology of Religious Studies*. New York: Oxford University Press.
Gregory, Karen. 2016. "In the Cards: From Hearing 'Things' to Human Capital." In Katherine Behar (ed.), *Object-Oriented Feminism*, 225–245. Minneapolis, MN: University of Minnesota Press.
Grogan, Jane. 2017. "Style, Objects, and Heroic Values in Early Modern Epic." *Studies in English Literature, 1500-1900* 57(1): 23–44. https://doi.org/10.1353/sel.2017.0001
Harris, Peter. 2015. "The GOP Must Be The Big Tent Party." *National Interest* (February 19). Retrieved from http://nationalinterest.org/blog/the-buzz/the-gop-must-be-the-big-tent-party-12283.
Hinnells, John (ed.). 2010. *The Routledge Companion to the Study of Religion*, 2nd edition. New York: Routledge. https://doi.org/10.4324/9780203868768
Hood, Emily Jean, and Amelia M. Kraehe. 2017. "Creative Matter: New Materialism in Art Education Research, Teaching, and Learning." *Art Education* 70(2): 32–38. https://doi.org/10.1080/00043125.2017.1274196

Hughes, Jennifer Scheper. 2012. "*Mysterium Materiae*: Vital Matter and the Object as Evidence in the Study of Religion." *Bulletin for the Study of Religion* 41(4): 16-24. https://doi.org/10.1558/bsor.v41i4.16

Jelfs, Tim. 2017. "Matter Unmoored: Trash, Archaeological Consciousness, and American Culture and Fiction in the 1980's." *Journal of American Studies* 51(2): 553-571. https://doi.org/10.1017/S0021875816000578

Jones, Lindsay (ed.). 2005. *Encyclopedia of Religion*, 2nd edition. 15 vols. Detroit, MI: MacMillan Reference.

Josephson, Jason Ānanda. 2012. *The Invention of Religion in Japan*. Chicago, IL: University of Chicago Press.

Kippenberg, Hans. 1997. *Die Entdeckung der Religionsgeschichte*. Munich: C. H. Beck; English translation: *Discovering Religious History in the Modern Age*. Princeton, NJ: Princeton University Press, 2002.

Kohl, Karl-Heinz. 2003. *Die Macht der Dinge: Geschichte und Theorie sakraler Objekte*. Munich: C. H. Beck.

LaMothe, Ryan. 1998. "Sacred Objects as Vital Objects: Transitional Objects Reconsidered." *Journal of Psychology and Theology* 26(2): 159-167. https://doi.org/10.1177/009164719802600202

Lease, Gary. 1994. "The History of 'Religious' Consciousness and the Diffusion of Culture: Strategies for Surviving Dissolution." *Historical Reflections / Réflexions Historiques* 20(3): 453-479.

Leuba, James H. 1912. *A Psychological Study of Religion: Its Origin, Function, and Future*. New York: Macmillan.

Lincoln, Bruce. 1996. "Theses on Method." *Method and Theory in the Study of Religion* 8(3): 225-227. Reprinted in *Method and Theory* 17(1) [2005] 8-10. https://doi.org/10.1163/157006896X00323

Lorenzen, David N. 1999. "Who Invented Hinduism?" *Comparative Studies in Society and History* 41(4): 630-659. https://doi.org/10.1017/S0010417599003084

Mack, Burton. 2000. "Social Formation." In Willi Braun and Russell T. McCutcheon (eds.), *Guide to the Study of Religion*, 283-296. New York: Cassell.

Martin, Craig. 2009. "Delimiting Religion." *Method and Theory in the Study of Religion* 21: 157-176. https://doi.org/10.1163/157006809X431015

Masuzawa, Tomoko. 2005. *The Invention of World Religions, or, How European Universalism was Preserved in the Language of Pluralism*. Chicago, IL: University of Chicago Press. https://doi.org/10.7208/chicago/9780226922621.001.0001

McCutcheon, Russell T. 1997. *Manufacturing Religion*. New York: Oxford University Press.

McCutcheon, Russell T. 2001. "Redescribing 'Religion' as Social Formation: Toward a Social Theory of Religion." In Russell T. McCutcheon, *Critics not Caretakers: Redescribing the Public Study of Religion*, 21-39. Albany, NY: SUNY Press.

McCutcheon, Russell T. 2003. *The Discipline of Religion: Structure, Meaning, Rhetoric*. New York: Routledge.

McCutcheon, Russell T. 2014. "A Brief Response from a Fortunate Man." In Russell T. McCutcheon, *Entanglements: Marking Place in the Field of Religion*, 59-72. Sheffield: Equinox. Original publication in *Culture and Religion* 1:1 (2000) 131-140. https://doi.org/10.1080/01438300008567147

McCutcheon, Russell T. 2015. "The Category 'Religion' in Recent Publications: Twenty Years Later." *Numen* 62: 119-141. https://doi.org/10.1163/15685276-12341358

Meyer, Birgit, with David Morgan, Crispin Paine, and S. Brent Plate. 2015. "Material Religion's First Decade." *Material Religion* 10(1): 105-111. https://doi.org/10.2752/175183414X13909887177628

Michaelis, Adolf. 1885. "Sarapis Standing on a Xanthian Marble in the British Museum." *Journal of Hellenic Studies* 6: 287–318. https://doi.org/10.2307/623403

Nicholson, Andrew J. 2010. *Unifying Hinduism: Philosophy and Identity in Indian Intellectual History*. New York: Columbia University Press. https://doi.org/10.7312/nich14986

Niditch, Susan. 2015. "Material Religion, Created and Experienced: Burial Sites, Symbolic Visions, and Sign Acts." In Susan Niditch, *The Responsive Self: Personal Religion in Biblical Literature of the Neo-Babylonian and Persian Periods*, 90–105. New Haven, CT: Yale University Press. https://doi.org/10.12987/yale/9780300166361.003.0006

Nongbri, Brent. 2013. *Before Religion: A History of a Modern Concept*. New Haven, CT: Yale University Press. https://doi.org/10.12987/yale/9780300154160.001.0001

Orsi, Robert A. 2003. "Is the Study of Lived Religion Irrelevant to the World We Live In? Special Presidential Address, Society for the Scientific Study of Religion, Salt Lake City, November 2, 2002." *Journal for the Scientific Study of Religion* 42(2): 169–174. https://doi.org/10.1111/1468-5906.t01-1-00170

Orsi, Robert A. 2007. "When 2 + 2 = 5." *The American Scholar* (March 1). Retrieved from https://theamericanscholar.org/when-2-2-5.

Orsi, Robert A. 2012. "The Problem of the Holy." In Robert Orsi (ed.), *The Cambridge Companion to Religious Studies*, 84–105. New York: Cambridge University Press. https://doi.org/10.1017/CCOL9780521883917.006

Orsi, Robert A. 2013. "Robert Orsi at the NYS Writers Institute in 2013." Online video. Lecture from the Researching New York 2013 Conference. Uploaded by New York State Writers Institute, December 3, 2013. Retrieved from www.youtube.com/watch?v=qnFQu7ukAAY.

Orsi, Robert A. 2016. *History and Presence*. Cambridge, MA: Harvard University Press.

Otto, Rudolf. 1967. *The Idea of the Holy*, trans. John W. Harvey. New York: Oxford University Press. Originally *Das Heilige*, 1917. English translation 1923.

Plate, S. Brent. 2014. *A History of Religion in 5 1/2 Objects: Bringing the Spiritual to Its Senses*. Boston, MA: Beacon Press.

Plate, S. Brent (ed.). 2015. *Key Terms in Material Religion*. London: Bloomsbury Academic.

Saler, Benson. 1987. "*Religio* and the Definition of Religion." *Cultural Anthropology* 2(3): 395–399. https://doi.org/10.1525/can.1987.2.3.02a00070

Saler, Benson. 1999. *Conceptualizing Religion: Immanent Anthropologists, Transcendent Natives, and Unbounded Categories*. New York: Berghan.

Schilbrack, Kevin. 2010. "Religions: Are There Any?" *Journal of the American Academy of Religion* 78(4): 1112–1138. https://doi.org/10.1093/jaarel/lfq086

Schilbrack, Kevin. 2014. *Philosophy and the Study of Religions: A Manifesto*. Malden, MA: Wiley Blackwell.

Schmidt, Jalane D. 2006. "Religious Objects, Objections, and Objectives: Recent Books on Afro-Cuban Religions." *Material Religion* 2(3) 383–388. https://doi.org/10.2752/174322006778815135

Sinhababu, Supriya. 2008. "Interview with J. Z. Smith." *Chicago Maroon* (June 6). Retrieved from www.chicagomaroon.com/2008/06/02/interview-with-j-z-smith.

Slingerland, Edward and Brenton Sullivan. 2017. "Durkheim with Data: The Database of Religious History." *Journal of the American Academy of Religion* 85(2): 312–347. https://doi.org/10.1093/jaarel/lfw012

Sloop, John M. 1998. Review of *Twilight Zones: The Hidden Life of Cultural Images from Plato to O.J.*, by Susan Bordo. *The Southern Communication Journal* 64(1): 86–88.

Smith, Jonathan Z. 1982. *Imagining Religion*. Chicago, IL: University of Chicago Press.

Smith, Jonathan Z. 2004. *Relating Religion: Essays in the Study of Religion*. Chicago, IL: University of Chicago Press.

Stevens, Wallace. 1919. "Anecdote of the Jar." *Poetry* 15(1) (October). Retrieved from www.poetryfoundation.org/poetrymagazine/browse?contentId=14575.

Suzuki, Michiko. 2017. "Reading and Writing Material: Koda Aya's Kimono and its Afterlife." *Journal of Asian Studies* 76(2): 333–361. https://doi.org/10.1017/S0021911817000043

Taylor, Mark C. ed. 1998. *Critical Terms for Religious Studies*. Chicago, IL: University of Chicago Press.

Tweed, Thomas A. 2016. Presidential Address. "Valuing the Study of Religion: Improving Difficult Dialogues Within and Beyond the AAR's 'Big Tent'." *Journal of the American Academy of Religion* 84(2): 287–322. https://doi.org/10.1093/jaarel/lfw019

Van Beek, Gosewijn. 1996. "On Materiality." *Etnofoor* 9(1): 5–24.

Van Elk, Michiel, et al. 2016. "Priming of Supernatural Agent Concepts and Agency Detection." *Religion, Brain, and Behavior* 6(1): 4–33. https://doi.org/10.1080/2153599X.2014.933444

Von Stuckrad, Kocku. 2013. "Discursive Study of Religion: Approaches, Definitions, Implications." *Method and Theory in the Study of Religion* 25: 5–25. https://doi.org/10.1163/15700682-12341253

Wiebe, Don. 2009. "Religious Studies: Toward Reestablishing the Field." *Religion* 39(4): 372–375. https://doi.org/10.1016/j.religion.2009.09.002

Wilken, Robert L. 1989. Presidential Address. "Who Will Speak For The Religious Traditions?" *Journal of the American Academy of Religion* 57(4): 699–717. https://doi.org/10.1093/jaarel/LVII.4.699

Chapter 7

The Red Hot Iron: Religion, Nonreligion, and the Material

Petra Klug

The Material Turn and the Phenomenological Temptation

In the last decades of the twentieth century, and particularly since the beginning of the twenty-first century, material entities (objects, media, and art, but also ritual, gender, sexuality and bodily experiences) have gained a new attention in the study of religion. That has led to what David Chidester (2000) in his review-turned-manifesto has termed a "New Materialism." Although this new materialism is not to be confused with previous forms of materialism, "whether naturalistic, empiricist, positivist, cultural, historical or otherwise," Chidester sees in it the potential for "a more substantial critique of the material conditions under which basic categories in the academic study of religion have been generated," as well as for a new perspective on the "social life of things," as he calls it in reference to Arjun Appadurai (1986), and on the "political economies of the sacred."

Those high expectations outlined by Chidester have been slightly moderated but result indeed in a higher appreciation for material objects and bodily experiences. Through the "material turn" objects become seen as more than just illustrations of theology. Instead, as the editors of the journal *Material Religion* state, "objects bear traces that yield valuable material evidence, sometimes almost the only evidence we have of the everyday lives of devotees." Furthermore, it allows one to see matter and spirit as unified: "Religion is unable to do without things, places, or bodies" (Meyer et al. 2010). This new focus helps to de-center a discipline that for a long time has privileged not only the textual aspects of religion over the practice of laypeople, but also the Protestant tradition over all others.

But the material turn also led to a comeback of phenomenology. Or, as Russell T. McCutcheon has observed: The "turn toward material and embodied religion sounds suspiciously like a reborn form of phenomenology of religion" (McCutcheon 2015: 121). Matthew Baldwin (Chapter 6, this volume) specifically criticizes the idea of objects possessing agency or being manifestations of the sacred, as well as seeing materiality as something "real" that is not accessible to a discursive approach. Further, he criticizes the approach of lived religion for its uncritical acceptance of participant's experiences as actual encounters with transcendent agents.

I share much of this critique. Indeed, in order for objects to possess religious agency independent from the imagination of the practitioner one would have to imply a religious power. For an object to be a manifestation rather than an illustration of the sacred, such a sacred would need to exist. And if religious experience is the measure for scholarly study, we are back with Rudolf Otto, who in his book *The Idea of the Holy*[1] instructs the reader:

> to direct his mind to a moment of deeply-felt religious experience, as little as possible qualified by other forms of consciousness. Whoever cannot do this, whoever knows no such moments in his experience, is requested to read no further; for it is not easy to discuss questions of religious psychology with one who can recollect the emotions of his adolescence, the discomforts of indigestion, or, say, social feelings, but cannot recall any intrinsically religious feelings. (Otto 1923: 8)

The study of religion, or in this case better called "religious studies" with such a phenomenological approach, requires the scholar to use religious perspectives and therefore not only excludes nonreligious scholars from the field but also leads to an unavoidable religious bias. A focus on experiences and objects might aid such an approach, as it can cover up the societal embeddedness of religion, particularly if it ignores "the situated, temporal, interested and human uses of individual material objects," as Baldwin has put it (Chapter 6, this volume).

However, I think that phenomenology is not intrinsic to the material approach and the new attention to objects, rituals, experience, and the body that it entails. Certainly, there are scholars who cross over to phenomenological spheres on the back of such material helpers, as Baldwin demonstrated nicely. But neither is clinging to material objects the only way to get there, nor does all scholarship concerned with material objects end up on this other side. At the same time, there are also non-phenomenological works on material religion, which substantively add to method and theory in the study of religion (e.g., Klinkhammer and Tolksdorf 2015; Brosius et al. 2013). And I would go even further to state that the attention to material implications of religion can even be of benefit to a *critical* study of religion.

The problem lies—and here I would agree with Baldwin—in what we define as religion. But I don't think that it is entirely encompassed in the distinction between emic and etic or in a critique of religion as a *sui generis* category because common definitions of religion usually frame what is understood as religion through its meaning for the religious alone. What religion means for the rest of society—for the nonreligious and religious non-conformists as well as for the critical study of religion—is not included, and leaves a blind spot in such a definition of religion.

Defining Religion—for the Religious Alone?

In disciplines that deal with different cultures, researchers usually distinguish between emic and etic perspectives (Pike 1967). While emic means according to the terms of the studied groups, etic means through the lens of the observer

(McCutcheon 1999: 15–22). But the problem that I want to point out here is not sufficiently addressed with this distinction. Even scholars who work with etic definitions of religion still define religion primarily or exclusively through its meaning for the religious. I'll refer to this as an *implicit emic perspective*, which means that it is an etic attempt to define what religion is on the emic level of its followers, instead of defining religion in terms of its role in society and culture.

This is rooted in large part in the impact of theology on the study of religion, maybe most importantly in that of Friedrich Schleiermacher. He distinguishes between morals and metaphysics on the one hand, which are responsible for all the violence in the name of religion, and the *true* religion, which is passive:

> Religion neither seeks like metaphysics to determine and explain the nature of the Universe, nor like morals to advance and perfect the Universe by the power of freedom and the divine will of man. It is neither thinking nor acting, but intuition and feeling. It will regard the Universe as it is. It is reverent attention and submission, in childlike passivity, to be stirred and filled by the Universe's immediate influences. (Schleiermacher 1994: 277)

By defining religion as passive and delegating religious persecution to morality and metaphysics, religion is dismantled from its normative effects.

But theology does not claim to describe or explain religion and its role in society. The more problematic development was that, through the impact of theology upon the study of religion in other disciplines, Schleiermacher's romantic idealization of religion was taken as a blueprint for a *description* of religion. Also, sociology and cultural studies tend to define religion primarily through its meaning for the religious. Such an implicit emic perspective is not identical with sharing these emic or religious perspectives, but means that religious perspectives are the only ones considered. That religion also has an impact upon the nonreligious remains systematically understudied.

Because the space here is limited, I'll discuss only a few particularly influential examples (for a more extensive review of definitions, see Klug 2015). Usually definitions are categorized as either substantive or functional. Perhaps the most influential substantive definition is from Edward Burnett Tylor, who defined religion as "belief in Spiritual Beings" (1974: 383). But by reducing religion to belief, this definition misses not only its implications for nonbelievers, but the normative dimension of religion altogether.

This normative dimension was addressed by Émile Durkheim, who in his functional theory defined religion as a "unified system of beliefs and practices relative to sacred things, that is to say, things set apart and forbidden—beliefs and practices which unite into one single moral community called a Church, all those who adhere to them" (Durkheim 1968: 47). In Durkheim's definition, the problem of the implicit emic perspective becomes strikingly obvious. Religion is defined for its adherents, which it binds into one community. The implications of religion for those who do not belong to it, or for a society that consists of religious and nonreligious people, are not included in this focus.

Another popular way to define religion is to determine its "dimensions." An example of this can be found in Ninian Smart (1997), who offers such a dimensional analysis in order to prevent lopsided descriptions of religion. Yet, he still primarily considers its dimensions for adherents or what Charles Glock (1973) had called "religious commitment." Smart distinguishes between the practical dimension, the doctrinal dimension, the narrative dimension, the experiential dimension, the ethical and legal dimensions, the organizational component, and the material dimension. And although the ethical and legal dimension actually could include the impact of religion upon others, he sees a political component only in Islam. The ethical-legal dimension of Christianity would be "love" (Smart 1997: 1–14).

Of course, an implicit emic definition does not necessarily prevent scholars from considering the impact of religious norms and practices on outsiders. But it often creates both a religious bias and lack of clarity about what counts as religion, such as when certain definitions cannot accommodate the possibility that religions can cause conflict and violence. In other words, to define religion as something that is of relevance primarily for religious people themselves amounts to another form of *caretaker mentality* because it allows one to define the much-debated issues of violence and terrorism as outside of the religious realm.

Furthermore, the academic discourse on "nonreligion" also oftentimes perpetuates such a one-sided approach. It does that by defining nonreligion through its relation to religion without considering the reverse side of that relationship—namely, the way the nonreligious are constructed, perceived, and treated by the religious. The classical blueprint for this is Colin Campbell's definition of irreligion, which establishes its term through its relation towards the established religion. For Campbell "irreligion is those beliefs and actions which are expressive of attitudes of hostility or indifference toward the prevailing religion, together with indications of the rejection of its demands" (Campbell 1971: 21). In scholarship following this one-sided idea of the relationship between religion and nonreligion, the implication of religion as passive is reproduced and—in case of conflicts—nonreligion is often framed as an attack on religion or as "anti-religious" (for details, see Klug 2017).

The implicit emic perspective on religion, alongside this definition of nonreligion as one-sidedly relating to religion, together perpetuate the theological discourse of religion as passive, exempt religion from critique, and obscure a better understanding of the entanglements of religion and societal power structures. In order to generate more critical and self-reflective scholarship, we need to fundamentally extend our perspective and include also the *impact of religion upon its others*.

The Religious Normation of the Outsider

In societies with strong religious populations or governments, religious norms influence many areas of public and private life, thereby affecting the nonreligious, too. Religious norms create power structures, especially when they are implemented in political processes or when majorities stand against minorities.

I want to call that *religious normalization* or *normation* in the sense that religion norms society and individuals.

The term normalization is usually employed in reference to Michel Foucault, who used it to describe the establishment of a norm from the typical or "normal" distribution of certain traits, risks, and abilities throughout the population in what he calls the apparatuses of security (Foucault 2009: 85–91). Foucault distinguishes normalization from "normation," which he sees as more common in earlier historical formations characterized through disciplinary power. Here, the norm is thought of as being prior to the normal, and subjects are formed according to it. Normation consists in "positing a model, an optimal model that is constructed in terms of a certain result" and in "trying to get people, movements, and actions to conform to this model, the normal being precisely that which can conform to this norm, and the abnormal that which is incapable of conforming to the norm" (ibid.: 85).

Religion's impact upon society can include elements of both normalization and normation. One could argue that American Civil Religion results from an average distribution of religion through the society, and therefore could be called normalization. However, religious norms often do not represent the average or normal but the extraordinary, pure, and total. Those cases would be better described as normation. Furthermore, in a pluralistic society like that of the United States, for example, we find different kinds of norms that sometimes even compete with each other, and therefore, do not even form a "normal" but can be normative nevertheless. As a result, I think that the term normation is more instructive for studying religion and needs to be adapted for pluralistic societies.

Religious norms divide people into "us" and "them." They construct the righteous believers on the one hand and the blasphemer, the savage, the pagan, the heathen, the heretic, the unbeliever, the atheist, the irreligious, the profane, the Gentile, the Kafir, the secular, and the antireligious on the other. But this constructed distinction has very material consequences for both the nonreligious as well as the critical study of religion, which are often not visible if we focus on an intellectual discourse alone.

Religious normation of the nonreligious, of nonconformists to religious rules, and even of minority religions, is present not only in theology and religious practice but in politics, law, business, and the private sphere. It manifests itself in structural mechanisms, in social interactions, and sometimes even in violence. While political, legal, or other decisions might be based upon religious norms, the consequences that emerge from this often *bind or affect everyone*. This impact is easily overlooked if we focus only upon religious texts and tune out their material significance.

The Material Impact of Religion upon the Nonreligious and Nonconformists

I want to illustrate that briefly with some examples from my Ph.D. project[2] about anti-atheism in the United States. The US is a religiously pluralistic country and claims freedom of religion. But the concept of God has always played an important role in American politics and citizenship. Despite the constitutional separation of church and state, religious—and usually monotheistic—norms and symbolism are prevalent in government and in the public.

Material manifestations that immediately come to mind are the display of the *Ten Commandments* in court rooms or on government grounds, the imprint "In God We Trust" on currency, and the ritual of pledging allegiance to a "nation under God." However, beside those well-known and much debated issues, religion has affected and still affects the nonreligious, and arguably also the study of religion, for example, through: laws limiting "legitimate" expression, restrictions of access to positions of power, the scriptural legitimization of inequality, and even violence and terrorism. Therefore, extending our view from theology and belief to the material impact of religion upon society and nonconforming individuals can help to develop a more critical approach to the study of religion by reflecting on the role religion has played in upholding societal power relations and exclusion, as well as the consequences its critics faced.

Religious norms can define legitimate and illegitimate expressions regarding religion, whether through laws, theological scholarship, or public opinion. For example, the 1697 Massachusetts Act against Atheism and Blasphemy ruled:

> That if any Person shall presume willfully to blaspheme the holy Name of God, Father, Son, or Holy Ghost; either by denying, cursing or reproaching the true God; his Creation or Government of the World ... [or] the holy Word of God; that is the canonical Scriptures contained in the Books of the Old and New Testaments ... shall be punished by Imprisonment, not exceeding six Months, and until they find Sureties for the good Behaviors; by sitting in Pillory; by Whipping; boaring thorow the Tongue, with a red hot Iron; or sitting upon the gallows with a Rope about their Neck. (General Assembly of Massachusetts-Bay in New England s.a. [1697])

Of course, a law is an ideological rather than a material thing. But the walls of the prison are material, and so is the "red hot Iron" used against the blasphemers. These tools also served to instill fear in nonconformists and the nonreligious, discouraging them from expressing their thoughts in the first place. Through such laws, religion's impact upon society has also limited the institutionalized study of religion tremendously, as well as scientific scholarship in general. Once we extend our definitions of religion and include the impact it has upon its others, there is much to be gained by observing its material aspects even for those who are not concerned with texts and theology. It allows us to explore the role of religion in maintaining its position of power and, at the same time, power relations within society.

The Bible was one of the most important legitimizations of slavery in the early United States in its distinction between believers and nonbelievers or "heathens." In Leviticus, it states:

> Both thy bondmen, and thy bondmaids, which thou shalt have, shall be of the heathen that are round about you; of them shall ye buy bondmen and bondmaids. Moreover of the children of the strangers that do sojourn among you, of them shall

ye buy, and of their families that are with you, which they begat in your land: and they shall be your possession. And ye shall take them as an inheritance for your children after you, to inherit them for a possession; they shall be your bondmen for ever. (Lev. 25:44-46, King James Version)

This part of the Old Testament was used to provide a specifically religious and hence ultimate legitimization of slavery and therefore had quite material consequences in the form of bondage, slave labor, sexual exploitation, whipping and lynching, bombing, and the burning crosses of the Ku Klux Klan. Of course, there were also religious abolitionists and, understandably, in progressive religious scholarship those passages were not seen as authoritative. However, mistaking progressive religious scholarship as the essence of religion or even as a blueprint for its scientific description not only borders on phenomenology but also tunes out more fundamentalist religious views, which were influential nevertheless.

Religion also limited access to societal positions of influence and power for those critical towards its norms in both religious and public institutions. The early Women's Rights Movement, for example, was met with strong religious opposition from clergy and churches. The General Association of the Congregational Churches of Massachusetts in 1837 addressed their members in a Pastoral letter, pointing out

> the dangers which at present seem to threaten the female character with widespread and permanent injury. The appropriate duties and influence of woman are clearly stated in the New Testament. Those duties and that influence are unobtrusive and private, but the source of mighty power. When the mild, dependent, softening influence of woman upon the sternness of man's opinions is fully exercised, society feels the effects of it in a thousand forms. The power of woman is her dependence, flowing from the consciousness of that weakness which God has given her for her protection, (!) and which keeps her in those departments of life that form the character of individuals, and of the nation. There are social influences which females use in promoting piety and the great objects of Christian benevolence which we can not too highly commend. We appreciate the unostentatious prayers and efforts of woman in advancing the cause of religion at home and abroad; in Sabbath-schools; in leading religious inquirers to the pastors (!) for instruction; and in all such associated effort as becomes the modesty of her sex; and earnestly hope that she may abound more and more in these labors of piety and love. But when she assumes the place and tone of man as a public reformer, our care and protection of her seem unnecessary; we put ourselves in self-defence (!) against her; she yields the power which God has given her for her protection, and her character becomes unnatural. (General Association of Massachusetts cited after Cady Stanton, Anthony, Gage 1881: 81–82; parenthetical emphasis as cited by Cady Stanton et al.)

Here the Biblical gender roles were applied to women within the church, whose services were valued, but whose influence they limited, and also to women outside of the church, who were met with an open threat. And although this letter was clearly, itself, a text, it yielded such material consequences like upholding gender norms that forbade women to seek employment outside of the few women-specific realms or to own property. If the new materialism is serious about including gender aspects, we cannot just focus on how women practice religion different from men. We need to include also women's oppression through religion, their experience of anger and their resistance: "No man," stated Elizabeth Cady Stanton, "can fathom the depths of rebellion in woman's soul when insult is heaped upon her sex, and this is intensified when done under the hypocritical assumption of divine authority" (Cady Stanton 1881: 419).

Furthermore, religion, or more precisely, religiously motivated actors, are not just passive. They possess agency. Some actively seek to transform society according to their religious norms. And this can have quite material consequences. For the Christian anti-abortion terrorists, the self-declared Army of God, their work was explicitly religious even where it was violent. In their 1992 *Manual* they described their motivation as follows:

> Beginning officially with the passage of the Freedom of Choice Act—we, the remnant of God-fearing men and women of the United States of Amerika [*sic!*], do officially declare war on the entire child-killing industry. After praying, fasting, and making continual supplication to God for your pagan, heathen, infidel souls, we then *peacefully, passively presented our bodies* in front of your death camps, begging you to stop the mass murder of infants. Yet you hardened your already blackened, jaded hearts. We quietly accepted the resulting imprisonment and suffering of our passive-resistance. Yet you mocked God and continued the holocaust. No longer! All of the options have expired. Our Most Dread Sovereign Lord God requires that whosoever sheds man's blood, by man shall his blood be shed. Not out of hatred for you, but out of love for the persons you exterminate, we are forced to take arms against you. Our life for yours—a simple equation. Dreadful. Sad. Reality, nonetheless. You shall not be tortured at our hands. Vengeance belongs to God only. However, execution is rarely gentle. (Army of God 1992)[3]

The Army of God explicitly rejected a reduction of their religious commitment to a passive one and described how their religious convictions require them to become active and violent against those who breach their religious norms—thereby exposing the idea of religion as passive as a scholarly construction.

Of course, scholars debate whether religious terrorism can count as religion at all, because in the romantic idealization that many since Schleiermacher have produced, religiously motivated violence doesn't exist. When people claim such motivations for their violent behavior, it must be somehow separated from religion. Such a compartmentalization can be seen not just in academic scholarship but also in the political and public sphere. After the terror attacks of 9/11, George W. Bush said that the terrorists "profane a great religion by committing murder in its name" (Bush 2001). But, in the spiritual manual that was found in the belongings of three of the attackers, they were instructed to consider it a specifically religious mission (Kippenberg and Seidensticker 2006: 15). This manual, in large part, consists of religious instruction such as recitations of the Quran and prayers. It promises virgins waiting for the martyrs and other pleasures of paradise. But maybe most importantly, the manual stated that violence is legitimate only if it is "for the sake of God." It even included a story of Ali Ibn Abi Talib, son-in-law and cousin of Mohammed, in order to illustrate that:

When he once fought against an unbeliever, the unbeliever spat on him. Ali then let his sword pause and did not strike him. Only afterwards did he strike him. After the battle, one of the companions asked him why he had done so, why he had not struck the unbeliever, and first left off and only later struck him. Ali answered, "When he spat on me, I feared I would strike him out of vengeance. Therefore I held my sword", or how he said. When he had called the intention to mind, he turned to him and struck and killed him. All this means that the human being should prepare his soul in a very short time, and then all he does is for the sake of God. (Unknown author cited in Kippenberg and Seidensticker 2006: 16–17)

In the case of 9/11, Muslims were the ones executing religious normation. This shows that the problem is not exclusively Christian, nor is it necessarily connected with the majority. Of course, religious convictions are rooted in a variety of reasons, including political and economic conditions. However, it seems dangerous to ignore the specifically religious motives for such acts and therefore also the specifically religious momentum that they bear.

I limited my examples to those concerning the United States. But even here, the list is by no means complete. Religious norms have a material impact upon people's norms and bodies, whether they are religious or not: Laws regulating issues like stem cell research, medically assisted suicide, and abortion are influenced by religious doctrine but apply to all citizens, whether believers or not. If parents decide that they prefer faith healing to seeking medical help, the children are materially affected whether they are old enough to understand or not. Religious rituals like female genital mutilation and male circumcision alter bodies without leaving a choice to the people to whom those bodies belong. In the twenty-first century, Biblical stories are used to legitimate child abuse. Even economics are impacted by religion directly, from faith based initiatives to people hiring employees because they are "good Christians." And if the Trump administration succeeds in repealing the Johnson Amendment, which keeps tax-exempted non-profits from endorsing political candidates, churches will gain indefinitely more influence in the political process.

So, if the material religion approaches would broaden their conception of religion and study also the effects on religion's others—if they would include the religious impact upon societal power relations and gender roles, as well as the experiences of pain and suffering that are *caused by religion*—they could serve as a corrective to the theological construction that paints a picture of religion as relevant only for the religious themselves, as passive, and as therefore exempt from critique. But this leads us to the question of how scholarship on religion is ideologically and institutionally entangled with religious power structures.

Methodological Challenges for the Study of Religion and Materiality

If we want to develop a more critical scholarship of religion, we need to reflect upon the power relations in which our subject developed and still develops. In a Marxist framework: What are the material conditions that require religion? Or as McCutcheon (2003: 116) asks: "Why [do]some human beings, at specific points in time, make reference to and invoke nonempirical, transcendent beings?" And what follows, in turn, from that for the power ingrained in religion?

Furthermore, we need to reflect upon the conditions under which scholarship about religion is produced; first in regard to the religious impact upon the broader society in the form of blasphemy laws and societal restrictions for the nonreligious; and second in terms of the specifics of a field that developed out of theology and is oftentimes still bound to religious organizations. We need to show the ways in which "the Academy" continues to dismiss critical subjects, critical theories, and critical scholars. This includes inquiring how theology, religious studies and the study of religion defines what counts as data for religion, what is rendered outside of its realm. It also includes studying how the category of nonreligion is constructed through both religious and academic discourse.

I think we would miss a crucial point by excluding material aspects of religion. But to reflect upon the material aspects of the relation between religion and power is not done by simply including material objects in the study of religion as we know it. It would be crucial that a material approach would not only be interested in the "lives of devotees," as the editors of *Material Religion* have phrased it, but also in the impact of religion upon the rest of society. The question of how religion has constructed, excluded, or exterminated its others is at the center of that. What were the bodily experiences or the material impacts that the nonreligious and nonconformists were facing for their critique? Who was or is excluded from material and artistic expression? And how does religion intersect with other societal power relations?

A critical approach to materiality also needs to reflect upon the power relations that lead to different material representations: Who was or is able to own objects, to create and pay for architecture? Who was or is able to express their experiences? Do such approaches implicitly privilege the narratives of those in power? And aren't such approaches necessarily biased against those who are oppressed most in a society or who did not survive—in Gayatri Chakravorty Spivak's words—the subaltern who "cannot speak" (Spivak et al. 2008)?

If we focus on materiality, we also need to ask how we can include something that has been defined as negativity through religion and the study thereof. It is possible, as Lois Lee (2012) has suggested, to find material expressions of nonreligion. But we need to consider that it might not be possible to study something which is primarily characterized through the *absence of religion* in the same way we study religion itself, without reproducing the implication of religion as the norm, and nonreligion as modelled upon it. What we can show, however, is how religiously induced processes of exclusion have played out quite materially for the nonreligious or those who breached religious norms. In this chapter I have tried to give some glimpses into such processes.

Baldwin (Chapter 6, this volume) has rightly pointed out that material religion approaches tend to produce phenomenological and religious scholarship. This is not intrinsic to material approaches. But it is also not a coincidence either. That material religion approaches seem to come with their own material "evidence" invites us to ignore the entanglement of religion with societal power relations, its origin in societal power structures, and also its powerful impact upon society, including those who do not share the religious norms that are involved. This, however, only exacerbates pre-existing methodological problems that the study of religion is facing.

In German, a "red hot iron," *ein heißes Eisen,* is also a metaphor for a subject that is too dangerous to be touched. But maybe it has to be touched in order for us to become at least fully aware of its continuing materiality.

Petra Klug obtained a Master's Degree in Sociology and Cultural Studies, as well as a Master's Degree in Religious Studies, from the University of Leipzig. In 2018, she finished her dissertation about Anti-Atheism in the United States at the University of Bremen before starting her postdoctoral project on early and forced marriages. Currently, she is Guest Professor for Critical Theory at Justus-Liebig-University in Gießen. Klug has authored a book on the German discourse on Islam (*Feindbild Islam?*), as well as several articles about religion, non-religion, gender, and human rights.

Acknowledgments

In addition to the participants in the study and my supervisors Gritt Klinkhammer and Phil Zuckerman, I want to thank the German National Academic Foundation (Studienstiftung des deutschen Volkes), German Research Foundation (Deutsche Forschungsgemeinschaft), University of Leipzig, Pitzer College Claremont, University of Texas, and University of Bremen for the support provided for the realization of this research project, as well as Marc Burckhardt and Tom Byrne for their help.

Notes

1   The German title *Das Heilige* translates more accurately as "The Holy," which, similarly to "the Sacred," does not allow for a differentiation between calling something holy and acknowledging that holiness as real. In saying the word holy, this holiness is already acknowledged.
2   My research project deals with the normation of atheists in the US. So far, research about the relationship between the religious and the nonreligous has almost exclusively focused on the relation of the nonreligious towards religion. The other side of that relationship, namely the way atheists are perceived and treated by the religious, has been systematically understudied. Therefore, my dissertation focuses particularly on the perception of nonreligious atheists as a group that violates the most basic religious norm: to be religious. I conducted 158 qualitative interviews with atheists and believers of different religious affiliations or without religious affiliation. It is therefore probably the biggest qualitative data set about the topic worldwide. I work with an exploratory research design approach, which is based on qualitative data analysis influenced by the Grounded Theory of Barney Glaser and Anselm Strauss (2006 [1967]).
3   The version of this *Manual* cited here can be found on the internet (Army of God 1992). However, as the author of the original document is unknown and the actual document seems to be open for changes, the quotations might not be exact. The manual was last accessed March 10, 2017. See also Jefferis (2011).

References

Appadurai, Arjun (ed.). 1986. *The Social Life of Things: Commodities in Cultural Perspective.* Cambridge: Cambridge University Press. https://doi.org/10.1017/CBO9780511819582

Army of God. 1992. *The Army of God Manual*, 3rd edition. Retrieved from www.google.com/search?q=army+of+god+manual+&ie=utf-8&oe=utf-8&client=firefox-b (accessed March 10, 2017).

Brosius, Christiane, Axel Michaels, and Paula Schrode (eds.). 2013. *Ritual und Ritualdynamik: Schlüsselbegriffe, Theorien, Diskussionen.* Göttingen: Vandenhoeck & Ruprecht.

Bush, George W. 2001. "Address to the Nation Announcing Strikes Against Al Qaida Training Camps and Taliban Military Installations in Afghanistan." Retrieved from www.presidency.ucsb.edu/ws/print.php?pid=65088 (accessed December 31, 2016).

Cady Stanton, Elizabeth. 1881. "Lucretia Mott." In Elizabeth Cady Stanton, Susan B. Anthony, and Matilda Joslyn Gage (eds.), *History of Woman Suffrage: In Three Volumes*, 407–440. Retrieved from https://archive.org/stream/historyofwomansu01stanuoft/historyofwomansu01stanuoft_djvu.txt (accessed June 14, 2019).

Cady Stanton, Elizabeth, Susan B. Anthony & Matilda Joslyn Gage (eds.). 1881. *History of Woman Suffrage: In Three Volumes.* Retrieved from https://archive.org/stream/historyofwomansu01stanuoft/historyofwomansu01stanuoft_djvu.txt (accessed June 14, 2019).

Campbell, Colin. 1971. *Toward a Sociology of Irreligion.* London: Macmillan. https://doi.org/10.1007/978-1-349-00795-0

Chidester, David. 2000. "Material Terms for the Study of Religion." *Journal of the American Academy of Religion* 68(2): 367–379. https://doi.org/10.1093/jaarel/68.2.367

Durkheim, Émile. 1968. *The Elementary Forms of Religious Life.* London: George Allen & Unwin.

Foucault, Michel. 2009. *Security, Territory, Population: Lectures at the Collège de France, 1977-1978.* New York: Picador/Palgrave Macmillan.

General Assembly of Massachusetts-Bay in New England. s.a. [1697]. "An Act against Atheism and Blasphemy." Retrieved from https://en.wikipedia.org/w/index.php?oldid=651383460 (accessed 14 December 2015).

Glaser, Barney G., and Anselm L. Strauss. 2006 [1967]. *The Discovery of Grounded Theory: Strategies for Qualitative Research.* New Brunswick, NJ: Aldine Pub. Co.

Glock, Charles Y. 1973. "The Dimensions of Religious Commitment." In Charles Y. Glock (ed.), *Religion in Sociological Perspective: Essays in the Empirical Study of Religion*, 9–11. Belmont, CA: Wadsworth Pub. Co.

Jefferis, Jennifer L. 2011. *Armed for Life: The Army of God and Anti-abortion Terror in the United States.* Santa Barbara, CA: Praeger.

Kippenberg, Hans G., and Tilman Seidensticker. 2006. *9/11 Handbook: Annotated Translation and Interpretation of the Attackers' Spiritual Manual.* London: Equinox Publishing.

Klinkhammer, Gritt, and Eva Tolksdorf (eds.). 2015. *Somatisierung des Religiösen: Empirische Studien zum rezenten religiösen Heilungs- und Therapiemarkt.* Bremen: Universität Bremen.

Klug, Petra. 2015. "Der Religionsbegriff der Religionswissenschaft im Spiegel von Nichtreligion und Nonkonformität." *Zeitschrift für Religionswissenschaft* 23(1): 188–206. https://doi.org/10.1515/zfr-2015-0003

Klug, Petra. 2017. "Varieties of Nonreligion: Why Some People Criticize Religion, while Others just Don't Care." In Johannes Quack and Cora Schuh (eds.), *Religious Indifferences: Between and Beyond Religion and Nonreligion*, 219–237. Berlin: Springer. https://doi.org/10.1007/978-3-319-48476-1_11

Lee, Lois. 2012. Locating Nonreligion in Mind, Body, and Space: New Research Methods for a New Field. *Annual Review of the Sociology of Religion* 3: 135–157. https://doi.org/10.1163/9789047429470_008

McCutcheon, Russell T. (ed.). 1999. *The Insider/Outsider Problem in the Study of Religion: A Reader*. London: Cassell.

McCutcheon, Russell T. 2003. *Manufacturing Religion: The Discourse on Sui Generis Religion and the Politics of Nostalgia*. New York: Oxford University Press.

McCutcheon, Russell T. 2015. "The Category 'Religion' in Recent Publications: Twenty Years Later." *Numen* 62(1): 119–141. https://doi.org/10.1163/15685276-12341358

Meyer, Birgit, David Morgan, Crispin Paine, and S. Brent Plate. 2010. "The Origin and Mission of Material Religion." *Religion* 40(3): 207–211. https://doi.org/10.1016/j.religion.2010.01.010

Otto, Rudolf. 1923. *The Idea of the Holy: An Inquiry into the Non-rational Factor in the Idea of the Divine and its Relation to the Rational*. London: Oxford University Press.

Pike, Kenneth L. 1967. *Language in Relation to a Unified Theory of the Structure of Human Behavior*. The Hague: Mouton. https://doi.org/10.1515/9783111657158

Schleiermacher, Friedrich. 1994. *On Religion: Speeches to its Cultured Despisers*. Westminster, VA: John Knox Press.

Smart, Ninian. 1997. *Dimensions of the Sacred: An Anatomy of the World's Beliefs*. London: Fontana Press.

Spivak, Gayatri Chakravorty, Alexander Joskowicz, Stefan Nowotny, and Hito Steyerl. 2008. *Can the Subaltern Speak? Postkolonialität und subalterne Artikulation*. Vienna: Turia + Kant.

Tylor, Edward B. 1974. *Primitive Culture: Researches into the Development of Mythology, Philosophy, Religion, Art, and Custom*. New York: Gordon Press.

Chapter 8

Surprised by History: Encountering Data in Religious Studies

Holly White

Matthew Baldwin reminds us in "Objects and Objections" (Chapter 6, this volume) that religious studies scholars are busy, productive people. While some of our scholarly objects for study have been unreflexively imported from European Christendom and the legacies of its colonialism, Baldwin claims that the proper domain of scholarship is the constructive enterprise, carried out through procedures of objection and contest. As scholars, we generate our field through our deliberations. We deploy terms and excite concepts through the juxtapositions of evidence, derived from a chain of contingent authorities that are up for re-engagement and revisitation as the conversation turns. I use "we" here with specificity: Baldwin clarifies that participation in institutions of pedagogy, presentation, and publication construct the field, and thus constitute what goes by the proper name, religious studies. Baldwin reviews how deliberative procedure and institutional relations are instrumental for delivering good data. Relying on assumed or "given" objects bypasses the scholarly labor of reflecting on how those objects are selected and set-apart. The self-conscious scholar comes to know her work not as data presentation but an investigation into data production.

It is the mechanisms of data production that frames my own engagement with Baldwin. What activities belong to the scholar and what, if any, are those of the objects themselves? This "themselves" harkens to or has a whiff of phenomenology—a discourse that Baldwin works to dismiss from religious studies for its haunting of universal, ultimate, or remote agents outside of critique. Data production, as Baldwin reiterates, is social reproduction. We, as scholars, are creating this data, and then can use our tools of socio-political critique on ourselves: first, to describe what is being said, written, and discussed in our journals, books and conferences; and second, to make use of that data to explain some phenomena. Picking apart our own naturalizing procedures as scholars, Baldwin depends on a method of historicization to highlight the constructedness of the categories we use, advocating a historicized materialism that brings to light the "situated, temporal, interested, and human use of individual material objects" (Chapter 6, this volume). The objects, be they material objects like bones or stones or the more diffuse or abstract categories like rituals or world religions, are, through Baldwin, only available through discursive and literary practices and are more properly social events than things that you venerate or accidentally choke on.

But what of the data mechanisms of the objects themselves? As I read him, it is not so much that Baldwin objects to materialism as much as he objects to unreduced materiality or unreflective, first-order justification for specific choices of materiality. The second half of his essay reviews recent scholarship on materialism that commits either of those errors.[1] Baldwin questions the recuperation of "material religion" where it appeals to "abundance, excess, overflow, unknowability, ineffability, irreducibility, incommensurability, etc." (Chapter 6, this volume). Scholarship which starts with these perceived qualities and then uses these qualities as justification is not new in any way. To Baldwin's frustration, the objects of the new materialists "are never merely particular, peculiar, local, social, economic, interested, ordinary, or otherwise *mundane* signs of intersubjective human behavior" (ibid.). An adjacent concern is those arguments which seek to appeal to some reality other than what is discursively available. While I share Baldwin's criticisms of these materialist approaches which inadequately interrogate the conditions of givenness of data or depend on sensation as the primary cause for investigation, I want to propose that there are historical and particular ways of considering the excesses without the appeals to universals or eternals. I make this proposal because it is a kind of excessiveness and surplus which continues the drive of scholarship and what funds Baldwin's religious studies. I agree with Baldwin's assessment of the routes of phenomenology but see other ways to explain the abundance. Situating objects as thoroughly historical, historicizable objects does the productive work of locating objects while also giving due to the expansive swaths of historical contingencies that invite our work.

Baldwin's text provides a point of entry for my outline of the historical production of data through his careful reading of Jonathan Z. Smith's account of scholarly surprise. Surprise is a multivalent term to Baldwin's ears and can translate as "wonder, amazement, amusement, bemusement, shock, horror, awe, dismay, disapproval, or commendation" (Chapter 6, this volume). It interests me that there is something Otto-ian about some of these terms yet that we (as critical scholars) know cannot be the case. What can provide the distinction? Baldwin gives some direction and notes that these are to be ideological and political perturbations, not surprising things. In reading this description in Baldwin's work, I found the choice of surprise, well, surprising. "Surprise" and its synonyms are, through Baldwin, being rewritten through Smith as distinctly historical and discursive events—a qualification that Baldwin insists on at every turn to fund the rightful sources of scholarly objects. This revision of these classically phenomenological—and even theological—terms invites my curiosity. These are, at least, humanistic terms. How do they work within Baldwin's frame of social process that produces objects for religious studies?

For more information on the nature of scholarly surprise, I turn to Baldwin's source in Smith's collection of essays, *Relating Religion*. Within this set, Smith references three basic dimensions of surprise. These are all centered in the activity of a subject—the scholar. The first is that surprise can derive from the task of comparison, either of the same across time or of a difference in space, such as from classification. This is another way of considering the repetition with a difference (see Chapter 6, this volume; Smith 2004: 163). The surprise is deliberate in this case, a "process of 'defamiliarization'" and thus, can be produced by effort in the scholar's studio.[2] The second dimension of surprise is what is created through applying second-order discourse or a category. Here, the surprise comes not from like objects in comparison, as is his first example, but from the surprise of a category's fitness for that object. This makes use of what happens when one concept or term can replace another. Smith uses Durkheim's translation of "religion" to "society" as a familiar and enduring example of this surprise that still has purchase in our field. Another is observation of where in the New Testament "religion" displaces the more commonly used "faith" (ibid.: 208). The third case of surprise from Baldwin's list of Smith is found in the last essay of the collection, "A Twice-Told Tale" and rounds out the collection. Here, surprise is, as above, in difference and explanation but with emphasis on the ever-social nature of labors of representation. With an emphasis on languages, Smith makes the case that scholarship involves translation. Description is much like the translator's tool of paraphrase and as such, is simply weak translation, according to Smith. For scholarship to make its mark, it needs to be mindful of the change that happens in any representation (ibid.: 372). Taken together, surprise is mixed into the sober practice of scholarship, located in scholarly efforts of explanation and not in animated materiality.

So as not to risk merely repeating Smith without translation, I want to apply Smith's cases of scholarly surprise for my own understanding of the excess of materiality in religious studies. The procedures of data production are, by Baldwin and Smith, cognitive operations. It is as if matter is silent or inert until made to speak by the scholar's keystrokes. I can agree with this theoretically. However, practically, the social, using and creating objects, is already in motion and making noise by the time the scholar arrives at her desk. Objects are already animated by use, and concepts overdetermined by their repetition. Baldwin understands this mix of reworking with inherited objects and making new ones when he delivers his precise and elegant definition of religious studies in his essay that centers our discourses as ones "concerned with the management (and creation!) of surprise" (Chapter 6, this volume). The scholar's work involves both mutually deliberate and deliberative effort. Thus, the scholar interrupts the already-in-motion stream of objects and manipulates them. What I want to emphasize from Baldwin's and Smith's work is that the instances of constructed surprise may or may not occur exclusively within the bounds of the scholar's studio but may have been generated with some deliberateness for different, unscholarly purposes, by others of times and places to make for their own contextual surprises. Scholars, in the business of the management of surprise, are inheritors to an unruly set of others' already formed juxtapositions and expositions. Giving an account of the forcefulness of those social formations that precede our scholarship and their entanglement with materiality bears more attention than what Baldwin has raised.

Smith includes his own examples of these preprocessed surprises, calling out that surprise is whatever occasions thought and prompts cognitive reworking. In the case of the first example of defamiliarization through comparison, Smith extracts his example from Victor Turner's explanation of masks and the exaggerated features that provoke thought. In their local use, the masks' combinations, Turner maintains, "startle neophytes into thinking about objects, persons, relationships, and features of their environment they have hitherto taken for granted" (Turner 1967: 105; cf. Smith 2004: 162–163). Smith identifies with this ritual moment: scholarly thinking is jumpstarted when the habits of human thought are interrupted and these interruptions are contiguous with what might be, at first thought, an irrational or supernaturally-intoned moment. The second sense of surprise—categorization—preserves a quality of excess by the inherent limits of translation. As Smith avers, "translation is never fully adequate. There is always discrepancy. (To repeat the old tag: 'To translate is to traduce.')"[3] By this account, there will always be a remainder that is beholden to historicization and human science. I glean here from Smith an influencing dimension to data production not, at first, at hand in Baldwin's essay. This is the profusion of constructions of non-scholars that are at work faster and both behind and ahead of scholarly production. This profusion is its own sort of source that generates the overdeterminded objects that render occasions for analysis—occasions that are seized on by scholars and nonscholars alike in their efforts to order and interact with their proliferating environments.

Excess, wonder, shock, horror, or awe will prompt thought of both the scholarly and nonscholarly variety; however, the outcomes of both will differ in crucial ways. One mark of scholarship is claim to the recursivity of production—the mutually formative conditions that make us producers and products simultaneously. In what remains of my essay, I take up this labor, describing how critical scholarship offers tools for this delicate, incessant task of watching the mechanisms of production and being caught—surprised—by the ways the scholar, like others, is always produced and thus, vulnerable to surprise from without. To this end, I revisit some of the field of historical critical method that girds Baldwin's work, including how a neo- Marxist history might account for the impersonal surprise. I then offer two objects for analysis for the way they demonstrate different dimensions of scholarly surprise.

Using a historical-critical method opens the social field to scrutiny, revealing the gaps that Smith identifies as surprise. In order for data to register as surprise, there needs to be an inversion of some expectation. One node in the social field registering surprise is the subject. Triggering some sort of cognitive or affective skip, the surprise could be seen to be seated in the subject registering the event. Thinking through a social constructivist lens focuses the subject as an intersection of social formations. Through the term "social formation," what might be more first thought as a subject is known for its multiple socially set identities (see Mack 2000; McCutcheon 2001). One account, then, is that surprise could be the eclipse or gap from these intersecting formations, with enough consistency between subjects to register these surprises as relevant or compelling enough for further attention. This approach to analyzing surprise, however, requires some method of tracking or accounting for the types of formations that generate these disjuncts, with the possibility of proliferate intersections. While much scholarship in social theory makes use of this route, I want to focus attention away from the site of individual subjects or particular striations of the social field towards the fabric of history that generates those striations in the first place. To attend to surprise at the site of social and historical disruption is to consider the kind of impersonal character that attracts the nomenclature of sacred or religious in the first place.

To match surprise to history, then, I want to pass through a dimension of Marx's thought on dialectical materialism and his revision of Hegelian contradiction. Keeping with a Hegelian totality but with an inversion, Marx names material conditions and political economy as the engine behind history. Contradictions are not merely objects of thought desperate for resolution or "aufhebung": history moves by the gears of human creativity transforming unmarked landscapes into habital space and usable goods (see Marx 1978: 158–159; also Giddens 1979). The "resolutions" attach human effort to raw material. However, under capitalism, the contradictions of thought that Hegel encounters are made of muscle, sweat, and hunger. Marx never lets his readers forget this. Surprise, in Marxian terms, then, is a derivation of material contradiction. Where what is at first, with Hegel, the oppositions of thought systems in conflict at the level of ideas, are, with Marx, conflicts at the level of ideas modeled on conflicts of uneven distribution of goods and services between their producers and consumers. Surprise includes with it the fundamental contradiction evident in social life: some have a lot and others have little. Contradiction, then, is both the unpleasant experience of cognitive dissonance of incompatible premises and the disjoint of social organization that both sustains and undermines society itself.

This explication of Marxian contradiction funds my own interpretation of Baldwin's character of surprise. First, it tethers Baldwin's scholarly tasks of adjudicating differences and querying claims of authenticity and legitimacy to political and ideological systems via materiality. Thus, the starting point for surprise is always at once material and discursive because of the social nature of materiality in Marx's thought. Second, this approach also expands theoretical field around the occasion for thought. This is in line with Smith's emphasis on the social nature of the occasion in his "A Twice-Told Tale" description of surprise. Through Marxian contradiction, that social field is more precisely defined and explained. The character of wonder that prompts thought is then at all times material and social. What is impersonal is tethered to human activity and worldly concern.

What then renders this moment particularly excessive, inaccessible, or in abundance? The totality of history, conceptually available in the nineteenth century for the European theorist, is no longer a tenable formula. The well-known label for the end of this conceptual moment, postmodernity, with its correspondent economic moment of late capitalism, has taken new twists and turns as the technological reach collapses distance and transforms the liberal binaries of public/private (see Zuboff 2016). What was once conceivable—a sweeping account of the ways of things-cannot be sustained, and other epistemologies challenge the supremacy of this mode. Scholarship has adapted and offers the particular and local in response. Yet, despite the impossibility to fully imagine the social relations and the extent of history, theories of social construction are indebted to the formulation of a web of material-historical-social life crossing the globe. A contradiction erupts for the scholar where she both depends on and rejects the possibility of explanations of history.

Here, I turn to Fredric Jameson, who offers several handholds for the scholarly enterprise with reference to Marxian history. Out of this condition (which is its own kind of surprise), Jameson offers the first of two tools I think that bear on the management of surprise. The first is methodological. Jameson devises a mode for historical work distinct for the postmodern moment, what he calls "cognitive mapping":

> An aesthetic of cognitive mapping—a pedagogical political culture which seeks to endow the individual subject with some new heightened sense of its place in the global system—will necessarily have to respect this now enormously complex representational dialectic and invent radically new forms in order to do it justice ... The political form of postmodernism, if there ever is any, will have as its vocation the invention and projection of a global cognitive mapping on a social, as well as a spatial scale. (Jameson 1991: 54)

At a moment where full explanation is foreclosed, some degree of explanation has to suffice. Yet that explanation cannot exhaust the historical, economic, and political connections which extend in every direction from any single object or data point. A map must suffice for the density and extension that is the sum of the social-ideological-material data that while not infinite, is innumerable.[4] Cognitive maps can be of use for religious studies where the scholar acknowledges the press of historical-social-economic connections at work but is at limitations to do so. This can apply to the contingencies of scholarly production, such as Baldwin does in delimiting the scope of publication data or in the historicization of the common terms like "religion." It can also apply to the periodizing of our present moment as "neoliberal" and tracking the differences in technology and cultural influence because of this decisive shift.

In cooperation with this methodology of cognitive mapping, Jameson supplies a second tool for scholars to confront the present condition of thought: a theory of history amended for our era and location. This is a moment cognizant of the limited site distances monitored by the postmodern scholarly awareness of difference. With the impossibility of knowing fully, Jameson assumes the interconnectivity of the global (a material reality for sure) and assigns this web of time and space the proper name "History."[5] The density and expanse of History comes ever more into view as it simultaneously recedes from capture. One thinks here of History manifest in a North American cultural context: global media networks pumping increasingly more images into our news feeds; scientific tools for data collection and analysis generate ever more information while the particular lives of African elephants and Korean pop stars bob into awareness by way of social media; the teeming details of diverse lives are ever more present. The effect is an unthinkable surplus that ruptures and then reknits events into a succession that is taken as the more familiar "history." Jameson emphasizes how History is larger than received narratives of winners and losers. It is, instead, inclusive of social interaction and repressed interactions layered with the technologies of production. This blending of psychoanalytic and Marxian discourses, consistent with Jameson's interpretation of culture, allows a dialectic of subject and social. What may be perceived as a "phantasmagoria" of sense experience is, by Jameson, always thoroughly social and material (see McCutcheon 2003: 6–7). History provides a concept for an immanent frame of subjective affect, social interaction, and modes of production.

This concept of History provides an orientation for critical scholars rejecting the promises of transcendence or phenomenological excitements. History, with the capital H, is mundane and ordinary but perhaps so much so that it does not receive much attention at first. This can lead to scholarly projects like the uses of early twentieth century cookbooks as theological texts (see Bailey 2012). Such mundane History, however, can also shock and mark loss, like memorials to war dead that keep their body count through shoes or soldier's boots.[6] History, in this telling, is not only the number of dead but the specificity and particularity of each life, each work day and each home and the social impact of each life and each death, rippling into the present with its remembrance. The material-social expanse of History appears through Marxian material-social contradiction—the cognitive and affective sense that my own humble shoes are and are not the boots of the soldiers or those of a genocide victim.

The benefit of framing the extending networks of social and material productions as not just history but History is that social formations or epistemologies left out of hegemonic accounts of history are known for their repressed and surprising dimensions as they are recovered and rewritten. What motivates the critical scholar *except* what new gems History might give up if we mine the right archive? Religion scholar Constance Furey uses Jameson's proper noun of History for her own explorations of what critical scholarship offers in its revisiting of the archive to map counter narratives to hegemony. In an effort to loosen historicism from its authoritarian posture, Furey follows the turn from philosophies of history to situate histories of context. Furey, noting the influence of Michael Foucault and Joan Scott on scholarship of retelling, sees the political potential in the logic that "telling a different story about the past will somehow expand our options today" (Furey 2008: 389). History, in Jameson's frame, is always in need of reading but it is in surplus of what can be interpreted by any one scholarly project. Our projects, when in reference to this History, are then animated by the necessity of their limitations.

Jameson's methodological and theoretical apparatus can be helpful not only for how to account for scholarly surprise in Smith and Baldwin but also for expanding the work of other religious studies scholars. My own, more subdued surprise came in reading recent scholarship that firmly situates itself in commodity culture. In reflecting on what objects are and do for religious studies scholarship, I wanted to explore the transposition of ordinary and extraordinary. I was most interested in scholarship that was self-reflexive about its own scholarly production and could see this in concert with the social production of "religious" objects. I turn now to these objects to discuss how particular scholars account for the religiousness of objects by means of history, appealing to materiality and its excessiveness without appeal to phenomenological method. I am interested in how the scholarship shuttles the reader to consider the mundane made religious and the religious made mundane. After considering these works independently, I will revisit how they contribute to the mapping and the limits of mapping the historical material fields of present global culture.

The first of these two mundane objects comes from Kathryn Lofton in *Consuming Religion* (2017). Lofton introduces her book with her own surprise: religious references sprinkled through an in-flight magazine article. Using this commercial product to occasion analysis, Lofton tracks the interfaces of religious discourses and commodities in contemporary US culture. Reflecting Durkheim's overlay of religion with society, the neoliberal epoch has us refining our self-presentations through commodities such as clothing, media preferences, and tech hardware. Popular religion is not only how traditional religions adopt contemporary market logics or tools but also how popularity is a means of authorizing and legitimating oneself through distinction *itself* and that these alliances map us in a field of social relations. This is to take up religion as not disappearing but transforming itself as new authorities ask and receive our allegiances. Lofton sees American religion both in economic life and *as* economic life, with the "marketplace as the primary archive of religion" (Lofton 2017: 7).

Religion *in* popular culture and popular culture *as* religion is not always obvious. Naming "popular religion" forces the scholar to make and defend choices with the kind of reflective responsibility that category formation commands. Teasing commodity culture for what may be theorized as "religion" defamiliarizes both the banal surface of popular media and consumer habits and the received assumptions of set-apart religiousness. The commonality of popular culture triggers reflection on the mechanisms of promotion into awareness, the channels of media, and social formation. What is close at hand—the in-flight magazine—surprises for the way it is not readily known as an object of religion. Forced into view are the mechanisms of their assembly and the contradictions they hold, such as how reachable a travel destination seems when profiled with glossy, macro-focused pictures or how "normal" a celebrity seems when on *Ellen*. These condensations create the kind of animated, auretic fetish objects that at first glance, glow with that kind of untheorized "surprise" Baldwin is anxious towards and that religion scholarship is well-positioned to redescribe by other discourses than those handed to us by normalizing media.

A mundane, at-hand object worth analysis for Lofton is soap. Soap is not an object for veneration (though advertisers would like it to hold some mystical promise) but, through Lofton's lens, becomes an occasion to analyze the weave of Protestant hegemony, the missionary dimensions of advertising, and the mutual construction of knowledge. Through interpretations of nineteenth and twentieth century visual and textual culture from the United States, Lofton unfolds the invention of the modern cult of ablution. This helps us to consider differently the little altars in our hotel bathrooms. The history of soap is one that is transformed through advertising and efforts of newly formed educational arms of industry that promoted soap use for social benefit via the language of science. Lofton herself scours the archive of the industry group the American Soap and Glycerin Producers to lift examples from its companion group, The Cleanliness Institute. Active through the early decades of the twentieth century, the Institute published a journal, handbooks, children's books and even a hymnal.

Lofton uses soap not only to unpack how cleanliness discourses produced class-based Christian respectability but also to examine how these objects—concrete and abstract—mark a more encompassing shift of subjectivity inscribed in a neoliberal religious order. Some characteristics of this neoliberal moment from Lofton's introduction include a continuity with modernity through technological utopianism and industrial education models; the rational authority of markets; global flows of culture and money in multiple directions with nodes of nation states and transnational corporations; the increase of capitalist structures; the increase of speed of cultural transmission and economic activity by way of technological change; the generation of producers and consumer identities; and an emphasis on spiritual values aligned with buying power and wealth. À la Durkheim, soap is one more religious object in our "cult of capitalism" that organizes us into our totems of consumption. In charting the path of cleanliness discourses from different moments of American capitalism, the distinctive features of the present neoliberal moment sharpen. Via soap, Lofton shows how a specific, mundane material commodity can be a lens for an investigation into a range of behaviors, ideologies and thus, give insight into the overdetermined object of American religion. In a gesture that is reminiscent of Jameson's cognitive mapping, Lofton owns that a study of American religion and its particularly industrial, corporate quality would require a "messy and maddening history, including tales of profit-seeking Buddhist monks and monomaniacal television evangelists, parables of gender-busting activity nouns, and jeremiad wails through wartimes and supply sides." (Lofton 2017: 98). The mundane is still mundane but becomes a lens for the surprises historicization offers.

The second object has the more conventionally religious, but perhaps for us suspiciously, liturgical ring: Icons. In her book *Global Icons: Apertures to the Popular* (2011), literary scholar Bishnupriya Ghosh takes apart and reassembles the potential of popular images for political movements. Like Lofton, Ghosh uses the regimes of representation in neoliberalism but expands to transnational context to consider the circulation of images to organize social life. She adopts the religiously-toned "icon" to point to the symbolic density of some images. If icons hint at "magical technologies," it is, as she avers, because of the loop of social signifiers and sensory indexes (Ghosh 2011: 9). What makes an image an icon is its condensation of shared cultural knowledge, its references to the physical infrastructures of media for its circulation (from film studios to printed reproductions) and the physical body of its subject. Cognition and affect are both under revision in the face of the icon, as its formal properties mobilize particular relations to time and space. Icons point to a historical past but selectively erase elements of that past to indicate a collective future. In this way, they seem timeless.

The image becomes an icon when the density of social life is such that it can only point off-screen to something recognizable but not accessible—except by its substitution.

What sets Ghosh's analysis apart for critical religious studies is the way she sees contemporary images as icons within a global moment, referencing both historical icon/image research, economic-political contexts of South Asia, and the emergent epistemologies of a region differently impacted by commodity culture than the US. Her examples include profiles like activists Mahatma Gandhi and Arundhati Roy but also commodities like Coca-Cola. She never leaves behind how all of these images—political, economic or religious—are consumer goods and dependent on a marketplace. The calendar page of Gandhi or the Coca-Cola sign can be revised or effaced, creating new iconography that renarrates an Apple iPod or a local resistance to water shortages. What differentiates Ghosh from the historicization of Baldwin or Lofton, however, is a more sustained semiological analysis of icons that disclose the play of temporal and spatial habits of thought. What generates an icon, be it Christ or a sweaty Coca-Cola bottle, is in part, its ability to point to a time or a place that has been foreclosed by history. It isn't that the icon is a material window to the sacred but instead, holds a place for the ambivalent relationship to the density of history, and points to events which are only ever made present again in our representations.

The icon, through Ghosh, adds to my argument for the management of surprise of religious studies by its willingness to speak back to the religion of image culture in South Asia. First, Ghosh's work revises conventional categories of East/West, religion/secular, virtual/material, and religious/political by periodizing the moment of global cultural and economic flows. Ghosh instructs the religion scholar on current thought in visual culture, training scholars in visual literacy for ideology critique in a more image-saturated, less textual historical moment. Through the revised category of "global icon" and its historicization of image culture in neoliberalism, Ghosh's icon delivers an occasion to examine the layers of condensed social and material culture. As discussed above with regards to Fredric Jameson's concept of History, the "surprise" of materiality is in the density of social relations that cannot be easily mapped but are attempted through the critical study of religion. Such studies, like Tomoko Masuzawa's investigation of religious studies' fascination with origins, show how historicizing procedures make meaning out of given categories (see Masuzawa 1993). In Mazuzawa's case, origin is interrogated as a dimension of repetition, which is historicized as a part of the nineteenth and twentieth centuries. Origin stories may once have appealed to scholars of form for their seeming ubiquity across different religions and thus, primed for comparative approaches in an era focused on philology. Masuzawa contributes by not simply in pointing out the false historic unity of origin stories but in exploring the scholar's fascination with origins of all sorts. Discourses of beginnings play out tensions of renunciation and gratification through narrative. However, Masuzawa notes the technological correlate in the developing tools of photography and film. In the early twentieth century, the ritual drama of beginning/repetition mirrored the historical moment's emergent material concern with the original/copy dynamic carried out in the mechanical reproduction of images (see Masuzawa 1993: 13–33; Benjamin 1968: 217–251). In Masuzawa as in Ghosh, historicizing situates and contexualizes but it also suggests that even as a scholar revisits the time to look for clues to explain the phenomena, the return to investigate suggests that there is always more there and that past as an archive is impossible to exhaust because the present will make increasing demands for new insight.

Ghosh's work is similar in that she too situates her study of icons for how sacrality is arrived at through repetitions that are always political. Thus, the icon's reach towards something like a "deep alterity" is suspicious because of its "danger potential to bind affect to hegemonic political projects" (Ghosh 2011: 79). What I take from Ghosh for my own reading of the surprise is that even in the more phenomenological intonation of Ghosh's sensual encounters with icons and her appeal to the physiological activity of perception, Ghosh's account of veneration is the emphasis on the collective, and thus, political dimension of every layer of the icon's generation, reception, or use.

Having considered how objects reference their moments of production, a second temporal dimension comes into play with Lofton and Ghosh. Using objects in ritual layer repetition in their meaning. Production and ritual are both historical dimensions that Jameson's History makes clearer. The condensations of material things and their animated natures rely on ritualization, lending them their fetishized quality. Like layers of shellac that make the object harder, ritual distinguishes itself through the layering of repetition with a difference. Thinking about these objects with Jameson's concept of History allows for new dimensions of working at the layers of historicization and to consider how history has surprising elements of its own to prompt the scholar to her work.

Constructing objects demands a historicizing process, as discussed with Baldwin. Be they icons or soap, these material objects, as we have seen, are dead matter but are not silent. And as Baldwin and the other papers in this series remind us, there is no such thing as dead matter anyway—only what can be shared and circulated, recognized by the tugs and pushes of social contact. In some responses, everything has the potential for animation by the lights of critical religious studies methods of historicization. Focusing on the material brings the social relations of production into relief and concretizes the conceptual work that our methods of history offer. History points us back and forward and has us look around, placing and connecting. Whatever appears is brought to life by, to borrow Baldwin's words, the "situated, local, material, and practical concerns of actual people" (Chapter 6, this volume). The construction of objects for analysis is ongoing by scholars and non-scholars alike, though it is the scholar who is beholden to show her work. This constructive process, known for its contradictory quality, is still wholly historical and social, yet a little more lively and fraught than what might be intoned by scholarly surprise.

Holly A. White received her Ph.D. from Syracuse University in the Department of Religion. Her dissertation addressed the modern aesthetic figure of Utopia and its relationship to critical methods in religious studies. Her areas of research include material culture, social theory, and modern literature.

Notes

1. Baldwin's discussion centers on both particular articles and a set of publications that have set the tone of "new materialism", most prominently the journal *Material Religion: The Journal of Objects, Art, and Belief* that launched in 2005. Baldwin addresses several articles that argue for ascribing animation to objects. For example, he sees Jennifer Scheper Hughes (2012) as retreating to Otto-ian language in her interest in adopting "horizontal" rather a "vertical" theory that permits humans and objects as both "co-agentive beings." He spends the bulk of his time with the larger projects and approaches of S. Brent Plate (2014) and Robert Orsi (2016) who both preserve Rudolf Otto (1967) in either Orsi's assurance that religion is universal or Plate's insistence that religion scholarship would be amiss if it did not have materiality for its study. As this essay argues, I agree that terms like Orsi's "abundant events" have some purchase but only through second-order discourse—a move that Orsi resists.
2. Smith's investment in defamiliarization for scholarship is first, for distinguishing itself from being the transmission of religion, and second, for sustaining nimbleness of mind to resist what, I would call, ideologies of self-evidence. To show how defamiliarization works, Smith constructs a fictional scenario of Durkheim presiding over a legal argument. In this example, Smith imagines Durkheim defending that the commercialism of Christmas does not render its symbols secular (and thus permissible for public display) but another kind of religion (see Smith 2004: 383–389).
3. Smith cites this twice in his text (ibid.: 208, 371) but doesn't explain its origins. This aphorism is a translation of the Italian proverb "*Traduttore, traditore*," and literally is translated as "translator, traitor" (see Rubenstein 2014: 23–25).
4. In my own speculation, the cognitive mapping of Jameson, while not related textually, is coincident theoretically with Jonathan Z. Smith's own interest in religious studies scholarship to promote "maps" over "territory." To rely on "maps," or second order discourse, in place of "territory," or first-hand accounts or primary discourse, is to not deny the territory but privilege the map. Smith is cautious to remind readers that "maps are all we possess" (Smith 1978: 309). This would seem to circumscribe territory as itself just another map. My own thinking is not to animate territory but to give credence to the potentiality of map making—what precedes or gives rise to map-making.
5. Jameson explains this concept earlier in his long career but continues to make use of it at other stages. In this early essay, Jameson connects Marxist and psychoanalytic frames, pulling at how History is another way of discussing the Lacanian "Real." History is a dense material process not readily accessible to any one mode of interpretation, be it Marxist, psychoanalytic, humanistic, or social scientific. Jameson continues to pull from each of these discourses through his career (see Jameson 1982: 338–395).
6. The travelling exhibit "Eyes Wide Open," curated by the American Friends Service Committee, displayed a pair of boots for every American serviceperson killed in the Iraq and Afghanistan wars. Initially on tour from 2004 to 2007, it divided and then expanded to include pairs of shoes to track the cost of Afghan and Iraqi lives and was used to attract attention to local death counts in specific cities and states as regional exhibits as recently as 2013. The permanent exhibit of holocaust shoes at the United States Holocaust Memorial Museum in Washington DC displays the shoes as a heap.

References

Bailey, Emily. 2012. "Historical Cookbooks in the Study of American Religion." *Bulletin for the Study of Religion* 41(4): 24–33. https://doi.org/10.1558/bsor.v41i4.24

Benjamin, Walter. 1968. "The Work of Art in the Age of Mechanical Reproduction." In Walter Benjamin, *Illuminations: Essays and Reflections*, ed. Hannah Arendt, trans. Harry Zohn, 217–251. New York: Schocken Books.

Furey, Constance. 2008. "Utopian History." *Method and Theory in the Study of Religion* 80(1): 385–398. https://doi.org/10.1163/157006808X371851

Ghosh, Bishnupriya. 2011. *Global Icons: Apertures to the Popular.* Durham, NC: Duke University Press. https://doi.org/10.1215/9780822394242

Giddens, Anthony. 1979. *Central Problems in Social Theory: Action, Structure, and Contradiction in Social Analysis.* Berkeley, CA: University of California Press.

Hughes, Jennifer Scheper. 2012. "Mysterium Materia: Vital Matter and the Object as Evidence in the Study of Religion," *Bulletin for the Study of Religion* 41(4): 16–24. https://doi.org/10.1558/bsor.v41i4.16

Jameson, Fredric. 1982. "Imaginary and Symbolic in Lacan: Marxism, Psychoanalytic Criticism, and the Problem of the Subject." In Shoshana Felman (ed.), *Literature and Psychoanalysis: The Question of Reading Otherwise*, 338–395. Baltimore, MD: Johns Hopkins University Press.

Jameson, Fredric. 1991. *Postmodernism, or the Cultural Logics of Late Capitalism.* Durham, NC: University of North Carolina Press.

Lofton, Kathryn. 2017. *Consuming Religion.* Chicago, IL: University of Chicago Press. https://doi.org/10.7208/chicago/9780226482125.001.0001

Mack, Burton. 2000. "Social Formation." In Willie Braun and Russell T. McCutcheon (eds.), *Guide to the Study of Religion*, 283–296. New York: Continuum.

Marx, Karl. 1978. "The German Ideology: Part I." In Robert C. Tucker (ed.), *The Marx-Engels Reader*, 2nd edition, 146–200. New York: Norton.

Masuzawa, Tomoko. 1993. *In Search of Dreamtime: The Quest for the Origin of Religion.* Chicago, IL: University of Chicago Press.

McCutcheon, Russell T. 2001. *Critics not Caretakers, Redescribing the Public Study of Religion.* Albany, NY: State University of New York Press.

McCutcheon, Russell T. 2003. *The Discipline of Religion: Structure, Meaning, Rhetoric.* New York: Routledge.

Orsi, Robert. 2016. *History and Presence.* Cambridge, MA: The Belknap Press of Harvard University Press.

Otto, Rudolf. 1967. *The Idea of the Holy*, trans. John W. Harvey. New York: Oxford University Press. Originally Das Heilige, 1917. English translation 1923.

Plate, S. Brent. 2014. *A History of the Religion in 5 1/2 Objects: Bringing the Spiritual to Its Senses.* Boston, MA: Beacon Press.

Rubenstein, Marv. 2014. *American English Compendium: Portable Guide to the Idiosyncrasies, Subtleties, Technical Lingo, and Nooks and Crannies of American English*, 4th edition. Lanham, MD: Rowman & Littlefield.

Smith, Jonathan Z. 1978. *Map Is Not Territory: Studies in the History of Religions.* Leiden, The Netherlands: E. J. Brill.

Smith, Jonathan Z. 2004. *Relating Religion: Essays in the Study of Religion.* Chicago, IL: University of Chicago Press.

Turner, Victor. 1967. *The Forest of Symbols: Aspects of Ndembu Ritual.* Ithaca, NY: Cornell University Press.

Zuboff, Shoshana. 2016. "The Secrets of Surveillance Capitalism." *Frankfurter Allgemeine* (March 5). Retrieved from www.faz.net/aktuell/feuilleton/debatten/the-digital-debate/shoshana-zuboff-secrets-of-surveillance-capitalism-14103616.html (accessed January 15, 2018).

Chapter 9

Governance and Public Policy as Critical Objects of Investigation in the Study of Religion

Peggy Schmeiser

Matthew Baldwin's "Objects and Objections: Methodological Reflections on the Data for Religious Studies" (Chapter 6, this volume) is a constructive and thought-provoking essay that invites readers to revisit the subject matter of our investigations not only as a field, but as individual scholars. His survey of the multiple ways that the "data" of the field of religious studies might be discovered, analyzed, and challenged lays a foundation for better understanding the forces and topics that have helped to shape and inform our field as it continues to evolve. Although Baldwin is open to considering a variety of different approaches and discursive intentions among scholars affiliated within the discipline, he does not support nor permit an *anything goes* approach to the *stuff* of our analyses. Rather his interest in objects that are "intersubjectively available" through "scientific, genealogical, sociological or historical" methods (Chapter 6, this volume) provides an essential opportunity for not only asking *what* we study but *how* we justify our selection. And while the responses to these questions may forever elude us, I believe this self-reflection and critique is imperative to the survival of our field and discourses.

As I read and re-read Baldwin's essay, several moments spanning decades of my academic life in the study of "religion" seem particularly poignant. The first was as a graduate student in the 1990s attending the American Academy of Religion annual conference. One particular year, a major publisher was distributing a poster that began with a sentence akin to the following: "Books about religion are about ..." The text then went on to list what seemed like an endless array of topics such as life, death, education, families, economics, politics, violence, sex, law, etc. Students like me grabbed multiple copies of the fiche to share with colleagues, family and friends, feeling somewhat superior that our discipline had the whole range of human and social experience as our object of study. When confronted by others with the all too familiar view that our academic pursuits in religious studies would either lead to ordination or nowhere (given the perceived limited real-world applications for our research), we now had a tool to illuminate the relevance of our learning. Later sharing my enthusiasm about the breadth of our academic scope with a professor, he responded dryly. "Peggy," he said, "if everything is religion, then nothing is religion." Then, to extend my confusion at the time even further, he added words like the following: "If I told you I go home at night and talk to my fuzzy pink rabbit about my day and about who said what to me and how it made me feel, you'd think I was crazy. But if I call that fuzzy confidante *God*, you'd think that's about religion and worthy as an object of investigation."[1]

Flash forward and I'm researching debates around the constitutionality of Canada's polygamy laws in light of practices of a break away sect in western Canada with links to the Fundamentalist Church of Jesus Christ of Latter Day Saints. Two bishops with multiple wives are under investigation at a time when a case is also underway in the Supreme Court of Ontario regarding the constitutionality of Canada's prostitution laws. An editorial cartoon (Rice 2010) emerges at the time showing two sex-trade workers under a lamppost. One is holding a newspaper with a headline that reads: "Law against polygamy violates Charter's [i.e. the Constitution's] right to religious freedom, lawyer says." The sex-trade worker reading the paper remarks to the other: "One person—multiple partners: that's where we went wrong. We should have started our own religion ..."

More recent still, I'm interested in a 2015 Supreme Court ruling now prohibiting municipalities from opening their meetings with a prayer on the basis that it would be in breach of the state's duty of neutrality (*Mouvement Laïque québéque v. Saguanay (City)* 2015). However, a lower court has already indicated that a municipality's crucifix and Sacred Heart statue that gets plugged in to make the chest glow red "were works of art that were devoid of religious connotation" (ibid.: para. 21) and therefore permissible. As strange as it seems, such findings are not altogether rare. Similar juxtapositions had arisen in the context of ongoing Government of Quebec attempts to implement legislation under state religious neutrality or laïcité that proposed public restrictions on wearing certain religious garb in public spheres while at times dismissing the idea of removing the large crucifix in the Assemblée Nationale on the grounds it was a symbol of heritage, not religion.

I share the above examples as illustrations of what many of us have come to conclude in this diverse field we co-inhabit. That is, that whatever we think we are studying when we study "religion" often defies definition, the boundaries of what is to be included in the category are subjective, malleable and ever-changing, and terms like "religion," "religious," "non-religious," or "secular" can be manipulated in innumerable ways for diverse academic, social, legal and political purposes.

I am grateful to Baldwin for so ambitiously, succinctly and courageously delineating where we find ourselves in debates about the object or objects of our studies. He reminds readers of the historical tendency in our field to focus on what is now often associated with "material religion," meaning the "material elements ("objects") associated with particular social formations that are identified by one criterion or another as 'religious'" (Chapter 6, this volume). In contrast to this material approach to our disciplinary objects or data however, Baldwin provides an alternative entry point that will likely prove more promising in inviting scholars to think about "objects" not in terms of tangible items but rather, as the "focus" of our investigations (ibid.). He further proposes that our data include everything that is subject to objection and argumentation, to what he calls "intersubjectively available matters" established through scholarly methods (ibid.).

As Baldwin's work briefly observes, numerous theorists have illuminated the historical and biased origins of notions about the category of "religion" and "world religions" in academic and political discourse. Relatively new scholarship in what is often referred to as "critical religion" offers a theoretical approach that integrates notions about identity, colonialism, power and statecraft to challenge academic and social assumptions about religion as a universal, fixed, and discernible component of society through which certain beliefs, behaviors, and objects can meaningfully be classified. In calling into question the processes by which certain human phenomena are presumed to be "religious" versus "secular" or mundane, this theoretical framework also destabilizes assumptions about what some might regard as religious, sacred, or spiritual objects and practices.

Publications in the field of critical religion illuminate how the category of "religion" and discourse about "world religions" can be traced to sixteenth- and seventeenth-century Christian European academic writings that gave rise to problematic binaries and classifications of systems and objects as secular or religious and public or private (McCutcheon 1997; Fitzgerald 2000; Dubuisson 2003; Masuzawa 2005; Arnal and McCutcheon 2012; Nongbri 2013). While some scholars in our field examine how colonialist and imperialist notions bias research by projecting western notions of religion onto non-western and ancient cultures (King 1999; Chidester 2014; Barton and Boyarin 2016), others question the impacts of this destabilization for the field of religious studies (Cotter and Robertson 2016). Positing that religion is not a "timeless universal to be found in all societies, but a historically and ideologically specific emergent," Fitzgerald criticizes the academy's construction of a category that "it purports to describe" (2016: 308). This theoretical framework thus offers new ways to consider how power relations within the academy, along with multiple political, historic, economic, or social factors, support the classification of certain beliefs, practices, and objects as religious or non-religious to the benefit of certain groups. Not only does this scholarship expose how modern western conceptions of religion have impacted and biased understandings about diverse societies and historic periods (King 1999; Barton and Boyarin 2016), it also illuminates how certain presumptions about religion can bias the selection of the very objects of our investigations.

I share Baldwin's bewilderment that any of our colleagues can persist in ignoring and dismissing the implications of this "critical scholarship on 'religion' as a category employed in human thought" (Chapter 6, this volume). There is no universal, identifiable and distinct component of society and human experience called "religion" that can somehow bestow on us the tangible items and goods that are all too often presumed to be the necessary objects of our analysis. Moreover, acknowledging that there is no "it" called religion to locate and mine for data need not signal an end to our discipline. Spoiler alert: Acknowledging there is no Santa Claus but rather only narratives that conjure a guy that tends to be white, bearded, and in the company of reindeer has certainly not limited academic interest in that subject matter. Google scholar suggests no fewer than 94,800 links to work about Santa in areas relating to economics, psychology, literature, computers, political science, sports and the environment. Presuming the scholars who study Santa don't really think there is one, we can be assured ourselves that not having a stable object called religion to study need not preclude our analysis of all of the uses and motives involved in the construction of that concept. (Now granted, one might arguably object that the analogy of Santa with religion is undermined by the fact one can see Santa in the malls but one can't necessarily see "religion." And yet, one could also reasonably counter that, like "religion," there is never any real Santa in the mall per se, only observable reflections or manifestations of an idea or narrative.) As Baldwin so poignantly points out, our task is not mystification, nor devotion, but rather, it's about understanding "*what is going on ...*" (Chapter 6, this volume).

Based on this analysis, there is or should be a cataclysmic shift in the field of religious studies. The most important and valued objects of our investigations can no longer be the mystified material items that have acquired sacred status in some peoples' view. Nor can they be the sentiments and beliefs that have somehow beatified these objects. Rather, it is the mundane and banal range of instruments and mechanisms by which certain items, beliefs, and behaviors come to be categorized or labeled as "religious" that should interest us. And if we wish to be truly relevant, we should also turn our attention to developing a deeper understanding of how this classification system functions as a governance tool in historic and geographic contexts. This approach would reflect a new trajectory in our field that propels scholars to what Barton and Boyarin refer to as "self-critical consciousness" that supports reflection on how presumed "concepts and categories organize and configure our ... world" (2016: 7). As Fitzgerald so eloquently argues, if religion is no longer seen as a "self-evident part of the furniture of the world" (2016: 308), the imperative shifts to interrogating the specific components of culture that the category gathers and sometimes conceals. It may be that our most promising and, dare I say, reasonable, source of data lies in the productive and strategic path proposed by Brent Nongbri (2013) in the conclusion to his ground-breaking study, *Before Religion: A History of a Modern Concept*. That is, for us to consider,

> ... what is at stake for those who think it is important to adhere to this or that *particular* definition of religion ... *Who* is doing the defining and *why*? In other words, a good focus for those who would study "religion" in the modern day is keeping a close eye on the *activity* of defining religion and the *act* of saying that some things are "religious" and others are not. (Nongbri 2013: 155)

While modern conceptions of "religion" and "world religions" have a checkered genealogy in late Renaissance intellectual traditions, several recent publications highlight how it is the state, through public policies and law, that plays the central role in assigning these designations. As a tool of governance, religion impacts every sphere of our lives, whether it be through education, health, immigration, security, the economy, the environment, or justice. Through a range of laws and policies, politicians and legislators govern culture and diversity based on a number of social identifiers and classifications linked to religion. The courts are then charged with interpreting and enforcing those governance initiatives within pluralistic societies. As several recent publications, including *Religion as a Category of Governance and Sovereignty* (Stack, Goldenberg, and Fitzgerald 2015) illuminate, identifying the people, beliefs, practices and objects that qualify for unique protection or restrictions under the rubric of religion is a key element of statecraft. And yet, as Trevor Stack observes, "few scholars have paid attention to the way in which governments classify institutions, practices and persons as 'religious' and non-religious'" (ibid.: 3).

My objects of investigation are therefore not drums, chalices, nor prayer beads. They are government documents, consultation transcripts, court submissions and rulings to understand what is obscured and at play when the category of religion is invoked in public contexts. Elsewhere, I examine the central role of law and the courts in state determinations of the boundaries and impacts of religion in western democracies. I have framed this analysis through an examination of underlying assumptions about the category of religion that are at play in public discourse. More specifically, I examine what I've termed "religious S-P-I-N," an acronym to denote religion's presumed Scope and Privilege as derived from its supposed Inherent Nature (Schmeiser forthcoming) that can often lead to inconsistent and inequitable treatment under the law.

Constitutional references to "religion" rarely define the term, leaving it to the courts to establish a definition based on already biased traditional western and Christian-centric notions about the inherent nature of the category. As work by scholars like Winnifred Sullivan (2005) demonstrates, the "impossibility of religious freedom" affects religious groups and society in general when no one can *prove* what precisely constitutes "religion" under the law. Meanwhile, the government and courts also engage on a regular basis in determinations about what is to be included in or excluded from the scope of "religion" and freedom of religion provisions. The above examples regarding the perceived heritage, art or religious status of biblical statues and crucifixes in public spaces so poignantly illustrates this practice. Finally, the institutions that are deemed within the scope of the "religious" may be accorded privileges, exemptions or restrictions by the state, including under human rights legislation that otherwise aims to support equality. Examples like the sanctioned refusal by religious organizations to ordain women and perform same-sex marriage ceremonies despite state prohibitions against discrimination on the basis of gender and sexuality reveal the uneven application of the law and the privileging of certain forms of thought over others when religion is at play. Alternatively, certain practices like prayer may be prohibited in public forums based on freedom of religion claims advanced by others (Carpay 2016).

If law is the enforcer, public policy is the enabler for state control over the category of religion. Through legislation and regulation, the state manages diversity in pluralistic contexts based on multiple factors including concepts like religion. As the work of numerous scholars like William Arnal and Russell McCutcheon (2012) underscores, notions about religion are inherent to notions of the profane. Public policies that appear secular or neutral under operating clichés like "the separation of church and state" are eternally caught up in delineating the boundaries, rules and permissions related to what is considered religious or non-religious in any given context. Whether it be legislative bills that seek to regulate dress codes and religious symbols in public spheres, the treatment of Indigenous beliefs and ceremonies like smudging in schools, or exemptions for religious institutions to deny services under legislation associated with assisted dying, the always ambiguous and ultimately untenable category of religion poses no end of conflict for politicians, bureaucrats and legal practitioners in western societies. Some scholars, including James Beckford (2017), however, would underline that even in human rights cases such as rules governing accommodations for religious observances in prisons, religion is seldom the dominant issue of concern for the state. Rather, he would argue, religion only becomes a public issue when it interferes with other state priorities such as security.

So what does all of the compelling, relatively recent deconstruction of the category of religion mean for our present debate on the sources of data and evidence for our investigations? If notions about religion and the category of religion itself are always in flux, does this mean there is no *real* or accessible *stuff* for analysis in the field of religious studies? If further reflections on Santa only offer limited comfort, recent titles such as Barton and Boyarin's (2016) *Imagine No Religion* and Naomi Goldenberg's (2016) "There is No Religion in the Bible" should reassure us that there is still ample material for our field despite, or perhaps more accurately, *because* of the shortcomings of its defining referent. As Baldwin himself concludes, one may "agree with Jonathan Z. Smith that 'there is no data for religion' [but] it is not possible to claim that 'there is no data for religious studies'" (Chapter 6, this volume).

Ironically, some of the most exciting and innovative opportunities to deepen analysis in our field may exist beyond our own current scholarship and in the methods and metrics of other disciplines. There has already been an undeniably rich history of integrating theoretical frameworks from other fields like sociology, history, psychology, and feminist studies into the field of religious studies. But as we look to recent world events and concerns over human migration and security, there will only be increasing need for broader understanding and theoretical frameworks that can adequately address the intersections of notions about religion with other spheres of governance. Thought-provoking work like Micah Schwartzman's "What if Religion is Not Special?" (2012) and Nelson Tebbe's "The End of Religious Freedom: What is at Stake?" (2014) and *Religious Freedom in an Egalitarian Age* (2017) may present our best opportunities for re-focusing our attention on data emerging from the social conflicts that now permeate our daily lives. Take as examples:

1   The case in Canada of a high profile convicted terrorist appealing his sentence on the grounds that racist biased perceptions of how a radical Islamist would behave and speak impeded recognition by the court and defense lawyers of his schizophrenia that went undiagnosed at the time of his trial (Warnica 2017).

2 President Trump's regulations introduced in the fall of 2017 permitting businesses to refuse insurance coverage for contraceptives for women on the basis of religious liberty (Pear, Ruiz, and Goodstein 2017).

3 Seemingly welcoming Royal Canadian Mounted Police that greeted primarily Muslim refugees entering Canada from the American border in the fall of 2017 with entry surveys asking their views on the hijab, their prayer frequency, and their political views on certain Islamic regimes (Shephard 2017).

4 Opposition from religious groups to measures that would have restricted the use of Canadian government funding to hire summer students for work focused on pro-life or anti-abortion activities (Platt 2018).

5 Historical legal uses of the category of "religion" in efforts to either suppress or advance the rights of Indigenous people as reflected in litigation regarding smudging and the failed attempt by the Ktunaxa Nation to stop development of a ski resort (*Ktunaxa Nation v. British Columbia (Forests, Lands and Natural Resource Operations)* 2017; Ruecker 2014).

As the above controversies reveal, the category of religion exists in perpetual tension with other social movements and concerns. As we ask ourselves about the objects and data we choose to interrogate, I believe it is incumbent on us as scholars of religion to move beyond narrow and ill-defined conceptions of the category to examine the inconsistent and inequitable ways that the state understands and regulates what it considers to be religious to the detriment of certain segments of the population. The most enriching and impactful scholarship of any discipline emerges when thinkers dare to demystify the people, beliefs, practices and objects that reinforce traditional hegemonies at the expense of those who lack the legal, political and economic means to subvert them.

For those who fear that this evolution in our discourse away from the items and objects that have characterized what have most often been identified as "religion" constitutes a slip down the rabbit hole, it is helpful to recall Baldwin's citation from a short poem, "Anecdote of the Jar," by Wallace Stevens, at the start of his essay. Though a classic of American literature, this poem is still unknown to many, particularly outside its country of origin. At its most basic level, the rather curious poem describes nothing more than a jar on a hill, the wilderness that "sprawled around, no longer wild" and how the glass container "took dominion everywhere" (Stevens 1919).

The mostly awkward yet critically acclaimed poem has often been analyzed in terms of humanity's relationship with nature. Others have offered alternative visions: Donald Gutierrez has described the poem as a "metaphor about the magnetic power of mind and art to order a void"; Pat Righelato regards it as an anecdote "which leads nowhere"; and Frank Letrricia rather observantly describes it as "a faceless totality of authority" in which the "the jar is into every damn thing" (Modern American Poetry undated). Despite these articulate analytic musings however, we fortunately have Roy Harvey Pearce to thank for discovering what Stevens most likely had in mind when he wrote the mysterious poem – a rather bland Canadian fruit canning jar with the word Dominion emblazoned on the side that was in use in Tennessee, possibly for drinking moonshine, when Stevens traveled there (ibid.). Taken in this light, the poem may be very apt for our exchange on the objects and objections that comprise our field of religious studies. Evidently, jars can have a variety of uses, multiple discursive meanings and may well be into every damn thing. So too it appears, with the narratives, practices, items, and ideologies that constitute the data of our own investigations.

Peggy Schmeiser, Ph.D., is a faculty member at the Johnson Shoyama Graduate School of Public Policy, a joint initiative of the University of Saskatchewan and University of Regina. Prior to this, she worked for many years in university government affairs and with the Canadian government in domestic and international policy areas relating to culture, equality, and the economy. Peggy has taught at four universities, is proficient in French, and has researched, published and lectured internationally on a wide range of topics relating to religion, secularism, public policy, culture and gender.

Note

1   These unpublished remarks were made to me by Professor Peter Beyer at the University of Ottawa.

References

Arnal, William, and McCutcheon, Russell. 2012. *The Sacred is the Profane: The Political Nature of "Religion."* Don Mills, ON: Oxford University Press. https://doi.org/10.1093/acprof:oso/9780199757114.001.0001

Barton, Carlin, and Boyarin Daniel. 2016. *Imagine No Religion: How Modern Abstractions Hide Ancient Realities.* New York: Fordham University Press. https://doi.org/10.2307/j.ctt1dfnt8f

Beckford, James. 2017. Unpublished comments as participant in the session, "Does the State Have a Legitimate Interest in Regulating Religion? Is Diversity Something to be 'Managed'?" Religion and Diversity Project Conference, University of Ottawa, October 26.

Carpay, John. 2016. "Keep Smudging and Other Religious Rituals Out of the Classroom." *Huffington Post* (May 12). Retrieved from www.huffingtonpost.ca/john-carpay/religious-rituals-in-school_b_13432298.html.

Chidester, David. 2014. *Empire of Religion: Imperialism and Comparative Religion.* Chicago, IL: Chicago University Press. https://doi.org/10.7208/chicago/9780226117577.001.0001

Cotter, Christopher, and Robertson David (eds.). 2016. *After World Religions: Reconstructing Religious Studies.* New York: Routledge. https://doi.org/10.4324/9781315688046

Dubuisson, Daniel. 2003. *The Western Construction of Religion: Myths, Knowledge, and Ideology*, trans. W. Sayers. Baltimore, MD: John Hopkins University Press.

Fitzgerald, Timothy. 2000. *The Ideology of Religious Studies.* Oxford: Oxford University Press.

Fitzgerald, Timothy. 2016. "Critical Religion and Critical Research on Religion: A Response to the April 2016 Editorial." *Critical Research on Religion* 4(3): 307–313. https://doi.org/10.1177/2050303216676524

Goldenberg, Naomi. 2016. "There is No Religion in the Bible." Unpublished paper.

King, Richard. 1999. *Orientalism and Religion: Postcolonial Theory, India and 'The Mystic East'*. Oxford: Oxford University Press.

Ktunaxa Nation v. British Columbia (Forests, Lands and Natural Resource Operations), 2017 SCC 54.

Masuzawa, Tomoko. 2005. *The Invention of World Religions: Or How Universalism Was Preserved in the Language of Pluralism*. Chicago, IL: University of Chicago Press. https://doi.org/10.7208/chicago/9780226922621.001.0001

McCutcheon, Russell. 1997. *Manufacturing Religion: The Discourse on Sui Generis Religion and the Politics of Nostalgia*. New York: Oxford University Press.

Modern American Poetry. Undated. "On 'Anecdote of the Jar'." Retrieved from www.english.illinois.edu/maps/poets/s_z/stevens/jar.htm.

Mouvement Laïque québéque v. Saguanay (City), 2015 SCC 16

Nongbri, Brent. 2013. *Before Religion: A History of a Modern Concept*. New Haven, CT: Yale University Press. https://doi.org/10.12987/yale/9780300154160.001.0001

Pear, Robert, Ruiz, Rebecca, and Goodstein, Laurie. 2017. "Trump Administration Rolls Back Birth Control Mandate." October 6. Retrieved from www.nytimes.com/2017/10/06/us/politics/trump-contraception-birth-control.html.

Platt, Brian. 2018. "How the Canada Summer Jobs program became a freedom-of-religion controversy." January 21. Retrieved from http://nationalpost.com/news/politics/how-the-canada-summer-jobs-program-became-a-freedom-of-religion-controversy.

Rice, Ingred. 2010. Editorial cartoon. *Saskatoon Star Phoenix*, November.

Ruecker, Michael. 2014. "Dances With 'Religion': A Critical History of the Strategic Uses of the Category of Religion by the Government of Canada and First Nations, 1885 to 1951." Unpublished Masters dissertation.

Schmeiser, Peggy. Forthcoming. "Vestigial State Theory and Law in Canada: A Critical Response." In Kathleen McPhillips and Naomi Goldenberg (eds.), *The End of Religion: Feminist Appraisals of the State*. New York: Routledge.

Schwartzman, Micah. 2012. "What if Religion is Not Special?" *University of Chicago Law Review* 79: 1351–1427. https://doi.org/10.2139/ssrn.1992090

Shephard, Michelle. 2017. "RCMP Officers Screened Quebec Border Crossers on Religion and Values, Questionnaire Shows." *The Toronto Star* (October 11). Retrieved from www.thestar.com/news/canada/2017/10/11/rcmp-officers-screened-quebec-border-crossers-on-religion-and-values-questionnaire-shows.html.

Stack, T., Goldenberg, N. R. and Fitzgerald, T. (eds.). 2015. *Religion as a Category of Governance and Sovereignty*. Leiden: Brill.

Stevens, Wallace. 1919. "Anecdote of the Jar." *Poetry* 15(1) (October). Retrieved from www.poetryfoundation.org/poetrymagazine/browse?contentId=14575.

Sullivan, Winnifred. 2005. *The Impossibility of Religious Freedom*. Princeton, NJ: Princeton University Press.

Tebbe, Nelson. 2014. "The End of Religious Freedom: What is at Stake?" *Pepperdine Law Review* 41: 963–982.

Tebbe, Nelson. 2017. *Religious Freedom in an Egalitarian Age*. Boston, MA: Harvard University Press. https://doi.org/10.2307/j.ctvc2rms2

Warnica, Richard. 2017. "Esseghaier Terrorism Case Highlights Tricky Collision Between Mental Illness and Extremism." *The National Post* (July 28). Retrieved from http://nationalpost.com/news/canada/esseghaier-terrorism-case-highlights-tricky-collision-between-mental-illness-and-extremism.

Chapter 10

Negative Dialektik and the Question Concerning the Relation Between Objects and Concepts

Lucas Wright

If the debate surrounding so-called critical religion has achieved anything of lasting philosophical value, it is, perhaps, the recognition that in each and every attempt to account for, to figure, the relation between objects and concepts one finds oneself in danger of saying precisely that which "critique" is meant to deny—that is, of lapsing into a so-called normative, or more appropriately called, an ontotheological,[1] register of expression. A regression appears to lie at the heart of critical positing, a regression which seems unavoidable. For how could one think critically if not through the practice of, at once, deploying normative criteria in the criticism of an allegedly given state of affairs? Language and logic seem to require, for critique, a circularity, rather than a hard binary between "what is really going on" and the situatedness of speaking and analysis. In short, the critique of the givenness of a specific configuration of heterogonous constructs and exercises of power requires a regression into a kind of thinking according-to-givenness, a regression back to normative language, as the condition for the possibility of critique itself. Elliot R. Wolfson, in a recent chapter entitled "Zeitliche Entzweiung und offenes System," makes this point well when he writes, "The categorical claim that we cannot recognize the truth can only be true if it is false," insofar as "without the ability to get out of a given context, it would be totally impossible to cultivate the knowledge we require to determine the parameters of context" (Wolfson 2017: 124).

Such a regressive tendency, as the condition of critical thought, is too easy to ignore in the desire to locate new targets of obfuscation (i.e. theological bias, the promotion of devotion, perennialism) making, as this desire does, the real fact of socio-political enmeshments the only identifiable fact. As a result, this tendency fails to acknowledge, in the reification of social construction, the aforementioned condition for situatedness itself—namely, the ability to figure and identify the parameters of construct and context from outside a given state of affairs. The real question posed by the religious studies scholar's inquiry into the "objects we study," then, is one regarding the existential condition of thinking itself, the dialectic between subjective implication and objective reality, between critical positing and the regression to a normative foundation.

In the present chapter, I focus attention upon this regressive tendency by way of explicating a shared source for thought between Baldwin (Chapter 6, this volume) and myself—Theodor Adorno's conception of a "negative dialectics." I do so with particular attention paid to the existential concepts of finitude and historicity in the formulation of the epistemological categories in question—namely, the categories of subject and object. I frame my argument around Baldwin's piece, taking as my point of departure Baldwin's excellent identification of the basic epistemological stakes of the question concerning the relationship between subjectivity, collective or otherwise, and objectivity. I then proceed to explicate my own position in reference to Baldwin's own. What is clear in the final analysis, above all of the particular claims made by Baldwin or myself, is that the particular *niche* in the academic study of religion in which this question concerning concepts and objects is posed, requires a larger engagement with broader philosophical concerns, which underpin the critical scholar of religion's desire to expose to light the constructed character of allegedly given phenomena. When we ask these sorts of questions on the theoretical level in religious studies, we are asking about the condition of thought, of life, itself, filtering these larger concerns through the particularity of our disciplinary lives. In these instances, from the moment the scholar begins reflexively questioning the conditions for perception and description, the religious studies scholar steps out of the circumscribed area of sheer description into the philosophical register of discourse. It is, then, the order of the day for those of us trained in philosophy to begin treating these debates in religious studies as specific occasions for thought, which index larger questions by focusing them into a particular frame of reference. I offer my argument as one attempt to articulate this demand.

Matthew Baldwin's Argument

Baldwin (Chapter 6, this volume) posits seven theses, which I now review for the sake of my own analysis. These theses are as follows:

1. When we ask about the "what" we study when we study religion, we are indeed dealing with "objects," a discrete classification as opposed to, say, "sheer matter."

2. "Objects" only exist, are themselves constituted, through a relation to perception, to the act of positing.

3. The relation of objects to perception bears an intersubjective character.

4. Due to the constitutive role of the act of positing in relation to the construction of objects, and the intersubjective character that this relation bears, objects are always "subject to objection," are constituted, phenomenologically[2] and ideologically, through the myriad of intersubjective processes unceasingly at work in a given lifeworld.

5. Because "objects" always bear the mark of the act of positing within an intersubjective register of thought and social life, "everything

which we make subject to objections can still be thought of as some kind of an object"—again, this is to reinforce the particularity of the classification "object" as opposed to a more ambiguous notion of "sheerness."

6. That objects so understood "must be established as objects through methods that are best termed either *scientific, genealogical, sociological,* or *historical.*"

7. That the task of the religious studies scholar, having admitted the above, is "not to promote mere appreciation, let alone devotion or mystification, but rather critical understanding of *what is going on.*"

The core of Baldwin's argument, and corresponding diagnostic analysis of the state of the field, is a combination of claims 1–5, though claims number 6–7 are not irrelevant, but rather follow logically from claims 1–5. The main point is that "objects," as a discrete classificatory concept, are intersubjectively produced through a variety of processes, sociopolitical and otherwise, such that the object becomes a datum for the scholar through the methods described in claim number 6. The claim that the object is constituted through its relation to the act of positing, and that this relative constitution of the object is inherently intersubjective, then, is the key claim that I wish to focus upon in my response.

With regard to the intersubjective character of the relation between object and perception, Baldwin notes that the presupposition of communication about objects is that such communication is an activity involving more than one person—namely, the person speaking about the object, person A, and the person or people to whom person A speaks, Persons B, C, etc. He writes:

> In philosophy, the fraught epistemological discussion of the relationship between "object" and "subject" all too often conceals this triadic relationship, misrepresenting it in both regnant models as merely dyadic. Objects properly so termed are object to at least two subjects. This triadic relation is embedded in the communicative structure of language, itself, making objects a subject for semiology. (Chapter 6, this volume)

It is upon precisely this claim that the earlier critiques of the turn to the "excess" of the object, of material religion, and lived religion, rest. The problem of reifying objectivity as an ontologically discrete sphere is, according to Baldwin, that this move does not account for the mediatory effects of the act of perception, but rather takes the immediacy of a given phenomenon for granted in its givenness by turning a blind eye to the inextricable activity of the act of perception itself. Baldwin needs this claim in order to support his subsequent assertions that there are particularly "academic" methods by which scholars construct objects and data, corresponding as these methods do to the task of "critically understanding what is going on" in a given situation. In order to further explicate the stakes of his position, Baldwin cites a text describing the position of Theodor Adorno. He notes:

> Adorno attempts to overcome the internal contradiction of the *intentio obliqua* (and to move past the naïve realism of the *intention recta*) through his notion of "the primacy of objects." But note that "the primacy of objects" does not point the way to the flat ontology of Object-Oriented speculative realism, but rather to a sublation of subject and object resulting in critical theory. (Chapter 6, this volume)

This citation of Adorno is particularly interesting given Baldwin's theses, insofar as this aspect of Adorno's thinking may serve at once to support most of what Baldwin asserts, while simultaneously challenging his last two claims—namely, the claim regarding the circumscription of method, which seems to presuppose ahead of critical investigation the stability of the structure of thought (*Denkarchitekture*) required for such circumscription, and the claim about explaining "what is really going on" posed in binary contrast to the promotion of mystification. While Baldwin is correct in claiming that any account of something should be critically attuned to the subjective implications and power structures of an allegedly given state of affairs, upon further scrutiny this setup runs the risk of reifying subjective implication—bias—itself in such a way as to reinscribe the very thing Baldwin seeks to deny—namely, a totalized assured point for thinking to hold onto at the expense of acknowledging the contingent character of thinking, an acknowledgment I hold as necessary for critical theoretical thinking. Such an acknowledgment would imply by definition some degree of mystification, or unknowing, that functions as the phenomenological horizon for thinking generally, a point which I think too important, and also too often misunderstood given the fraught history of religious studies in relation to its theological past, to leave untouched in this response. I proceed now to explain this point, summarizing first Adorno's general project, and concluding with remarks regarding the import of this project for the critical scholarly study of religion.

Adorno and the Preponderance of the Object

Theodor Adorno (1903–1969) was a philosopher, sociologist, musicologist, and one of the founders of what became known as the first generation of the Frankfurt School of critical theory, associated with the Institute for Social Research (*Institut für Sozialforschung*). Arguably, the first major text produced in relation to what became known as critical theory was Adorno and Max Horkheimer's co-authored *Dialektik der Aufklärung* (1944), or *Dialectic of Enlightenment*. The last text produced by Adorno, at least prior to his death, was his *Negative Dialektik* (1966), or *Negative Dialectics*. Space does not permit for an adequate summary of critical theory as a whole. However, I take the following description of the aim of first generation critical theory by Horkheimer and Adorno to be a good starting point for understanding Adorno's work. They write of the *Dialektik der Aufklärung*, "The fragments, that we have collected here show, then, that we must give up every trust" (Horkheimer and Adorno 2006: 1). Trust in what? Namely, in a manner similar to Walter Benjamin's denunciation of the progressive eschatological view of history in his *Über den Begriff der Geschichte*,[3] the ontotheological surety of progressive enlightenment.

> The aporia that we found over-against our work, apparent (*erwies*) itself as the first object that we had to investigate: the self-destruction of the Enlightenment. We harboured no doubt—and herein lies our *petitio principii*—that the freedom of society is inextricable from enlightened thinking. Therefore, we believe to have identified precisely that the concept even of this thinking, not less that the concrete historical forms, the institutions of society, in which it is interwoven, already contains the germ of every regression, which generally occurs today. (Horkheimer and Adorno 2006: 3)

The project of the *Dialektik der Aufklärung*, and for Adorno moving forward, is to sort out the relationship between positive freedom on the one side, and the necessity of criticizing all seemingly "given" facts. Stated otherwise, Adorno recognizes the requirement of rigorous critical interrogation of all seemingly apparent categories and states of affairs for the positing of freedom. Only through the recognition of the composite nature of reality does anything resembling the recognition of truth become possible.

The goal for Adorno is twofold with regard to both the philosophical and socio-political aspects of his project. First, Adorno seeks to conceive a notion of thinking as *praxis*, which is capable of yielding to the resistance the Thinking-I encounters when confronted by the sphere of the Not-I—the so-called objective sphere, a reversal of what Adorno observes as a hegemony of subjectivity reinforced in certain idealist conceptions of "system." The goal is to retain a sense of systematicity rooted in the development of objects themselves without projecting ontotheological priority onto said objects.

> System, in the expressly, emphatic, truly philosophical sense, would be—over against this concept of systematicity as an ordered schema of subjective reason, a schema of order that one can design according to the task of classification—the development of the object (*Sache*) itself from a principle, dynamic, as a movement, which draws everything into itself, which captures everything, and is at the same time a totality, and with the claim of objective validity in the way that nothing, as is generally the case with Hegel, that nothing between heaven and earth can be thought outside such a system. Perhaps the most thoroughly implemented type of such a system is Fichtean in the strongest sense. Fichte actually sought to derive everything from one idea, namely the-I, the absolute subject, and also ... the not-I. (Adorno 2003: 59)

Here Adorno posits the need to develop a mode of thinking according to the self-integrity of objects, taking over an aspect of Fichte's work that he seeks to recuperate. According to Fichte, all comprehensive science must be just that—namely, comprehensive, on the basis of a non-derivative ground,[4] which, according to Adorno, he then identifies with the cognitive capacity of the self (i.e. the thinking-I). This earlier notion of system is one which, according to Adorno, could only accept the primacy of subjective reason as the originator of meaning in reference to the status of objects. The presupposition of this notion of system is the identity between subject and object, which turns out to be only the affirmation of the self, rather than an emphasis upon non-identical difference. "In idealism the highly formal principle of identity, by virtue of its own formalization, has affirmation as its content" (Adorno 1966: 149). In contrast, Adorno seeks a mode of thinking that retains the desire for some measure of coherence, which he identifies as the driving impulse of Fichte's work, without lapsing into a metaphysical or theological mode of discourse—namely, a notion of system developed according to that which is unfamiliar in relation to subjectivity.

In opposition to the past sense of identity between subject and object, Adorno writes of his own project, "It [negative dialectics] should be a dialectic, not of identity [between subject and object], but rather of *non-identity*" (Adorno 2003: 15). What this means, for Adorno, is that one should seek to think according-to the gap, which appears as the contradiction, between any concept and the manifold of what-is in-the-world. Where the principle of identity in former systems thinking collapsed the gap between object and concept into the demand for a better figuration, a concept that would accord itself more accurately to what-appears to consciousness, Adorno instead relies upon the fact that no concept is capable of accounting for the whole, the fact that at the heart of every positing is contradiction between the posited and what-is. Thus, every concept is deficient (ibid.: 17–18)[5] and by definition, so too all critical thought, insofar as contradiction is always already *in*, constitutive of, rather than between, every object and concept (ibid.: 17).[6]

It is the positing of the non-identity of subject and object that must lie at the heart of what Baldwin's above quotation identifies as the sublation between the object and subject. This is a notion that cannot—according to the appeal to non-identity, wherein the opposed term "identity" is equivalent with the eradication of the tension, the alterity, which subsists between the two terms—imply the dissolution of either pole, subject or object, such that one triumphs over the other. The appeal to this notion of identity would be to reinscribe a kind of totalizing identity between the two poles—that which Adorno perceives as the dangerous temptation of a Hegelian notion of synthesis, which turns every point of irreconcilable particularity into a reconciled whole.

> It must be clear above all, that the theory of Hegel, which is not wholly arbitrarily given the name Objective Idealism, turns against this concept of negativity qua subjectivity; that this concept of negativity does not have the last word in the Hegelian dialectic, but rather that the Hegelian dialectic ... is a positive dialectic. (Adorno 2003: 26–27)

Rather, a negative dialectics, a critical theoretical approach to the question of the objects we study when we study, would aim to think-according-to—to exploit—the Übermaß, the excessive "irreconcilability" (*die Unversöhntheit*) between subjects and objects that conditions, but does not destroy as in naively idealist or object-oriented approaches, our relation to the objects we study.

> It [the concept of negative dialectics] works according to the model of a philosophy, which does not presuppose the concept of identity between being and thinking, and also does not terminate in this concept, but rather the opposite, a philosophy

which wants to actualise the alterity of concept and object (*das Auseinanderweisen von Begriff und Sache*), of subject and object, and their irreconcilability. (Adorno 2003: 15–16)

Baldwin correctly notes that Adorno intends to sublate subject and object, and that it is this sublation that leads to what, arguably, is the core of Adorno's conception of critical theoretical work. Yet, this description risks misconstruing the dialectical movement Adorno imbues to his thinking regarding the sublation of object and subject in accordance with the focus upon contradiction. This is the case insofar as the emphasis upon sublation, as a support for the constructivist notion of the object versus the *a priori* existence of objects, misses the larger appeal to the facticity, and historicity, of the subject as possessing an objective character. For Adorno, each subject is itself constructed through each subject's objective situatedness in-the-world, through the subject's contingent character—in the place of the preponderance of subjectivity appears, now, a preponderance of the object. "Realized critique about the identity works (*tastet*) according to the preponderance of objects" (Adorno 1966: 182). Just as the epistemological beginning point lies in the constitutive gap between concepts and objects, so too does the beginning point of thinking, including the self-reflexive identification of the-self as such, arise from the distance of relation in-the-world between, not the identity of, a person, other persons, and entities in the world. In short, subjectivity is contingent upon the materiality, upon the being-there (*da-sein*), of each person (ibid.: 182–183).[7]

This is not to say, however, that Adorno has simply taken over the structure of domination present in the subject's hegemony, replacing the subject with the object—this would be to turn the negativity of the subject's dependence upon the objective sphere into a positive surety. Rather, the point here is to draw attention to the objective contingency itself of the subject as the origin of thought, without making this objectivity anything other than that upon which thinking depends. This contingency upon, contingency as, objectivity is itself the commonality shared by beings, and it is for this reason—that the coherence of reality, which is required for positing, exists in the shared objectivity of beings—that Adorno can affirm the possibility of a new notion of critical theoretical thinking, the aforementioned new notion of system that begins from the coherence of objectivity as that which all thinking must presuppose (Adorno 2003: 65).[8] Socio-politically, this notion of contingency itself appears as the main point of the theoretical core of Adorno and Horkheimer's *Dialektik der Aufklärung*, wherein they locate the fear of contingency itself as the source of the need to resolve the dialectical tension between the subject's recognition of itself as such, and the contingency of the subject upon an objective finitude, which the subject is unable to master (Horkheimer and Adorno 2006: 9–13).[9] In the end, for Adorno, the order of the day is not for an eradication of the dialectical tension between known and unknown, but rather a critical *praxis* that takes as its sole principle the fact of contingency and finitude.[10] The facticity, then, of one's finite being-there, the dialectic of being-alive and the certainty of death, appears as the phenomenological condition for the possibility of cognition—the existential as the necessary presupposition of the epistemological. That one is-there, with all cognitive ability and particularity of bias, is not in question by this formulation. Indeed, cognition is affirmed and forms one constitutive pole of the existential and epistemological dialectic. It is rather the case that such cognition, like the existential affirmation of being-there and the inverse of its demise in-death, is recognizable as such only against the backdrop of its inverse—the objective unknown upon which it is contingent. It is under this existential-epistemological condition that one should understand the passage from Adorno, which Baldwin cites in favour of the constructivist position regarding the object.[11]

Against Reifying Social Construction

I return now in conclusion to the main issues Baldwin raises regarding the construction of objects in scholarly discourse. I can see the work that the rejection of a dyadic notion of intersubjectivity does for Baldwin's argument, and the way the invocation of Adorno functions as one possible example for what such a rejection looks like when fleshed out into a broader systematic project. Yet, I see problems with the rejection of the dyadic notion, and Baldwin's corresponding rejections of the "excess" of the object and the appeal to objectivity in material religions work, insofar as Baldwin does not seem to fully ground his rejection in an account of the aforementioned epistemic and existential dialectic of contingency. Such an account characterizes Adorno's own work, and the work of a speculative realist such as Quentin Meillassoux, whose project I take Baldwin to also be at odds with given his general rejection of the object oriented and speculative realist approaches.

A question I pose to Baldwin, then, is: from whence does the demand to seek a "critical understanding of what is going on" appear, if not from some sort of grounding-conviction that there is indeed some-thing, material or otherwise, that critical inquiry presupposes in order to form a judgment regarding a particular state of affairs—even if this presupposition is, as for Adorno and Meillassoux, only the fact of contingency? The philological analysis that Baldwin uses to support his claim that objects are only ever "for-us," betrays already just such a presupposition when he writes that the word object "only stands for something else." It is that "something else," which manifests indirectly through the "trace of reference," that escapes Baldwin's account, despite the fact that he himself invokes this language, as the condition of possibility for the construction of the object in discourse, and thus for critical inquiry into "what is really going on." The failure to account for this aspect, in the end, undermines his rejection of the excess of the object, further compounding the impasse between those who seek, rightly, to emphasize the ideological construction of objects and data, and those seeking to attune their scholarly attention to the material conditions that make such discursive activity possible. What is needed is, as stated earlier in my citation of Elliot Wolfson and in my explication of Adorno, a perspective capable of withstanding both the implication of the subject and the ability to recognize subjective context as such, through the ability to step out of a particular situation.

My own suggestion for a possible way forward is to revisit the notion of dialectics as immanent critique that undergirds so much of critical social theory in relation to the questions concerning how to conceive the interplay between excess and construction. Baldwin's argument, I believe, provides a strong starting point for such research, insofar as he lays bare for the religious studies audience the core epistemological tensions at play in the discussion regarding objects in religious studies. What remains outstanding is a more precise reassessment by religious studies scholars working in theory and method of their relationship to philosophical and critical theoretical material at large, and the more specific existential concerns such as those mentioned above. A more general question, which I think essential for future research, is what it might look like to begin to see these theory and method debates as larger occasions for philosophical reflection beyond the confines of our specific theoretical location in the academy.[12] I take my own suggestion regarding the reassessment of critical social theory to be a push in this direction. Absent such a reassessment, I am not confident that progress regarding the theorizing of the objects of religious studies will be made, though this failure to reassess this relationship is not a forgone conclusion, as I hope the present chapter makes clear.

Lucas Scott Wright (M.A. UCSB) is a PhD student in the German Programme in the Department of European Languages and Studies at the University of California, Irvine. His current research focuses generally on modern Jewish thought, theology, and European history, thought, and culture in relation to the study of mysticism and contemporary trends in continental philosophy and critical theory.

Notes

1. Space does not permit for a full explication of this Heideggerian term. However, we may, as Elliot R. Wolfson does, define ontotheology as "thinking metaphysically of being in relation to entity," that is, as eliding the distinction between being-as-such and beings. Such a definition accords with Heidegger's own distinction between traditional philosophy and his approach when he writes, "Wir sprechen von der *Differenz* zwischen dem Sein und dem Seienden. Der Schritt zurück geht vom Ungedachten, von der Differenz als solcher, in das zu-Denkende. Das ist die *Vergessenheit* der Differenz." See Wolfson (2014: 42) and Heidegger (2006: 59) respectively.
2. Here it important to clarify my strictly philosophical use of the designation "phenomenological," in contradistinction to the use of the term in religious studies material. Philosophically, one may accept as a general definition for phenomenology something like the following: "literally, a 'science of the phenomenon,' but not 'phenomenon' in the usual sense of a brief, dazzling coruscation. More literally, a phenomenon is something that *appears*; strictly speaking, it is the *appearance* itself. Phenomenology does not attempt to speak about things, but only about the way they manifest themselves, and hence it tries to describe the nature of *appearance as such*. It asks the question of whether or not it is possible to say anything with absolute *certainty* about the nature of appearance in general. When something appears, does that appearing have any general features which we can identify? Does manifestation have an essence? Thus phenomenology focuses not on *what* appears, but on *how* it

appears" (Lewis and Staehler 2010: 1). A description of phenomenology as applied in the study of religion is available as something like the following: "Phenomenologists *study religion in and of itself* and not as an epiphenomenon of other more primary subjects ... Only phenomenology provides for the academic study of religions a distinct methodology, justifying its claim to be a field of study in its own right, *sui generis*" (Cox 2006: 3–4; first italics are mine).

In this second description, the focus upon appearance, in particular the identification of discrete—common—characteristics of an appearance, which is described abstractly in the first citation, is now linked to an implied ontological claim regarding the signifier "religion" and the adjective "religious," and the adverb "religiously"—namely, that what appears as religion, as religious, as being done religiously, corresponds to something given-to-perception *sui generis*, and correspondingly, at least implicitly, given from an *a priori* existent position. Religious studies scholarship in the present, generally speaking, contrasts this emphasis upon "how" appearance appears in itself, qualified by the question regarding the identification of "general features which we can identify," with a concern for an allegedly "critical" inquiry, which would illustrate that there is no simply "given" appearance that is not already interpolated and conditioned by a myriad of sociopsychological factors. Such an aversion to the alleged surety of a "given" phenomenon should, however, only be in the face of the aforementioned implication that whatever one associates grammatically in the register of "religion" is *sui generis* insofar as it exists *a priori*—in short, insofar as religion is taken to be onto-theologically "real," and its appearances, thus, capable of being simply given. The phenomenological as a methodology for, and a discursive mode of, describing appearances, however, is not by necessity implicated by the criticism of the scholar of religion. As such, what is at stake in my explication of Adorno is not a rejection of either phenomenology nor ideological criticism, but rather how scholars of religion should negotiate epistemologically their relation to the former by way of the latter.

3   See Benjamin (1991: 22). Here Benjamin, in a manner reflective of his famous commentary on Klee's "Angel of History" painting in the same text, associates the belief in the secured progressive movement of history with the policies of the social democrats, now shown to be inadequate in the face of fascism. For Benjamin, only criticism of this belief in a progressive eschatological notion of history, identical to criticism of the solidity of the *status quo* itself insofar as this belief lends onto-historical and theo-historical validity to the present state of affairs, is sufficient for addressing the rise of fascist violence. "Die sozialdemokratische Theorie und noch mehr die Praxis, wurde von einem Fortschrittsbegriff bestimmt, der sich nicht an der Wirklichkeit hielt, sondern einen dogmatischen Anspruch hatte ... Die Vorstellung eines Fortschritts des Menschengeschlechts in der Geschichte ist von der Vorstellung ihres eine homogene und leere Zeit durchlaufenden Fortgangs nicht abzulösen. Die Kritik an der Verstellung dieses Fortgangs muß die Grundlage der Kritik an der Vorstellung des Fortschritts überhaupt bilden."

4   See J. G. Fichte (1798).

5   Adorno makes this point by demonstrating how abstraction, which he thinks is necessary for thinking, functions through creating unreal, in the sense of a direct correspondence to what-is, but nonetheless real, in the sense that the mind can synthesize a variety of objects by locating commonalties, abstract concepts. "Wenn ich irgendeine Reihe von Merkmalen, eine Reihe von Elementen unter einen Begriff subsumiere, dann ist es in der üblichen Begriffsbildung so, daß ich von diesen Elementen ein Merkmal abstrahiere, das sie miteinander gemeinsam haben: und dieses

eine Merkmal soll dann der Begriff sein, nämlich die Einheit von all den Elementen, die dieses Merkmal haben." Yet, this process of abstraction does not somehow account for the totality of those entities from which the thinking person abstracts commons characteristics. Rather, the manifold array of what-is, even when indirectly named through conceptual thinking, is always more and otherwise than the abstract, reductive, concept can hold. "Ein jedes B, von dem gesagt wird, es sei A, ist immer auch ein *anderes* und ist immer auch *mehr* als das A, als der Begriff, unter den es in dem prädikativen Urteil gebracht wird." It is precisely this excessive feature of the objective sphere that Adorno seeks to exploit in his own thinking.

6 Here Adorno mobilizes, in his description of how his approach is a dialectics, the notion of "contradiction" [*Widerspruch*] as a way to illustrate that when one thinks from the bottom-up, rather than from the top-down, the source of thinking must be the recognition of irreconcilability. "Trotzdem hat das, was Ihnen als negative Dialektik soll vorgeführt werden, mit dem Begriff der Dialektik etwas Entscheides zu tun—und das ist doch nun auch vorweg einmal zu sagen. Nämlich: der Begriff des Widerspruchs, und zwar des Widerspruchs in den Sachen selbst, des Widerspruchs *im* Begriff, nicht des Widerspruchs *zwischen* Begriffen, wird in dem, was wir besprechen, eine zentrale Rolle spielen."

7 "Vom Subjekt ist Objekt nicht einmal als Idee wegzudenken; aber vom Objekt Subjekt. Zum Sinn von Subjektivität rechnet es, auch Objekt zu sein; nicht ebenso zum Sinn von Objektivität, Subjekt zu sein…Das »meine« verweist auf ein Subjekt als Objekt unter Objekten, und ohne dies »meine« wiederum wäre kein »Ich denke«." It is this point regarding the recognition of the objective, concrete, character of subjectivity that I take to be one of many similarities between Adorno, Rosenzweig, and Heidegger, respectively less or more uncomfortable as the identification of these similarities may be.

8 Adorno writes, "Es ist also in Philosophie etwas vom System zu retten: nämlich daß die Phänomene objektiv—und nicht erst in ihrer vom erkennenden Subjekt ihnen auferlegten Klassifikation—einen Zusammenhand bilden. Dieser Zusammenhang in der Sache selbst ist aber nicht zu hypostasieren, also nicht zu einem Absoluten zu machen, und ist auch nicht von außen an sie heranzubringen; sondern er ist in ihnen selbst, in ihrer inneren Bestimmung aufzufinden." Here the desire on the part of Adorno to retain the systematic coherence of systems thinking, without the structure of ontological domination that occurred in previous systems, comes strikingly close to the desire of a more recent figure—Quintin Meillassoux. In his *Après la finitude: Essai sur la nécessité de la contingence*, Meillassoux writes, "On peut donc dire qu'il est possible de *démontrer l'absolue nécessité de la non-nécessité de toute chose* … on peut établir—par voie de démonstration indirecte—la nécessité absolue de la contingence de toute chose" (Meillassoux 2006: 84).

9 An adequate explication of this text beyond the scope of the present chapter. However, it is important to note that the epistemic argument advanced by Adorno in *Negative Dialektik* follows the same overarching concern regarding what he sees as a self-annihilating tendency of enlightenment thinking to deny human contingency— self-annihilating because this denial of contingency means the ultimate denial of the condition for the possibility of human being, finitude. Framing the problem of enlightenment around the denial of all myth, Adorno and Horkheimer, in of the more striking passages of the first chapter, make a direct connection between the denial of anthropomorphism—the denial of the theological reification of self-projection—on the part of enlightenment thinking and the denial of the self, a conceptual suicide.

10 On this point I again note the similarities to the work of Rosenzweig and Heidegger. Rosenzweig in particular, well-ahead of Adorno's work, diagnosis the same problem in enlightenment thinking. He writes of this need to escape finitude in the opening pages of *Der Stern der Erlösung*, for example, "Vom Tode, von der Frucht des Todes, hebt alles Erkennen des All an. Die Angst des Irdischen abzuwerfen, dem Tod seinen Giftstachel, dem Hades seinen Pesthauch zu nehmen...Alles sterbliche lebt in dieser Angst des Todes, jeder neue Geburt mehrt die Angst um einen neuen Grund, denn sie mehrt das Sterbliche ... Aber die Philosophie leugnet diese Ängste der Erde" (Rosenzweig 2002: 3). Admitting the particularities of their respective projects, the target of critique appears remarkably similar—the denial of contingency, the burying of one's head in the face of the dialectical truth that I am indeed "here" but I will not always be so—the dialectical condition for the possibility of all cognition. Regarding my claim that Adorno's project is a *praxis*, rather than a static system à la the idealist systems he rejects, see Robert Antonio (1981: 330–345).

11 Baldwin cites the aforementioned passage regarding the sublation of the subject and object from the chapter "On Subject and Object" from Theodor Adorno (2005). Later on in the text, however, Adorno qualifies the sublation he is enacting, framing it around the negative dialectical model I explicate in my argument. Adorno writes, "The difference between subject and object slices through subject as well as through object. It can no more be absolutized from thought. Actually everything that is in the subject can be attributed to the object ... Object, though attenuated, also is not without subject. If object itself lacked subject as a moment, then its objectivity would become nonsense ... The antithesis between universal and particular too is necessary as well as deceptive. Neither one can exist without the other, the particular only as determined and thus universal, the universal only as the determination of a particular and thus itself particular. Both of them are and are not. This is one of the strongest motives of nonidealist dialectics" (Adorno 2005: 256–257).

12 I owe my attention to this question to Joel Harrison, who pointed out early in my graduate career the possibility of framing religious studies theory and method concerns in terms of epistemological problems more generally.

References

Adorno, Theodor. 1966. *Negative Dialektik*. Frankfurt am Main: Suhrkamp Verlag.

Adorno, Theodor. 2003. *Vorlesung* über *Negative Dialektik*. Frankfurt am Main: Suhrkamp Verlag.

Adorno, Theodor. 2005. *Critical Models, Interventions, and Catchwords*. New York: Columbia University Press.

Antonio, Robert. 1981. "Immanent Critique as the Core of Critical Theory: Its origins and Developments in Hegel, Marx, and Contemporary Thought." *The British Journal of Sociology* 32(3): 330–345. https://doi.org/10.2307/589281

Benjamin, Walter. 1991. *Gesammelte Schriften*, vol. 1. Frankfurt am Main: Surhkamp Verlag.

Cox, James. 2006. *Guide to the Phenomenology of Religion*. New York: Continuum.

Fichte, J. G. 1798. *Über den Begriff der Wissenschaftslehre oder der sogenannten Philosophie*. Jena und Leipzig: Christian Ernst Gabler.

Heidegger, Martin. 2006. *Identität und Differenz*. Heidegger Gesamtausgabe, vol. 11. Frankfurt am Main: Klostermann.

Horkheimer, Max, and Theodor Adorno. 2006. *Dialektik der Aufklärung: Philosophische Fragmente*. Frankfurt am Main: S. Fischer Verlags.

Lewis, Michael, and Tanja Staehler. 2010. *Phenomenology: An Introduction*. New York: Continuum.
Meillassoux, Quentin. 2006. *Après la finitude: Essai sur la nécessité de la contingence*. Paris: Éditions du Seuil.
Rosenzweig, Franz. 2002. *Der Stern der Erlösung*. Freiburg im Breisgau: Universitätsbibliothek.
Wolfson, Elliot R. 2014. *Giving Beyond the Gift: Apophasis and Overcoming Theomania*. New York: Fordham University Press. https://doi.org/10.5422/fordham/9780823255702.001.0001
Wolfson, Elliot R. 2017. "Zeitlich Entzweiung und offenes System: Die Atonalität der Kabbala und Heideggers anfängliches Denken." In Michael Friedman and Angelika Seppi (eds.), *Martin Heidegger: Die Falte der Sprache*, 121–167. Vienna: Verlag Turia + Kant.

Part III
Scholars

Chapter 11

"The Thing Itself Always Steals Away": Scholars and the Constitution of their Objects of Study

Craig Martin

> [T]he thing itself always steals away
> —Jacques Derrida, *Voice and Phenomenon*[1]

According to the call for papers, this year's NAASR program focuses on

> the things that we, as scholars of religion, study. What, for instance, counts as data? How is it imagined, handled, or constructed? ... There exist longstanding and still active debates in the field regarding whether the items that we study pre-exist our approaches or whether our approaches actually create the conditions in which the former come into existence. It should come as no surprise, then, that the inter-relationship between theory, method, and data is complex and hardly settled. (NAASR 2017)

My contribution to this discussion comes, in part, from a place of anger and frustration. Throughout my career I have consistently argued that scholars constitute their objects of study through the use of discourse. As such, from my perspective scholarship ought to take into account the active role of the scholar in the production of knowledge. This position is based on—at this point—more than 15 years of study of anti-realist philosophers, from G. W. F. Hegel to Edmund Husserl, Martin Heidegger, Jacques Derrida, Michel Foucault, Judith Butler, John Dewey, Hilary Putnam, and Jan Westerhoff. None of these scholars is naively anti-realist. None of them argue that reality is made of discourse or that scholars can magically produce their objects of study by using words like magic wands. And yet, anti-realism is often caricatured as making such claims and cavalierly dismissed on the basis of such caricature.

For instance, recently I posted to Facebook the following quotation, found in Kocku von Stuckrad's excellent work, *The Scientification of Religion*: "[n]o discourse, no grid of classification, however familiar it may appear, has ever been derived 'from the things themselves'; it is the other way round and discourse and classification generate the order of things" (Sarasin 2003: 36; quoted in von Stuckrad 2015: 7). In the online conversation that followed, one friend objected: "a person with one arm cannot by discourse become a two armed person." When I pointed out that no poststructuralist has ever argued such a thing, my interlocutor claimed his statement was a *reductio ad absurdum*—apparently the idea that discourse functions like magic is a logical consequence entailed by the claim that discourse is constitutive of reality. Although the format of Facebook places limits on the depth and subtlety of philosophical engagement, this still struck me as a crude response. Similarly, I was recently accused—in print—of failing to distinguish between discourses and the objects of discourse; apparently poststructuralists— or so was the allegation—"just collapse everything into discourse" (Bush 2017).

These cavalier dismissals anger me. Perhaps it is merely because I hate being caricatured. Or perhaps it is because—much like the logic that sustains the practices of hazing—I feel that since *I* went through the pain of reading and digesting the most difficult writings of Hegel, Derrida, or Butler, others ought to as well. Either way, in what follows I offer a detailed defense of the claim that reality is mind-dependent and that scholars therefore produce—via discourse—what they study. The essay is painfully long, dense, and technical, and for that I apologize to my respondents. Nevertheless, I am persuaded that we must do our homework, so to speak, and understand the views we might want to criticize before dismissing them. We would never credit a scholar of the Hebrew Bible who did not know ancient Hebrew, or a scholar of the Vedas who did not know Sanskrit. Similarly, I do not think we should credit rejections of poststructuralist anti-realism that are based on little more than passing familiarity with the claim that "there is nothing outside of the text." (Shockingly, I've found that more than a few dismissals of Derrida's work depend merely on a reading of secondary sources about his work.) If I am wrong about realism and anti-realism (which is entirely possible), and if scholars do not in fact produce their objects of study, scholarly integrity nevertheless requires that that conclusion must be reached *after rather than before* a careful study of poststructuralist literature.

Realism and Anti-Realism

Philosophical anti-realism asserts, in some form or another, that "reality" is in some way mind-dependent or consciousness-dependent; that is, reality is in part dependent upon the constitutive work of the mind (or minds) in constructing that reality. Social constructionism is a form of anti-realism that emphasizes, on the one hand, that the construction of reality is social rather than individual, and, on the other hand, that the realities we construct are historically variable. Michel Foucault and Judith Butler are perhaps among the most strident anti-realists devoted to historicizing the social construction of gender, sex, and sexuality; in addition, they demonstrate clearly what is at stake in these debates. Arguments about whether reality exists independently of consciousness can, at times, seem insignificant at best and, at worst, a distraction from more important social, political, or philosophical questions. The works of Foucault and Butler press us to consider what social and political consequences follow from the assumption that gender, sex, and sexuality exist as real—and as fixed—independently of human consciousness or culture. For such theorists, realism *naturalizes* historically specific social categories; strident anti-realism, by contrast, sets as its task the *denaturalization* of our systems of classification.

In his early works—from the 1960s and 1970s—Jacques Derrida extends Martin Heidegger's "destruction" of Western philosophy by offering immanent critiques of the works of Plato, Jean-Jacques Rousseau, Immanuel Kant, G. W. F. Hegel, Edmund Husserl, and Heidegger, among others. This body of work provides a substantial and, arguably, damning critique of philosophical realism. At the same time, Derrida draws special attention to how Western philosophy's categories or systems of classification were part and parcel of European imperialism and colonialism—Derrida's own contribution to denaturalizing historically specific concepts. His most famous—or infamous—anti-realist statement comes from *Of Grammatology*, in which he claimed that "[t]*here is nothing outside of the text*" (Derrida 1976: 158; emphasis original). In Euro-American scholarship on Derrida, this single sentence—which appears in the midst of Derrida's commentary on Rousseau's *Confessions*—has too often been read apart from the surrounding context on pages 158 and 159 of Gayatri Chakravorty Spivak's translation. Removed from its context, this sentence has inspired two broadly popular but unfortunate interpretations, both of which, at times, have served as metonyms for Derrida's work in general, or, worse, for poststructuralist anti-realism in general.

The first of these two interpretations reads Derrida as a sort of linguistic Berkeleyanism. Writing in the eighteenth century, George Berkeley—in *Principles of Human Knowledge* and *Three Dialogues*—advances a form of philosophical idealism which claims that the material world does not exist; on the contrary, that all "things" are merely "ideas" that appear to the senses of spirits, and those ideas were causally produced by God rather than a material world. Berkeley writes:

> the various sensations or ideas imprinted on the sense ... cannot exist otherwise than in a mind perceiving them. ... The table I write on, I say, exists, that is, I see and feel it; and if I were out of my study I should say it existed, meaning thereby that if I was in my study I might perceive it, or that some other spirit actually does perceive it. ... [However,] as to what is said of the absolute existence of unthinking things *without any relation to their being perceived*, that seems perfectly unintelligible. Their *esse* is *percipi*, nor is it possible they should have any existence, out of the minds or thinking things which perceive them. (Berkeley 1996: 25; emphasis added)

Following his exposition and defense of this view, Berkeley concludes: "it follows that we have no longer any reason to suppose the being of *matter*" (ibid.: 56).

For those who naïvely read Derrida in this manner, "there is nothing outside of the text" apparently means that all we have is discourse or language (rather than ideas, as Berkeley would have it). Perhaps we are even in a "prison house of language," with nothing on the other side of the prison walls. As one commenter writes:

> With the "linguistic turn" of deconstruction, the radical disjuncture from social reality becomes even more pronounced. With deconstruction, for example, such ideas as "truth" and "history" do not exist outside of language, if at all. ... [I]t is not unfair to say that under the linguistic turn, nothing could exceed language, except language itself. But even this excess amounted to a "chain of signifiers"

that slid away like a sloughed-off snakeskin to hover around its own coiled body. If it pointed to anything, it was only to itself. (Barkesdale 2013)

In *More Than Belief: A Materialist Theory of Religion*, Manuel A. Vásquez accuses both Judith Butler and Derrida of a form of "linguistic idealism," which he claims—citing Ian Hacking—is "descended from Berkeley's ideal-ism [sic]" (Vásquez 2011: 147). As we will see below, unfortunately this interpretation ignores the fact that merely three sentences after stating "there is nothing outside of the text," Derrida explicitly allows for "the real life ... existences of 'flesh and bone,' beyond and behind what one believes to be circumscribed as Rousseau's text" (Derrida 1976: 159).

The second unfortunate interpretation, which appears in the secondary literature far more often than the linguistic Berkeleyan interpretation, reads Derrida as a linguistic Kantian: in lieu of Kant's opposition between phenomenological experience and the noumenal thing-in-itself, we are led to believe that the statement "there is nothing outside of the text" opposes discourse or language to a noumenal thing-in-itself.[2] This reading implies that Derrida is, in some way, a dualist who separates reality from its reception in consciousness or language. For instance, in Lee Braver's otherwise sophisticated history of continental anti-realism, *A Thing of This World*, Braver claims that this passage means that "we cannot get outside of thought, systems, ideas to reach reality itself" (Braver 2007: 443), or that, although signs refer "to an external world, ... our access to this world is always mediated by more signs" (ibid.: 446). Similarly, Edward Slingerland, in *What Science Offers the Humanities*, interprets "there is nothing outside of the text" in this manner:

> Of course, Derrida is not actually denying the existence of an extralinguistic reality of objects. What he *is* denying is the possibility that we can have any kind of direct access to the objects *an sich*; they are known to us only as discursive objects, strands in the woven text that makes up the humanly knowable world. (Slingerland 2008: 79)

Slingerland asserts that Derrida and other theorists in the humanities are reproducing a centuries old distinction between mind and body, or between spirit and nature. For Slingerland, "such a rigid dualism is a serious mistake" (ibid.: 4). Although not talking about Derrida in particular, Titus Hjelm, in *Social Constructionisms*, mocks this sort of linguistic dualism:

> From this perspective, the "world out there" and perceptions of that world are radically separated, with no access to the former, except through discourse. It is one thing to say that the *meaning* of, say, gravity is dependent on our ways of talking about it ... It is another thing for me to jump out of a sixth story window and assume a safe landing because I'm shouting "I'm not falling!" on the way down. (Hjelm 2014: 93)

While such a view would deserve mocking, these critiques grossly misunderstand Derrida's poststructuralist anti-realism, which explicitly and vehemently opposes any such dualism.

In this chapter, I will turn to where Derrida most explicitly discusses the cognition of "extra-linguistic" objects: in his discussion of Husserl's idealism. I will provide an exposition of Derrida's critique of Husserl, demonstrating that Derrida arrives at an anti-realist view that is neither a linguistic Berkeleyanism nor a linguistic dualism. My exposition of Derrida's writings will of necessity be simplified and one-sided; the texts I'll cite are about *far more* than the cognition of objects, but for my purposes I'll avoid themes that stretch beyond the present agenda. I will demonstrate that a careful reading of Derrida's texts supports neither the linguistic Berkeleyanism nor the linguistic dualism interpretations of his work. If we are going to reject the poststructuralists' insistence that scholars create their own objects of study, it will have to be on grounds other than the sort of *reductio ad absurdum* offered by Hjelm and my Facebook friend.

Husserl, Objects, and Ideality

In several major works, from *Logical Investigations* and *Ideas* to *Experience and Judgment* (dating from the turn of the twentieth century to posthumous publications in the late 1930s), Husserl attempts, among other things, to account for the phenomenological conditions that make cognition of objects *as objects* possible for human consciousness. For Husserl, because objects do not fully appear as such to phenomenological consciousness, they must be constructed or idealized for us, by us: the objectivity or ideality of objects is *a posteriori* for consciousness.

All of Derrida's earliest works offered immanent critiques of Husserl's corpus, often focusing on elements related to this question of the objectivity of objects. These works include his graduate thesis, *The Problem of Genesis in Husserl's Philosophy* (Derrida 2003; originally written in 1953–1954), his first book-length publication, a translation and introduction to Husserl's "Origins of Geometry," (1989; first published in 1962), and his first book, *Voice and Phenomenon: Introduction to the Problem of the Sign in Husserl's Phenomenology* (2011; first published in 1967; although published in the same year as *Writing and Difference* and *Of Grammatology*, the former was merely a collection of previously published essays and the latter was written after *Voice and Phenomenon*). In what follows, I will focus on Derrida's reading of Husserl in his introduction to "Origins of Geometry" and *Voice and Phenomenon*, whose critiques of Husserl are largely parallel to one another.[3]

Husserl's phenomenological starting point for a consideration of the ideality or idealization of objects involves a reflection on what I will call "mid-sized objects" within one's visual range. For my purposes, I'm defining a "mid-sized" object as one that an adult human could manipulate and observe all sides of without too much difficulty, barring objects whose details are too small to see without aided vision. For example, for objects one might find in a household, mid-sized objects could include anything from a bread crumb or push-pin to a desk, bed, or dresser. (The size of the object *relative to human bodily capacities* is not an insignificant aspect of this definition, since the way we cognize these mid-sized objects is very different from the way we cognize objects like "religions" or "nations.") Husserl notes that the immediate phenomenological experience of an object is constantly changing; for instance, as one moves, as the object moves or rotates, or as the light source over the object changes, whatever appears in the visual field changes as well. In *Ideas I*, Husserl's example is that of a table:

> Let us start from an example. Looking the whole time at this table, moving around it in the process, altering my position in space as always, I am continually conscious of the existence (as bodily there) of this and the same table, and, to be sure, of the same one, remaining completely unchanged in itself. The perception of the table, however, is a perception that is constantly changing; it is a continuity of changing perceptions. I close my eyes. My other senses are not in any relation to the table. Now I have no perception of it. I open my eyes and I have the perception again. *The* perception? Let us be more precise. Recurring, it is under no circumstances individually the same. Only the table is the same, and I am conscious of it as identical in the synthetic consciousness that joins the new perception with memory. (Husserl 2014: 71)

A couple of things are significant here. First, Husserl attributes unity and fixity to the table in-itself, but disunity and multiplicity to the changing phenomenological consciousness of the table. The thing-in-itself is what it is—a single, unchanging object—while consciousness of said object continually varies. Second, not only does phenomenological consciousness of the object shift, change, or flow, but it also disappears as one closes one's eyes. However, because the table has a consciousness-independent existence, it persists as a thing-in-itself even when it is not seen; "the perceived thing can be without being perceived, ... and it can be without changing" (ibid.). As Derrida will point out, Husserl's description here is a site where classic western philosophical oppositions—with us since Heraclitus and Plato—between identity and difference, logic and experience, or reason and empiricism are played out.

A crucial element of Husserl's account of the experience of the "now" moment in phenomenological consciousness involves what he calls *retention* and *protention*. Retention consists of recalling what has passed out of immediate phenomenological consciousness, while protention consists of anticipating what may come next. The phenomenological experience is thus divided between a "*re-membering*" and an "*anticipation*" (Husserl 2014: 140). In the passage we're considering, Husserl draws attention only to retention and the unstable now: "the now of perception incessantly transforms itself into the following consciousness of the just-passed and at the same time lights up a new now, and so forth" (ibid.: 72). As such, the now moment is not only not stable but also not self-sufficient; all nows refer to what is other than the now.

Consider the phenomenological experience of a spoken sentence, such as the following: "Is a bell making that sound?" Upon hearing the first four syllables, one will not as yet necessarily have heard the words "Is a bell make-"ing. Rather, until one hears "-ing that sound," the words one might have heard could very well have been "Isabel make-"s, as in, "Isabel makes her own marinara sauce." The identity of the word is *not at all existent in* the phenomenological experience; its identity is ideal not empirical. The identity of the "bel" syllable is necessarily constituted on the basis of what came before and what came after. This is, of course, why the talk-to-text features on our phones often change the first words spoken as one continues one's sentence. For example, when I speak "Husserl and Derrida" into the Google Search feature on my phone, it first translates my speech as "Husserl and Jerry. Die"—presumably because protention anticipates that the syllables which sound like "Derr-ee" are much more often going to have referred to "Jerry" for English speakers than to an obscure French philosopher—before going on to correct to "Husserl and Derrida." The phone itself relies on protention and retention to "understand" the words said. Without protention and retention, phenomenological experience would consist of unrelated, punctual moments without continuity; the experience would be like that of a film in which every single frame is randomly chosen from other films. Protention and retention permit phenomenological consciousness a continuity it otherwise would not have.

Husserl also provides the example of experiencing a melody (Husserl 2014: 143): because a melody is experienced across moments of time, it can never appear in a simple, present now. "[T]he *essence* of something of which one is in this way conscious entails the possibility of reflecting on its having-been-perceived" (ibid.: 143). Husserl insists that "the *entire* phenomenological time-field of the pure ego" is made up of all "*three* dimensions of the before, afterward, simultaneous" (ibid.: 159). Only when we have the "*entire stream* of temporal unities of experience" is that stream "strictly closed off and self-contained" (ibid.). The logic is trinitarian: "*One* pure ego—*one* stream of experience, replete in all three dimensions, essentially hanging together in this repleteness" (ibid.). This unity is, of course, belied by the very terms Husserl uses: at the very least, if retention involves "re-membering," then consciousness is dealing with "members" that must be joined, and as such do not constitute a simple, closed unity. The identity of what we experience is constructed by consciousness independently of each empirical, punctual now; the identities of the "things" we "perceive" are essentially non-empirical.

Returning to the previous passage under consideration, Husserl goes on to emphasize that the thing-in-itself, *as a whole*, exceeds immediate perception: "[l]ike the perceived thing generally, so, too, anything and everything accruing to it in terms of parts, sides, inherent aspects necessarily transcends the perception" (Husserl 2014: 72). For example, because the whole table does not appear to phenomenological consciousness at once—the whole as "whole" transcends any individual perception or now moment, for example, as I cannot see the bottom and the top at the same time—we must idealize it through protention and retention of various phenomenological moments. Its ideality—its unity and identity—is, for us, constructed out of various moments of perception.

Husserl further considers the phenomenological experience of an object's color:

> The color of the seen thing is intrinsically no really obtaining inherent aspect of the consciousness of color; it appears but while it appears, the appearance can and *must* continually change in the course of ostensive experience of it. The *same* color

appears "in" continuous manifolds of *shades* of color. (Husserl 2014: 72; original emphasis)

That is, as we walk around a table, the angles between the light source, the light reflecting off of the table, and the distance and vector of that light to our eyes is constantly changing. Arguably, in "reality" (and, as should be clear, "reality" is what is at stake here), we see shifting shades of the "same" color. As a result, the "sameness" of the color is a product of our idealization, and is not at all present in the phenomenological experience in and of itself.

This extends beyond the experience of color: "Something similar holds for sensory quality and equally for each spatial shape. One and the same shape (given in person *as* the same) appears continuously again and again "in a different way," in profiles of shapes that are always different" (Husserl 2014: 72). For instance, a pyramid could appear as a two-dimensional triangle from one side, or as a two-dimensional square from the bottom. Husserl insists that the shape is "given ... *as* the same," but his phenomenological description belies that: the "same" pyramid is given through different "profiles," and its sameness is constructed in consciousness. This holds for an object's spatial depth as well. "A profile is an experience. But experience is only possible as experience and not as something spatial" (ibid.: 73). That is, for example, one's experience of a pyramid is necessarily two-dimensional rather than three-dimensional or spatial; at any particular moment, we only experience at best a profile of the three-dimensional object. "What is profiled, however, is intrinsically possible only as something spatial (it just is essentially spatial) but it is not possible as experience" (ibid.). We cannot directly experience the thing-in-itself as an object with depth; we construe its spatiality after the fact, through protention and retention of the various profiles we've experienced.

At one point Derrida uses the word "substruction" to refer to this process of idealization that Husserl describes: substruction constructs in part by subtracting inessential, empirical differences.[4] Consider the imagination of geometrically perfect shapes: we start with "*more or less smooth* surfaces, sides, lines, or *more or less rough angles*, and so on. ... '[P]roceeding from the factual, an essential form becomes recognizable'" (Derrida 1989: 123). From empirical "roundness" we imagine "pure" roundness, "*under* which is *constructed* the geometrical ideality of the 'circle'" (ibid.: 124; original emphasis). However, the imagined, pure roundness "is not to be confused with the multiplicity of natural shapes which more or less correspond to it in perception" (ibid.). An object's ideality or identity is never present to phenomenological consciousness, only the object's various empirical manifestations appear.

Derrida also draws attention to the fact that the ideality or substruction of the object is necessarily contingent upon repetition of the "same" in different phenomenological experiences *across time*. Time—an essential condition of protention and retention—makes the ideality of the object possible, since we cannot construct the object in consciousness on the basis of a single phenomenological now. At the same time, however, in a way time separates the thing from itself in our immediate experience: the "it" appears now one way, and now another way, and now a third way. Phenomenological experience of a thing is a continual process of it looking like *this*, then *not* looking like this, but now *that*. Pure nows, without protention and retention, would be punctual moments of perpetual difference. And, crucially for Derrida, protention and retention are *not* in the object but in the subject. As such, the empirical object has as its condition of possibility non-empirical (or no longer empirical) elements and processes. The ideality of the three-dimensional pyramid *at any particular moment* depends upon now moments that are *no longer present or which are not yet present*, except in a subject. The presence of the object's ideality—its identity and unity—is, for us, contingent upon what is absent in perception of the object itself. An object's ideality is, *essentially*, in part non-empirical. Derrida writes, "one sees an irreducible non-presence recognized as a constituting value, and with it a non-life or a non-presence of the living present, a non-belonging of the living present to itself, a non-originarity that cannot be eradicated" (Derrida 2011: 6). The "sameness" of the object is shot through-and-through with difference, and difference which is *irreducible*. If we remove the differences, we cannot construct the object. In addition, "[t]his relation to non-presence ... radically destroys every possibility of self-identity in its simplicity" (ibid.: 56). For Derrida, these conditions of possibility of the substruction of objects are *also conditions of impossibility for simple, self-identical objects*. This is, of course, a Hegelian theme: the being of beings is constituted in and through difference and negativity.

For Derrida, another consequence of the fact that the ideality of the object for us is contingent upon time is that "it" is *always open to future reconstruction* (the "it" is in scare quotes because, once reconstructed, the "it" is necessarily a different "it"). What we first take to be a two-dimensional triangle is, once turned 30 degrees to the right and 10 degrees down, reconstructed or re-idealized as a three-dimensional pyramid. However, who is to say that the pyramid could not be turned once again, at which point we might discover that there is no "back" or fourth wall to the pyramid, in which case it's more like a tent with one side open. There is, *a priori*, no way to make the pyramid's ideality appear directly to phenomenological consciousness. The pyramid's ideality is necessarily and inescapably non-empirical.

We might, with some level of confidence, assure ourselves that such a mid-sized object could be manipulated or turned over in our hands long enough that our idealization of it could be closed; we could arrive at a point where its identity would no longer be revisable. However, consider that—apart from infants or toddlers in their nurseries or play rooms—most "objects" of consciousness or discourse are not mid-sized objects. As Nelson Goodman notes in *Ways of Worldmaking*:

> Once in awhile someone asks me rather petulantly "Can't you see what's before you?" Well, yes and no. I see people, chairs, papers, and books that are before me, and also colors, shapes, and patters that are before me. But do I see the molecule, electrons, and infrared light that are also before me? And do I see the state, or the United States, or the universe? I see only parts of the latter comprehensive entities, indeed, but then I also see only parts of the people, chairs, etc. (Goodman 1978: 71)

As a professor, I regularly make judgments about objects like "students," the "student body," a particular student's "grade," the "faculty," the "administration," and so forth. Consider just one: the faculty. The faculty as a whole rarely appears before phenomenological consciousness all at once, and even when it does—for instance, at a commencement ceremony—one learns very little about the faculty other than their outward physical appearance (or at least those parts of physical appearance that aren't covered by regalia). But when I think of my college's "faculty" as an object, the physical appearance is typically of little importance; much more important is what the faculty "thinks"—about assessment, for instance, or the college president's new agenda for the college. The view of the faculty about the president's new agenda could be constructed through retention or memories of, perhaps, phenomenological consciousness of interactions with individual faculty members, open discussions in full faculty meetings, nonverbal signals and gestures accompanying such a discussion, rumors of conversations in other departments, bitching sessions over beers at the local pub, and so on. On the basis of such a substruction, one might claim: "the faculty will not like phase two of this new initiative." But with what level of certainty can we make such statements? As should be clear, temporality here provides ample opportunity for the "faculty" to be open to radically different reconstructions. *Temporality makes the substruction of the object both possible and essentially open-ended* (and this is to say nothing of the extent to which the construction of such objects is contested and agonistic, which results in our certainty about the bounds and characteristics of such objects receding further). And, again, most of the "objects" of interest to us are not mid-sized objects: our economy, our environment, our state, our state policies, our jobs, our salaries, our budgets, our debt, our retirement accounts, our future, etc.

Matters are further complicated when we consider one of Husserl's philosophical goals, particularly in his essay, "Origins of Geometry": to authorize as objective the truths of (Euro-American) math and science. In this essay, Husserl is caught in a double bind: he accepts that objective truths—like the Pythagorean theorem—do not descend from the heavens; however, as a type of foundationalist, he nevertheless wants to defend the objectivity of the truths of geometry. Since he doesn't accept that their truth is founded on a transcendent origin, he must ground their truth in human history and consciousness, but it cannot be merely subjective or culturally relative. Husserl writes,

> geometrical existence is not psychic existence: it does not exist as something personal within the personal sphere of consciousness: it is the existence of what is objectively there for "everyone" (for actual and possible geometers, or those who understand geometry). Indeed, it has, from its primal establishment, an existence which is peculiarly supertemporal and which—of this we are certain—is accessible to all men, first of all to the actual and possible mathematicians of all people, all ages. (Husserl 1989: 160)

As with all sciences, "tradition" is an inescapable part of this achievement of objective truth: "We know of [geometry's] handed down, earlier forms, as those from which it has arisen ... [I]t is not only a mobile forward process from one set of acquisitions to another but a continuous synthesis in which all acquisitions maintain their validity" (Husserl 1989: 159). A mobile process: idealization—to objective truth—requires time and synthesis and the accumulation of tradition. However, the European Enlightenment has as one of its central principles the axiom that a claim is not true simply because it has been inherited from an authoritative tradition. How does Husserl bridge the gap between historically relative, specific human consciousnesses and objective truth?

According to Derrida, Husserl for all practical purposes makes recourse to a Hegelian teleology, whereby we dialectically sublate—or synthesize, to use Husserl's term—empirical evidence until we arrive at an ideal end, albeit one which is sometimes not yet reached. *Ideally*, phenomenological experience will be transformed into objective truth. Over time—and time, as Derrida notes, is essential to the process Husserl describes—we go from empiricism to reason, from existence to logic, from body to spirit:

> The sensible utterances have spatiotemporal individuation in the world like all *corporeal* occurrences, like everything embodied in *bodies* as such; but this is not true of the *spiritual* form itself, which is called an "ideal object." In a certain way ideal objects do exist objectively in the world, but it is only in virtue of these two-leveled repetitions and ultimately in virtue of sensibly embodying repetitions. (Husserl 1989: 160–161; emphasis added)

The spiritual object appears at the end of a series of repetitions of representations of empirical objects to ourselves; repetition and time are the levers that lift us from the subjective to the objective. Crucially, the product does not exist independently of those spiritual repetitions or representations, but neither does it exist independently of the empirical. *Both* empirical evidence in phenomenological consciousness *and* repetitions in cognition are essential conditions of possibility of objective truths. Husserl is neither an empiricist nor a rationalist or idealist, but rather both. As Paola Marrati writes, for Husserl and Derrida "[i]deality and empiricity appear at the same time; they are produced by the same movement and it is for this reason alone that any attempt to separate them absolutely is doomed to failure" (Marrati 2005: 83).

To summarize the points thus far,

- the ideality of objects are constructed for consciousness, in time, through protention and retention of various empirical now moments in phenomenological consciousness;

- the ideality produced depends on and simultaneously discards varying empirical evidences;

- the process of idealization is necessarily open-ended, as future phenomenological experiences may produce evidence that requires us to revise the objects at hand for consciousness; and

- this process is neither strictly empiricist nor idealist, but rather both.

Ideality and Language

Husserl goes on to note that *language* is a further condition of possibility of this process of idealization, at least as concerns the truths of geometry. When introducing language in "Origins of Geometry," he makes three points. The first is an off-hand comment apparently unrelated to the two points that follow: words, like "things," are themselves similarly idealized. Second, although words are necessary to *refer to* idealized objects—like geometrical figures—those objects have an existence independent of the words or consciousnesses that refer to them; that is, Husserl wants to be realist about such objects. Third, the objectivity of the truths to which such words refer can be certain once we arrive at *invariant* constructions. I'll discuss each of these claims in turn.

(1) *Language and words are themselves idealized.*
Husserl writes:

> language itself, in all its particularizations (words, sentences, speeches), is, as can easily be seen from the grammatical point of view, thoroughly made up of ideal objects; for example, the word *Löwe* occurs only once in the German language; it is identical throughout its innumerable utterances by any given persons. (Husserl 1989: 161)

Löwe, or "lion" in English, is substructed from all the empirical instances of the word, and—presumably—it refers to the "same" idealized concept in each case. The "same" word "lion," like a pyramid, can appear empirically different each and every time, and still be the same word. It can be spoken aloud, pronounced in a wide variety of ways, in various voices, or even sung in different notes or keys, but it is still the "same" word. Similarly, we could write "lion" in Times New Roman, in a sans serif font, write it in cursive, or print it, but the different marks would all refer to the "same" word.

While Husserl offers this as an offhand, throwaway comment, this point is of more than a little importance to Derrida. Derrida draws special attention to the fact that signs of words, by definition, must be repeatable. "A sign that would take place only 'once' would not be a sign" (Derrida 2011: 42)—it would be a singular event, a gasp, or an exclamation.

> A signifier (in general) must be recognizable in its form despite and across the diversity of empirical characteristics that can modify it. It must remain the *same* and be able to be repeated as such despite and across the deformations that what we call the empirical event makes it necessarily undergo. (Derrida 2011: 43)

Not only must the signifier be indefinitely repeatable, but the idealized word, sign, or concept to which signifying marks refer, strictly speaking, *does not exist empirically*; rather, the ideal is *referred to* by the various empirical instances. Those empirical instances of the word are not the thing-in-itself. As Vernon W. Cisney writes:

> Language itself is therefore constituted essentially on the basis of this paradoxical entanglement of singularity (irreplaceable, empirical, "reality" in each of its operations) and ideality—this entanglement, in other words, and hence the essential inseparability of reality and representation, is what makes language what it is. (Cisney 2014: 110)

Derrida notes the irony here: despite Husserl's opposition to Platonism, which makes the *really real* exist in a non-empirical world, here Husserl similarly locates the object (i.e., the ideal object) in a non-empirical space. "By determining the *ontos* as *eidos*, Plato was doing nothing else" (Derrida 2011: 45).

Derrida notes that Husserl is making claims at three different levels here. *Words* refer to *concepts*, and concepts refer to *objects*. However, in each case the object at hand (word, concept, or extra-linguistic referent) is idealized or substructed from multiple empirical instances in a way that is mind-dependent. By no means does Husserl deny the non-empirical reality of the ideal to which he is referring. Indeed, as Marrati puts it, "the cost" of ideality is the reduction of the "existence of the transcendent world. ... [T]he site of ideality [is] the neutralization of factual existence" (Marrati 2005: 67). In *Ideas I*, Husserl explicitly emphasizes the role of fantasy in constructing the objects of sense (given the importance of this admission, I quote at length):

> Like the geometer, the phenomenologist can only make limited use of an originary givenness as a means of assistance. To be sure, all the main types of perception and envisaging stand at his free disposal as something given in an originary way, namely, as perspective exemplifications for a phenomenology of perception, phantasy, memory, and so forth. ... [T]he freedom of research of essences necessarily demands operating in phantasy.
>
> ... Thus, if one loves paradoxical talk, one can actually say—and if one properly understands the ambiguous sense involved, one can say in strict truth—that *"fiction" makes up the vital element of phenomenology,* ... that fiction is the source from which knowledge of the "eternal truths" draws its nourishment. (Husserl 2014: 127)

As Derrida puts it in his gloss on this point, fantasy or imaginary reproduction "opens ideality" (Derrida 2011: 47); representation is the *a priori* of ideality. Thus, despite all of Husserl's attempts to separate the idealized object from its representation, representation appears to be absolutely irreducible to the ideality of the object. This is, of course, a radically anti-realist claim: *if representation opens ideality, the objects represented do not exist for us prior to their representation.* As with the pyramid we turned over in our hands, the object's ideality is, quite literally, *never* immediately present to phenomenological consciousness and—as such—is in part nonempirical. "[T]he thing itself always steals away" (ibid.: 89).

A further point: insofar as the ideality of a word is iterable—the "same" word can be stated over and over again while remaining, at least theoretically, self-identical—the ideality of a word is no more fully present to phenomenological consciousness than the objects to which it refers. As Leonard Lawlor writes, "an ideality can be repeated to infinity, while a fact is singular. But, insofar as being iterable, an ideality can never in fact be given as such in an [empirical] intuition; it can always be repeated beyond the limit of this intuition" (Lawlor 2002: 203). As such, not only does the thing itself steal away, but so does the word.

The consequences of Derrida's point here are radical. For a thing to appear it has to be represented—in part via retention—to the self as an idealized thing; apart from its repetition in retention we would have the blooming, buzzing confusion of difference in the experience of pure, isolated nows. The identity of the thing for us *depends on* idealization over time at different moments. But, insofar as that identity is substructed for us through representation, repetition of the thing *is constitutive of its thingness in the first place*—there are no things for us without their representation. Thus representation of the thing has a logical priority over the thing-in-itself, insofar as representation is the thing's condition of possibility. There are not things for us that are *then* represented; rather, there are secondary representations that make things possible for us in the first place. Thus the paradox already noted: for us, *the representation of the thing pre-exists what is represented*.

To return to Husserl's claims about language in "Origins of Geometry": despite the fact that the truths of geometry are idealized in language, he insists that (2) *the objects to which words refer exist independently of language or consciousness*. In his own words:

> the idealities of geometrical words, sentences, theories—considered purely as linguistic structures—are *not the idealities* that make up *what is expressed and brought to validity as truth in geometry* ... Wherever something is asserted, one can distinguish what is thematic, that about which it is said (its meaning) *from* the assertion ... And what is thematic here is precisely ideal objects, and quite different ones from those coming under the concept of language. (Husserl 1989: 161; emphasis mine)

This makes for an odd sort of realism: the objects of geometry are real, and real *independently* of language—and yet, despite the fact that he claims they're "quite different" objects, everything else Husserl has already said about such objects explicitly claims that they're formed, intersubjectively, through repetition in language and in *exactly the same way* as the words that refer to them. Since we've already discussed at length how objects are substructed, I'll consider here Husserl's insistence on the importance of *written language* in the production of the objective truths of geometry. To begin with, the construction of math or the sciences is never an individual affair: it requires a *civilization*. "Clearly it is only through language and its far reaching documentations, its possible communications, that the horizon of civilization can be an open and endless one" (Husserl 1989: 162). In addition, *written* language is crucial for communication of "the objectivity of the ideal structure" of objects across space and time (ibid.: 164). Third, the development of sciences is cumulative: "scientific thinking attains new results on the basis of those already obtained" (ibid.: 166). Fourth, scientific thinking is not passive discovery, but rather a human production: "Making geometry self-evident ... requires ... methodical production ... [c]arried out systematically" (ibid.: 173). Again, this is an odd sort of extra-linguistic realism: geometrical objects and truths exist independently of language, but they are *not discovered*; rather, they must be *produced* in language.

(3) *The objectivity of the truths to which such words refer can be certain once we arrive at invariant constructions.* The sublation of the empirical and the substruction of ideality takes place in history, using the tools of language, but eventually arrives at a "universal a priori" (Husserl 1989: 174). When do we know we have arrived at the end, at an objective truth about geometrical objects? For Husserl, this takes place when we come to an unrevisable truth that can be infinitely repeated *without variation*: a truth is objective "[o]nly if the apodictically general content [is] invariant throughout all conceivable variation," that is, when it "can be understood for all future time and by all coming generations of men and thus capable of being handed down and reproduced with the identical intersubjective meaning." (ibid.: 179). Unlike "time-bound" truths, geometry "is valid with unconditioned generality for all men, all times, all places, and not merely for all historically factual ones but for all conceivable ones" (ibid.). For Husserl, perhaps historically-specific languages are the condition of the possibility for the original substruction of such truths—they serve as the ladders that we can use to climb from history to objectivity—but once their invariant, universal forms are found, we can apparently kick the ladder away.

For Derrida, here Husserl is writing checks that—empirically—he cannot cash. The future to which he appeals, a long future in which geometry will no longer be revisable, is not present today to any phenomenological consciousness. The truth of geometry is ultimately based upon absent evidence and, as such, is non-empirical. Despite the fact that Husserl elsewhere insists that all truths must be based on empirical evidences that appear to phenomenological consciousness—a premise that Husserl calls "the principle of principles," as Derrida reminds us (Derrida 2011: 46)—here Husserl establishes the truths of geometry on the basis of a leap into the future, and thus beyond the empirical. Once again, the *really real*—as something uncreated by humans, independent of consciousness, and unanchored by history—recedes further and further from the empirical. Those things which he takes to be most secure lack the level of security required by his very own "principle of all principles."

In summary:

- the representation of objects in and through language is a necessary condition for their ideality or substruction, particularly objects such as geometrical figures or theorems;

- as such, for us the representation of such objects is logically prior to the objects themselves;

- Husserl claims that the objective truths of, e.g., geometry, have a mind-independent reality, but, as Derrida notes, describes them as essentially dependent; and

- Husserl claims that the universal objectivity of such truths is secured by their invariant repetition throughout time, but, as Derrida notes, this claim is completely unwarranted according to the standards of empirical evidence Husserl sets for himself.

Three Sticking Points

At this point I would like to draw attention to three sticking points against realism that follow from the previous discussion of Husserl and Derrida, each of which I'll discuss in turn, with a special emphasis on the second:

1. The thing-in-itself is necessarily for-us.
2. Object individuation is discourse-relative and variable.
3. Matrices of individuation and claims about objects are essentially and indefinitely revisable.

The Thing-in-itself is Necessarily For-us

Because things never appear in their entirety to phenomenological consciousness, their identity or ideality is constructed in consciousness *a posteriori*. The in-itself we arrive at—and "arrive" is an appropriate word, since ideality or substruction takes place *in time* and via *movement*—is *ours*. And we cannot say anything about any object without engaging in the movement of ideality or substruction.

The obvious realist objection is that, of course, *for-us* objects might be subject to the movement of ideality, but, arguably, the objects in-themselves—apart from any observer or speaker—exist independently of the processes of ideality. Common sense tells us that, even if we substruct the table for ourselves, what we end up calling—*at the end* of the movement of ideality—the "table" will exist even when we close our eyes; we can still stub our toe on the table while making our way to the kitchen in the dark.

First, however, we have no direct or unmediated empirical evidence from which we can speak of the table-in-itself. We only have indirect empirical evidence for the table—*because that is the only sort of evidence we can ever have for objects that do not appear in their fullness all at once* (that is—for all objects). Second, the anti-realist needn't deny the realist's last objection that we can stub our toes on tables we cannot presently see: of course our idealized constructions are often not only warranted on the basis of prior empirical evidence but exceedingly reliable in predicting how the stuff of the world can and will push up against our consciousness. But a subject stubbing her toe on a table entails a consciousness: toe-stubbing is, here, mind-dependent. In addition, the point that the realist seems to be pressing is tantamount to saying that the table can make impressions when no one is impressed, or that the table looks a certain way when no one is looking. Such assertions remind us of the famed one hand clapping: what kinds of contact can be made when no contact is made? The realist pursuit of a mind-independent reality makes odd turns.

Object Individuation is Discourse-relative and Variable

For Derrida, (1) object individuation requires substruction, and (2) substruction is, for us,[5] a discursively dependent process; (3) this makes "things" dependent on both consciousness and language for their existence *as* things. Note what is not asserted here: it does not follow from this that all of the stuff of the world is mind-dependent, only that the *individuation of* the stuff of the world is mind-dependent. This matters because *not all discourses individuate the stuff of the world in the same manner*, and there is insufficient warrant for the assumption that one matrix of individuation is superior to or closer to "reality" than another—although some matrices of individuation might be more *useful*, depending on a subject or a group's interests.

For an example, let me turn to *Defining Reality: Definitions and the Politics of Meaning* (2003), in which Edward Schiappa provides an account of how the definition of the word "wetlands" changed in the United States during the early 1990s.[6] At the time, conservationists who wanted to protect wetlands were in competition with developers who wanted to build houses, strip malls, etc. on existing wetlands, and each group substructed "wetlands" in a different manner.

For the conservationists, the keys to defining a "wetland" were threefold. (1) The soil had to be sufficiently saturated with water such that (2) less oxygen could get into the soil, creating conditions in which (3) only certain types of plants adapted to soil with less oxygen—called "hydrophytes"—could thrive. Their definition was not random, and nor was it based on a simple description of patches of land that were sort of wet. On the contrary, the conservationists were concerned first with protecting those species of plants and animals that could only live in these types of wetlands. Second, wetlands—at least on this construction—absorb and hold sediments that we, as humans, don't want in our drinking water, keeping the water table cleaner. Third, this sort of soil can also absorb excess water during heavy rainfall, thus protecting humans to some extent from possible floods. So the conservationists fabricated a definition of "wetland" precisely because they wanted to save certain plants and animals, improve drinking water, and protect us from floods. By contrast, developers had another sort of human interest: they wanted to make money by building on the properties designated and protected as "wetlands."

When George H. W. Bush was running for president of the United States in 1992, "wetlands" were a crucial political issue, and Bush needed to earn the votes of those citizens sympathetic to the conservationists. Consequently, one of his central campaign promises was that under his presidency he would ensure that no wetlands would be lost to development. However, at the same time he also wanted to please the developers so as to continue to get their support. When Bush finally came into office, he signed into existence legislation that protected "wetlands," but the legislation changed the substruction of "wetlands" in ways designed to serve the interests of the developers. Specifically, the legislation said that wetlands had to be *very wet*, not just below the surface of the soil, but also at the surface. Bush said, "I've got a radical view of wetlands. I think wetlands ought to be wet" (Schiappa 2003: 87). This benefitted the developers because this greatly reduced the number of "wetlands," as, based on the definition of the conservationists, not all of the "wetlands" were really wet or had water on the surface.

Estimates suggested that probably 30–50 million acres of land that had been "wetlands" on the conservationists' definition were reclassified as "not wetlands"—reducing the number of wetlands by a third or by half—so that the developers could build houses and strip malls. A great deal of money could be made, and Bush could claim he kept his campaign promise: he *did* in fact approve legislation that protected the "wetlands," even as he redefined the term to suit his purposes. It was a successful bait-and-switch.

The conservationists, of course, were unhappy with these results, insofar as the "really wet" wetlands were so different from the "wetlands" they had singled out that the new legislation no longer served their interests. "Really wet" wetlands couldn't absorb sediments dangerous to human drinking water in the same way, couldn't absorb floodwaters, and didn't sustain the types of endangered species that thrived in the type of "wetlands" that fit their definition. On the new definition, all of the desires of the conservationists were thwarted.

For Schiappa, what is interesting about this case is that both definitions of "wetlands" are tied to human interests, just different sets of interests. What is a wetland? The answer to that question apparently depends on whether one wants a clean water table and to avoid floods, or if one wants to build a suburb. Note: we cannot simply answer that question by going out and looking at one. The substruction of such an object is, *a priori*, not an empirical matter. The very same patch of land might look like a wetland for the conservationists but not for Bush and the developers. The thing's identity is, ultimately, nonempirical.

Another crucial point for Schiappa is that these definitional decisions are always related to political power, which is why they're so contested. At the end of the day, what is politically crucial is the legal definition *enforced by the state*. Conservationists can define "wetlands" differently all they want, but their definition has no real-world consequences as long as the state is endorsing and enforcing another definition.

Schiappa concludes that abstract questions like "what is a wetland?"—especially when considered outside of any social or political context—are generally useless. Rather, "the questions to ask are 'Whose interests are being served by this particular definition?' and 'Do we identify with those interests'" (Schiappa 2003: 82)? Do we want to make money or save houses from floods?

Returning to the anti-realist point, here the individuation of objects is clearly discourse-dependent. Without the discourses of conservationist scholars, we would not have individuated "wetlands" in the first place. Their existence *as wetlands* is a product of their discursive substruction. The things of the world do not individuate themselves; had humans never evolved, no one would ever have individuated wetlands. As Hägglund puts it in his discussion of Derrida's commentary on Emmanuel Levinas' body of writings, "discrimination has to be regarded as a constitutive condition. Without divisional marks—which is to say, without segregating borders—there would be nothing at all" (Hägglund 2008: 82). I would qualify the point: it's not that there would be nothing at all, it's that there would be no "things" at all.

Here it is worth returning to the realist's primary objection, posed above: "of course, *for-us* objects might be subject to the movement of ideality, but, arguably, the objects in-themselves—apart from any observer or speaker—exist independently of the processes of ideality." John R. Searle is one of the most strident advocates of this view. In *The Construction of Social Reality*, he defines realism as "the view that there is a way that things are that is logically independent of all human representations" (Searle 1995: 155; emphasis removed). Searle allows that all *descriptions* of the "brute facts" of reality—including, for instance, the "brute fact" that "Mount Everest exists independently of how or whether I or anyone else ever represented it or anything else"—are discourse-relative: "[a]ll representations of reality are made *relative to* some more or less arbitrarily selected set of concepts" (ibid.: 161; emphasis added). However, he insists that the "brute facts" that discourses describe *exist independently* of discourse and make discourses about them possible; for Searle, conceptual relativism "seems to presuppose realism, because it presupposes a language-independent reality that can be carved up or divided up in different ways" (ibid.: 165). The problem, from the perspective of this chapter, is in the phrase "there is a way that *things* are": for Derrida, "things" *entails* individuation and individuation *entails* the intentional consciousnesses that Searle wants to exclude from the "brute facts" of reality.

As should be clear from Schiappa's example, stating that "wetlands" exist *as wetlands* independently of the process of their substruction makes little sense: of *which particular* type of wetlands are we speaking? Of course, the anti-realist could rightfully allow the following: those things that conservationists eventually individuated as wetlands existed prior to when conservationists individuated them. As Searle rightly notes:

> We arbitrarily define the word "cat" in such and such a way; and only relative to such and such definitions can we say, "That's a cat." But once we have made the definitions and once we have applied the concepts relative to the system of definitions, whether or not something satisfies our definition is no longer arbitrary or relative. (Searle 1995: 166)

However, prior to formulating a definition of "wetland," that referent to which the term *now* refers did not exist *as* wetlands then, because to exist *as* a wetland, or to be individuated *as* a wetland, is always to be *for-us*. Were we to remove the conservationists' individuation or the *for-us*, the resulting claim—"wetlands existed prior to when conservationists individuated them"—would be far more problematic. Such a claim could not be verified as true without investigation of the "extra-linguistic" referent for the word "wetland," and such an inquiry would *necessarily* require reference back to the linguistic discourses of the conservationists, or the *for-us*—in which case we're back in anti-realist territory. *The "extra-linguistic" referent is dependent for its individuation on language.*

This second sticking point is perhaps the most important one because it draws attention to the social and political consequences of realism: *realism naturalizes historically specific matrices of individuation.* Realism insists that a table is just a table, as if that were the final word on the matter, as if what some might call a "table" could not be individuated differently—as a desk, as fuel for a house fire, or as garbage or debris in a landfill. While naturalizing the individuation of a table might be largely politically innocuous or irrelevant, the same is not true of objects like "primitive savage," "woman," or "homosexual." Not all matrices of individuation substruct "woman" in the same manner, but naturalizing one individuation over others can have considerable social consequences—and *that's the risk always taken by the realist approach* to objects. Or, to use another example, a realist for whom the claim that "life begins at conception" is fully naturalized is liable to have difficulty understanding or communicating with those who individuate "human life" in a different manner. For them, "life" just is what it is. In such cases, realism is a considerable barrier to historicization. Similarly, I once got into an argument with a biologist who insisted that "sex" is, by definition, based on XX and XY chromosomes; when I pointed out that, throughout history, other biologists defined "sex" differently, the retort was: "No, *sex is based on DNA.*" Because the terms had been thoroughly naturalized for her, thinking in terms of alternate matrices of individuation was apparently impossible.

One needn't be a "radical" poststructuralist to come to such a conclusion about the relativity of object individuation. Euro-American analytical philosophers provide us with similar arguments. In his classic *Ways of Worldmaking*—cited briefly above—Nelson Goodman notes that "[i]dentification rests upon organization into entities and kinds. The response to the question 'Same or not the same?' must always be 'Same what?' ... Identity or constancy in a world is identity *with respect to* what is within that world *as organized*" (Goodman 1978: 8; emphasis mine). Hilary Putnam defends a similar view, calling it "conceptual pluralism." He writes:

> we might describe "the contents" of a room very differently by using first the vocabulary of fundamental physical theory [i.e., "as consisting of fields and particles"] and then again the vocabulary of tables and chairs and lamps ... [W]e can use both of these schemes without being required to reduce one or both of them to some single fundamental and universal ontology. (Putnam 2004: 48–49)

Putnam concludes by noting that "[t]he whole idea that the *world* dictates a unique 'true' way of dividing the world into objects, situations, or properties, etc., is a piece of philosophical parochialism" (ibid.: 51). From such a perspective, there is no final or unrevisable ontology or matrix of individuation.

A side point: it is because of these two sticking points that I find it so terribly problematic when scholars use the "lens" metaphor to talk about their use of theory. The metaphor is typically employed to suggest that theory or theoretical discourses function like lenses to open vision on a particular subject matter, perhaps from a particular perspective. For instance, one might say that "feminist theory is a lens through which we can read a text, a lens that enables us to focus on the patriarchal social practices described therein." Note what the metaphor implies: reality is *out there*, beyond the lens, and—despite the fact that the lens enables vision—the lens gets *between us and reality*—perhaps even distorting or coloring vision in some way. The lens metaphor is extremely close to—if not identical with—the linguistic Kantian view whereby theoretical discourses get between us and the noumena of the world.

By contrast, according to the two sticking points I've attended to here, there are no noumenal "things" out there, as the individuation of objects in the first place is discourse-relative. As such, feminist discourses don't get *between* us and patriarchal practices; rather, they *individuate* those practices *for us* in the first place. The lens metaphor invites a worrisome epistemological anxiety: perhaps our lens distorts or colors our access to reality? By contrast, seeing a matrix of individuation as constitutive implies no separation between subjects and the things individuated, any more than a knife used to divide one slice of bread from the next separates those slices from the slicer. The words in a matrix of individuation are the knives that give us the slices, but *they do not get in between us and the slices*. There are many epistemological anxieties about which we should be worried, but the fear that constitutive discourses separate us from the world should not be one of them; individuation carves one object from the next but does not create a barrier between subjects and objects.

Matrices of Individuation and Claims about Objects Are Essentially and Indefinitely Revisable

The third sticking point is that matrices of individuation are indefinitely revisable. Time or temporality is the horizon of possibility for the substruction of objects, but openness to temporality simultaneously makes the closure of substruction theoretically impossible. Protention haunts every present now moment: it could always be the case that some future will come along that force us to revise our matrices of individuation. This could be for several reasons. First, by turning objects in our hands—in the case of mid-sized objects—or by gathering new data—for instance, by performing scientific experiments—we may see a side or profile of the objects we've individuated that have never appeared to us before. Second, "things" change and thus the objects we individuate may present new or previously unprecedented features, characteristics, or behaviors. Third, changing interests may invite us to individuate objects in a novel ways, as when George H. W. Bush's political interests directed his administration to individuate "wetlands" in a different manner.

In summary, things are individuated as things *for-us*, and matrices of individuation are both historically relative and indefinitely revisable. As such, speaking of the "real" existence of "things" independently of their individuation for consciousness makes little sense—such talk refers to things prior to the construction of their thingness.

Conclusion

Although my defense of anti-realism ultimately might not be persuasive to many readers, I hope to have demonstrated, first, that Derrida's views are neither unargued (as Searle claims about Derrida: see Searle 1995: 159) nor simplistically naïve—as if they could not tell the difference or recognize a distinction between a word and a referent. Second, I hope to have shown that the stakes of the discussion are not simply esoteric; insofar as realism can be used to naturalize or have the effect of naturalizing particular matrices of individuation, the question of anti-realism matters socially and politically.

I would like to reiterate one of the points with which I began: it is quite possible that poststructuralists are wrong about the fact that we construct our objects of study—I, for instance, would argue (based on recent studies on infant cognition) that the individuation of mid-sized objects is not, in fact, completely discourse relative in the way Derrida implies. However, we cannot reject poststructuralist anti-realism without a consideration of their arguments and simultaneously pretend to be responsible scholars.

It no more follows from the claim that scholars create their objects of study that we're not subject to gravity than it follows from the Madhyamika claim that we have no selves that Buddhists then must not have to pay taxes. The *reductio ad absurdum* depends on a complete misconstrual of the argument at hand. And, while we would never tolerate silly dismissals of the doctrine of *anatta* by scholars who've never read a single primary source from the Madhyamika tradition, realists apparently have free reign to caricature poststructuralism based on secondhand knowledge of the philosophical sources. Despite the fact that this paper has been painfully dense and technical, responsible scholarship typically requires us to do our due diligence before mocking a position we reject. I assert that realists should be held to the same scholarly standards.

Craig Martin, Ph.D., is Professor of Religious Studies at St. Thomas Aquinas College. His work focuses on method and theory in the study of religion, as well as discourse analysis and ideology critique of modern rhetoric on religion. His recent works include *Capitalizing Religion: Ideology and the Opiate of the Bourgeoisie* and *A Critical Introduction to the Study of Religion*.

Notes

1. This quote is from Derrida's *Voice and Phenomenon* (Derrida 2011: 89).
2. Richard Rorty notes that, from a realist perspective, anti-realists are often accused of being "some newfangled kind of transcendental idealist[s]" (Rorty 1991: 101); Rorty notes that the point for the anti-realist is, instead, that "she can find no use for the notion" of things-in-themselves (ibid.).
3. Derrida's analysis in *The Problem of Genesis* is dissimilar in many respects, as the point of entry of his critique was considerably different at the time.
4. There is a great deal of excellent secondary literature on Derrida's early work on Husserl. In particular, my reading of Derrida has been shaped by the following resources: Vernon W. Cisney's *Derrida's Voice and Phenomenon* (2014), Edward Baring's *The Young Derrida and French Philosophy, 1945-1968* (2011), Martin Hägglund's *Radical Atheism: Derrida and the time of Life* (2008), Leonard Lawlor's *Derrida and Husserl: The Basic Problem of Phenomenology* (2002), and Paola Marrati's *Genesis and Trace: Derrida Reading Husserl and Heidegger* (2005).
5. The clause "for us" is crucial here, insofar as non-human animals could, conceivably, substruct objects without the use of language.
6. I've used this example in print before (see Martin 2017).

References

Baring, Edward. 2011. *The Young Derrida and French Philosophy, 1945–1968*. Cambridge: Cambridge University Press. https://doi.org/10.1017/CBO9780511842085

Barkesdale, Amiri. 2013. "Postmodernism, the Academic Left, and the Crisis of Capitalism." *Insurgent Notes: Journal of Communist Theory and Practice* (March 11). Retrieved from http://insurgentnotes.com/2013/03/postmodernism-the-academic-left-and-the-crisis-of-capitalism.

Berkeley, George. 1996. *Principles of Human Knowledge and Three Dialogues*. Oxford: Oxford University Press.

Braver, Lee. 2007. *A Thing of This World: A History of Continental Anti-Realism*. Evanston, IL: Northwestern University Press. https://doi.org/10.2307/j.ctv47w24v

Bush, Stephen. 2017. "Religion and Belief after the Turn to Power: A Response to Craig Martin." *Method and Theory in the Study of Religion* 29(4–5): 334–339. https://doi.org/10.1163/15700682-12341398

Cisney, Vernon W. 2014. *Derrida's Voice and Phenomenon*. Edinburgh: Edinburgh University Press.

Derrida, Jacques. 1976. *Of Grammatology*, trans. Gayatri Chakravorty Spivak. Baltimore, MD: Johns Hopkins University Press.

Derrida, Jacques. 1989. *Edmund Husserl's "Origins of Geometry": An Introduction*. Lincoln, NE: University of Nebraska Press.

Derrida, Jacques. 2003. *The Problem of Genesis in Husserl's Philosophy*, trans. Marian Hobson. Chicago, IL: University of Chicago Press. https://doi.org/10.7208/chicago/9780226143774.001.0001

Derrida, Jacques. 2011. *Voice and Phenomenon: Introduction to the Problem of the Sign in Husserl's Phenomenology*, trans. Leonard Lawlor. Evanston, IL: Northwestern University Press.

Goodman, Nelson. 1978. *Ways of Worldmaking*. Indianapolis, IN: Hackett Publishing.

Hägglund, Martin. 2008. *Radical Atheism: Derrida and the Time of Life*. Stanford, CA: Stanford University Press.

Hjelm, Titus. 2014. *Social Constructionisms: Approaches to the Study of the Human World*. New York: Palgrave Macmillan. https://doi.org/10.1007/978-1-137-41396-3

Husserl, Edmund. 1989. "Origins of Geometry." In Jacques Derrida, *Edmund Husserl's "Origins of Geometry": An Introduction*, 155–180. Lincoln, NE: University of Nebraska Press.

Husserl, Edmund. 2014. *Ideas for a Pure Phenomenology and Phenomenological Philosophy: First Book: General Introduction to Pure Phenomenology*, trans. Daniel O. Dahlstrom. Indianapolis, IN: Hackett Publishing. https://doi.org/10.4324/9781315823577

Lawlor, Leonard. 2002. *Derrida and Husserl: The Basic Problem of Phenomenology*. Bloomington, IN: Indiana University Press.

Marrati, Paola. *Genesis and Trace: Derrida Reading Husserl and Heidegger*, trans. Simon Sparks. Stanford, CA: Stanford University Press.

Martin, Craig. 2017. *A Critical Introduction to the Study of Religion*, 2nd edition. London: Routledge. https://doi.org/10.4324/9781315474410

NAASR. 2017. "Call For Papers." Retrieved from https://naasr.com/2017/01/08/call-for-respondents-the-things-we-study-when-we-study-religion.

Putnam, Hilary. 2004. *Ethics without Ontology*. Cambridge, MA: Harvard University Press.

Rorty, Richard. 1991. *Objectivity, Relativism, and Truth: Philosophical Papers Volume 1*. Cambridge: Cambridge University Press. https://doi.org/10.1017/CBO9781139173643

Sarasin, Philipp. 2003. *Geschichtswissenschaft und Diskursanalyse.* Berlin: Suhrkamp.
Schiappa, Edward. 2003. *Defining Reality: Definitions and the Politics of Meaning.* Carbondale, IL: Southern Illinois University Press.
Searle, John R. 1995. *The Construction of Social Reality.* New York: The Free Press.
Slingerland, Edward. 2008. *What Science Offers the Humanities: Integrating Body and Culture.* Cambridge: Cambridge University Press. https://doi.org/10.1017/CBO9780511841163
Vásquez, Manuel A. 2011. *More than Belief: A Materialist Theory of Religion.* Oxford: Oxford University Press.
Von Stuckrad, Kocku. 2015. *The Scientification of Religion.* Berlin: De Gruyter. https://doi.org/10.1515/9781614513490

Chapter 12

Scholars and The Framing of Objects

Vaia Touna

My contribution in this edited volume, to quote Craig Martin's opening line in his essay (Chapter 11, this volume), also "comes from a place of frustration." In my own work I've been interested in how the past—that is, ancient artifacts (whether texts or material artifacts)—through scholarly and non-scholarly discourses acquire specific meanings, meanings which tells us more about the people who produce and use those modern discourses than about some actual meaning associated with the artifacts themselves. For example, in my book *Fabrications of the Greek Past* (Touna 2017), which looked at the characterization of "traditional" villages in Greece, I argued that the classification of some villages *as* "traditional" had less to do with some essential quality they possessed and more with economical, political, and social interests of the time when those characterizations became prominent within Greece, sometime in the 1970s and onwards. Furthermore, the act of characterizing some villages *as* "traditional" involved not only the people of those villages and the Greek state, but also far wider institutions, such as the European Union and UNESCO (ibid.: 116–139). Therefore, as I've argued there, discourses on "tradition" are always historically situated and not only mirror but also reproduce contemporary interests. But in the various discussions that I have often found myself in—whether at conferences or when discussing my own work with colleagues—I have sometimes met a specific (and, yes, frustrating) push-back that sounds something like this: "But there *must* be something we can say about the past" or "But things had to have *happened* in the past." Both of these statements surely suggest many things that we could examine, but I'll discuss here just two that I find of relevance to our current conversation. On the one hand, such statements suggest, whether implicitly or explicitly, that, in focusing on modern narratives about the past, I deny that "things happened" or that "things exist"; and on the other hand, it is presumed that there is *a* reality, *a* meaning, *an* identity in those artifacts, and that the role of the scholar is, through a constant refinement of their tools (e.g., methods and language), to access those meanings and those realities as much or as closely and accurately as possible. In other words, the presumption is that scholars need to develop, through their methodologies, a conceptual system that somehow corresponds to ancient realities (thereby rehabilitating or perhaps reanimating them), thus offering a plausible or probable understanding of *what really happened.*

So as I was reading Craig Martin's chapter, which, though not as interested in the specific issue of discourses on the past, nonetheless deals with the contest between realism and anti-realism (trying, as he writes, to "offer a detailed defense of the claim that reality is mind-dependent and that scholars therefore produce—via discourse—what they study") the lyrics of a Greek poem written by George Seferis in 1935, came to my mind. Concerning what contemporaries do with the various pasts that they inherit, he writes:

> I woke up with this marble head in my hands
> that exhausts my elbows and I don't know where to put it down.
> It was falling into the dream as I was coming out of the dream
> thus our life became one and it will be very difficult for it to separate again.
> I look at the eyes. Neither open nor closed
> I speak to the mouth, which keeps trying to speak
> I hold the cheeks, which have broken through the skin.
> I have no more strength[1]

I see the scholar's relationship with her or his object of study to be similar to the marble head that falls into the poet's hands, the one who doesn't know what to do with it, because its importance is not self-evidently there; in fact, at times the burden of what we end up studying, and the debates we enter with those who we disagree, can be exhausting. But, to me, the even more interesting thing is found in the line that reads: "our life became one and it will be very difficult for it to separate again." For items from the ancient world *became* meaningful objects, *became* part of our world, through scholarly (and, I would also say, non-scholarly) discourses; for if the thing, i.e., the marble head, only exists *in relation to* and *for the purpose of* particular interests, then it *becomes* an item worth studying only because of those interests (whether scholarly or not—such as my current project: studying the various ways archaeologists *and* Greek villagers signify their present by appeals to the past).

This brings me to Martin's discussion of Derrida's reading of Husserl and Hegel, where he arrives at three points that he sees as functioning against realism:

1 The thing-in-itself is necessarily for-us.

2 Object individuation is discourse-relative and variable.

3 Matrices of individuation and claims about objects are essentially and indefinitely revisable.

The examples that I could draw upon in regards to, and in support of, Martin's points are so overwhelmingly many that, to be honest, writing this essay has been painfully tiring because I have recently written several papers (which were presented at the Society of Biblical Literature conferences in 2016 and 2017) about this very topic: on discursive and pre-discursive realities, on whether or not we can say what an ancient author *really meant*. For how, as many in the field seem to assume, can we access the meaning of ancients texts, oftentimes existing in only fragmentary form, and sometimes non-existent but attested to from secondary and tertiary primary sources? As you may have already guessed, I would say, no, we cannot. But phrasing it in this way is what probably gets me into trouble in the first place, because it seems to suppose that *there is* a meaning, and the problem is just that we are unable to access it. So let me rephrase this a bit, to be a little clearer. It's not that we cannot say anything about the texts, or, artifacts that we are dealing with, but what we *do* say, or, what we *can* say, is on the level of discourse and is said for the purpose of *our* theoretical questions—so what we say about some inscription or some marble statue is not in some kind of sync or correspondence with the "really real," for the "the marble head" of the poem, is meaningless; instead it's the *becoming* that we are dealing with, such as the way a generic item becomes signified and then circulates among a group; furthermore, claims to the contrary when they are made, are for the purpose of authorizing that modern discourse and the author who makes the claims, and in successfully doing so they seal such claims off from critical scrutiny.

Consider, for example, a large body of artifacts, known as terracotta figurines, found along the coast of the eastern Mediterranean region and dating between the so-called Bronze (3300–1200 BCE) and Iron (1200–700 BCE) ages.[2] Those artifacts of various sizes and shapes depict figures in various positions and have been the object of various interpretations (see for example Mina et al. 2016). Although scholars admit to the difficulty at arriving at a conclusive interpretation of those artifacts, regarding their meaning and function (due in part to the fragmentary knowledge they have of that long gone world and thus the period of time that divides us from them), their descriptions quickly become prescriptions, and therefore difficult to separate from each other. Browsing the online site of The Museum of Cycladic Art in Athens, Greece (whose mission follows that of the N. P. Goulandris Foundation—which was also the primary donor of the collections—that is: "the study of Aegean civilization, research on prehistoric, Classical and modern Greek art, as well as its dissemination and promotion"; Museum of Cycladic Art undated a), which is mostly dedicated to the exhibition of artifacts from that period, with a focus on the Cycladic, Mycenean, and Cypriot art, we read: "The meaning and function of Cycladic figurines is kind of an enigma. In the absence of written records, any interpretation has to be based exclusively upon archaeological finds and reasonable assumptions" (Museum of Cycladic Art undated b).

But what are those reasonable assumptions that are based exclusively upon our reading of archaeological finds? Elsewhere on the museum's site, describing a particular type of figure known as the psi-type (borrowing the name from the letters of the Greek alphabet, Ψ [psi], to indicate the shape of those artifacts, namely a figure with upraised arms), we read:

> Schematic female figurines with arms folded or raised in an attitude of supplication are the commonest types of Mycenaean cult objects. They are small in size, handmade and are called conventionally Phi-type, Psi-type and Tau-type because of their similarity to the corresponding letters of the Greek alphabet (Φ, Ψ and T). (Museum of Cycladic Art undated c)

Here we see how easily the description becomes a prescription; the idea of "supplication" and "cult objects" immediately classifies a body of peculiar and enigmatic artifacts within a specific, modern interpretive frame that allows the item to be studied and compared with other artifacts, in rather particular ways. Several articles that deal with those artifacts make similar claims and, despite minor differences and disagreements, there is an underlying similarity that may go unnoticed. For example, in an article that was published in the *Hesperia Supplements*, entitled "The Survival of the Goddess with the Upraised Arms: Early Iron Age Representations and Contexts," the author, Mieke Prent, seems to take a rather critical position as to whether there are clear indication that those figurines represent a deity, yet she concludes her paper by suggesting otherwise:

> The recurrent representations of a female with upraised arms in Protogeometric B and later funerary contexts further suggests a special connection with beliefs concerning the afterlife. Perhaps there was a wish to entrust the dead to the care of an ancestral goddess, who was represented as displaying a gesture known of old.
>
> It is even possible that these images were connected with Persephone, a goddess whose yearly descent to Hades and subsequent return to earth symbolized the cycle of death and life. Although firm evidence for a Bronze origin of this goddess is lacking, the familiarity of Hesiod with the Eleusinian myth of Demeter and Persephone suggests that it was already "a well-known and ancient story" in his time. Regardless of the name (or names) of this goddess, the main point to be made here is that an old image was both adopted and adapted, and thereby it was given new relevance in a changing world. (Prent 2009: 238)

What I find of particular interest about this claim is the persistence of a specific kind of discourse that prevails implicitly in this case (and explicitly in other scholars)—that is, the discourse on religion that frames those objects in such a way that it is difficult to separate the discourse from some inherent quality in the artifact. Even when contexts are discussed for their better understanding, they already come prepackaged with a religious frame. Are they found in graves? Then this signifies religion. Are they found in public spaces, which are often described (that is, prescribed) as sanctuaries and therefore with clear religious connotations (despite the fact that scholars widely recognize that in the ancient world such distinctions as sacred/profane or religion/politics where not as clear cut as we understand them today)? Then they are religious symbols, etc. Although there is an overwhelming amount of publications that understands those artifacts as having some kind of religious reference, there are publications that describe those artifacts in more mundane terms; for example, if their size is small enough they might be just toys. Or, other scholars less interested in identifying religion in the ancient world but more interested in their economy understand those artifacts as commodities in a system of exchange within the Mediterranean world (see Borgna 2013; Merker 2003). But what we should not forget, paying attention to what Russell McCutcheon (2000: 206) asks in his chapter on myth in the *Guide to the Study of Religion*, is "[h]ow can the descriptive 'is' so smoothly become the prescriptive 'ought'?" This is something that we, as scholars, should always pay attention to and perhaps our task is not to smooth the gap between the two but to point out when such a smoothing is happening and "identify the strategies that construct the set-apartness of various conventions, beliefs and practices in the first place" (ibid.: 207) and, I would add, identify the strategies that make mere stuff from the past objects worth studying.

So, although an artifact of a figure, with its hands raised upwards, is just that—an artifact of a figure with its hands raised upwards—it quickly *becomes* a religious symbol, a figure that is praying or worshipping, a representation that experiences awe, perhaps, or maybe even a goddess of fertility, an item of ritual practice, a toy, a commodity within a system of economic exchange, or perhaps an item of exhibit in a museum that tries to link modern identities to their origins. It *becomes* all of these things only because the speaker frames it as such, all due to her interests. Meaning thus follows framing. Without the frame (we can also call it the context, the discourse, etc.) I'm not sure if scholars would even have an object of study, for without such a frame how would the archaeologists even know where to dig or be able to distinguish among items in a pile of fragmentary and broken pieces of the past? But what frustrates me is the lack of awareness on the part of scholars who assume that the framework they used, that allowed them to piece together those fragments and fill in their inevitable gaps in the first place, is taken as self-evident—despite the inevitable use of qualifiers (e.g., perhaps, might, possibly, etc.) that, although they function as glue that fills those gaps, point also implicitly to our fragmentary knowledge (i.e., that which fills the gap can't help but draw attention to it at the same time).

But let me go back to the poem. "I look at the eyes ... I speak to the mouth, which keeps trying to speak ... I hold the cheeks ... I have no more strength," the poet writes. Notice the use of the first person pronoun and the verb: "I look," "I speak," "I hold," "I have." Scholars, I find, often try to devalue or steer away attention from their own *active* role in how *they* look, *they* speak, *they* hold, and I would say, how *they* construct their object of study. Hayden White, in his book *Tropics of Discourse: Essays in Cultural Criticism* (1985), when discussing the role of nineteenth-century historiography (which I think still applies for some twenty-first-century scholarship), writes:

> Historians continued to believe that different interpretations of the same set of events were functions of ideological distortions or of inadequate factual data. They continued to believe that if one only eschewed ideology and remained true to the facts, history would produce a knowledge as certain as anything offered by the physical sciences and as objective as a mathematical exercise.
>
> Most nineteenth-century historians did not realize that, when it is a matter of trying to deal with past facts, the crucial consideration for him who would represent them faithfully *are the notions he brings to his representation* of the ways parts relate to the whole which they comprise. *They did not realize that the facts do not speak for themselves, but that the historian speaks for them, speaks on their behalf, and fashions the fragments of the past into a whole whose integrity is—in its representation—a purely discursive one.* (White 1985: 125; emphasis added)

This sort of criticism of the way that we overlook, and thereby naturalize, our own agency, can still be applied to scholars who, today, deal with ancient material and past events. There still persists the idea that facts, often in the form of texts or material artifacts from the past, can still speak to us in the present, should we, of course, pay closer attention to their contexts, or should we retool our discourses.

Now, of course, no scholar would deny the role of discourse but, as Martin rightly observes, more-often-than-not, discourses are understood as a "lens." As he writes:

> Theory and theoretical discourses function like lenses to open vision on a particular subject matter, perhaps from a particular perspective ... Note what the metaphor implies: *reality is out there*, beyond the lens, and—despite the fact that the lens enables vision—the lens gets *between us and reality*—perhaps even distorting or coloring vision in some way. (Chapter 11, this volume)

This is similar to White's idea of "ideology." So, even when they acknowledge, for example, in their books' introductions or afterwords, the role of discourse or their role in the production of interpretations, they still proceed in the rest of the book as if they didn't make such an acknowledgment and, instead, propose "plausible" and "probable" insights of what so-and-so ancient author said, thought, or felt, as well as what the text *really* means, what some long dead audience felt. This is where my frustration can sometimes overwhelm me, because then aren't their acknowledgments in the introduction or afterword at best irrelevant, and at worst uncritical or insincere on their part? Shouldn't such an acknowledgment produce rather different kinds of scholarly works? Shouldn't it prompt us to make a shift in our work, and pose, and then answer, different kinds of questions?

When I began my Ph.D. in Canada, under the supervision of Willi Braun, and while reading scholars such as Michel Foucault, Bruce Lincoln, Jonathan Z. Smith, Hayden White, Jean-Francois Bayart, Russell McCutcheon, Aaron Hughes, etc., along with my involvement in the Culture on the Edge group (with, among others, Craig Martin), just such a shift in my approach to the past began to take shape. More specifically, I started to understand that the task of a scholar who deals with the past as being different from that of a mythmaker, in the way that Bruce Lincoln described it in his 2002 book, *Gods and Demons Priests and Scholars*. That is, while the work of mythmakers is to "revise the origin story as they like *and to reshape the world in so doing*," the task of a historian, according to Lincoln, is:

> [F]irst to recover as much of the past as possible with as much accuracy and interpretive acumen as possible; second, to acknowledge where gaps in the evidence make such recovery difficult, tentative, or even impossible; and third, to challenge those who would fill such gaps with their tendentious inventions. Among the strongest instruments of a historian's critique are doubt, hesitation, reticence, skepticism, and modesty (sincere, and neither affected nor self-deluded)—items generally lacking from the mythmaker's arsenal. (Lincoln 2002: 62)

But I also became interested in a different set of questions—not so much on rectifying meanings and better understanding ancient worlds but, rather, on seeing how meanings are *our* meanings, and how they are produced in the present, working towards an effect. Of course, this shift also entails understanding that no meaning, not even my own (such as when I suggest what some ancient tragedy might have meant) can be seen as more authoritative than any other, and thus no closer to some kind of ancient source or past reality—and I don't see this as a problem to overcome but as an acknowledgement that motivates me to ask different questions. For now I can see that my reading of some ancient play, or maybe even the words of a recent Greek poet (such as the one I used in the opening of my essay), are involved in contemporary debates and thus are ways to make evident the modern contests that we wage using yellowed and crumbling materials.

In conclusion, then, and despite the poet's lament, "I have no more strength" (which reminds me of scholars' lament for their inability to have the thing speak for itself and failures to build a coherent past from their fragmentary sources), I think that what the shift that Martin describes in such detail enables us to do is far more interesting—should we, of course, take seriously the "I," that is, our own active involvement in the production of knowledge—than being satisfied with pondering merely plausible and probable understandings of what might have really happened. For now we leave such a qualified endeavor to the mythmakers.

Vaia Touna is Assistant Professor in the Department of Religious Studies at the University of Alabama, Tuscaloosa. She is author of *Fabrications of the Greek Past: Religion, Tradition, and the Making of Modern Identities* (Brill, 2017). Her research focuses on the sociology of religion, acts of identification and social formation, as well as methodological issues concerning the study of religion and the past in general.

Notes

1   The original is as follows:

> Ξύπνησα μὲ τὸ μαρμάρινο τοῦτο κεφάλι στὰ χέρια
> ποὺ μοῦ ἐξαντλεῖ τοὺς ἀγκῶνες καὶ δὲν ξέρω ποῦ νὰ τ' ἀκουμπήσω.
> Ἔπεφτε στὸ ὄνειρο καθὼς ἔβγαινα ἀπὸ τὸ ὄνειρο
> ἔτσι ἑνώθηκε ἡ ζωή μας καὶ θὰ εἶναι πολὺ δύσκολο νὰ ξαναχωρίσει.
> Κοιτάζω τὰ μάτια. Μήτε ἀνοιχτὰ μήτε κλειστὰ
> μιλῶ στὸ στόμα ποὺ ὅλο γυρεύει νὰ μιλήσει
> κρατῶ τὰ μάγουλα ποὺ ξεπέρασαν τὸ δέρμα.
> δὲν ἔχω ἄλλη δύναμη

The English translation is my own.

2   Although the division between so-called Stone Age, Bronze Age, and Iron Age as various stages of human civilization according to historians, archaeologists, etc. can be attested worldwide, the time period when they occurred varies according to region. So even those distinctions are ways by which scholars try to frame chronological periods in order to proceed with their own studies, and which, further, result in the creation of particular modern fields within the academy that specialize in the various chronological and geographical periods that they in fact construct.

References

Borgna, Elisabetta. 2013. "Ai Limiti Della Periferia: Sulla Funzione Delle Figurine Micenee Nello Scambio Interregionale." *Archaeologia Austriaca* 97/98: 115–130.

Lincoln, Bruce. 2012. *Gods and Demons, Priests and Scholars: Critical Explorations in the History of Religions*. Chicago, IL: University of Chicago Press. https://doi.org/10.7208/chicago/9780226035161.001.0001

McCutcheon, Russell T. 2000. "Myth." In Willi Braun and Russell T. McCutcheon (eds.), *Guide to the Study of Religion*, 190–208. London: Cassell.

Merker, Gloria S. 2003. "Corinthian Terracotta Figurines: The Development of an Industry." *Corinth* 20: 233–245. https://doi.org/10.2307/4390726

Mina, Maria, Sevi Triantaphyllou, Yiannis Papadatos (eds.). 2016. *An Archaeology of Prehistoric Bodies and Embodied Identities in the Eastern Mediterranean*. Oxford: Oxbow Books.

Museum of Cycladic Art. Undated a. "The Museum: History." Retrieved from www.cycladic.gr/en/page/istoria (accessed January 28, 2018).

Museum of Cycladic Art. Undated b. "Cycladic Themes: Art." Retrieved from www.cycladic.gr/en/page/techni (accessed January 28, 2018).

Museum of Cycladic Art. Undated c. "Female Figurine (Psi Type)." Retrieved from www.cycladic.gr/en/exhibit/kp0010-ginaikio-idolio-tipou-ps (accessed January 28, 2018).

Prent, Mieke. 2009. "The Survival of the Goddess with Upraised Arms: Early Iron Age Representations and Contexts." *Hesperia Supplements* 42: 231–238.

Seferis, George. 1935. "Γιῶργος Σεφέρης—«Μυθιστόρημα»." Retrieved from http://users.uoa.gr/~nektar/arts/tributes/george_seferis/novel.htm (accessed January 25, 2018).

Touna, Vaia. 2017. *Fabrications of the Greek Past: Religion, Tradition, and the Making of Modern Identities* Leiden: Brill. https://doi.org/10.1163/9789004348615

White, Hayden. 1985. *Tropics of Discourse: Essays in Cultural Criticism*. Baltimore, MD: Johns Hopkins University Press.

Chapter 13

Serial Killers and Scholars of Religion

Martha Smith Roberts

> While there is a staggering amount of data, phenomena, of human experiences and expressions that might be characterized in one culture or another, by one criterion or another, as religious—there is no data for religion. Religion is solely the creation of the scholar's study. It is created for the scholar's analytic purposes by his imaginative acts of comparison and generalization. Religion has no existence apart from the academy. For this reason, the student of religion, and most particularly the historian of religion, must be relentlessly self-conscious. Indeed, this self-consciousness constitutes his primary expertise, his foremost object of study. (Smith 1982: xi)

Craig Martin's discussion of the realist/anti-realist debate and the ways in which discourse constructs reality (Chapter 11, this volume) is instructive in many ways. The task of thinking through the stakes of this debate, as well as my own taken-for-granted social constructionism, has been a worthwhile exercise. In crafting a response, I was interested in the creative power of discursive classification in terms of a practical application for scholars and teachers in the field of religious studies. Following the earlier papers, this discussion offers us a chance to think about not only the ways that scholars constitute their objects of study, but also the ways in which the process of constituting *religion* is also constituting *scholars* of religion. The co-construction of subject and object also has institutional implications, as scholars negotiate their places within their fields, departments, and universities. If we take seriously, as Martin asks us to, the claim that discourse is constitutive of reality, then these scholarly negotiations are important acts of world-making, acts that involve not magic, but power.[1] A particularly illustrative example of discursive construction can be found in a recent pop culture rendering of the historical development of an object and field of scholarly research a bit outside of religious studies.

The Netflix series *Mindhunter* details the origins of the serial killer in American criminology. This work of historical fiction follows two FBI agents and an academic (a psychologist) as they study the people who commit multiple murders. While our topic of religion and anti-realism may seem a far cry from television crime dramas, *Mindhunter* illustrates some of the problems we are grappling with in reference to the existence of objects, subjects, and scholars in the academic study of religion. Here we have an example of the social construction of a particular reality, the serial killer, but also the ways in which construction and discovery are conflated and confused. In the series, the behavioral sciences unit, a newly created division, is not only documenting "multiple murderers" by interviewing past killers and recording what they find, but also creating a taxonomy and language for describing their object of study and a method for utilizing the data for future cases. In one important scene near the end of season one, this process of discovery and creation is particularly well illustrated:

> The "serial killer" scene is a conference-room scene between Holden Ford, Greg Smith, Bill Tench [FBI agents], and Wendy Carr [the psychologist]. Wendy tries to come up with a term for murderers who carefully prepare for their kills versus those who go on a spontaneous rampage. Smith asks if that isn't simply *organized* versus *disorganized* killers. Wendy says, no, that refers to the process during the crime, not the pattern behind it. (Collins 2018)

The difference between the patterns, random or sequenced, poses the next classificatory debate, so they press on:

> Killers like Charles Whitman or Richard Speck, she says, take *random* victims during rapid-fire rampages, so their existing term of art "*sequence* killer" doesn't work. "Whitman was on a spree," Holden says, with Wendy and Greg backing him up. Bill agrees too, but then expresses doubt about the "sequence killer" label for a killer like Ed Kemper: "It feels too ... cadenced," he explains ... "It should feel like a long story," Holden follows up, "continually updated." "A *series* of killings," Bill replies. "*Serial?*" Holden murmurs. "*Serial murderer?*" Greg suggests. "*Serial killer?*" Bill says, refining the concept, and you can see on everyone's face that he's hit the mark. "That's better," Wendy says, impressed. "Let's see if it sticks." (Collins 2018)

The scene highlights the synchrony of creation and discovery. In the rapid-fire brainstorming session, the unit works together to make sense of their evidence—to create their taxonomy. The unit did not invent multiple murderers; there were already humans in the world committing multiple murders. But by giving language to this phenomenon they begin to discursively construct the reality of the serial killer, a term and object that takes on a life of its own in the American cultural imagination. This scene is a climactic moment in the show, and it comes after the team has collected data, created templates, developed classifications, and covered the walls in notecards full of information. The acts of discovering a pattern and creating an object of study are bound together in the discursive negotiations of the unit.

More interesting, perhaps, than their creation of an object of study—the serial killer—is the creation of the behavioral sciences unit itself. Their development as "experts" and their varying levels of discomfort with their work is a major part of the drama. The questions that arise for them are not unlike our own scholarly self-construction: How much do they identify with their object of study? What makes them experts? What is the value of their work? In a sense, the show is an apology for the work of the behavioral sciences unit. Viewers watch the team identify and classify a phenomenon, and then use their knowledge to solve cases that no one else has the tools to take on. The characters must actively prove the value of their unit: within the FBI, to local police investigations, and to society in general. In other words, *Mindhunters* underscores the anti-realist nature of disciplinary invention by illustrating the confluence of creation and discovery in both the subjects and objects of study.

While the discursive construction of religion may not be as thrilling as capturing serial killers, the principles remain the same. In relation to our own field, I wonder if we can harness the power of anti-realist critique to highlight the value of studying religion. This means interrogating the discursive construction of both religion and scholars of religion. Seeing the internal machinations of the behavioral science unit does not lead to the conclusion that they are magically creating serial killers out of the darkest recesses of their own imaginations. In fact, the fascination viewers have with the show is with the tension between discovery and creation, the suspense that accompanies the very real need to understand and classify human behavior. Some of the drama is also connected to the unit securing the resources, funding, and staff to accomplish their research. This may seem to be the most relevant parallel between the show and our own departments. What these negotiations reveal, however, are the ways in which the creation of taxonomies can construct realities on multiple levels.

The significance of the discourse of realism is the way it normalizes and naturalizes the contingent by granting it a reality outside of these power relations. It is a way of avoiding critical thinking about discursive human behaviors. To employ anti-realist strategies then requires that scholars of religion are self-reflexive about the constructed nature of their own categories, objects of study, scholarly roles, and fields of study. It means questioning the classificatory power at work in the construction of each of these levels of our field. With this in mind, we can appreciate Craig Martin's use of Edward Schiappa's suggestion that abstract "realist" definitional questions, such as "What is a wetland?" when considered outside of social and political contexts, are generally useless. Instead, it is more important to ask questions that interrogate the social and political world, such as "Whose interests are being served by this particular definition?" and "Do we identify with those interests?" (Chapter 11, this volume). These are the questions that we ask when we study the discursive construction of religion in a variety of settings, and these are the questions we must also ask outside of our research, in the classroom and university.

The former, realist, line of questioning is a type of essentializing that assumes that definitions are ends in and of themselves; they "simply," neutrally, describe reality. However, when we use our own field as an example, we know that the answer to "what is religion?" or "what is a religion?" is not at all merely descriptive. In fact, examining how one answers these questions is an exercise in the latter series of questions: Whose interests are being served by this definition? And do we identify with them? The ways in which scholars define and deploy this term "religion" creates a variety of different objects of study; it also creates a variety of scholars. Those scholars then have to defend the legitimacy of their work in different institutional contexts, further reifying the study of religion as important.

The usefulness of recognizing anti-realism at work in the construction of religion has been successfully addressed by others in the field before us. Jonathan Z. Smith repeatedly encouraged our field to recognize these power relations. In an essay entitled "'Religion' and 'Religious Studies': No Difference at All," Smith explains,

> I take it we can agree that the term "religion" is not an empirical category. It is a second-order abstraction. This changes our previous mode of discourse. While it is possible to speak of theorizing about religion in general, it is impossible to "do it" or "believe it" or be normative or descriptive with respect to it. Ways of meaningful speaking of first-order phenomena have become impossibly conjoined to a second-order abstraction resulting, at the very least, in misplaced concreteness. What meaning, then, can the word "religion" have in such a situation? (Smith 2013: 79)

He goes on to discuss some of the ways in which the study of religion is religion (ibid.: 80). This argument is essential to the understanding of the value of religious studies in the university. Religion is a second-order category used to make sense of the world. It is a mode of thinking, classifying, and constructing. This can be a confounding way to teach religion to students. Smith himself noted issues that arise for students in taking courses that focus on religion as a discursive production. However, his conclusion was that there is a value in teaching students to "become adept in the 'hermeneutics of suspicion'" (ibid.: 27). Teaching religion, not simply as an assumed or expected *content*, but also as a *form* of analysis, as a mode of critical thinking, is valuable.[2]

However, I wonder if the realist/anti-realist split can be a useful way to think about the ways in which the construction of the scholar of religion, and the negotiations of power that go along with that, are themselves evidence of the value of anti-realist theorization. In fact, I might go so far as to say that we can use anti-realist logics to construct/create/constitute not only religion, but also the value of scholars of religion in the university and in the public sphere. As my own department is currently revising our requirements for majors, I find this reflection on how scholars construct their objects of study quite timely. We sit around a table, debating the language of concentrations versus areas, and then again of what those classifications will be and contain. Should there be three or four? Which classes are in the area of "critical approaches to religion and society"? Which belong to a global or American context? Where do methods have a place in all of this? What about ethics? History? Biblical studies?

We have also found that students on our campus think that studying religion is a confessional practice. Their stereotypes have been instructive in our own debates. We know what they think we do. And it is not what we think we do. And so, my department obviously recognizes that there is a lot at stake in how we answer the question "what is religion?" Hence all of the meetings. We are all invested in the idea that we can and do construct our department, our major, our courses, their content, and thus.... religion (and I should mention, I'm in a "religion" department—not "religious studies" or "theology" or "history of religion," or a number of other possibilities). We are actively designing curriculum aimed at de-naturalizing our students' understanding of religion. In this sense it is a thoroughly anti-realist endeavor.

The central question at work here is not just "What is religion?" but, of course, "Whose interests are being served?" As we classify and categorize our courses' form and content, we are also classifying ourselves. We are creating a space in the university for our work as legitimate and important scholarship. This is also the creative power of classification. These, to quote Martin, "matrices of individuation and claims about objects are essentially and indefinitely revisable" as "the openness to temporality simultaneously makes the closure of substruction theoretically impossible" (Chapter 11, this volume). As language constructs the referents of religion, so it constructs the referents of scholars of religion. And both of these are indefinitely revisable. My department is in a moment of conscious revision.

There are other practical problems as well: We want to draw in more majors. We want to keep our tenure lines. We want continued institutional support. And our claims as scholars, that what we do is important and needs to continue, is bound to the realist/anti-realist debate in multiple ways. Not least of which is that we claim that a "religion" major will learn not just "what religion is," but instead, the ways in which the answer to that definitional question organizes human worlds. And the ability to go beyond a search for realist definitions and see instead how realism naturalizes and normalizes particular constructions of reality—that—is an infinitely transferable skill set. As our field struggles to perpetuate itself in many ways: not enough jobs, low funding for graduate students, few majors, overall decline in humanities, rise in contingent labor, etc., how do we show our relevance? Can we use anti-realist logics to constitute our disciplinary value? Russell McCutcheon addresses this in *Critics Not Caretakers*, where he highlights that the work of the field is critical thinking:

> Scholarship in public universities entails pushing beyond mere description of subjective self-disclosures and reports on this or that experience, as if these experiences somehow predate the sociohistorical world; scholarship requires one to generate theories of human minds and societies, to engage in cross-cultural comparison of the human doings that our theories help us to see as significant, to contextualize our subjects' reports on their doings within the larger settings that make both the doings and their reports possible and meaningful in the first place, and then to explain *why* just these similarities or just those differences exist between various human communities, their doings, and their self-perceptions. (McCutcheon 2001: 8)

Rather than argue that we study religion because religion is important, can we argue that we study how, why, and to whom religions are important? Can we show our students and administrations that religion is not a "real" (be it a supernatural or material) object that scholars simply describe and categorize and that is inherently worthwhile ... but instead that religion is a way of thinking about—and challenging—power and normativity? Can we describe our work in a way that recognizes an "openness" and "infinite revisability" that draws upon a longer tradition of critical analysis—"religion" as form, not just content? (And as this volume's main chapters argue, this means critiquing our own construction of traditions as well; denaturalizing our own individuations as best we can). If we can use anti-realism in this way, if we can show, as Craig Martin argues, that our work is not a linguistic Berkeleyanism (nothing outside text) or linguistic dualism (no direct access between language and object), that it is not a "radical disjuncture from social reality," but rather, that it is an examination of the social and linguistic in multiple realities, then, I think, we constitute religion and scholars of religion as valuable to society.

A look back to the founding of many religious studies departments reveals that this has not been the standard of the field. Lucia Hulsether's analysis of the pluralist framework that has created and maintained the field since the mid-twentieth century is telling. As she highlights the move away from theology and toward pluralism, we might all recognize what has come to be a paradigmatic way of describing the value of religious studies in the university. Theology fell out of vogue, but pluralism offered a language of "cross cultural encounter" and "sympathetic dialogue" that administrators could understand and embrace (Hulsether 2018). This may sound like progress, but her work is a cautionary tale about the ways in which the framework of pluralism reproduces a study of religion that is uncritical of the power relations at work in its discursive production, in essence, the very charges leveled at theology are also at work in pluralism. Relying on a pluralist legitimation for the value of religious studies merely replicates the reification of religion as an object of study, with a notable expansion from one tradition to many, solidifying the world religions paradigm as the core of the field.[3]

As we attempt to show the value of an academic study of religion, an anti-realist discourse analysis of the field, scholars, and objects of study can help us to understand the various ways that this project has been undertaken in the past and offer possibilities for the future. Diversity, inclusion, and pluralism have in many cases become empty signifiers of liberal and progressive values; can we still claim them as our reason for existence? Arguing that a religion department will help the university understand (and perhaps even promote) diversity and pluralism simply reifies the ideas of diversity and pluralism. Again, anti-realism challenges scholars to deconstruct these terms, to ask whose interests they serve. Moving forward, we cannot rely on these concepts to show the value of our work, but we can analyze these concepts to show the value of our work. In my own classes, I ask students to critically analyze both diversity and pluralism. To examine their historical contexts, the changes over time, and the ways in which our contemporary definitions have become normative prescriptions for how religions should exist together in the American context. We analyze these concepts not as "real," but as discursive constructions that emerged out of struggles for power. I am not teaching my students pluralism; I am teaching them about pluralism. And with that knowledge, they are better equipped to answer the challenges of a world full of diverse interpretations of reality; they are better equipped to deal with diversity and pluralism because they can see them as claims to power.

Here I want to return to Craig Martin's Facebook friend, who argued that a one-armed man could not generate limbs by speaking them into existence, an undeniable fact that proved conclusively that discourse does not construct reality. Their claim here reduces anti-realism to magical thinking that has no real-world value because it does not regenerate body parts out of thin air. And they are right about the second part; it does not. However, that is exactly the magic, the creative power, of social construction. Discourse does create bodies, but it does not require the power of cell regeneration. So, is it real? Yes, but not the way they think. Because "religion" is not always a mid-sized object (an arm, the table), it requires more complicated realist/anti-realist theorizing. However, this makes it an even more useful tool for thinking though the real-world effects of anti-realism, or, the ways in which the social construction of reality is important in the creation and maintenance of the material world and the scholars that inhabit it. As my department is repackaging and re-describing "religion," we are attempting to show that there is a value in the study of religion that is not simply about proving that a stable, essential religion exists in the world, nor is it about getting all of the diverse religions to accept each other. We are creating scholars (ourselves and our students) who not only describe and classify a reality, but who also analyze what is at stake in the way a variety of discourses construct realities.

Craig Martin's call for serious attention to anti-realist claims and their value in our scholarship can serve as a baseline for our own projects. Isn't anti-realism, as a form of rigorous analysis of the power relations involved in making the contingent non-contingent, exactly what we want to be doing? If so, I ask, how can we make this clear in a department mission statement and learning objectives at a SLAC? Or, in the set of "Religious Literacy Guidelines for College Students" which the AAR is currently designing? Must we state that students should be able to "discern, describe, and distinguish" religion in the world? Perhaps we take a step back from these essentialist frames and find ways to implement anti-realism into the institutional framework of the study of religion. What that looks like, and what its practical implications will be is still open; it is, of course, infinitely revisable. Anti-realism creates the possibility for the academic study of religion to self-reflexively create value that can perpetuate the field.

To conclude, I want to return to *Mindhunter*'s behavioral sciences unit, actively creating and classifying serial killers in the 1970s. The series not only reveals the creative possibilities of discursive construction, it also contains a cautionary tale. We must be mindful of the dangers of realism that are the very context for the show. In proving their value as a unit, the need for their existence, their classificatory work begins to move into the realm of the real. Not only do others start to agree with their classifications, the term they coin begins "to stick" in ways they did not anticipate. They begin to believe that "serial killer" not only describes a taxonomy of behavior, but also an inherent, essential human identity that they can now find in the world. Creation and discovery are blurred. Members of the group start to reify the concept themselves, destroying the lives of people who they assume to be serial killers. Their category becomes a mode of power. The lesson that serial killers have for religion then, is the danger in normalizing our own categories, of granting ourselves the ability to discover our creations in the real world, existing somehow apart from the negotiations of their construction.

Martha Smith Roberts is Assistant Professor of Religion at Denison University. Her primary research is a critical analysis of post-racial and post-ethnic theories of American religious pluralism. Roberts is also working on a co-authored manuscript analyzing the various spiritualities emerging within the hula hooping subculture. She is the Executive Secretary and Treasurer for the North American Association for the Study of Religion, and she also serves on the Board of Directors for the Institute for Diversity and Civic Life in Austin, Texas.

Notes

1. Craig Martin's chapter delves into the foundational work of postmodern philosophy, including Derrida, Husserl, and Hegel, in line with his aim of taking these anti-realists seriously. Martin's own introductory textbook illustrates some of the ways in which these theories can be put into pedagogical practice in the field, and the work of Bruce Lincoln, Tomoko Masuzawa, Russell McCutcheon, and Jonathan Z. Smith similarly underpin my discussion. See Lincoln (2000, 2014), Masuzawa (2005), Martin (2017), McCutcheon (2007, 2014), and Smith (2004).
2. A recent example of this can be found on the Practicum Religion Blog. In a post titled "Teaching Discourse Analysis as a Practical Tool" Tenzan Eaghll discusses how centering critique and discourse analysis in a course can work for graduate students. In terms of undergraduate work, Russell McCutcheon discusses a pedagogical application in which students are required to dramatize the discursive issues of the field in videos based on the critical book, *Religion in 5 Minutes*. See Eaghll (2018), McCutcheon (2018), and Hughes and McCutcheon (2017).
3. This statement can be further elucidated by work on the nature of the world religions paradigm. See Masuzawa (2005), Cotter and Robertson (2016), and Owen (2011).

References

Collins, Sean T. 2018. "The 'Serial Killer' Is Born in a *Mindhunter* That Shows the Team at Their Best—and Worst." Retrieved from www.avclub.com/the-serial-killer-is-born-in-a-mindhunter-that-shows-1819785689 (accessed February 2, 2018).

Cotter, Christopher R., and David G. Robertson (eds.). 2016. *After World Religions: Reconstructing Religious Studies*. New York: Routledge. https://doi.org/10.4324/9781315688046

Eaghll, Tenzan. 2018. "Teaching Discourse Analysis as a Practical Tool." Retrieved from http://practicumreligionblo.blogspot.com/2018/02/teaching-discourse-analysis-as.html (accessed February 5, 2018).

Hughes, Aaron, and Russell T. McCutcheon (eds.). 2017. *Religion in Five Minutes*. Bristol: Equinox Publishing.

Hulsether, Lucia. 2018. "The Grammar of Racism: Religious Pluralism and the Birth of the Interdisciplines." *Journal of the American Academy of Religion* 86(1): 1–41. https://doi.org/10.1093/jaarel/lfx049

Lincoln, Bruce. 2000. *Theorizing Myth: Narrative, Ideology, and Scholarship*. Chicago, IL: University of Chicago Press.

Lincoln, Bruce. 2014. *Discourse and the Construction of Society: Comparative Studies of Myth, Ritual, and Classification*, 2nd edition. New York: Oxford University Press. https://doi.org/10.1093/acprof:oso/9780199372362.001.0001

Martin, Craig. 2017. *A Critical Introduction to the Study of Religion*, 2nd edition. New York: Routledge. https://doi.org/10.4324/9781315474410

Masuzawa, Tomoko. 2005. *The Invention of World Religions: Or, How European Universalism was Preserved in the Language of Pluralism*. Chicago, IL: University of Chicago Press. https://doi.org/10.7208/chicago/9780226922621.001.0001

McCutcheon, Russell T. 2001. *Critics Not Caretakers: Redescribing the Public Study of Religion*. Albany, NY: State University of New York Press.

McCutcheon, Russell T. 2007. *Studying Religion: An Introduction*. New York: Routledge.

McCutcheon, Russell T. 2014. *Religion and the Domestication of Dissent: Or, How to Live in a Less Than Perfect Nation*. New York: Routledge.

McCutcheon, Russell T. 2018. "Lights, Camera, Action." Retrieved from http://practicumreligionblog.blogspot.com/2017/12/lights-camera-action_11.html (accessed February 9, 2018).

Owen, Suzanne. 2011. "The World Religions Paradigm: Time for a Change." *Arts & Humanities in Higher Education* 10(3): 253–268. https://doi.org/10.1177/1474022211408038

Smith, Jonathan Z. 1982. *Imagining Religion: From Babylon to Jonestown*. Chicago, IL: University of Chicago Press.

Smith, Jonathan Z. 2004. *Relating Religion: Essays in the Study of Religion*. Chicago, IL: University of Chicago Press.

Smith, Jonathan Z. 2013. "'Religion' and 'Religious Studies': No Difference at All." In Christopher I. Lehrich (ed.), *On Teaching Religion*, 77–90. New York: Oxford University Press. https://doi.org/10.1093/acprof:osobl/9780199944293.003.0009

Chapter 14

Caffeinated and Half-baked Realities: Religion as the Opium of the Scholar

Jason W. M. Ellsworth

In his essay, Craig Martin (Chapter 11, this volume) notes that he has painstakingly read and digested some of the most difficult writings of a number of theorists. My response comes from a place where I am situated in that struggle as well, developing my own thoughts—including the response here which is a representation of some of my current thinking on the subject matter. Martin's use of the word "digesting" is particularly relevant to my interest in food studies that takes up much of my current research. In the following chapter I open with a discussion on food labels—or more specifically claims such as fair trade. This type of terminology is meant to persuade consumers that the food they are buying and consuming is in some manner socially just. However, as can be seen in many studies on tea and coffee, fair trade is not a homogeneous label, but rather is a contested name that can be manipulated in bureaucratic fashions for the purpose of capitalist accumulation. I use this as a segue into Martin's work on anti-realism, and particularly my own interest in the study of religion. I argue that religion is the opium of the scholar, where religion as a category does not describe the world, but instead acts like opium to hide underlying symptoms in society and conceals the scholar's involvement in the very construction of the category. For the scholar, when "religion" is deployed as a descriptive tool, it obscures the process wherein the scholar produces the very objects of study via a discourse. "Religion" hides the grounds upon which a whole enterprise of comparative scholarship is built upon. I end with a few notes on how commodity chain studies, such as those on fair trade, might offer insight on how one might approach the study of "religion."

Caffeinated and Half-baked Realities

Grocery store shelves are lined with products adorning labels such as fair trade, organic, sustainable, and local. These labels are often meant to indicate processes whereby food is produced in an ethically sourced manner. Compared to products from what are considered conventional markets, fair trade products are meant to guarantee greater social justice for small scale farmers around the world (such as higher income and better working conditions). It is a movement and certification process meant to make trade fairer for farmers and workers. Similarly, organic labels are meant to act as the benchmark for the most environmentally safe produced products, compared to those without the certification. In a globalized food economy, these symbols, logos, and labels are important to consumers who hope to understand where their food comes from and make informed decisions on their food choices. Yet, as has been shown by many, these terms can be misleading and contradict the very processes that produced the products (Besky 2014; Roseberry 1996; Collins 2000; Fischer and Benson 2006; Lyon 2009; Hetherington 2013; Wilk 2008). In this sense, food labels do not so much tell us about the product, but rather act as a cloak that hides the process of production—constructing romantic images of the local, traditional, and authentic (Pratt 2008). Labels such as organic, fair trade, or local do not convey which activist, corporate, or political agendas are being carried out (ibid.: 54).

The caffeinated beverages of coffee and tea are two long time focuses of food studies, dating back to the work of Sidney W. Mintz (1985). Mintz's work examines the growth and evolution of sugar as a single food (category and commodity) from an exotic upper-class commodity to a common substance found on every table in Europe. One of the most commonly cited works in the anthropology of food, Mintz focuses on food as a social substance that illuminates how people define both themselves and others. By linking sugar to aspects of slavery, flavoring, global movement, aspects of privilege, production, and consumption, Mintz displays how the meaning of sugar (and the meaning it gave over time) changed depending on the context. In this sense, Mintz explains how one deals with natural environments is a social act, symbolically constructing universes (ibid.: 8). It is a study of how power relations are exercised:

> The first sweetened cup of hot tea to be drunk by an English worker was a significant historical event, because it prefigured the transformation of an entire society, a total remaking of its economic and social basis. We must struggle to understand fully the consequences of that and kindred events for upon them was erected an entirely different conception of the relationship between producers and consumers, of the meaning of work, of the definition of self, of the nature of things. What commodities are, and what commodities mean, would thereafter be forever different. And for that same reason, what persons are, and what being a person means, changed accordingly. In understanding the relationship between commodity and person, we unearth anew the history of ourselves. (Mintz 1985: 214)

Mintz (1985, 1996) deploys a political economy approach, centering on the structural powers that create the food supply and dictate consumer choices. This point is drawn on by many in the study of other food commodities such as tea, coffee, broccoli, grapes, soy, and other cuisines around the world (Besky 2014; Roseberry 1996; Collins 2000; Fitting 2011; Fischer and Benson 2006; Lyon 2009; Hetherington 2013; Wilk 2008).

Recent studies on fair trade goods build on Mintz, asking what is "fair trade" and whom does it benefit? Who defines the terms of fair trade? Can it ever truly be an alternative commodity network with its own marketplace, especially if it continues to be systematically entrenched in the neoliberal paradigm of free market economics that currently dominates trade across the globe? This is the paradox of fair trade: it is an alternative market process and at the same time a niche market within capitalist or neoliberal free trade models.

William Roseberry (1996: 763) notes that coffee is much like wine, beer, or cheese where one can cultivate tastes and identify with particular places via consumption. He points out that "specialty coffees are supposed to taste better than mass-market coffees" and thus why those typical mass-market coffees (such as Maxwell House) have joined the "speciality" trend (ibid.: 762). However, specialty coffees were originally meant to be new modes of purchasing that challenged the coffee giants (such as being able to buy from small distributers that worked more closely with the peasant farmers that produced the beans) (ibid.: 763). Roseberry points to a constructed image of the past as a time of genuine coffee production that today is being used to market coffee to those looking for a purer coffee (i.e. natural, whole, fresh) (ibid.: 764).

Roseberry historicizes coffee in the United States from an elite expensive beverage, to the inexpensive drink of the working class and then to a segmented market that contains a specialty niche that sells both to the elite and the working class (thus marketing to various class and generational segments). In this vein "coffee is the beverage of US capitalism" and coffee can provide like other commodities "a window through which we can view a range of relationships and social transformations" (ibid.: 770). The process of coffee consumption is a structured set of relationships whereby the producer can conceal the alienated labor by casting the illusion that the consumer knows the full scope of the products they are buying. It is the free market model that leads to the standardization of gourmet (specialty) coffee as political commodity (ibid.: 774).

The specialty tea and coffee markets are particularly partial to using the labels fair trade and sustainable. It infuses food with a sense of social justice and solidarity with workers to pitch products to consumers. Sarah Besky's *The Darjeeling Distinction: Labor and Justice on Fair-Trade Tea Plantations in India* (2014) is one example that examines the manufactured capitalist extraction of Darjeeling tea as a luxury beverage about taste and value within place, labor, its products, and the production consumption paradigm through a food system perspective. Besky questions the extent that such certification systems actually help the laborer or small farms. Many of the fair trade plantations are hard to imagine as "small" and are owned by larger multinational corporations rather than what might be conceived of as small-scale peasant farmers. The irony is that some of the most expensive tea is produced by the tea industry's "worst-paid workers" (ibid.: 15). Theoretically, Besky builds on Bourdieu and Marx, examining the realms of taste, value, social relations and the political in connection to how actors (tea plantation laborers) view moral and economic markets (ibid.: 15–16). Besky points out how "commodities mask the (unjust) conditions of their own production" and that what masquerades as justice does not challenge market capitalism (ibid.: 20). The very geographical imaginary of where Darjeeling tea is produced is also a vast distance from where it is consumed, *hiding* both how and by whom the tea was produced. Besky shows how a specific higher quality taste is not inherent in itself but a constructed notion, that is predicated on the exotic image of the tea from a distant land, the moral high ground built up in its certification, and the very distance from the production that can help sustain that image by not showing the truth of the laborer.

Another helpful study is Daniel Jaffee's work that systematically examines the effects of fair trade on the coffee growing region of Oaxaca, Mexico. His work explores coffee beans as one product that is part of "larger ongoing commodity crises that have ravaged large sectors of peasant agriculture in the global south" (Jaffee 2014: xxi). Jaffee's work in the end, is to understand how peasant coffee producers experience fair trade and the tangible benefits it brings to the farmers via economic well-being, food security, access to education, ecological benefits and the need for supplemental income (ibid.: 3). While fair trade is often compared to free trade in an oppositional manner, Jaffee also presents fair trade as a "paradox" within itself for it "utilizes the mechanism of the very markets that have generated" injustices that have hurt farmers worldwide (ibid.: 1). In a sense, it is a "hybrid" model that is both a social movement and an alternative market within the large market (ibid.). Fair trade in large part cuts out many of the intermediaries of the commodity chain and "signifies that products come from democratically organized farmer or artisan cooperatives" (ibid.). While fair trade may deliver benefits to the participants, the various actors (from producers to retailers) have very different notions on what essentially is the nature and purpose of fair trade.

Fair trade emphasizes factors other than price to make sure producers have a "fair" life. However, it has been shown that fair trade can be manipulated by corporate groups such as Starbucks and Procter & Gamble who see fair trade as a "lucrative niche market" (Jaffee 2014: 4). It begs the question: whose fair trade? Who decides on what is "fair," especially when some commodities bearing the fair trade logo focus more on meeting certification standards, ignoring the actual social aspects of production (particularly labor) that it purports to protect. In one study on commodities and coffee, Christopher M. Bacon (2010: 112) states, "Fair Trade governance, like that of other third-party sustainability certification programmes, continues to be a deeply contested, socially embedded process, subject to an array of political economic constraints, personal convictions and path-dependent contingencies." And, as Lyon and Moberg (2010: 7) note, rather than creating an alternative marketplace, fair trade commodities receive legitimacy through their certification that presents them as socially just products. This is the "paradox" of creating a supposed socially just commodity within the neoliberal (free market) economy. In effect, corporations are able to create the illusion of "socially just" products under the banner of fair trade to increase profits. Yet "free trade" is difficult to point to, as the label is contested. So, while it can be argued fair trade may offer some form of "fairness," it can also be seen as being diminished within the free market model—as prices and profits of corporations have dominated the process. This politics of free trade and free market economics argues for an unregulated system; corporations are able to bend the fair-trade concept to their needs, rather than the laborer.

Elizabeth Fitting's (2011) work in Mexico, which focuses on the uncertainty faced by small-scale maize producers within an intensified neoliberal regime in respect to genetically modified corn, offers some insight. While not focused on fair trade, a note by Fitting is rather relevant:

> Theses narratives about the Mexican countryside are not simply words and ideas; they are an inherent part of social practice and have material effects in the world. There is power in the process of naming. The ways policy makers and experts view and describe the countryside, its problems and remedies, make their way into policy and state practices, although these policies are implemented and received in uneven and unintended ways. (Fitting 2011: 13)

The take away—there is power in naming and there are material consequences within this process. When we name things, we construct models of reality and turn names into things. Power derives here in the ability to neatly package food with "ethical" sounding food labels, while hiding or concealing the actual mode of production. Fair trade and organic are not things easy to point to as a stuff or object in the world, but rather are socially constructed discourses with much at stake. The social constructionist line of critique here is not meant to make a positive or negative stance on fair trade, but rather show that not all products labeled fair trade are equivalent—instead they are variable. Even with certification processes in place variability takes place. The food studies previously mentioned go beyond the label and may offer insight into how one might go about approaching other socially constructed categories such as "religion."

Religion is the Opium of the Scholar

Once, in a lecture at Lafayette College, British primatologist, ethologist and anthropologist Jane Goodall described how another primatologist was trying to understand how a chimpanzee's mind works. To quote Goodall:

> Some of the signing chimps love to draw and paint. One particular young chimp, I think she was about 5 years old. Normally she did very complex drawings or paintings, but this time, she just made a line like this. Her teacher handed it back and said, "Finish it." She said, "Finished." The teacher asked her what it was, and she said, "A ball." Now what has she drawn? She's drawn the movement of a ball. That tells you something about what they're thinking. It's amazing. (Goodall 2013)

Now linguistically one may simply say that there is a linguistic translation or interpretation that is at issue here. However, I would like to take it as stated—in this sense—a ball is both the material elements (the stuff) and the movements—and perhaps at the same time neither. The subjective perception of the primatologist and the chimpanzee offer varying versions of what or how a ball is defined—particularly at different points of time.

Returning to the essay to which I am responding, a "ball" falls within the range of objects Craig Martin discusses as mid-sized objects—the single fixed unchanging object that exists as a thing-in-itself (Chapter 11, this volume). However, there is a constant shifting of the phenomenological consciousness of the object. Martin's chapter dives theoretically deeper into this, but I am left with a few questions—what is a specific thing (material or conceived), who decides, and what does the story about the above ball really tell us? Perhaps the simple take away is that the primatologist and the chimpanzee have two different notions of how to represent a ball. But I would be more inclined to agree with Martin's contention that scholars produce the objects we study via discourse. And, since the primatologist is telling the story, we are only left with that story. It thus tells me more about the primatologist who at first looks for a singular solid answer in how a ball is represented. The answer the primatologist looks for is not "out there" in the world waiting to be discovered, but rather is already pre-conceived in the very phenomenological notion of what constitutes a ball. Or as Martin notes "there are no things for us without their representation" and that the representation of these objects arise prior to the object itself (there are no things for us).

Marx's commodity fetishism allows us to consider mid-sized objects in relation to the realist and anti-realist notion of material objects.[1] We might consider Marx's examination of the commodity, such as a table, where the table can have three values or sets of social relations—use value, labor value, and exchange value. Marx notes, "as [the table] emerges as a commodity, it changes into a thing which transcends sensuousness" (Marx 1990: 163-164). The table becomes something outside the producer... "it is nothing but the definite social relation between men themselves which assumes here, for them, the fantastic form of a relation between things" (ibid.: 165). Marx endeavors to point to commodities not as things, but some form representative of values. Marx grounds the commodity in the social relations of social necessary labor time (see also Harvey 2010). The transcendent and magical language that Marx uses to describe the commodity and the economic free markets is something I find particularly useful (see Graeber 2001). However, one could argue that Marx is also making equally magical moves to state his own case—in a way to delegitimize the supply and demand models—to naturalize Marx's own theory of labor value. How then does one get beyond this magical discourse?

Slavoj Žižek (2001) has a way of describing commodity fetishism or fetishism in a manner that sees the fetish as a lie, something that hides the symptom. The symptom is not cured by the fetish: "that is to say, symptom is the exception which disturbs the surface of the false appearance, the point at which the repressed truth erupts, while fetish is the embodiment of the Lie which enables us to sustain the unbearable truth" (ibid.). Perhaps in some way the fetish is needed for the symptom to continue on without actually being corrected—the two are intertwined. The lie and symptom are connected. This is reminiscent of Marx's notion that religion is the opium of the people:

> The basis of irreligious criticism is this: Man makes religion, religion does not make man. Religion is, indeed, the self-consciousness and self-awareness so long as he has not found himself or has lost himself again. But man is not an abstract being, squatting outside the world. Man is the human world, the state, society. This state, this society, produce religion which is an inverted world consciousness,

> because they are an inverted world. Religion is the general theory of this world, its encyclopedic compendium, its logic in popular form, its spiritual point d'honneur, its enthusiasm, its moral sanction, its solemn complement, its general basis of consolation and justification. It is the fantastic realization of the human being inasmuch as the human being possesses no true reality. The struggle against religion is, therefore, indirectly a struggle against that world whose spiritual aroma is religion.
>
> Religious suffering is, at one and the same time, the expression of real suffering and a protest against real suffering. Religion is the sigh of the oppressed creature, the heart of a heartless world, and the soul of soulless conditions. It is the opium of the people. (Marx and Engels 1978: 54)

I do not know if it is possible to uncover the full extent of what Marx truly "meant"—it goes beyond the text and many argue about the specifics. However, the one common interpretation is that opium was in Marx's time a pain reliever. Opium concealed the suffering that people endured. On the surface, Marx uses the colloquial sense of the term religion, to mean such things as Christianity. If Marx was to be more specific, it could be said that Christianity is the opium that relieves the suffering people endure under capitalism. However, suffering is not removed but hidden. Opium constructs a different "reality" for people. So, what, then, happens if we take opium simply as something that conceals or hides something else—constructing a different or new reality?

The scholar can be viewed as the starting point of the construction of "religion," and in this construction, the scholar conceals the thing she or he looks to study. "Religion" as an object of study cannot be known as a thing in itself. It is the discourse surrounding this construction that makes an interesting place of inquiry. As stated by Jonathan Z. Smith:

> But man, more precisely western man, has only had the last few centuries in which to imagine religion. It is this act of second order, reflective imagination which must be the central preoccupation of any student of religion. That is to say, while there is a staggering amount of data, of phenomena, of human experiences and expressions that might be characterized in one culture or another, by one criterion or another, as religious—there is no data for religion. Religion is solely the creation of the scholar's study. It is created for the scholar's analytic purposes by his imaginative acts of comparison and generalization. Religion has no independent existence apart from the academy. For this reason, the student of religion, and most particularly the historian of religion, must be relentlessly self-conscious. Indeed, this self-consciousness constitutes his primary expertise, his foremost object of study. (Smith 1982: xi)

If the scholar creates "religion"—constructs a thing—concealing something else, is *religion the opium of the scholar*? In this sense, religion is both created for and by the scholar. Today most people do not use opium as they once did; other pain relievers or concealers sometimes are used to help describe the situation such as Tylenol, so maybe today it should be religion is the Tylenol of the scholar—but that is another matter. What is concealed beyond these objects, or things, are actually processes, in constant flux, never really things within themselves—they are without an essential element.

In *Capitalizing Religion*, Martin (2014: 6) argues that "the ideology of individualism does not make people more individualistic, but rather masks the extent to which "individuals" are collectively constituted." I would argue that the notion of "religion" for the scholar is similar. The scholar constructs religion as a tidy box for comparative use for the scholar. Within a discourse, "religion" is one that produces realities, masks the social relations taking place, and conceals the scholar's involvement. It ends up being a one-dimensional ball, that only tells us about what the scholar sees in a phenomenological sense in the mind.

This is where I find the story of the chimp helpful in understanding the position of the scholar—and perhaps the chimp can help us understand a ball as not one essential thing but something constantly in motion—moving—the object is made up of more than our rigid definitions. So while religion is the opium of the scholar, a constructed category—object or thing—concealing the bundles of relationships, it should be noted that these constructions by the scholar place the scholar themselves into the very field, making them often part and parcel of the thing itself they are wishing to study or explain—part of the fetish, and thus part of the motion and processes they look to explain. In part then, for the scholar, "religion" as opium hides or conceals the very scholar themselves and their involvement in the very process.

Food for Thought on "Religion"

If religion is the opium of the scholar, concealing what is beneath and at the same time constructing new realities—a similar methodology that is used in commodity studies may be helpful for uncovering the underlying bundles of relations to understand what is at stake. It is about getting beyond the label to understand the web of relations, discourses, power dynamics, and material consequences of such naming processes.

The question might now be how to approach or untangle this ball? Perhaps it is similar to unveiling the contradictory aspects of food process that are often hidden beneath the labels and marketing tactics of corporations. Studies of global commodity chains can illuminate how unequal relations of power are entangled in commodity production. Many of the fair-trade studies I touched on earlier in this chapter utilize a commodity chain following methodology to help expose the hidden aspects of a commodity. Rather than taking fair trade as a given, the studies unveil the contradictory aspects of food production that are often hidden beneath the labels and marketing tactics of corporations. At the same time, studies of global commodity chains can illuminate how unequal relations of power are entangled in commodity production. For as Wolf (1982) shows there is power in naming things, "concepts like 'nation,' 'society,' and 'culture' name bits and threaten to turn names into things. Only by understanding these names as bundles of relationships, and by placing them back into the field from which they were abstracted, can we hope to avoid misleading inferences and increase our share of understanding" (ibid.: 5). In a similar vein, one must be wary that terms such as fair trade or organic are not treated as things, but rather view these labels as bundles of relationships. Relationships built on varying power dynamics where the stakes can be high for many involved. Power derives here in the ability to neatly package food with "ethical" sounding food labels, while hiding the actual mode of food production (that may include exploitive practices) and the social construction of fair trade discourse.

When food study scholars examine fair trade, they do not only look at the label or the food stuff, but at how the very idea of fair trade is socially constructed for particular agendas. My intention here is to lay out a thorough methodology, it is to simply point out that for those of us that study "religion" and other social constructions, commodity chain studies may offer an interesting approach to the subject matter moving forward to uncover how "religion" is produced.

Jason W. M. Ellsworth is a doctoral candidate in the Sociology and Social Anthropology Department at Dalhousie University and is a Sessional Lecturer at the University of Prince Edward Island in both the Religious Studies and Sociology and Anthropology Departments. His research interests include the anthropology and sociology of religion, Buddhism in North America, food studies, marketing, economy, and transnationalism.

Note

1 This points in this paragraph were inspired by Craig Martin's first draft of his chapter presented at the NAASR meetings in 2017 in Boston, where he addressed mid-sized objects in relation to the realist and anti-realist notion of material objects via the commodity fetishism of Marx.

References

Bacon, Christopher M. 2010. "Who Decides What is Fair in Fair Trade? The Agri-environmental Governance of Standards, Access, and Price." *Journal of Peasant Studies* 37(1): 111–147. https://doi.org/10.1080/03066150903498796

Besky, Sarah. 2013. *The Darjeeling Distinction: Labor and Justice on Fair-Trade Tea Plantations in India*. Berkeley, CA: University of California Press.

Collins, Jane L. 2000. "Tracing Social Relations in Commodity Chains: The Case of Grapes in Brazil." In A. Haugerud, P. Little and P. Stone (eds.), *Commodities and Globalization: Anthropological Perspectives*, 97–109. New York: Rowman & Littlefield.

Fischer, Edward F., and Peter Benson. 2006. *Broccoli and Desire: Global Connections and Maya Struggles in Postwar Guatemala*. Stanford, CA: Stanford University Press.

Fitting, Elizabeth. 2011. *The Struggle for Maize: Campesinos, Workers, and Transgenic Corn in the Mexican Countryside*. Durham, NC: Duke University Press. https://doi.org/10.1215/9780822393863

Goodall, Jane. 2013. "Thomas Roy and Lura Forrest Jones Visiting Lecture for 2012–13 at Lafayette College: Transcript of Jane Goodall's Speech and Q&A Session." Retrieved from https://news.lafayette.edu/2013/05/08/transcript-of-jane-goodalls-speech-and-qa-session.

Graeber, David. 2001. *Toward an Anthropological Theory of Value: The False Coin of Our Own Dreams*. New York: Palgrave. https://doi.org/10.1057/9780312299064
Harvey, David. 2010. *A Companion to Marx's Capital*. London: Verso.
Hetherington, Kregg. 2013. "Beans Before the Law: Knowledge Practices, Responsibility, and the Paraguayan Soy Boom." *Cultural Anthropology* 21(1): 65–85. https://doi.org/10.1111/j.1548-1360.2012.01173.x
Jaffee, Daniel. 2014. *Brewing Justice: Fair Trade Coffee, Sustainability and Survival*, revised edition. Oakland, CA: University of California Press.
Lyon, Sarah. 2009. "'What Good Will Two More Trees Do?' The Political Economy of Sustainable Coffee Certification, Local Livelihoods and Identities." *Landscape Research* 34(2): 223–240. https://doi.org/10.1080/01426390802390673
Lyon, Sarah, and Mark Moberg. 2010. *Fair Trade and Social Justice: Global Ethnographies*. New York: New York University Press. https://doi.org/10.18574/nyu/9780814796207.001.0001
Martin, Craig. 2014. *Capitalizing Religion: Ideology and the Opiate of the Bourgeoisie*. New York: Bloomsbury.
Marx, Karl. 1990. *Capital*, vol. 1, trans. Ben Fowkes. New York: Penguin.
Marx, Karl, and Friedrich Engels. 1978. *The Marx-Engels Reader*, 2nd edition, ed. Robert C. Tucker. New York: W. W. Norton & Company.
Mintz, Sidney. 1985. *Sweetness and Power: The Place of Sugar in Modern History*. New York: Penguin Books.
Mintz, Sidney. 1996. *Tasting Food, Tasting Freedom: Excursions into Eating, Culture, and the Past*. Boston, MA: Beacon Press.
Pratt, Jeffrey. 2008. "Food Values: The local and the Authentic." In Geert De Neve, Peter Luetchford, Jeffrey Pratt, and Donald C. Wood (eds.), *Hidden Hands in the Market: Ethnographies of Fair Trade, Ethical Consumption, and Corporate Social Responsibility*, 53–70. Bingley: Emerald JAI. https://doi.org/10.1016/S0190-1281(08)28003-0
Roseberry, William. 1996. "The Rise of Yuppie Coffee and the Reimagination of Class in the United States." *American Anthropologist* 94(4): 762–775. https://doi.org/10.1525/aa.1996.98.4.02a00070
Smith, Jonathan Z. 1982. *Imagining Religion: From Babylon to Jonestown*. Chicago, IL: Chicago University Press.
Wilk, Richard. 2008. "'Real Belizean Food': Building Local Identity in the Transnational Caribbean." *American Anthropologist* 101(2): 244–255. https://doi.org/10.1525/aa.1999.101.2.244
Wolf, Eric. 1982. *Europe and the People without History*. Berkeley, CA: University of California Press.
Žižek, Slavoj. 2001. "Self-deceptions: On Being Tolerant and Smug." *Die Gazette* (August 27). Retrieved from www.lacan.com/zizek-self.htm.

Chapter 15

On the Seminal Adventure of the Trace

Joel Harrison

"Truths are illusions," writes Nietzsche, "about which it is forgotten that they *are* illusions" (Nietzsche 1989: 250). This famous passage from "On Truth and Lying in an Extra-moral Sense" prefigures much of what we would today call "post-modern" or "post-structural" work in philosophy. There, Nietzsche argues that what we call "truth" is actually figurative: metaphors, metonyms, anthropomorphisms, "in short, a sum of human relations which were poetically and rhetorically heightened, transferred, and adorned, and after long use seem solid, canonical, and binding to a nation" (ibid.: 250). Nietzsche's point in this essay is that we often think the meanings of words are somehow *natural* when, in fact, they are not—a problem with language Craig Martin notes in his contribution to this volume (Chapter 11). Thus, even to say a proposition is "true" or "false" for Nietzsche turns on a host of cultural associations, valuations, histories, etc. rather than correspondence with some pure experience of reality. Martin attributes a similar view to the French philosopher Jacques Derrida and argues throughout his contribution to this volume that this view (i.e. that words have no natural referents) entails a commitment to reality as in part mind-dependent. This is a positive consequence of such a view of reality since it troubles problematic notions of race, gender, class, and, importantly for religious studies scholars, religion.

However, I am not convinced that a partly mind-dependent reality is what concerns either Derrida or Nietzsche. Furthermore, their views ought to be distinguished because, as I will argue in what follows, language is *self-referential* for Derrida. It is clear from Nietzsche's essay that language is *meant to be* referential, but that, in Kantian fashion, it cannot penetrate "the veil" to get to things as they are in themselves. "The word 'appearance' contains many seductions," Nietzsche laments, "and so I avoid it as much as possible. For it is not true that the essence of things appears in the empirical world" (Nietzsche 1989: 252). But our obsession with "the empirical world" *is precisely the problem* for Derrida. The nature of language, as we will see, is not determined by its relationship to the empirical because words can only refer to other words. Instead, language is determined by its inevitable *play*, its tendency to slip away from us, say what it does not intend, and unsettle, complicate, and obscure that which we think is fixed, natural, and clear.

The aim of this response is two-fold. First, I want to put my reading of Derrida in dialogue with Martin's in order to show that Derrida's position is actually more radical than Martin makes it out to be. Second, through this critique, I want to show that the appeal of Derrida in particular for critical approaches to religion is in how deconstruction moves us away from debates over religion's ontology (whether religion is "real" or not, what religion "is," etc.) and toward a critical analysis of the ways the category of religion "slips away" from those who deploy it—lay folk, politicians, and, perhaps especially, scholars. Regarding the first part of the response, I argue Martin makes two primary mistakes in his account. First, he conceives of the impossibility of a totalizing language (i.e. a naturalized language that closes the meaning of a word as final) according to what Derrida calls "the classical style" of non-totalization[1]: "[O]ne then refers to the empirical endeavor of either a subject or a finite richness which it can never master. There is too much, more than one can say" (Derrida 1978: 289). In other words, according to this version of non-totalization, empirical data provides us with an *infinite field* that can never be covered by finite language. All words, all descriptions, all explanations are infinitely revisable as new empirical data is presented. However, this emphasis on the empirical, Derrida says, misunderstands the nature of language. Words do not refer to an inexhaustible empirical reality. Words only refer to other words; therefore, "the nature of the field—that is, language and a finite language—excludes totalization" not because finite language cannot cover the infinite field of experience but because "there is something missing" from the field of language (ibid.: 289). This claim and this "something" will require much more explanation than is appropriate for an introduction, but we will arrive there in due course through comparing Martin's characterization of the field of language with what Derrida describes in his essay "Structure, Sign, and Play in the Discourse of the Human Sciences."[2]

The issue with Martin's mischaracterization of the openness of language leads directly to the second problem I see with his account. Martin does not explain what Derrida means by the "play" of language. I suspect this is in part because "play" characterizes the second version of non-totalization touched on above, and Martin seems committed to the first. This error is brought into sharper focus once one attends to how all of Martin's examples are grounded in the perception and intentional *naming* of the objects of our perception. This problem comes in most forcefully in trying to show that anti-realism is true by first simply assuming that Derrida is an anti-realist and then showing why Derrida is right.[3] Martin claims that critics of Derrida's so-called "anti-realism" err not because they are wrong to label him this way. Rather, they err because they reject anti-realism, which Martin argues is an unavoidable yet positive consequence of Derrida's view of language that ought to be embraced. As I will argue, Martin's assumption that Derrida is an anti-realist is based on faulty conclusions drawn from Derrida's critique of Husserl that are actually at odds with how Martin reads *Of Grammatology* in the conclusion to his essay. The assumption misunderstands Derrida's critique of presence (i.e. perception) as the central category of knowledge. In the passages from *Voice and Phenomenon* most central to Martin's argument, Derrida is interested in *discourse* about experience rather than the structure of experience. In other words, Derrida is not interested in what constitutes "reality," and he is not arguing that reality is in some sense "mind-dependent." Martin is right about Derrida "denaturalizing" language, particularly when it comes to the purported inherent value of particular words with regard to race, gender, and class. But he is wrong about how Derrida achieves this denaturalization. Language is denaturalized not because it is part of the mind-dependence of reality but because language can only refer to itself, and this self-reference is in a constant state of slippage that Derrida calls play.

My reasons for picking out this particular point, however, are not as pedantic as they may seem, and I would implore the reader to think with me about how the critique I am leveling here matters for religious studies—which is my second aim. Through this two-pronged critique, I argue that Derrida's analysis can offer religious studies a new entry point for critical discourse on religion—one that is no longer bound by arguments over the ontology of religion as a category. What some have taken to be "critical" approaches to religion, especially those involved in the North American Association for the Study of Religion (NAASR), are really nothing more than the negative image of theological metaphysics, an obsession with proving that religion, as a concept, is not ontologically existent. A commitment to the denial of presence is still a commitment to this metaphysics, as Derrida argues.[4] Deconstruction, then, gives us a different mode for critiquing the concept of religion, which has the potential to wrest us from the endless dichotomies that have plagued the discipline for more than fifty years now: empiricism, hermeneutics; real, unreal; explanation, interpretation; presence, absence.

Derrida's Fraught Legacy in the US

I am in agreement with Martin on the basic premise that undergirds his essay: post-structuralism provides religious studies with valuable analytical tools, and its rampant mischaracterization among detractors is based on extremely flawed readings of the primary texts or, sadly, *no reading at all*. The work of Derrida in particular has fallen victim to this problem for virtually the entire time it has remained in view of the American humanities academy.[5] My continued insistence at the outset on talking about *readings* of Derrida might, for some, raise a potential (but false) problem for any essay on Derrida, and it is worth addressing right now, since it is so characteristic of these mischaracterizations. To say that there can be flawed readings of Derrida or a proper way to understand Derrida may strike those with even (or only) a passing familiarity of his work as self-contradictory. After all, is Derrida not the great destroyer of meaning making, proper interpretations, and final words? In a word, no. Derrida, who is arguably the greatest "reader" of the twentieth century, is in fact arguing for a particular way to read using familiar texts (e.g. Plato's *Phaedrus*) to make his case. This is what deconstruction is first and foremost: a way of reading. Nowhere does Derrida write that his reading of these texts forecloses all other readings. Nowhere does he say that language is ultimately meaningless and, therefore, any reading is a good one. Rather, for Derrida, any reading is *possible*—no reading can be precluded at the outset on the basis of an authority, namely some kind of *inherent* meaning in language. However, that does not prevent us from talking about good and bad readings. And there are myriad bad readings of Derrida.

This kind of openness to possibility is, I would argue, one of the primary reasons Derrida's work never really lingered in religious studies in the way that it has in other humanities disciplines.[6] The beginning of Martin's essay expounds on this, especially with regard to the orientation some in NAASR seem to have toward post-structuralism. NAASR was founded on the premise that such "existential"[7] philosophies were actually *part of the problem* in defining and establishing religious studies as an academic discipline. Donald Wiebe, who co-founded NAASR in 1985, argues in *The Politics of Religious Studies* that *all approaches* to the study of religion that are not grounded in natural scientific methods are, in some sense, actually part and parcel with "religio-theological" approaches to the discipline and, therefore, not properly academic. While Wiebe certainly did not mean that all religious studies scholars must utilize the hard sciences for their work, his account of the history of the discipline very clearly precludes figures like Derrida and actually *accuses* them of contributing to the continued importation of "theological agendas" into religious studies.[8]

It is fascinating, then, for there to be a steady contingent of scholars within NAASR who are interested in what continental philosophy more broadly has to offer the study of religion. But this is not without its contradictions and cognitive dissonances. For example, at the 2016 NAASR conference, during the Q&A following Ann Taves's panel (on which I participated), a gentleman lamented all of our talk of a "theory of religion." Religion, he claimed, is like "bird." To have a theory of religion, then, is just as silly as having a "theory of bird."[9] Ornithologists would certainly have something to say about this, but the structure of this claim raises a contradiction that I think is peculiar to NAASR. One of the primary arguments leveled by NAASR members (I am thinking of Russell McCutcheon and Martin especially) is that religion *isn't real*,[10] which, for Martin, is presumably one of the major upshots of Derrida being cast as an anti-realist. Religion is not an object that exists in the world. *And yet*, if it isn't real, then how can it possibly be like "bird?" The gentleman's point, one assumes, was to say that religion isn't special and, therefore, should not require all of this "theorizing." Such theorizing only obfuscates the "natural facts" surrounding "religion." Theory only seeks to confuse the issue and muddy the waters when discourse about religion is and ought to be perfectly clear. Those invested in cognitive science of religion or other natural scientific approaches might not be troubled by the idea that there are "natural facts" regarding religion, but as someone invested in the politics surrounding the construction of the category—as I know McCutcheon, Martin, and others are—I am deeply troubled by the idea that there is anything "natural" about religion.

This is not to say that Martin or McCutcheon would not agree with me that the comparison between "religion" and "bird" is silly. But there is a thread of resonance between arguments I have seen them make, particularly on social media and blog posts, and the underlying point the bird commenter was trying to make: Our language about religion should be *clear*. An essay in the *JAAR* from a couple years ago[11] raised this kind of hell among NAASR members, McCutcheon, Martin, and Matthew Baldwin in particular, over the claim that discourse on religion was marked by a kind of *incommensurability* that ought to be taken into account in debates over whether the concept is useful. There was an insistence among the NAASR folk that "incommensurability" was precisely the kind of pseudo-scholarly language that prevents "actual" scholarship on religion from taking place (very clearly echoing Wiebe's criticisms of "existentialism.") As Martin's own essay shows, even if through a misreading of Derrida, and what I also intend to argue here is that post-structuralism reveals to us that language is *never clear*. Demands for the "clarity" of language or claims that the meaning of religion is "clear" should actually raise flags for us that something is amiss, perhaps even nefarious.

I raise these issues prior to presenting my response as a way of framing Martin's reading of post-structuralism. Martin's account of Derrida on Husserl is not necessarily wrong. It is his *conclusions* with which I take issue, namely that the point of the text is that it demonstrates Derrida is an anti-realist and that anti-realism is the correct orientation to understanding our relationship to reality. This analysis betrays a lingering commitment to the empirical, and Martin's commitment to the realism/anti-realism dichotomy is perhaps best understood in the context of the Wiebean legacy outlined above, though, as I say, with some apparent dissonances and contradictions. In critiquing Martin's account of Derrida as erroneously committed to the empirical, when Derrida is actually critiquing a philosophy of language that grounds itself in the empirical, I am also signaling a more general issue with the critiques of the concept of religion described above. These critiques and Martin's account are bound by a "metaphysics of presence"[12] wherein what appears to us—what is *real*—is always the locus of analysis.

Non-Totalization and the Crisis of Empiricism

Martin captures the Husserlian origins of Derrida's insights quite nicely in his essay, but the ends for which he uses these insights mischaracterize Derrida as being focused on the nature or structure of experience. However, Derrida is highlighting how the structure of experience subverts our discourse about experience, which is importantly different. Showing this in Martin's essay provides a helpful entrée into the first prong of my critique, that Martin is conceiving of non-totalization in the wrong way, because, as I explained above, Martin's mistaken account of non-totalization relies on him being committed to challenges presented by the empirical rather than challenges presented by language.

Martin's basic point in the Husserl section is that "[a]n object's ideality is, *essentially*, in part non-empirical" (Chapter 11, this volume) because in order for perception to be coherent at all, our minds must both recall and anticipate aspects of objects that are not in view in the present moment. Therefore, reality must be partially mind-dependent because every "now" requires this past and future information (retention and protention) that is "*not* in the object but in the subject" (ibid.). The key to this analysis is Derrida's emphasis on the aspect of "non-presence" in experience that this Husserlian structure of experience necessarily entails. For Martin, Derrida's analysis seems to be primarily about experience itself, i.e. the aspect of non-presence indicates mind-dependent reality and, therefore, anti-realism. It is an account whose aim is to examine our relationship to reality via the conditions of experience. But Derrida is actually *reading* this Husserlian explanation of experience in order to analyze our discourse *about* experience. In other words, it may very well be that Derrida's account and affirmation of certain aspects of Husserl's explanation of experience commits him to some form of anti-realism. But that is not his aim. Rather, Derrida highlights how our discourse about experience is fundamentally confused and that this actually reveals something to us about *language*, not experience. We *speak* as if our experiences are fully present to us in particular moments. We assume that when we are *describing* what we encounter in the "now," we are simply describing the objects of our experience without reference to any other "now." We think everything in the "now" is *fully present* to us. This is wrong, as Martin very carefully shows us, because every presence, every "now," is always constructed through non-presence, references to the past and future that are not available in immediate experience. But Derrida is leveling a critique of the metaphysics of presence *in language*—a critique of the way Western philosophical discourse privileges presence in various ways, including in its talk of "experience." It is not an argument for or about anti-realism.

This account of experience also entails, Martin says, that the objects of experience are "*always open to future reconstruction*" (Chapter 11, this volume) by which he means that our descriptions of our experiences can never be totalizing or closed. His explanation of this point, which is his and not Derrida's, brings us to the first prong of my primary critique: the problem with his account of this non-totalization. Martin gives a number of examples of the ways in which objects of experience are open to descriptive revision ("future reconstruction.") Most objects of consciousness, Martin says, are not the mid-sized objects that Husserl is talking about; they're large and abstract. Martin argues that if we consider an abstract object, such as the faculty of a university, the prospect of providing a closed account becomes complicated quickly. Notice, however, that Martin explains the impossibility of giving a closed account of such an abstract object by pointing to the infinite field of the empirical data:

> The faculty as a whole rarely appears before phenomenological consciousness all at once, and even when it does—for instance, at a commencement ceremony—one learns very little about the faculty other than their outward physical appearance (or at least those parts of physical appearance that aren't covered by regalia). But when I think of my college's "faculty" as an object, the physical appearance is typically of little importance; much more important is what the faculty "thinks"—about assessment, for instance, or the college president's new agenda for the college. The view of the faculty about the president's new agenda could be constructed through retention or memories of, perhaps, phenomenological consciousness of interactions with individual faculty members, open discussions in full faculty meetings, nonverbal signals and gestures accompanying such a discussion, rumors of conversations in other departments, bitching sessions over beers at the local pub, and so on. On the basis of such a substruction, one might claim:

"the faculty will not like phase two of this new initiative." But with what level of certainty can we make such statements? (Chapter 11, this volume)

We cannot bring the whole of the faculty "before phenomenological consciousness." We cannot know what the faculty is thinking because we cannot have the proper level of "certainty" about what the faculty will or will not like, i.e. what the faculty thinks or feels about a particular initiative, because we do not have the empirical data to make such claims. Even if we did, the data itself would be inexhaustible. We have here a crystal clear example of what I have already said Derrida calls "the classical style" of non-totalization: The impossibility of a totalizing, closed account of terms, experiences, objects of consciousness, etc. understood from the standpoint of the relationship between an infinite field of data and finite language.

In "Structure, Sign, and Play," Derrida notes the same way of thinking about non-totalization in the work of Claude Lévi-Strauss, and I want to draw attention to the similarities between Martin's account above and Derrida's account of the same in Lévi-Strauss. Derrida points out that this problem first arises for Lévi-Strauss when the phenomenon of the incest prohibition disrupts the classic anthropological binary between nature and culture.[13] Lévi-Strauss calls this disruption a *scandal*, and we might recall similar reactions among those in our own discipline who are scandalized by the disruption of, say, religious/secular as a clear and self-evident binary. However, it is only a scandal for the one who assumes there to be a strict—that is, closed—opposition between these terms in the first place. The incest prohibition calls the absoluteness of nature/culture into question because it is the site at which the binary can no longer be maintained. In the incest prohibition, the concept of "nature" bears within it the trace of its opposition and vice versa. Just as with Derrida's analysis of experience in Husserl, his point here is not to critique the nature/culture opposition as an end in itself (which was Lévi-Strauss's point.) Rather it is "only one [example] among others" that reveals to us "that language bears within itself the necessity of its own critique" (Derrida 1978: 284).

This necessity presents us with two choices. One, which Derrida calls "a first action," is to "question systematically and rigorously the history" (ibid.) of concepts like nature and culture, i.e. what we typically call a genealogical approach. The second, which Derrida identifies with Lévi-Strauss, "consists in conserving all these old concepts within the domain of empirical discovery while here and there denouncing their limits, treating them as tools which can still be used. No longer is any truth value attributed to them; there is a readiness to abandon them, if necessary, should other instruments appear more useful ... This is how the language of the social sciences criticizes *itself*" (ibid.).[14] The limits of the tools, Derrida continues, are given by the infinite set of empirical data:

[T]here is not a single book or study by Lévi-Strauss which is not proposed as an empirical essay which can always be completed or invalidated by new information. The structural schemata are always proposed as hypotheses resulting from a finite quantity of information as which are subjected to the proof of experience. ...

Totalization, therefore, is sometimes defined as *useless*, and sometimes as *impossible*. (Derrida 1978: 288–289)

Both Martin and Lévi-Strauss begin from a moment of *crisis*, which leads them to the same understanding of the impossibility of totalization. For Martin, the crisis is not his own but one belonging to our empiricist colleagues if they are convinced by his argument. Even though Martin understands this crisis in positive terms and Lévi-Strauss more negative, both come to the same conclusion: Totalization is impossible because the empirical data presents us with an infinite field that finite language cannot cover.

Center, Sign, Play

Derrida's critique of this version of non-totalization is also a critique of the way Lévi-Strauss understands language. If totalization is understood in terms of two fields, one empirical data from experience, the other language, then we're talking about a correspondence theory of language. It is clear that this is what Martin has in mind as well, since the essay is almost entirely focused on the relationship between language and reality. Take his example of "the wetlands" (Chapter 11, this volume). There, Martin points out that "wetlands" means three different things to three distinct groups in the 1990s: developers, conservationists, and the Bush Administration. Martin's point is that while there is a physical referent for "wetlands," it shifts depending on who is using it, despite the fact that all three groups lay claim to the "real" definition. This is meant to demonstrate how language is never fixed but can signify something different depending on who is speaking. Yet this kind of shifting of meaning is not what Derrida means by play. In this example, the meaning of "wetlands" is *chosen* and constructed. Play, on the other hand, happens unintentionally as a result of our inability to ground our discourse according to a unifying principle—what Derrida calls a center. The concept of play runs throughout Derrida's work and, as the wetlands example shows, could easily be confused with Martin's empirical account of the openness of language. Furthermore, play also serves as another flashpoint for misreading Derrida as an absolute relativist, i.e. as saying there are no good or bad readings of texts because language can mean anything we want it to. However, play does not refer to the meanings we assign. It is not mere relativism nor does it refer to the openness of language from the standpoint of experience. Rather it refers to an *undecidability*, a tendency in language for the meanings of words to always slip away *from us* into what they are not.

As Martin notes in his introduction, this misreading of Derrida, that language precludes us from accessing an external reality, is often sourced from a single line in *Of Grammatology*. It is poorly translated as, "There is nothing outside of the text" (*Il n'y a pas de hors-texte*). A better translation, "There is no *outside-text*," would indicate, not that we are cut off from some reality beyond the "veil" of language but that language cannot refer to anything *but itself*. This point is made right at the beginning of *Of Grammatology*, where Derrida, introducing the "secondary" position writing has to speech in Western thought as "the signifier of the signifier" points out that this "double" signification is actually already endemic in language generally:

> The secondarity that it seemed possible to ascribe to writing alone affects all signifieds in general, affects them always already, the moment they *enter the game*. There is not a single signified that escapes, even if recaptured, the play of signifying references that constitute language. (Derrida 1976: 7)

Language is a system of signs that only refer to themselves, not external referents.[15] The sign already contains within it the inextricable link between signifier and signified where the "word" or its "object" can occupy either position. That is, the word "tree" as signifier can evoke the image of a tree, signified, or the impression[16] of a tree can evoke the word (or something else entirely.) Signifier and signified are bound together like two sides of a sheet of paper to constitute the sign. The play of language is the play of signifiers and signifieds—the tendency for signifiers and signifieds to slip away from one another *unnoticed*.[17]

Recall that Derrida says the other way to conceive of non-totalization is from the standpoint of *play*. In order to grasp this better, we must understand *what* precisely is at play and how this structure of signs, just described, makes play possible. Derrida begins the "Structure, Sign, and Play" essay by noting that in the West all "systems" of thought or discourses that seek to give an explanatory account are trapped by a metaphysical logic that is focused on a "center"—a central, unifying concept that grounds theoretical/philosophical structures.[18] The relationship between theology and "God" is the obvious example, but religious studies and "religion" works equally well. In both cases, the center is intended to provide inflexible boundaries for the discipline or system, which allows for the possibility of a totalizing theoretical account of any term, event, etc. which falls within the purview of the discipline. In other words, the center is intended to limit the play of the structure. But the center, like the concept of presence in *Voice and Phenomenon*, is not what it seems to be. Though the center supports the structure, paradoxically it must also *escape* its structurality—otherwise it could not be the unifying concept that reductively grounds the structure.[19] "God" is an excellent example of this—the concept grounds the discipline of theology, yet *God as such* cannot be contained by the structurality of theology. Derrida provides myriad other examples: "*eidos, archē, telos, energeia, ousia*, ... transcendentiality, consciousness, ... man" (Derrida 1978: 279-280). The problem is strikingly similar to what Martin outlines in Derrida's critique of Husserl. Western discourse on presence—on the *center*—has operated as though it could ground the structures it supports (experience for example) for the purposes of totalization. And yet, the very nature of the thing it is meant to ground *excludes it* from this position.[20] Presence always determines the structure of experience by escaping it as non-presence. Presence is *never* "full presence" but always presence/non-presence. In short, it turns out that the "master concept," the center, that was meant to arrest the play of the contingent terms within the structure *is also at play*.

How should we think about the center once we recognize this paradox? The approach to the problem, Derrida says, is *not* to simply destroy the center, claim it is lost, or say it does not exist, because this keeps us trapped in the same metaphysical logic, replacing the former center with a new center—an absolute negation. This negation, as Martin points out and as I have said above, always contains within it the trace of its opposition. Thus the negation of "religion" in *something else* already bears the trace of the original concept (religious/secular is the obvious example.) The negation of metaphysics *entails* the logic of metaphysics.[21] It will not surprise us to learn that Lévi-Strauss thought of the incest prohibition scandal in terms of a lost center, which ties his misunderstanding of the center directly to his mischaracterization of the totalization problem, both of which have their source in his misunderstanding of language; namely, the center is lost and impossible to find because the empirical field we need to contain with language in order to find and totalize it is infinite.[22]

Yet if the signs that comprise language only refer to other signs, then this way of conceiving of non-totalization does not work because the empirical field *cannot* be the problem. On the view that language is self-referential, we must understand non-totalization in terms of the field of play, which is "a field of infinite substitutions only because it is finite, that is to say, because instead of being an inexhaustible field, as in the classical hypothesis, instead of being too large, there is something missing from it: a center which arrests and grounds the play of substitutions" (Derrida 1978: 289). If the concept of center were possible in the way that classical Western metaphysics claims it to be, it could arrest play within the system totally.[23] The language used to give account of the structure would be completely clear and unambiguous, without obfuscation or confusion. The concept of religion, for example, would no longer be a problem because its meaning would be fixed, arresting the play of concepts like belief, faith, prayer, ritual, sacred, etc. within the system and the play between opposed systems, i.e. religion and the secular. But such centers are *missing* from the field of language. There are no *absolute signs* where signifier and signified are permanently fixed. When we do attempt to fix signs—which *we cannot help but do*—we are providing a "temporary" center in the form of what Derrida calls a *supplement*:

> One could say ... that this movement of play, permitted by the lack or absence of a center or origin, is the movement of *supplementarity*. One cannot determine the center and exhaust totalization because the sign which replaces the center, which supplements it, taking the center's place in its absence—this sign is added, occurs as a supplement. The movement of signification adds something which results in the fact that there is always more, but this addition is a floating one because it comes to perform a vicarious function, to supplement a lack on the part of the signified. (Derrida 1978: 289)

Martin provides us with an excellent example of this supplementarity drawn from *Of Grammatology*, but he again emphasizes the flexibility of language in terms of choice. In the example of Rousseau's lovers, the missing center is the "mother-figure" which Rousseau supplements through the taking of various lovers and through masturbation. The episode comes at a point in Rousseau's text when he is "close enough to *Mamma* to see her and to nourish his imagination upon her but with the possibility of a partition. It is at that moment when the mother disappears that substitution becomes possible and necessary" (Derrida 1976: 152–153). The subsequent lovers and masturbation become a chain of supplements,[24] but again, Martin does not attend to the relevance of this episode for Derrida. Rousseau's *choosing* a new lover or choosing to masturbate is not what matters. As with the wetlands example, the intentional renaming of the sign is not the kind of flexibility in language that Derrida is talking about. To focus on Rousseau's *choice* misses the *play* of the supplement. Each time Rousseau chooses a new supplement, *it escapes him*. It fails to substitute for the maternal non-center because this non-center *exceeds* each supplement. Derrida's account of this episode in Rousseau attends to the play in the negative space of Rousseau's choices made possible by the maternal non-center, not the fact that Rousseau can choose.

Engineers and Bricoleurs

By way of conclusion I want briefly summarize what I have argued and gesture toward what these arguments might say about scholars in religious studies. My primary issue with Martin's account of Derrida is that it is mistakenly focused on the empirical. This means that Martin's account of reasons why the meanings of words can never be foreclosed depends upon the infinite field of empirical data rather than the play of language. The latter is a much better way of answering the critics of Derrida whom Martin identifies as thinking that Derrida says words literally generate reality. Derrida is obviously not saying that because, for him, words only generate other words. I have tried to show how this works for Derrida, and in doing so, have argued that the flexibility of language is not something that we have any control over. This is what it means to say that language is at play. Even if we recognize that there are no centers that would ground discourse, the moment we identify a supplement to take the place of the non-center, it has *already* slipped through our fingers.

What are scholars of religion to do *with the concept of religion* given this state of affairs? It would be lovely to know Martin's answer to that question. In lieu of that (for now), Derrida actually provides an answer that I find quite satisfying particularly because I know that it will trouble those who are committed to the clarity of language and the concreteness of empiricism. Derrida writes that in the wake of the crisis of method and the loss of center, Lévi-Strauss introduces the concept of *bricolage* to describe this center-less state of theory with himself as the *bricoleur*.[25] This is what we typically understand as theory today: a borrowing of a discourse from another field—usually philosophy, but sometimes economics (Marx), psychology (Freud), or others—for the purposes of our own analysis. All discourses, according to Derrida, are necessarily *bricolage* given the fact of the non-center—and we are all *bricoleurs*. Lévi-Strauss contrasts the *bricoleur* with the engineer, who "should be the one to construct the totality of his language, syntax, and lexicon." But if the center is in fact a non-center, then:

> [T]he engineer is a myth. A subject who supposedly would be the absolute origin of his own discourse and supposedly would construct it "out of nothing," "out of whole cloth," would be the creator of the verb, the verb itself. The notion of the engineer who supposedly breaks with all forms of *bricolage* is therefore a theological idea; and since Lévi-Strauss tells us elsewhere that *bricolage* is mythopoetic, the odds are that the engineer is a myth produced by the *bricoleur*. (Derrida 1978: 285)

This presents a significant challenge to those religious studies scholars who wish to simultaneously affirm the mythical engineer (via appeals to the clarity of language, accusations of obfuscation, and claims that natural science is somehow "above" these linguistic complications) and affirm the post-structural point that language is never a fixed field and, therefore, is *never clear*. The concept "religion" on the first view has a clear meaning, a clear (probably reductive) explanation. On the second view, scholars of religion "must make room for the possibility that religion *cannot be known about*—or known about in any way that is final, definitive, or absolute. Scholars of religion today, in short, must make room for the possibility of the unknowable more that exceeds both logic and language" (Dunn 2016: 887).

That there is an *excess* of the concept "religion"—that religion as supplement always slips away the moment it leaves our mouths or fingers is actually *freeing* for the discipline. Debates over whether religion is "real," what it *is*, how to properly define it, etc. fall into the Lévi-Straussian camp that mistakenly sees the totalization of concepts from the standpoint of infinite data rather than infinite play. We must learn to be better readers and *affirm* the play of language rather than try to arrest it. To that end, I will let Derrida have the final word:

> Turned towards the lost or impossible presence of the absent origin, this structuralist thematic of broken immediacy is therefore the saddened, *negative*, nostalgic, guilty, Rousseauistic side of the thinking of play whose other side would be the Nietzschean *affirmation*,[26] that is the joyous affirmation of the play of the world and of the innocence of becoming, the affirmation of a world of signs without fault, without truth, and without origin which is offered to an active interpretation. *This affirmation then determines the non-center otherwise than as loss of center*. And it plays without security. For there is a *sure* play: that which is limited to the *substitution* of *given* and *existing*, *present*, pieces. In absolute chance, affirmation also surrenders itself to the genetic indetermination, to the *seminal* adventure of the trace. (Derrida 1978: 292)

Joel Harrison holds a Ph.D. in religious studies from Northwestern University. His work focuses on the intersection between social theory, theology, and philosophy of religion at the turn of the twentieth century in Germany and questions of theory and method in religious studies.

Notes

1 The "non-totalization" of language is roughly analogous with what Martin means when he describes post-structuralist approaches to language as "anti-realist." Non-totalization refers to the impossibility of the meaning of words as fixed or

naturalized. As we will see, I have objections to characterizing this as "anti-realist." However, it is also important that the new technical language I introduce here find some grounding in the terms that Martin deploys—hence, I draw this parallel.

2 For a panel that was ostensibly about "scholars" in religious studies, it was surprising that Martin did not choose this essay, since it is explicitly about social scientists and the way they address the inadequacies of language in their work. It also presents a much more concise and clear (for Derrida) account of Derrida's major concepts than *Voice and Phenomenon* or *Of Grammatology*.

3 "In his early works—from the 1960s and 1970s—Jacques Derrida extends Martin Heidegger's 'destruction' of Western philosophy by offering immanent critiques of the works of Plato, Jean-Jacques Rousseau, Immanuel Kant, G. W. F. Hegel, Edmund Husserl, and Heidegger, among others. This body of work provides a substantial and, arguably, damning critique of philosophical realism. At the same time, Derrida draws special attention to how Western philosophy's categories or systems of classification were part and parcel of European imperialism and colonialism—Derrida's own contribution to denaturalizing historically specific concepts" (Chapter 11, this volume).

4 "There is no sense in doing without the concepts of metaphysics in order to shake metaphysics. We have no language—no syntax and no lexicon—which is foreign to this history; we can pronounce not a single destructive proposition which has not already had to slip into the form, the logic, and the implicit postulations of precisely what it seeks to contest" (Derrida 1978: 280–281).

5 We needn't rehash these debates here. It suffices to remind the reader that debates over "post-structuralism" and deconstruction in particular were at their height in the late 1970s and through the 1980s. Jeffrey Nealon's essay, "The Discipline of Deconstruction," from a 1992 issue of *PMLA*, captures the end of this era very well, albeit in literature departments. Nealon also touches on a number of ways in which Derrida has been misread in the American academy (see Nealon 1992: 1266–1279).

6 By "linger," I do not mean that Derrida has been read particularly well in these other disciplines. Rampant misreadings of Derrida are endemic to the American academy in general.

7 I use "existential" here in a broader, cultural sense rather than a more narrow, philosophical one. One might say that Derrida is a *kind* of existentialist insofar as he both eschews the possibility of any "inherent meaning" in a text and concerns himself with the failure of such meanings (that they are always already deconstructed) and the meanings that we manufacture in their place (which also fail by their own deconstruction.) That he is concerned with "meaning making" in this broad sense is enough to include him under the object of critique that so often appears in the objections of religious studies scholars to approaches that are not purely empirical.

8 Wiebe gives a repeated account of the history of the field, citing and criticizing Joseph Kitagawa in a number of the essays in this collection that touch on this point. However, I will draw attention to two specific locations in the text where Wiebe decries the dominance of "postmodernism" in the American humanities: "[I]t might be suggested that postmodernism is to be the savior of the religiously oriented study of religion; indeed, in showing that science as it once was conceived is not possible because objectivity is impossible, one presumes that the alternative, 'religio-scientific' study of religion, is as scientific as anything else. ... With the resurgence of religion in modern Western societies and the dominance of postmodernism and deconstructivism [*sic*] in humanities faculties undermining the prestige and role of science and scientific rationality, current conditions on many of our university campuses are most

hospitable to the humanist and the religious devotee. And this situation can only mapper the progress of the Science of Religion" (Wiebe 1999: 111, 288). This is not to say, of course, that all NAASR members are in lockstep with this interpretation of the field. However, I do think there is significant evidence to suggest that Wiebe's view and some permutations of it do dominate the disciplinary understanding of what it means to have a "critical" approach to religion.

9   In revising this chapter, it was brought to my attention that talk of birds and ornithologists has a bit of a legacy in religious studies, and that Martin actually cites the anecdote in his *A Critical Introduction to the Study of Religion*, which originally appeared in J. Z. Smith's work. Martin writes, "A critic of the academic study of religion once suggested that studying religion will not help people become religious; the critic used an interesting metaphor, comparing the study of religion to the study of birds: 'no amount of theory can help an ornithologist to fly' (see Smith 2004: 208). Another scholar responded by saying, 'Precisely! An ornithologist is not a bird *but one who studies birds*' (Smith 2004: 208; emphasis added)" (Martin 2017: 31). It's worth noting that this apparently well-known anecdote from Smith is not saying the same thing that the gentleman at the NAASR panel was saying. Here, the claim is that studying religion and being religious are not the same; one need not be a bird to study birds. However, in my anecdote, the claim is that *religion*, not religious people, is like *bird*; one should not need a theory to understand it, presumably because it is a "natural" phenomenon.

10 One of McCutcheon's primary arguments in *Manufacturing Religion*, for example, is that "religion" is not a *sui generis*, autonomous "object" in the world; rather, it "is a constructed, analytical tool with an occluded manufacturing history and disguised material implications" (McCutcheon 1997: 5). Martin's chapter in this volume, I think, speaks quite clearly to the question of whether religion is "real" or not.

11 From the abstract which struck up the negative response: "Against those who would argue for the reformation of religious studies as a species of the natural sciences, this article contends that there is something about religion that exceeds what can be observed in the material conditions of its existence. ... Specifically, the methodological approach to the study of religion proposed here is one that demands the juxtaposition of a multiplicity of incommensurate narratives, including the scholar's own autobiographical narrative, as a means of engineering an epistemologically-productive encounter between the historian and her temporally and spatially distant subject" (Dunn 2016: 881).

12 The "metaphysics of presence" is one of those somewhat opaque Derridean turns of phrase. It indicates a commitment found in Western philosophy to ground itself in terms of "presence." In other words, what Western thought *privileges* is presence *over* absence; it focuses itself on the meaning and nature of "being," "truth," "perception," etc. In *Of Grammatology*, Derrida provides the following brief list which serves as examples of the privileging: We already have a foreboding that phonocentrism merges with the historical determination of the meaning of being in general as *presence*, with all the subdeterminations which depend on this general form and which organize within it their system and their historical sequence (presence of the thing to the sight as *eidos*, presence as substance/essence/existence [*ousia*], temporal presence as point [*stigmè*] of the now or the moment [*nun*], the self-presence of the cogito, consciousness, subjectivity, the co-presence of the other and of the self, intersubjectivity as the intentional phenomenon of the ego, and so forth)." Here, Derrida is pointing out that there is a privileging of *hearing* the spoken word (as opposed to reading) and that this

privileging is part of a large set of privileges Western thought bestows to certain terms (including sight, the "self-presence" of consciousness in the cogito, etc.) which can all be grouped under a general privileging of "presence" (Derrida 1976: 12).

13 Derrida summarizes the problem: "The incest prohibition is universal; in this sense one could call it natural. But it is also a prohibition, a system of norms and interdicts; in this sense one could call it cultural" (Derrida 1978: 283).

14 This dichotomy should sound familiar to those of us in religious studies since it is the same general dichotomy that has characterized the field once the concept of religion was revealed to be just as *unnatural* as the nature/culture opposition. Without going too far afield from the point I am making here, it is worth noting that the concept "religion" appears *nowhere* in Martin's text as an example that would illustrate the utility of his analysis for the discipline of religious studies. This is *fascinating* to me since it forces us to ask how "religion" fits into Martin's account of Derrida as an anti-realist. I have serious doubts that Martin would be willing to say that the meaning of religion is simply "open to future revision." At the same time, I do not see how he could not be committed to that position.

15 Martin does explain this toward the end of his essay.

16 "Impression" here does not necessarily mean "empirical experience of." It means "our idealization of" which can bear resemblance to external reality, but signifier and signified are linguistic constructs. Once we experience something and name it, that sign has "entered the game" as Derrida says. The initial experience no longer matters—only our impression of it as signifier/signified.

17 This gets to the heart of what deconstruction is: *Noticing* how this slippage has occurred. We do not deconstruct. Discourse has *already* deconstructed itself. All we do, following Derrida, is read how it has done that.

18 "[S]tructure—or rather the structurality of structure—although it has always been at work, has always been neutralized or reduced, and this by a process of giving it a center or of referring to a point of presence, a fixed origin. The function of this center was not only to orient, balance, and organize the structure—one cannot in fact conceive of an unorganized structure—but above all to make sure that the organizing principle of the structure would limit what we might call the *play* of the structure" (Derrida 1978: 278; his emphasis).

19 "Thus it has always been thought that the center, which is by definition unique, constituted that very thing within a structure which while governing the structure, escapes structurality. This is why classical thought concerning structure could say that the center is, paradoxically, *within* the structure and *outside it*. The center is at the center of the totality, and yet, since the center does not belong to the totality (is not part of the totality), the totality *has its center elsewhere*. The center is not the center" (Derrida 1978: 279).

20 Think again of the presence/non-presence relationship Martin describes in which every present moment is made possible by its opposite, i.e. the non-presence of the past/future now.

21 See n. 4.

22 Martin shares this way of thinking non-totalization, as I have argued, but it is also worth noting that most in religious studies also conceive of non-totalization this way. Consider what it means to call religious studies a "big tent" discipline. That label signals this first kind of non-totalization. Presumably as more empirical data becomes available, the tent expands, seemingly with no end.

23 We can see this very clearly in our own discipline, for example in the work of Eliade who thought a totalizing system of "Religion" could then explain all of the variations of "religion" in the world.
24 Somewhat paradoxically, Martin is arguing here for language's self-reference even if in the beginning of the essay he was arguing that language is open on the basis of the infinite empirical field (see Chapter 11, this volume).
25 "The *bricoleur* is someone who uses 'the means at hand,' that is, the instruments he finds at his disposition around him, those which are already there, which had not been especially conceived with an eye to the operation for which they are to be used and to which one tries by trial and error to adapt them, not hesitating to change them whenever it appears necessary, or to try several of them at once, even if their form and their origin are heterogeneous—and so forth" (Derrida 1978: 285).
26 I began the essay contrasting Derrida and Nietzsche, but I have ended the essay with Derrida's endorsement of a "Nietzschean affirmation," by which Derrida is likely referring to Nietzsche's critique of traditional morality and of science as "the will to truth" in which Nietzsche argues for the subjectivity of valuation and a system of values that affirm life (the will to power) rather than deny it (asceticism) (see Nietzsche 1996).

References

Derrida, Jacques. 1976. *Of Grammatology*, trans. Gayatri Chakravorty Spivak. Baltimore, MD: The Johns Hopkins University Press.

Derrida, Jacques. 1978. "Structure, Sign, and Play in the Discourse of the Human Sciences." *Writing and Difference*, trans. Alan Bass. Chicago, IL: University of Chicago Press.

Dunn, Mary. 2016. "What Really Happened: Radical Empiricism and the Historian of Religion." *Journal for the American Academy of Religion* 84(4): 881–902. https://doi.org/10.1093/jaarel/lfw011

Martin, Craig. 2017. *A Critical Introduction to the Study of Religion*. New York: Routledge. https://doi.org/10.4324/9781315474410

McCutcheon, Russell T. 1997. *Manufacturing Religion: The Discourse on Sui Generis Religion and the Politics of Nostalgia*. Oxford: Oxford University Press.

Nealon, Jeffrey T. 1992. "The Discipline of Deconstruction." *PMLA* 107(5): 1266–1279. https://doi.org/10.2307/462879

Nietzsche, Friedrich. 1989. "On Truth and Lying in and Extra-moral Sense." *Friedrich Nietzsche on Rhetoric and Language*, ed. and trans. Carole Blair, Sander L. Gilman, and David J. Parent. Oxford: Oxford University Press. Originally published in 1873 (in German).

Nietzsche, Friedrich. 1996. *On the Genealogy of Morals*, trans. Douglas Smith. Oxford: Oxford University Press. Originally published in 1887 (in German).

Smith, Jonathan Z. 2004. *Relating Religion: Essays in the Study of Religion*. Chicago, IL: University of Chicago Press.

Wiebe, Donald. 1999. *The Politics of Religious Studies*. New York: St. Martin's Press.

Part IV

Institutions

Chapter 16

Finding the Devil in Indiana Jones: Mythologies of Work and the State of Academic Labor

James Dennis LoRusso

Raiders of the Lost Ark reached theaters when I was six years old and immediately captured my imagination. At that young age, I primarily experienced the film's protagonist, Indiana Jones, as a swashbuckling adventurer seeking rare treasures while fending off Nazis, the very face of evil for any middle-class American child of the 1980s. Amid these cinematic quests to find and protect history's lost relics from the clutches of profit-seeking charlatans or fascist fanatics, children of my age learned that Indiana Jones differed from the heroes of my parents' generation. He was neither a proper "superhero" capable of exceptional feats nor some brilliant crime-solving Sherlock. Rather, Jones's special power (if we may call it a "power") resides in his knowledge as an academic. It is his grasp of history and archaeology that drive his adventures, and it is the moral imperative to preserve the purity of our past and to protect it from those who would corrupt its legacy that he ultimately serves.

Through the tales of Indiana Jones, the collective vision of director Steven Spielberg and effects guru George Lucas offered us more than an action-packed cultural product; they gave us a powerful, if exaggerated, vision of academic labor. Jones is a faculty member at a university, whose occasional "fieldwork" is to track down rare antiquities for museum collections. In *Raiders*, we briefly witness Jones-as-professor, lecturing on his findings to a classroom comprised of sleepy-eyed boys and of girls enthralled by actor Harrison Ford's dreamy good looks. Clearly, we are meant to see "Dr. Jones" as the boring but necessary persona that he must perform for the "real" Indiana Jones—the one risking life and limb to save history—to thrive. While hyperbole, this image of academic life could easily echo the way many scholars envisage their vocation. Delivering quotidian lectures, dealing with the trivial concerns of unmotivated students, and tolerating Byzantine administrators permit the academic to pursue their true purpose: conducting and publishing research that advances human knowledge. As researchers, we return to the reason why many of us first chose an academic life; we tap into our inner "Indiana" and embark on an adventure into the unknown.

Of course, this romanticized version of academia hardly comports to the reality, but it does reveal an important way in which the work of academics gets prioritized, valorized, and mythologized not merely in American popular culture but in academia itself. Research is frequently preferred to teaching and scholarship, and often seen as a "pure" type of work, untouched by the base forces of market capitalism that the rest of society must endure. Like Indiana Jones, we scholars do our work in spite of capitalism, as a noble calling crucial to the advance of human progress that we do not for notoriety but because it is right and good ... Or at least, this is what we might tell ourselves.

In fact, academic work, like any other phenomenon we might potentially study, remains inextricable from the social structures, including market capitalism, upon which it is built, and therefore constitutes a form of "data" ripe for scholarly analysis. From this perspective, claims about the purity or nobility of academic work are not empirical descriptions of reality but rather mythologized accounts that highlight certain institutional dynamics while obscuring others. In other words, narratives like Indiana Jones may paint a spirited picture of academic work but they are hiding a devil within; they conceal the less rosy aspects of scholarly life while contorting, and I argue, even grossly misrepresenting the entrenched norms and practices of academic labor.

Assessing the State of Academic Labor

For anyone even remotely connected to academic institutions, the state of academic labor is no mystery. The most popular descriptor for the current situation of academia, particularly the humanities, is *crisis*, as a brief review of the statistics will easily confirm. *The Economist* (2010) reports that the academy produces approximately 100,000 new PhDs every four years, but during this time only 16,000 tenure or tenure-track positions will be available. On the balance therefore, doctoral programs will grant 6.25 PhDs for every professorship each year.[1] In simple statistical terms, these numbers suggest that the average recipient of a PhD has a sixteen percent chance of landing that coveted tenure-track position; however, the reality is more complex and much more troubling. While the academy presumably fills these 16,000 tenure-track positions every four years, the remaining job-seekers do not simply vanish from the academic job market but their numbers compound dramatically. Many hopeful early career scholars will remain on the job market for several years, exponentially increasing the pool of surplus labor. Of course, many will leave the job market each year, but it seems highly unlikely that those leaving the job market fully cancel out new entrants. The harsh truth is that even as these scholars develop their portfolio to improve their chances of attaining the faculty position, the annual flood of newly minted PhDs inevitably reduces these odds. According to a Royal Society report *The Scientific Century: Securing Our Future Prosperity* (quoted in Hankel 2015), less than one percent of all PhD earners will attain tenure.

Contrary to these essential facts, the norms and practices of academia generally privilege the tenured professoriate as the desired goal of graduate education and the scholar's ultimate trajectory. In theory, the ideal scholarly career advances along a clearly designated path—a *cursus honorum*—beginning with graduate school and culminating with an appointment as full professor with tenure. The specific steps might vary, as some early PhDs make a temporary "pit stop" as postdocs, visiting professors, or some other limited-term appointment. However, in the end, or so the story goes, even under the harshest of market conditions, hard work and perseverance will eventually yield the promised rewards. Yet, this itinerary fails to account for the structural constraints of the current academic job market, because given the dearth of tenure-track positions, it simply cannot comport to empirical reality. Therefore, in assessing the state of academic labor today, I wish move beyond a simple restatement of these abysmal numbers as others have done. Rather, in this chapter, I want to turn our theoretical and methodological toolkit back onto ourselves, to reposition the academy as our object of study—our "data"—to interrogate the governing norms, practices, and structural integrity of academia. This allows us to ask and attempt to answer, *why do academics—the self-appointed keepers of rationality and critical thinking—cling to such irrational expectations for the trajectory of their careers?*

Social Construction of Work and Academic Labor

To begin to answer this question on the state of academic labor, I wish to step back and consider how academic labor is connected to the broader concept of *work*. In contemporary society, work represents something that all, if we are able, are expected to perform. It can be an action ("I am working"), a designated place ("my place of work"), a period of time ("workday"), and even an identity ("my line of work"). Work can be paid or unpaid, physical or intellectual. Potentially, work can describe virtually any context. Given this nearly endless range of usage, what does it mean to talk about work?

All in all, work is an *idea*, an idea that most of us probably take for granted. Work, we learn from an early age, sustains our livelihood but also much more. It not only provides for basic sustenance but also confers dignity, social status, and a moral framework through which we make sense of our existence and evaluate our worth. Our work (or lack thereof) reveals who we are to ourselves and others; it is the measure of our rhythm and trajectory; it is a reservoir for meaning-making. My point is that the way we imagine work closely resembles how we ordinarily think about religion. They are what Charles Taylor refers to as "social imaginaries," fundamental, self-evident ordering principles of modern life (Taylor 2003).

Moreover, work and religion appear to us moderns as self-evident, ahistorical, and universal aspects of human experience. Whether hunter-gathers or computer programmers, people have always worked not only to survive but to fulfill some intrinsic need. For Jewish and Christian traditions, the Book of Genesis situates work as a central obligation predating the fall, stating "the Lord God took the man and put him in the Garden of Eden to work it and care for it" (NIV: Genesis 2:15). Some of the most influential intellectuals of the twentieth century have elaborated these assumptions through the lens of social science. Humanistic psychologist Erich Fromm defines the "productive orientation" as "man's ability to use his powers and to realize the potentialities inherent in him" (Fromm 1947: 84) In other words, we fully realize our humanity through the act of producing. Similarly, Mihaly Csikszentmihalyi declares that individuals achieve optimal contentment when they get into the "flow," a mental state facilitated by complete immersion in an activity (Csikszentmihalyi 1975).

Work may occupy a kind of sacred terrain in modern culture that transcends time and space, but like religion, it too is a social construction of relatively recent origin (Masuzawa 2005; Smith 1978). This ideology of work persists not because it points to some innate aspect of human experience but because it sustains the current capitalist social order, organized around private property rights and strict limitations on state intervention into the economic domain. By representing capitalist wage labor as an intrinsic and eternal human need, we mystify work. As Roland Barthes suggests, we fabricate a myth, transforming a product of history into human nature (Barthes 1972). Myths are a kind of "template" for reality, both the foundation of individual experience and the basis upon which society is constructed (Lincoln 2014: 23).

Discourses that mythologize work—that define work as essential to human flourishing—help to maintain the army of wage labor upon which capitalist economies rely by instilling within each of us the perceived need to become a laborer. Through this passive, almost imperceptible impetus, individuals are enlisted in upholding the social order. We can most clearly see the evidence of this education in popular culture, through films such as *Jerry Maguire* (1995) or *The Pursuit of Happyness* (2006), both of which feature protagonists who achieve fulfillment through hard work, entrepreneurial spirit, and perseverance in the face of harsh market conditions. *Jerry Maguire* tells the story of an eponymous sports agent (Tom Cruise), jaded by the impersonal realities of corporate life, who haphazardly strikes out on his own to start a small business. In his heroic act of entrepreneurship, he overcomes personal and professional adversity to realize success and happiness. Similarly, in the semi-biographical *The Pursuit of Happyness,* Will Smith's character is a struggling single father who must endure poverty and even homelessness in order to secure a coveted position at an investment bank. Such tales reinforce the conviction that individual initiative alone can conquer the structural inertia of capitalism. Of course, these works of fiction reflect not the actual experience of life under late capitalism but rather its utopian ideal. They are the exceptions that prove the rule by which most remain bound.

Academic Labor as a Class Position

In briefly exploring how mythologies of work perpetuate the status quo, we can begin to understand how academic laborers cling to unrealistic expectations. Discourses about academic labor gloss over important contradictions by masking the structural realities in which most aspiring academics are embedded. Like work, "academic labor" can signify numerous concepts. It could simply represent any work that academics perform in their role *as* academics. If one is working, they are by definition doing academic labor. Alternatively, academic labor could constitute a set of primary activities (researching, teaching, writing, etc.) distinct from other kinds of secondary labor in which academics might engage (filling out expense reports, submitting grades, miscellaneous administrative duties).

While these definitions might be used casually to describe academic labor, they hide certain elements that I believe crucial to any adequate assessment of academia. These definitions lack attention to context by flattening the social structure. Class analysis, on the other hand, designates "labor" neither as an activity nor as a professional identity, nor as a kind of mystified imaginary like "work" but as a shorthand for a specific social group who "are reduced to selling their labor-power in order to live" (Marx and Engels 2004). From this perspective, academic labor signifies a discrete subset of all labor, an exploitable class position within the institutional structure of the academy.

Of course, what counts as "exploitable" is a matter of debate, especially since even senior scholars—those with the most institutionalized authority—face increasing demands on their time and must frequently justify the existence of their positions and programs to austere administrations (particularly in the humanities). Despite the uncertainties and insecurities that these scholars experience, they remain apart from the proper academic "proletariat" who exist primarily to preserve the privileged status of the former. In fact, removing contingent labor from academic programs would imperil the stability of the entire system by rendering it economically unsustainable. Many departments depend on academic labor to reduce overall teaching costs and ensure continued survival.

In addition to lowering the teaching burden for traditional faculty, reliance on contingent labor disincentivizes the creation of additional tenure-track positions, which effectively elevates the prestige of the tenured professoriate. In all but the most well-resourced institutions, academic labor (i.e. the academic proletariat) keeps the structure from collapsing, a structure in which they wield little, if any, influence (except perhaps over their students). Academic elites—faculty and administrators—resemble historic formations of capital rather than Marxian conceptions of labor precisely because they profit not merely from selling their labor but by virtue of their advantaged position, from their ability to appropriate surplus value from the workers who create wealth (i.e. those who teach the students). It would be misleading therefore to suggest that the very real hardships facing the tenured professoriate are structurally similar to academics outside its well-defined boundaries. Their class positions, and thus their interests, remain utterly distinct. Any reasonable consideration of the state of academic labor should sharpen rather than obscure this difference. The survival of these elites as a group depends as much, if not more, on their ability to "live off" the benefits accrued through exploitation of the academic precariat as on their own labor. This is accomplished by enforcing a particular mode of production by its perpetual mystification via an elaborate set of cultural practices to which I will now turn.

Mythologizing Academia and Reproducing the Status Quo

Having noted the structural disadvantages facing academic labor as a class position, let us return to the question I initially proposed: Given the overwhelming evidence to the contrary, why would those aspiring to a career in academia continue to cling to a belief that they will succeed where so many have failed? Clearly, the system by design seems to render such hopes futile. Yet, rather than adjust our professional expectations accordingly, many of us (myself included) willingly subject ourselves to acute forms of material deprivation that would otherwise, in another career or line of work, appear absurd. We will surrender living wages, health insurance, and even the ability to plan our lives beyond the next few months of work, just to keep a foothold inside the academy, to work a little harder, to publish that next piece that might finally place among the most desirable candidates for faculty openings in our respective subfields. Why is this the case? A partial answer lies in the cultural norms, authorizing discourses, and practices that legitimize this system and consequently enlist the acquiescence of academic labor.

First, both within and beyond the academy, the humanities boast the remarkably anemic reputation that *advanced humanities education is designed to produce traditional academics*. Well-trodden tropes—"those that can't do, teach" or "a degree in _____ is worthless"—pepper quotidian discussions about the value of humanities education. Even former US President Barack Obama disparaged the value of a humanities degree in a 2014 speech.[2] While humanities scholars may craft quite reasonable rebuttals to such condemnations, they nonetheless persist in part because doctoral programs themselves by and large remain committed to equipping their students for a singular occupation: the institutionalized scholar. Doctoral education in the humanities prepares students for a narrow bandwidth of positions, the centerpiece of which continues to be the tenured professoriate. Only through the tenured professoriate can one fully utilize the training one has received, which means that anything else remains a consolation, something for which one "settles." Consequently, relegating those in "alt-academic" or non-traditional careers to second-class status effectively bolsters the prestige of the tenured professoriate.

A number of graduate schools and departments are certainly seeking ways to better equip their students for the structural conditions of the job market, but this status hierarchy is reinforced in other subtler ways. These well-intended efforts are hampered by maintaining a strict insider/outsider distinction in the humanities. Faculty searches typically look for candidates from within the traditional academy—early career or established scholars—rather than those who have "left" academia for other kinds of work (a topic which I address in more detail later). Thus, faculty are generally comprised of scholars who have little to no experience outside the academy, leaving them ill-equipped to mentor the majority of doctoral students who will inevitably fail to attain a faculty position. Other fields outside the humanities value experience beyond the academy. In the field of mass communication (advertising, marketing, journalism), for example, candidates without some form of industry experience are rarely considered for tenure-track positions. While this practice may not easily translate to humanities programs, the inadvertent refusal to recruit faculty from non-academic contexts simply perpetuates the assumption that the tenured professoriate is the exclusive domain for successful academics.

Another myth to which academic laborers acquiesce is the belief that *academia is a meritocracy*. Like Will Smith's character in *The Pursuit of Happyness*, those who possess the intelligence and work the hardest will earn entry into the highest ranks of academia. Given the nearly insurmountable structural limitations of the academic job market, however, this simply cannot be true. The "best and brightest" are beset by countless obstacles over which they have no control, but which they inevitably face once they enter the academic job market. As Russell McCutcheon notes in his *Theses On Professionalization* (McCutcheon 2012), for many job candidates, classroom experience and the quality of research may be less important than other factors, such as the reputation of the school from which they have earned their PhD. Nonetheless, a mixture of structural and cultural reasons perpetuates this governing narrative. At the structural level, the meritocratic myth persists precisely because it adequately accounts for the experience of scholars who wield institutional power: academic elites. For members of the tenured professoriate, meritocracy makes sense. They indisputably labored through graduate school to produce brilliant scholarship and subsequently attained the just reward of a lifetime academic career. However, in the vast sea of PhD recipients, their anecdotal experience represents a minority report. Through their privileged position, as gatekeepers of the professoriate, they misrepresent the particular as the general experience. While academic elites deserve every bit of recognition for their scholarly acumen, the belief that merit primarily accounts for their status grossly underappreciates exogenous factors.

Culturally, too, the academy upholds the meritocratic myth. As in any institution, titles matter, and in academia one's title can define how we encounter another's scholarship. Intuitively, we judge the *merit* of an argument by the prestige of its author. Pragmatically, of course, such distinctions are necessary, because it behooves scholars to read, cite, and critique the work of the most prestigious scholars in our respective fields. However, it is important to note that these practices also reinforce existing structures of privilege within the academy, even in our day-to-day conversations. For example, an early-career scholar criticized a close colleague of mine on a conference panel several years ago. Hours later, as my colleague debriefed with me, she dismissed the junior scholar's thoughtful critique with laughter, stating, "Well, I have a tenure-track job and he doesn't!" Fully complicit, I laughed as well, but an uncomfortable truth resides in the subtext here. Her status implies not merely higher status but bestows intellectual superiority as well. Even though she or I may have found the criticism *merited*, it did not merit attention. Here, the meritocratic myth simply serves to reinforce the prestige of the tenured professoriate.

To be fair, I am not suggesting that merit plays no role in the academy. On the contrary, merit remains a central part of the academic enterprise. Undoubtedly, academic elites have labored, often under the weight of enormous pressures, to advance their fields and serve as public intellectuals. In short, they are among the "best and brightest" who have earned their stripes. I merely wish to shed light on how these governing myths, in practice, can perpetuate the current "crisis" of academic labor. It engenders the idea that "failed academics" failed themselves and exonerates academic elites and institutions from culpability. Even these so-called failed academic laborers, who have suffered most acutely under this regime, not only recycle these myths but in their attempts to point out the injustices of the system, invent their own discourses that ultimately serve the status quo.

"Quit Lit" and the Complicity of Academic Labor

The anxiety produced by this crisis of labor appears no more clearly than in the recent emergence of the genre of scholarly writing known as "quit lit."[3] With increasingly frequency in recent years, scholars have taken to digital media to publicly announce their exit from academia. Despite the occasional declaration from a tenured or tenure-track professor, in many, if not most cases, these online confessionals come from the most vulnerable segments of academia: those actively seeking permanent employment in traditional academic jobs.

Quit lit serves as a space for the academic precariat to articulate counternarratives of academic labor that highlight the most acute consequences of the current conditions of academic work that run counter to the prevailing myths that uphold the status quo. These are not stories of justly rewarded effort or success but rather tales of frustrated expectations and undeserved suffering of those who have dreamed of but ultimately fallen short of that singular coveted goal: the tenured professoriate. Deciding to "leave" gives these individuals a sense of freedom to express their frank views on academia without the burden of consequences. At the beginning of the film *Jerry Maguire*, Tom Cruise experiences a similar catharsis when he publishes an interoffice memo exposing the wrongheadedness of corporate largesse. For disgruntled academics, "quit lit" jeremiads via blog posts or social media encyclicals are their "Jerry Maguire" moments when they can finally come clean about all of the abuse, injustice, and deceit to which they were subject over their scholarly career. Yet, these are equally their moments of failure, when they finally admit defeat and relinquish a dream to which they have clung for too long.

These accounts of fallen hopes and dreams offer a unique window into the localized suffering and perceived injustices that otherwise remains obscured or minimized. Its authors expose the chasm between the promise of academic life and its lived conditions. For instance, one author recounted in a piece titled "Why You Need to Leave Academia" (Hankel 2015) how he used public assistance and picked up supplementary employment while earning a PhD. "I made the last minute decision to apply for the [food] stamps in between lab experiments and hurried down to the building hoping my advisor wouldn't notice I was gone," he writes. Moreover, the author worked as an overnight janitor for a retail chain because "he didn't want any of the other graduate students to see me." This quit lit piece becomes the opportunity for this author to finally expose an acute form of suffering that was otherwise hidden from view in order to uphold the belief graduate student labor yields a living wage. Sometimes the failure to achieve a "living" wage is literal, as another quit lit piece explains:

> While I did get a small teaching stipend for those summer months, I did not have any health insurance. At the beginning of the 2003-2004 school year, I'd opted to pay for just 9 months of insurance (at a cost for my family of about one full month's salary, incidentally). So when my husband Anthony began to experience extreme and frequent heartburn and nausea over the summer months, he figured he'd just wait to see a doctor 'til I could pay the family's insurance bill again when the Fall Term started in September ... September 15, we again had insurance. September 16, he saw a doctor. The diagnosis: not something that a "little purple pill" could clear up ... Liver cancer. (Watters 2012)

In both of these cases, the authors specifically hold the normalized structures of academic labor accountable for material deprivation. The former cites anemic stipends while the latter points to the highly unstable rhythms of contingent work. The juxtaposition of lived experience and the governing myths of academia expose the presumed central deception. Hankel (2015) laments "the whole reason I worked so hard to become a PhD" was "a better life for myself and for my own family someday"; "I felt the promise of a professorship was a false one," writes Watters (2012), "A false promise to most grad students to be sure, and definitely a false promise to me."

Of course, quit lit is not without its detractors, particularly from within the academy, and just as quit lit unveils the dissonance between expectations and experiences of academic labor, critics suggest the genre promotes deceptions of its own. In one scathing attack, professor of media studies Ian Bogost offered harsh words for the quit lit crowd:

> Guess what. Working for a living is a pain in the ass. Nobody cares that I quit finance. Or advertising, retail, technology consulting, the entertainment industry, or anywhere else I've worked. The trick with quitting is that you want to throw a party for you when you do it. Quitpieces are the opposite of parties. If you're writing a quitpiece you've already lost. Everybody knows that quitters quit. (Bogost 2015)

Bogost first resituates academic labor within the broader social context of work and immediately reprimands quit lit for misrepresenting the nature of work. There's no guarantee that work, including academic labor, will be fun or intrinsically rewarding or meaningful, he suggests. Yet, in dismantling these misconceptions, Bogost implicitly offers a competing essentialist definition of academic labor: work is hard, it is indifferent, it is "a pain in the ass" and accordingly, it simply cannot be otherwise. So stop complaining, get back to trying, or get on with quitting. Characterizing work as inherently difficult, disappointing, or demeaning renders the existing state of academic labor impervious to any attack. Quitting therefore embodies a choice—the free act of a rational market actor—to give up of one's own accord and seemingly divorced from any of the structural constraints like illness or economic hardship actually cited in the literature. Of course, Bogost is a member of the tenured professoriate whose criticism of quit lit reflects his interest in protecting the status quo. He concludes that academia is "amazing" and does have "substantial problems," but ultimately quit lit simply represents "more fodder for legislators, corporations, and the general public to undermine the academy. It helps nobody in the long run," or more precisely, Bogost worries that quit lit does not help people like him—professors holding tenure at state universities.

Thus, both quit lit and its critics employ arguments that, intentionally or not, perpetuate the present conditions of academic labor. As much as quit lit might expose the injustices of academic labor, it does little to undermine its structural integrity. In fact, I want to suggest that quit lit carries out a vital function for academia by performing important boundary maintenance for what counts as academic labor. In one sense, the very existence of quit lit reinforces the notion that legitimate academic labor strictly represents the work done by institutional academics (or at least with the blessing of academic institutions). "Quitting" academia does not mean stopping intellectual work altogether but exiting the territory deemed "academic" and for which the academy (and its institutional actors) assumes responsibility. The genre recognizes this border by stating unequivocally that one is no longer beholden to the academy and, likewise, the academy owes them nothing. Whatever future endeavors upon which one may embark, it is no longer academic work.

Quit lit also polices the boundaries of academia by distinguishing between academic and non-academic labor. In one sense, Bogost's observation (see above) that academic work is no different from other jobs proves insightful. Academics *want* their labor to have intrinsic worth, to be fulfilling, and serve a greater purpose. In a blog post titled "Quit Lit and Academia as a Vocation," political theorist Andrew Biro keenly notes that one reason for the "horribly exploitative" conditions of academic laborers "is because of the belief that academic work is not just (or more than just) 'a job'" (Biro 2015). For academics (myself included), the work we do—the research, the teaching, the writing—represents more than a paycheck. It is a means and an end to which our professional and personal selves are bound, and quit lit publicly signals one's estrangement from this vocational identity. Quitting academia, on this view, means assuming a purely instrumental and vacuous form of labor, what David Graeber refers to as "bullshit jobs," jobs which contribute nothing of consequence and serve no social function other than to maintain the illusion of work itself as virtuous (Graeber 2013).

Yet, the desire for meaningful work is unexceptional and not distinctive to academic labor. In fact, it is a conventional rhetorical mode that became increasingly salient in the decades after the Second World War and saturates American attitudes towards work more generally today (LoRusso, 2017). People, regardless of their occupation, expect their working life to yield more than material rewards. Moreover, the discourse gets mobilized in ways that bolster the authority and status of elite institutional actors—be they corporate executives, trustees, administrators, or even tenured (or tenure-track) academics. Oftentimes, as my research into workplace spirituality illustrates, this desire enlists religious discourse as a way to mark a particular kind of work as sacred, in the Durkheimian sense, and quit lit proves to be no exception. In his own quit lit confessional, Oliver Lee, a former professor of history, describes the moment he realized his dissatisfaction with an academic career as follows:

> My friend asked me, in total sincerity, "Why aren't you doing something meaningful with your life?"
>
> "This *is* important," I insisted. But there was no passion behind my words. I was priest who had lost his faith, performing the sacraments without any sense of their importance. (Lee 2015)

For Lee, academic labor should differ from other work. It should be important, meaningful, and should, like that of a priest, enjoin the one to a cause beyond immediate material need. Once this sense of cause vanishes, it is as if Lee has lost his faith. Thus, quitting signifies an act of apostasy and quit lit becomes a type of narrative of spiritual catharsis.

Others, like Rebecca Schuman, view quitting not as a painful loss of faith but a fortunate escape. "In its insularity and single-mindedness," she declares in her assessment of quit lit, "academe is also very similar to a fundamentalist religion (or, I dare say, cult), and thus those who abdicate often feel compelled to confess" (Schuman 2013). Schuman seems to intimate that academia persists despite gross inequities by instilling within its members a religious devotion to its survival. In order to truly leave the academy, one must not only find work outside the academy but literally jettison an entire system of belief upon which one has depended for, in some cases, decades.

As scholars of religion, the appearance of religious language should peak our interest, not because academia *is* a religious cult into which academic labor has been collectively indoctrinated as adherents, but rather because the decision to describe academia in religious terms is hardly objective and instead quite arbitrary. It invites *redescription* (McCutcheon 2001), to ask what is at stake for Lee or Schuman, to consider the work being done by these terms. On one hand, equating academia to a fundamentalist religion (or cult) undercuts its legitimacy by linking the irrationality and illiberality associated with the latter to the former. On the other hand, however, Lee's conflation of academics with priests confers on scholarly work an exceptional quality, elevating her above the vapid tedium of the workaday world.

Nonetheless, whether evaluated positively or negatively, religious rhetoric produces one undeniable result: it considerably strengthens the salience of the boundary between academic and non-academic labor. In this respect, therefore quit lit, even as it lays bare the academy's systems of exploitation, nonetheless serves to insulate and maintain the integrity of these purportedly unjust structures. Even if it falls short of its promise, academic labor remains above the fray as a purer form of work than most alternatives. Rather than erasing this distinction, quit lit valorizes it, leaving outsiders to fend for themselves in a substantially different world from which they will likely never return and effectively exonerates institutional insiders from any culpability in the substantial and sustained "exit" of academic labor.

Where Do We Go from Here?

If readers find my portrayal of academic labor somewhat grim, it is because it is a personal and professional one. It stems from countless conversations over the years with colleagues about dashed aspirations and tempered expectations in the face of diminishing prospects, but also from my scholarly interest in the complex relationship between myth, society, and labor. The fact that we nonetheless persevere under these conditions testifies to the sheer potency of these governing myths and discourses. As scholars in the humanities, we devote much of our energy to exposing the cultural norms and practices that sustain socioeconomic injustices, but it is vital that we understand how our own operating assumptions create and maintain some of these same systems of exploitation.

In shedding light on how these governing myths and discourses function, however, reside opportunities for change. As Bruce Lincoln observes, although discourse "may be strategically employed to mystify the inevitable inequities of any social order and to win the consent of those over whom power is exercised ... discourse can also serve members of subordinate classes (as Antonio Gramsci above all recognized) in their attempts to demystify, delegitimate, and deconstruct the established norms, institutions, and discourses that play a role in constructing their subordination" (Lincoln 2014: 3). Acknowledging how "quit lit" or the meritocratic myth preserve the status quo allows us the chance to reshape the cultural and structural landscape anew by recognizing the socially constructed and arbitrary quality of academia and academic labor. It destabilizes the entrenched boundaries between the insider and outsider and forces a re-evaluation of accepted practices. It challenges the academy to assume responsibility for the fate of the vast army of reserve scholars it creates, to account for its ecological footprint (what economists refer to as "externalities"). Indeed, doctoral programs and graduate schools that are actively engaged in reform and redesign efforts are already advancing this cause (see Russell McCutcheon's 2018 blog post, "It's Time We Tackle This Directly," for further discussion of this issue).

Furthermore, in reframing academic labor as a class position over and against institutional elites, we see how academic laborers share more in common with the typical working-class individual than with the mystified professional classes to which they are more often coupled. Adjunct instructors, postdoctoral researchers, and limited-term or visiting professorships (like part-time and non-salaried workers) lack the basic material security and permanence associated with traditional faculty, whose material interests more properly reside alongside the managerial elites they frequently critique. Recent efforts to unionize contingent faculty and graduate student workers represent promising developments on this front. All in all, reworking these myths and discourses can disrupt their power, unmask the false consciousness to which academic laborers too often succumb, and reveal the devil hiding within our heroes. For most scholars, academic life does not, after all, culminate in the noble pursuit of a lost ark or a holy grail, but rather conscription into a system of exploitation and designed obsolescence. Perhaps the time has come to leave behind our inner Indiana Jones and craft new narratives that can more adequately account for academic labor.

James Dennis LoRusso is Associate Research Scholar for the Faith & Work Initiative in the Center for the Study of Religion at Princeton University. LoRusso is interested in theories and methods in the study of religion, the intersection of religion and business management thought and praxis, and the workplace as a site of production for the category of religion. He is the author of *Spirituality, Corporate Culture, and American Business: The Neoliberal Ethic and The Spirit of Global Capital* (Bloomsbury, 2017), which traces how "spiritual" discourses in business have contributed to the establishment and perpetuation of neoliberal capitalism. In his current role, he is co-researcher for a mixed-methods study of corporate chaplaincy in US companies and an ethnographic study of "spiritual labor" in secular and faith-based organizations.

Notes

1. The accuracy of data on PhD recipients versus tenure-track positions remains debatable. The ratio of 6.25:1 is generated from numbers provided by an article in *The Economist* (see Economist 2010), but other sources make competing, if slightly different, claims. For instance, see McKenna (2016), which argues that roughly half of all PhD recipients lack any job commitment upon graduation each year. Unlike the data cited in *The Economist*, the higher number accounts for those with positions outside tenure-track jobs such as lecturer, postdoctoral appointments, adjuncts, as well as private sector posts. Still, both data sets, though different, indicate the existence of a vast increasing pool of surplus PhDs who lack sustainable employment.
2. In a 2014 speech in Wisconsin for which he received criticism, President Obama stated "I promise you, folks can make a lot more, potentially, with skilled manufacturing or the trades than they might with an art history degree."
3. Google searches by the author yielded no results prior to 2012 for "quit lit," referring to quitting academia. Before 2012, the term produced search results primarily for advice for quitting tobacco usage.

References

Barthes, Roland. 1972. *Mythologies*, trans. Annette Lavers. New York: HarperCollins. Originally published in 1957 (in French).
Biro, Andrew. 2015. "Quit Lit and Academia as a Vocation." September 13. Retrieved from https://andrewbiro.wordpress.com/2015/09/13/quit-lit-and-academia-as-a-vocation.
Bogost, Ian. 2015. "No One Cares That You Quit Your Job." *The Atlantic* (September 9). Retrieved from www.theatlantic.com/notes/2015/09/no-one-cares-that-you-quit-your-job/404467.
Csikszentmihalyi, Mihaly. 1975. *Beyond Boredom and Anxiety: Experiencing Flow in Work and Play*. San Francisco, CA: Jossey-Bass.
Economist. 2010. "The Disposable Academic." *The Economist* (December 16).
Fromm, Erich. 1947. *Man for Himself*. New York: Holt.
Graeber, David. 2013. "On the Phenomenon of Bullshit Jobs: A Work Rant." *Strike!* (August). Retrieved from https://strikemag.org/bullshit-jobs.
Hankel, Isiah. 2015. "Why You Need to Leave Academia." *Cheeky Scientist*. Retrieved from https://cheekyscientist.com/leave-academia.
Lee, Oliver. 2015. "I have one of the best jobs in academia. Here's why I'm walking away." *Vox* (September 8). Retrieved from www.vox.com/2015/9/8/9261531/professor-quitting-job.

Lincoln, Bruce. 2014. *Discourse and the Construction of Society: Comparative Studies of Myth, Ritual, and Classification*. New York: Oxford University Press. Originally published in 1989. https://doi.org/10.1093/acprof:oso/9780199372362.001.0001

LoRusso, James Dennis. 2017. *Spirituality, Corporate Culture, and American Business: The Neoliberal Ethic and the Spirit of Global Capital*. London: Bloomsbury Academic.

Marx, Karl, and Frederick Engels. 2004. *Manifesto of the Communist Party*. Marxist Internet Archive. Retrieved from www.marxists.org. Originally published in 1848.

Masuzawa, Tomoko. 2005. *The Invention of World Religions, Or How European Universalism was Preserved in the Language of Pluralism*. Chicago, IL: University of Chicago Press. https://doi.org/10.7208/chicago/9780226922621.001.0001

McCutcheon, Russell. 2001. *Critics, Not Caretakers: Redescribing the Public Study of Religion*. Albany, NY: SUNY Press.

McCutcheon, Russell. 2012. "Theses on Professionalization." *The Religious Studies Project* (February 29). Retrieved from http://religiousstudiesproject.com/2012/02/29/russell-mccutcheon-theses-on-professionalization.

McCutcheon, Russell. 2018. "It's Time We Tackle This Directly." *Studying Religion in Culture* (April 3). Retrieved at https://religion.ua.edu/blog/2018/04/03/its-time-we-tackled-this-directly. https://doi.org/10.4324/9781351112079

McKenna, Laura. 2016. "The Ever-Tightening Job Market for Ph.D.s." *The Atlantic* (April 21).

Schuman, Rebecca. 2013. "'I Quit Academia,' an Important, Growing Subgenre of American Essays." *Slate* (October 24). Retrieved from www.slate.com/blogs/browbeat/2013/10/24/quitting_academic_jobs_professor_zachary_ernst_and_other_leaving_tenure.html.

Smith, Jonathan Z. 1978. *Map is Not Territory: Studies in the History of Religions*. Chicago, IL: University of Chicago Press.

Taylor, Charles. 2003. *Modern Social Imaginaries*. Durham, NC: Duke University Press.

Watters, Audrey. 2012. "The Real Reason I Dropped Out of a PhD Program." *Hacked Education* (August 29). Retrieved from http://hackeducation.com/2012/08/29/the-real-reason-i-dropped-out-of-a-phd-program.

Chapter 17

Teaching in the Ideological State of Religious Studies: Notes Towards a Pedagogical Future

Richard Newton

Teaching occupies a contentious place in the current state of religious studies. It is a work tethered not only to redeemable compensation, but also the opportunity to work "freely" within the university. Under other circumstances we would, *in deed*, call such an exchange a predatory trap on the part of the academy.

Increased institutional dependence on so-called "adjunctive" or "contingent" labor should suffice to underscore the usury before us. The trope of meritocracy, that "mechanistic" "tragedy," would have those dissatisfied with tenuous employment place blame on themselves for not having worked hard enough to work more (Baker 2017, 2018). This irrational, or as Hayden White prefers, "radical" interpretation of the university is the kind of dynamic to which the scholar of religion could be savvy (White 1978: 70). I suspect such an inference subtends my students' claim that lower-ranked faculty are more invested in teaching and thus the preferred choice at course registration time.

Even if you bristle at the rationale, you likely have something to say about the practice of assessment. Who are they to assess the worth of an instructor? Whether you approach your work with a historical, comparative, structural, or cognitive approach, I invite you to consider what else those students may be trying to convey. To borrow from Rebekka King, it may be precisely this kind of analysis—of truth's social effects—that we are after with them. It may be the first blush of their own "pedagogical impulse[s]." And that might just be the place from which we can "draw our students in[to]" the study of religion (King 2017: 152). Let us not take for granted that our students may be trying to join in—perhaps without knowing it.

What precisely they are joining into has been a matter of considerable debate for NAASR. Matthew C. Bagger advocates that we constitute religious studies more as a "field"—characterized by its object of study and questions related to it—than a discipline, defined by a specific set of theories and methods. To Bagger's point, insistence on a disciplinary regime begs to replicate the over-determinations we would otherwise investigate in our work (Bagger 2017: 139–140). However, King reminds us that it is as a discipline that we most frequently justify our place as collaborators in the institutional memory and operations of the academy at-large (King 2017: 151–152). This is an important discussion to be had, but it is moot if we disregard the landscape where it is taking place.

When thinking about teaching in the modern university, teacher-scholars would do well to consider the conditions under which we study religion. I am becoming increasingly convinced that our teaching is happening in an "ideological" state that could have us working harder to work more for ends that are not in the interest of our students, let alone ourselves (Althusser 2014: 232).

More specifically, I want to suggest that the uncritical commendation of the Scholarship of Teaching and Learning (SoTL) in higher education could serve a curricular agenda that stands in fundamental opposition to our field's work vis-à-vis conspicuous attempts to "rebaptize" the study of religion. SoTL refers to a genre of research focused on how teachers of any subject can better engage and express their message to learners. Simply put, it is an assessment of the professor as proselytizer. And while most of SoTL includes research on subjects other than "religion," its history involves a number of worrisome presumptions about the importance of religion. My fear is that if we enchant our work as intrinsically significant, we lose the critical distance to question the actions and institutions fostering its appearance as such. Our students do as well.

In response, I submit for consideration a meditation on Althusser's own reflections on teaching in an ideological state as a framework for imagining a model of student–scholar collaboration that would contribute to our work in religious studies as both field and discipline. My intent is that we too can put forward a compelling vision of teaching and learning—but one that actually takes into account the point of view of teachers. And in each and every class, the syllabus would be an argument for consideration rather than a doctrine to be learned.

My blatant privileging of the teacher is a necessary concession. *Homo academicus*, regardless of teaching load, is a political creature (Bourdieu 1988: xvii). Our learning objectives and outcomes impress a paradigm geared toward certain concerns. Yet if our data consists of value statements and those who would press them, then the only discipline to which we can coherently resolve to practice is one built upon the sanctity of the question. After demonstrating some of the reasons why such a commitment is not descriptive of the current ideological state of religious studies, I want to offer some proxy outcomes for an alternative state of teaching for religious studies.

Institutions such as the Association of American Colleges and Universities advocate for SoTL as a framework for documenting and developing best practices in valuable educational experiences. In 1990, Ernest L. Boyer, esteemed president of The Carnegie Foundation for the Advancement of Teaching, laid the foundations of the SoTL in response to the relatively low value of teaching when compared to research and administrative service in academic performance reviews. Boyer maintained that investigation into the praxis of teaching is itself a form of scholarship, for "[w]ithout the teaching function, the continuity of knowledge will be broken and the store of human knowledge dangerously diminished" (Boyer 1990: 24). For him, teachers belong to a storied lineage of cultural gatekeepers, a history intended to put us in, what Rudolf Otto might call, a state of trembling and fascination.

As if not to unduly preach to the pedagogical choir, Boyer heralds none other than research physicist J. Robert Oppenheimer to describe the state of teaching. Because "the specialization of science is an inevitable accompaniment of progress; yet is full of dangers...the role of the scientist is not to merely find the truth and communicate to [one's] fellow [scientists]" (Boyer 1990: 24). The "father of the atomic bomb's" rationale is rather poetic (Hijiya 2000: 125). Aside from his famed recitations of the Bhaghavad Gita's most tragic verses, he thinks it cruel that scientists, who understand what is "beautiful and enlightening" keep that knowledge to themselves rather than trying to share "the most honest and most intelligible account of new knowledge to all those who will try to learn" (Boyer 1990: 24–25). The presumed understanding of ontology comes with a deontology. Or in the words of mythmaker Stan Lee, "with great power comes great responsibility."

Thinking with Louis Althusser, we should take note how the sense of duty shared by these two scholars functions within the superstructure that is the United States of America. Boyer was a former US Commissioner of Education in the 1970s; Oppenheimer was deputized into the military. Their sense of responsibility is also one of disciplinary distinction. Boyer seeks to perfect teaching as a dependable transmission of knowledge; Oppenheimer, to produce a cohesive model of the world. Both men are operating out of disciplinary points of view designed to methodically reproduce a static façade over rather dynamic processes.

None of what I have said thus far need disqualify Boyer's call for higher education to reconsider the meaning of scholarship. But as Bagger warns, we might object to the implications of his disciplinary commitments. Case in point, we might take issue with two articles from the *Journal of the American Academy of Religion*. The first is Boyer's 1992 essay, "Teaching Religion in the Public Schools and Elsewhere." The second is a 2016 essay by Emily O. Gravett called "SoTL in Religious Studies." While the latter piece references Boyer's 1990 *Scholarship Reconsidered* as the genesis of SoTL, its bibliographic omission of the 1992 essay says volumes about the micro-myth buried within the Ur-text (Doniger 2011: 99). Lurking behind values-based education is a cautionary tale about the paradise lost without it.

In that 1992 essay, Boyer explicitly says that "no public school should teach religion or impose religious ritual on its students." Two sentences later, however, he presents his central theme:

> [I]t's simply impossible to be a well educated person without learning about how religion has, throughout history, consequentially shaped the human story in almost every culture. And I believe that the sacred texts of all the great religions should be introduced to students with reverence and intellectual insight. (Boyer 1992: 517)

For those curious, his genealogy juxtaposes Hindu cave paintings, the temples of ancient Greece, the cathedrals of the Middle Ages, and the art of Marc Chagall. Homer and Euripides are paired with T. S. Eliot and John Updike. Hildegard is matched with Leonard Bernstein. The inquiries of Marx, Weber, and William James are duly noted in a portrait of "the consequential role of religion." Having explored the possibility of the study of religion in public high schools, Boyer lamented religion's muted place in textbooks and hoped for what Daniel Bell called a return to "the sense of the sacred" to correspond with the then onset of STEM, or "Science, Technology, Engineering, and Mathematics" education (Boyer 1992: 518).

Boyer ends his piece depicting how American youth culture could benefit from a

> study of values; through a curriculum that shows coherence and what I view as divine patterns; through great teaching that nurtures the intellect as well as integrity and human justice; and through a term of service that demonstrates to students that to be truly human, one must serve. (Boyer 1992: 524)

When executing such a curriculum, would we be as disciplined as King's students to ask, "serve whom, how, and why?"

Boyer believed his program unimpeachable of judicial scrutiny against religion in public schools because of his insistence of religion as part of the fabric of language. He proclaims, "teaching about language is teaching about truth, and that every language class must be an ethics class, since communication without honesty is one of life's most dangerous destructive weapons (Boyer 1992: 519–520). Better religion teaching could replace mutually assured destruction with something more stable.[1]

Boyer's ethos is not subject to enforcement by what Althusser would call a "repressive state apparatus," unless one counts his role in the administration and granting machinery of the AAC&U. But in interpellative fashion, it is the ideological or seemingly self-inspired, work of the American Academy of Religion's members that have continued his initiative, though primarily in the context of higher education (Althusser 2014: 191).

Emily O. Gravett's "The Scholarship of Teaching and Learning in Religious Studies" presents a primer of SoTL for the uninitiated within the academy. Since Boyer's 1990 work, learning assessment has become a primary focus, joining Institutional Review Board-approved (IRB) student feedback, and explicit engagement with other SoTL literature—the SoTL Trinity, as it were (Gravett 2016: 592). Gravett's literature review does not map on to a religious agenda so much as it attempts to demonstrate the utility of substantive, evidence-based pedagogy. Ultimately the value of SoTL "for religious studies" is its ... "inevitable ethical character" on behalf of the students (ibid.: 607). In this way, Gravett continues the solipsism of religion, value, and teaching begun by Boyer.

I find Gravett's essay to be a useful introduction to the SoTL discourse despite its choice to distinguish itself from "more theoretical or conceptual scholarship written about teaching, which does not emerge from the author's own experiences or experiments within the classroom or with students." Learning assessment tools, IRB consultations, and collegial discussions of teaching experiences are all useful apparatuses for learning to teach religious studies better. On the other hand, SoTL seems to have substantially less interest in teachers' agency and—dare I say—the "moods and motivations" that inform their praxis within a cultural system (Geertz 2000: 97). I am particularly troubled by such exclusion given that it is always from our own embodiment within the ideological state of the university that we are trying to teach and theorize.

Thus to what extent would one's non-engagement with SoTL—by one's own volition or ignorance—disqualify the person from employment in the academy? Many teaching job advertisements and tenure portfolios require candidates to submit a teaching statement of some kind. The genre is predicated on the codification not of experience so much as how one's practices fit in line with techniques, strategies, and best practices documented in SoTL. Having been in a number of pedagogy workshops in the American Academy of Religion, Society of Biblical Literature, and other groups, I am comfortable saying that there is a great deal of consternation around appearing conversant enough with SoTL so as to merit the chance to work or keep working. Again I say, would we not call this datum "interpellation" in any other context?

This question could be written off as a thought experiment, though I suspect that the Boyer legacy in AAR will only appreciate. In a 2012 Oxford University Press book called *No Longer Invisible: Religion in University Education*, Douglas Jacobsen and Rhonda Hustedt Jacobsen contend that religion has long been intimately tied to the work of university education. They highlight six areas to observe the marriage including (1) religious literacy, (2) interfaith etiquette, (3) framing knowledge, (4) civic engagement, (5) convictions, and (6) character and vocation (Jacobsen and Jacobsen 2012: 56). Jacobsen and Jacobsen's "religion in the academy" project at Messiah College informs their work (ibid.: 159). The Brethren-in-Christ (BIC) institution where it is housed is also home to the Ernest L. Boyer Center, which houses the works of the one-time Messiah student and former BIC minister (Messiah College undated). Boyer's ecclesial commitments were the subject of an entire 2015 special issue of the peer-reviewed journal, *Christian Higher Education* (Ream 2015).

Jacobsen and Jacobsen's work has also received funding from the theologically inclined Lily Endowment and the John Templeton Foundation, as well as the support of Lee Shulman, another president emeritus of The Carnegie Foundation (Jacobsen and Jacobsen 2012: 159–160). And as you have no doubt heard, in 2016 the AAR began preparing its "religious literacy guidelines" to correspond with the AAC&U's "essential learning outcomes," an endeavor that is in intentional conversation with SoTL. The initiative is made possible by a five-year, $160,000 grant from the Arthur Vining Davis Foundation's efforts to promote "interfaith leadership and religious literacy" (American Academy of Religion undated).

Having benefited from the benevolence of so many of the institutions listed, I would be hypocritical to suggest that teachers should unequivocally refuse grant monies. In fact, one would be naïve to think that the economics of the landscape North American higher education—at least in the United States—would leave this investment to any one' teacher's choice. As Brad Stoddard has documented in Althusserian terms, philanthropic organizations such as the ones listed here have bankrolled the work of US religious studies scholars since the post-Cold War in ways that have established the discipline as a useful "ideological state apparatus" for reifying and advancing American capitalist interests (Stoddard 2017: 115–119).

To be clear, I am no more interested in championing these organizations as I am in demonizing them. But the data pertaining to these institutions' influence raises questions about "the interests advanced by assigning causation," which colleges and universities are all the ready to do. So to Gravett's point about the experience of the teacher, we might ask how much of our syllabi are determined by demonstrable outcomes reached by activities belonging to a canon of literature bolstered by funding agencies with confessional interests? I suspect that many teachers would feel an insecurity similar to that accompanying the attachment of anonymous student feedback to cases of tenure and promotion. To Craig Martin's point in his conclusion to *Capitalizing Religion*, "The key question at the end is, perhaps, not 'what is the cause?' but rather 'whose interests are advanced by assigning causation in this way rather than that way?'" (Martin 2014: 160). If the teacher's vocation as it were, is the business of unsettling presuppositions and preconceived notions, then what recourse will we have when our questions pose a clear and present danger to the curricula of the state or the intellectual comfort of the student?

Temptations abound in the ideological state of religious studies. When religious studies departments find themselves facing closure, teachers could hitch their fate to arguments of relevance. Former US Secretary of State John Kerry offers statements such as "religion is a multivalent force, not reducible to good religion and bad religion." Thus we could commend prospective students to learn from Kerry who upon the 2013 launch of his Office of Religion and Global Affairs said, "if I went back to college to day, I think I would probably major in comparative religion because that's how integrated [religion] is in everything that we are working on and deciding and thinking about in life today" (Kerry 2013).[2] Such a public relations coup could stem the tide of think pieces decrying the limited value of a humanities degree like religious studies.

I count any gains a Pyrrhic victory if our students get jobs that prohibit them from asking questions like "what are the implications of parsing terms like "religion" or "extremism" for the purpose of indexing social difference?" A place when we can no longer ask about interests and agendas is a place where we cannot do what we do—in spite of the personal conviction, civic duty, and market forces that make such positions attractive.

As teachers, we know too much about the psychology of militancy and the critical sociology of ideologies. They may not be directly involved, Michel de Certeau feigns, but they are always present in overtures of reform (1988: 183). The American Anthropological Association learned this when the CIA headhunted ethnographers during most of America's twentieth-century wars (Price 2000). More recently, the American Psychological Association is still reeling from the knowledge that some in their number may have added to the government's quiver of enhanced interrogation techniques and torture practices (Risen 2015).

So I caution against the salacious rhetoric that would reimagine religious studies as a natural fit for ethical reflection or its participants the paradigm for responsible research practices. After all, in 2014 the US State Department created the violent, 2014 anti-ISIS propaganda parody, "Welcome to ISIS Land," that mocked the neo-caliphate's attempt at recruiting fighters into Syria. To borrow from a *Washington Post* headline, "in a propaganda war against ISIS the US tried to play by the enemy's rule" (Miller and Higham 2015). The same Kerry State Department that oversaw the production of this video is the same Kerry State Department that sought a foreign policy informed by "a more sophisticated approach to religion" (Kerry 2014).

For Kerry, sophistication involves engaging religion as an ontological datum to be managed and not a social dynamic to be negotiated—let alone observed. The rising tide of pluralism plus religions' universal call for compassion and "the Golden Rule" make religion *something* to be "engag[ed]."[3] From this standpoint the State Department's chief concerns are that they will "mistakenly see religious influences when only political and social ones exist" or "overstep[ping] the separation of church and state laid out in the First Amendment. Expertise in religion would help the State Department "approach religion with a critical and sophisticated analytical lens" (Kerry 2014).

I invite teacher-scholars to consider whether Kerry's understanding of sophistication is congruent with the methods and theories with which we have come to approach "religion." Cultural theorist Bruce Lincoln's words come to mind: "the end result of our definitional labors ought to problematize, and not normalize, the model that prompted their inception" (Lincoln 2006: 2). And if we agree with him on this point, then being a natural fit in the ideological state of religious studies is antithetical to the order of inquiry we profess. The ideological state does not willingly allow for that kind of intrigue. The ideological state does not eagerly reward those dissatisfied with convenient truths.

We are where we are and we teach where we teach. And in reviewing the backchannel conversations happening on Twitter during my initial NAASR presentation, I saw that my Althusserian framing left some teachers dismayed. The neo-Marxist's stark conceptualization of institutions leaves little room for positive identification. For in the ideological state of religious studies, one either takes or is taken. But for those working harder to work more, hear Althusser's words for the profession of the educator:

> I ask the pardon of those teachers who, in dreadful conditions, attempt to turn the few weapons they can find in the history and learning they "teach" against the ideology, the system and the practices in which they are trapped. They are a kind of hero. But they are rare and how many (the majority) do not even begin to suspect the "work" the system (which is bigger than they are and crushes them) forces them to do, or worse, put all their heart and ingenuity into performing it with the most advanced awareness (the famous new methods!). So little do they suspect it that their own devotion contributes to the maintenance and nourishment of this ideological representation of the School, which makes the School today as "natural", indispensable-useful and even beneficial for our contemporaries as the Church was "natural", indispensable and generous for our ancestors a few centuries ago. (Althusser 2014: 252)

Rather than read Althusser as a fatalist, I cannot help but see him exposing the Achilles heel of the ideological state—namely, its dependence on an apparatus for modeling innovation. Whether in the revisiting—and thus, reconstruction—of the past (i.e. history), or in the expansion of intellectual horizons via the new idea—(i.e. learning), Althusser suggests that teachers have an opportunity to effectively counter the efforts of the state. He lauds those who are already doing so, just as he recognizes the struggles that have yet *to join in*.

But once again, the question is what exactly are *we joining*. The neo-Marxist says it is not the "new methods" or the "natural" school of thought, or the indispensable site that is the church. It is in the examination of the system and practices of the systems in which we are embedded. This is the sort of paradigm within which religious studies can thrive as a human science. It demands that its teachers poke and prod at every turn to expose pedagogy falsely so-called; our only aversion, heuristics that remove implication and mask effect.

With that proviso, I encourage us to imagine a different kind of radical relationship with the academy than the irrational investment of working harder to work more for ends that in few ways benefit works. I am calling for an understanding of our discipline as a commitment to pull at the threads of even seemingly seamless fabrications. My concern is for a generation of students who are learning to call out instances of social construction or cultural appropriation but are taught not to question the conditions under which groups bracket off some institutions as autonomous, self-sufficient originals. Being politically correct is not cultural critique, and cultural critique is not necessarily examining culture critically (Fitzgerald 2018). Thus we might also beware of institution's rush to parade the public intellectual who can peddle the simple narrative. Our attention should be on helping the student ask questions that make even us think twice.

Instead of conceding that social theory is too complicated to translate pedagogically, maybe it is time to create teaching circles where we troubleshoot course design. Do we have graduate students under our watch looking for teaching experience prior to formal forays into the job market? Maybe we can leverage members' national and international reputations against the need for institutions to appear cosmopolitan. When a theory-inclined department needs a short-term instructor, let them offer a teaching fellowship to the student of a colleague at another school. Such exchanges could bring the kind of prestige that students need to legitimate their professional advancement as productive teacher-scholars of renown.

I also do not think we need to completely reject SoTL. What if our schools become the labs and fields where we reframe SoTL? What does the cognitive science of religion have to say about assessment culture? Where in the hierarchical flowchart do our rubrics take unwarranted exception in the evaluation of students, faculty, staff, and administration? Where does the memory of glorified university histories trample on the freedoms of the forgotten? Cannot these be the projects of our students? And can we help each other frame our findings when it comes time to prove our quality?

I hope that we continue to create the resources—via the *Religion Bulletin: The Blogging Portal of the Bulleting for the Study of Religion* and our book imprints—that will support the classroom and the work we are doing there? The recently published *Religion in 5 Minutes* volume is a great example of this (Hughes and McCutcheon 2017). I would also commend the NAASR Working Papers series as a pedagogical resource for bringing students into the field.

I see no reason why there should not be a network wherein we share cross-campus opportunities for student research. If a professor is at a campus with a dedicated digital humanities facility or a psychology lab, what should keep that professor from making those resources available to the student at another campus? How much more could our collegiality mean if we invested in each other?

And perhaps most feasibly, how can we use annual meetings as a way to exchange ideas for helping students become savvy to the ideas, skills, experiences, and questions of religious studies? We have precedent for students using blog posts to reflect on how the debates of the guild's various annual meetings corresponded to the discussions they were having in the classroom. Their assessment of our gatherings present a chance to reassess what we are doing in ways that benefit research and teaching. I think pedagogy workshops—similar to our job market workshops for graduate students—could offer similar professional development to teacher-scholars.

As I look forward to the possibilities, I wonder whether they will result in us working harder to work more. Maybe there is no other option when teaching in the ideological state of religious studies. Though if we are going to work harder, then let us always be brave enough to ask how we can do so on behalf of our students.

Richard Newton is Assistant Professor of Religious Studies at the University of Alabama. His research examines the making of social difference in light of the anthropology of scriptures. He also curates the student–scholar multimedia collaborative, *Sowing the Seed: Fruitful Conversations in Religion, Culture, and Teaching* (sowingtheseed.org).

Notes

1. For a discussion of why offering a better religion or a better set of values is not befitting of critical pedagogues, see Newton (2017a, 2017b).
2. Initially this entity was named the Office of Faith-Based Community Initiatives.
3. This rhetoric and claims track closely with Karen Armstrong's presentation of the Axial Age thesis in her book *The Great Transformation: The Beginning of our Religious Traditions* (2007).

References

Althusser, Louis. 2014. *On the Reproduction of Capitalism: Ideology and Ideological State Apparatuses*, trans. G. M. Goshgarian and Ben Brewster. New York: Verso. Originally published in 1971.

American Academy of Religion. Undated. "Religious Literacy Guidelines for College Students." Retrieved from www.aarweb.org/about/religious-literacy-guidelines-for-college-students (accessed January 29, 2018).

Armstrong, Karen. 2007. *The Great Transformation: The Beginning of Our Religious Traditions.* New York: Anchor Books.

Bagger, Matthew. 2017. "The Study of Religion, Bricolage, and Brandom." In Aaron W. Hughes (ed.), *Theory in a Time of Excess: Beyond Reflection and Explanation in Religious Studies Scholarship*, 138–149. Sheffield: Equinox.

Baker, Kelly J. 2017. *Grace Period: A Memoir in Pieces.* Chapel Hill, NC: Blue Crow Publishing.

Baker, Kelly J. 2018. *Sexism Ed: Essays on Gender and Labor in Academia.* Chapel Hill, NC: Blue Crow Publishing.

Bourdieu, Pierre. 1988. *Homo Academicus*, trans. Peter Collier. Stanford, CA: Stanford University.

Boyer, Ernest L. 1990. *Scholarship Reconsidered: Priorities of the Professoriate.* New York: The Carnegie Foundation for the Advancement of Teaching. https://doi.org/10.1093/jaarel/LX.3.515

Boyer, Ernest L. 1992. "Teaching Religion in the Public Schools and Elsewhere." *Journal of the American Academy of Religion* 60(3): 515–524.

De Certeau, Michel. 1988. *The Practice of Everyday Life.* Berkeley, CA: University of California.

Doniger, Wendy. 2011. *The Implied Spider: Politics and Theology in Myth*, revised edition. New York: Columbia University.

Fitzgerald, Timothy. 2018. "Joel Harrison on Facts and Values, Critical Religion and on Bruno Latour." January 23. Retrieved from www.criticaltheoryofreligion.org/timothy-fitzgerald-joel-harrison-on-facts-and-values-critical-religion-and-on-bruno-latour (accessed January 29, 2018).

Geertz, Clifford. 2000. *The Interpretation of Cultures.* New York: Basic Books. Originally published in 1973.

Gravett, Emily O. 2016. "The Scholarship of Teaching and Learning in Religious Studies." *Journal of the American Academy of Religion* 84(3): 589–616. https://doi.org/10.1093/jaarel/lfw006

Hijiya, James A. 2000. "The 'Gita' of J. Robert Oppenheimer." *Proceedings of the American Philosophical Society* 144(2): 123–167.

Hughes, Aaron W., and Russell T. McCutcheon. 2017. *Religion in 5 Minutes.* Sheffield: Equinox.

Kerry, John. 2013. "Office of Faith Based Community Initiatives." Retrieved from www.c-span.org/video/?314438-1/sec-state-kerry-launches-faith-based-community-initiative (accessed January 29, 2018).

Kerry, John. 2014. "Toward a Better Understanding of Religion and Global Affairs." Retrieved from http://2007-2017-blogs.state.gov/stories/2015/09/05/toward-better-understanding-religion-and-global-affairs.html (accessed May 31, 2019).

King, Rebekka. 2017. "Precision and Excess: Doing the Discipline of Religious Studies." In Aaron W. Hughes (ed.), *Theory in a Time of Excess: Beyond Reflection and Explanation in Religious Studies Scholarship*, 150–154. Sheffield: Equinox.

Lincoln, Bruce. 2006. *Holy Terrors: Thinking about Religion after September 11*, 2nd edition. Sheffield: Equinox.

Martin, Craig. 2014. *Capitalizing Religion: Ideology and the Opiate of the Bourgeoise* New York: Bloomsbury.

Messiah College. Undated. "The Ernest L. Boyer Center." Retrieved from www.messiah.edu/info/22570/boyer_center (accessed January 29, 2018).

Miller, Greg, and Scott Higham. 2015. "In a Propaganda War Against ISIS, the US Tried to Play by the Enemy's Rules." *Washington Post* (May 8). Retrieved from www.washingtonpost.com/world/national-security/in-a-propaganda-war-us-tried-

to-play-by-the-enemys-rules/2015/05/08/6eb6b732-e52f-11e4-81ea-0649268
f729e_story.html?utm_term=.81b86079b610 (accessed January 29, 2018).
Newton, Richard. 2017a. "Locating Value in the Study of Religion." *Method and Theory in the Study of Religion* 29: 459–478. https://doi.org/10.1163/15700682-12341407
Newton, Richard. 2017b. "Signifying 'Theory': Toward a Method of Mutually Assured Deconstruction." In Aaron W. Hughes (ed.), *Theory in a Time of Excess: Beyond Reflection and Explanation in Religious Studies Scholarship*, 37–46. Sheffield: Equinox.
Price, David. 2000. "Anthropologists as Spies." *The Nation* (November 2). Retrieved from www.thenation.com/article/anthropologists-spies (accessed January 29, 2018).
Ream, Todd C. (ed.). 2015. "Creative Calls for Coherence: Ernest L. Boyer and Christian Higher Education." *Christian Higher Education* 13(1): 1–3. https://doi.org/10.1080/15363759.2014.850934
Risen, James. 2015. "American Psychological Association Bolstered C.I.A. Torture Program, Report Says." *The New York Times* (May 1). Retrieved from www.nytimes.com/2015/05/01/us/report-says-american-psychological-association-collaborated-on-torture-justification.html (accessed January 29, 2018).
Stoddard, Brad. 2017. "Show Me the Money": Big Money Donors and the Cognitive Science of Religion." In Aaron W. Hughes (ed.), *Theory in a Time of Excess: Beyond Reflection and Explanation in Religious Studies Scholarship*, 115–120. Sheffield: Equinox.
White, Hayden. 1978. *Tropics of Discourse: Essays in Cultural Criticism*. Baltimore, MD: Johns Hopkins University.

Chapter 18

Competencies and Curricula: The Role of Academic Departments in Shaping the Study of Religion

Rebekka King

On more than one occasion, the president of my institution has instructed department chairs that they are to think of their departments and its faculty as a family. While probably not his intention, these instructions conjure up Tolstoy's adage "all happy families resemble one another; every unhappy family is unhappy in its own way" (Tolstoy 1899: 1). Like the category of religion, "department" functions as a semiotic symbol to which meaning is assigned according to both the context and convictions of its interpreters. Academics presume to *know* what the department is because they themselves have "lived experience" and "thick descriptions" of the various roles they have performed within a department: ostensibly ranging from undergraduate students to esteemed faculty, and more accurately in various tenuous positions as teaching and research assistants, adjunct faculty, and visiting fellows.

For many the term *department* might evoke an almost Durkheimian conception of an identity embedded in space and accessed with a master key: a specific hallway, set of offices, or building where the department is physically located.[1] For others, the department might signify a group of individuals and personalities, likely the faculty, administrative staff, and students: all those who contribute to (or, in some instances, hinder) its daily operations. This observation echoes Craig Martin's chapter in this volume which unpacks the category of "scholars," envisioned as those holding specific degrees and disciplinary training denoted through academic regalia. In Martin's assessment, however, faculty is more likely understood as a collection of individual agents invested in ideas related to the university and its administration (which he notes could be constructed through various factors including, memories of how things have been done in the past, open dialogue and debate in faculty meetings, or the ever-satisfying "bitch" session over beer on a Friday afternoon).

For others, the department might be equated to a disciplinary placeholder. Here it is seen as a vehicle under which certain types of scholarship (and not others) might be conducted. In this context, boundaries are negotiated and stakes are claimed about the validity, necessity, and domain of the methods, theories, and datum which scholars take up within a given disciplinary realm. The idea that department denotes discipline provides insight to ongoing debates within religious studies about its identity as a discipline, field, or operating as an inter-, trans-, or multidisciplinary area of study (see Engler and Stausberg 2011).[2]

It is particularly noteworthy that little has been written on the comportment of departments. Like many classificatory systems, its attributes are endowed with an *a priori* status. No definition is thought to be required: the word is understood as a direct and universal referent. Certainly, as we think about departments, we can look to official designations. The Tennessee Higher Education Commission's Academic Policy A1.3, for example, offers the following definition of a department:

> Department: An instructional unit encompassing a discrete branch of study or organized around common and similar academic areas and is usually administered by a department chair [sic].[3]

This definition, grammatical errors aside, more or less speaks to the genre of department as an administrative unit but does little to give us a sense of its purpose, practice, or the particulars related to "a discrete branch of study" or "common and similar academic areas." On a more practical level, a department is a vehicle for administrative work: colleagues who share organizational responsibilities, such as student recruitment and retention, course delivery, committee work, program assessment, and the various events and services geared towards enhancing the educational experiences of our students and our own professional development. Alongside its lived experience and disciplinary focus, the department serves as a key administrative body at an institution. According to some studies, 80 percent of academic decisions are made at the departmental level (Carroll and Wolverton 2004).

Since my start at Middle Tennessee State University, my own conception of department has been ubiquitous with curriculum design and assessment. Likely, this focus does not reflect most junior faculty's experiences, but it has been mine. Over the course of my first four years at Middle Tennessee State University, I (along with my colleague, Jenna Gray-Hildenbrand) was tasked with building a religious studies program from the ground up. Thus, when I think about department, I tend to envision the layers of required and elective courses that work together to build a religious studies degree. I see the curriculum as the structure (or, to evoke Bourdieu, "a structuring structure") upon which all of the other components of a department—social, ideological, imagined, and concrete—attach themselves in such a way that they reflect a departmental *habitus* (cf. Bourdieu 1990).

In what follows, I draw upon my own experience of program design in order to provide introductory remarks that speak broadly to the architecture of a department vis-à-vis the study of religion. In doing so, I discuss the particulars of the recent development of the Religious Studies major at Middle Tennessee State University. I highlight the ways that broader shifts and orientations within the disciple of religious studies take an administrative form at the departmental level. My comments are intended to provide some general thoughts about the administrative and institutional works that we do in hopes that my experiences might be useful beyond the particular case of my institution. I see this linkage of curriculum and departments as imperative because on a practical level it effects the ways that we schedule courses, allocate resources, and hire faculty. While my discussion is focused on curriculum design, I suspect that similar conclusions could be teased out in the context of program review, outcomes assessment, and the regular work of faculty attempting to balance teaching, research, and service.

The Arc of Religious Studies

The original blueprints for Religious Studies departments and programs outline a shift from pre-seminary theological departments to the scholarly study of religion. In the aftermath of *Engel v. Vitale* (1962) and *Abington School District v. Schempp* (1963), a new emphasis on the historical and cultural value of studying religion emerged. These two Supreme Court decisions prohibited theological studies at public universities but asserted, in the words of Justice Clark, that "education is not complete without a study of comparative religion or the history of religion and its relationship to the advancement of civilization" (quoted in McCutcheon 2003: 67–68; cf. Engler 2006). As a result, universities and colleges attempted to diversify curricular offerings by incorporating a phenomenological approach that attended to different religions along a comparative and historically-oriented trajectory (King 2017).[4]

As religious studies departed from its origins in theology and broadened its scope, departments hired new faculty with expertise beyond Christianity. Herein lies the origins of world religions or comparative religions model. Such programs were designed with an underlying assumption that it would be problematic if a student were to undertake the academic study of religion without encountering the "other." According to this view, at many institutions students must demonstrate knowledge of different traditions through completing coursework in Eastern and Western religions. In many departments the importance of gaining insight into the history of religions and the imperative to study different religions resulted in the establishment of the world religions course as an introductory and often prerequisite course for more advanced studies.

I have a student who, on the occasion of our first encounter, plopped down in the chair in my office and pleaded to be admitted into my Jesus of Nazareth senior seminar, because he "really, really loves Jesus." This student explained to me that he had been "called" to take my class. Thinking someone was playing a trick on me, I glanced around for hidden cameras. Finding none, I explained to him that the course was full and the over-ride option was only available to majors and minors in the program. Without hesitation he pulled out his cellphone, went to the university registration website, and added a religious studies minor to his degree plan in order to gain admission into the course. A bit taken aback, I gave him a brief overview of the differences between religious studies and theology and expressed concern that he might struggle with scholarly deconstructions of Jesus. He remained undeterred. Acquiescing, I advised him to also enroll in our introductory Religion and Society course to balance out the content he would encounter in an advanced-level Jesus course. Instead, he opted for a second upper-level seminar, "The History of Christianity."[5]

This scenario, no doubt familiar to many faculty who teach in regions with highly religious demographics, exemplifies the ways that students pursue course offerings for theologically-oriented purposes. In an ironic return to origins, many students at public institutions see their religious studies coursework as makeshift training for ministry, missionary work, or religious devotion. While it remains to be seen what choices this particular student will make for his remaining three courses in the religious studies minor, his choices thus far provide fodder for the larger concern that he might complete a Christocentric program of study and fail to gain any relevant knowledge of religions apart from his own. A program breadth requirement in non-Christian (or non-Western) religions could be perceived to counter such tactics providing a firmer grounding in non-theological, scholarly approaches to religion.

The world religions model was introduced to challenge the theological paradigm that was its predecessor, but as has been routinely noted, in many instances, it works to reify theological presuppositions. In its most current reiteration, it is often redressed with skills such as religious literacy, cultural reflexivity, and global engagement. Here, the theological categories have been reshaped in a way that retains their *a priori* mold. Critics observe its universalizing plasticity and paradigmatic nature, relabeling its presuppositions and corollaries: The World Religions Paradigm (Cotter and Robertson 2016; Owen 2011). Attempts to dismantle the World Religions Paradigm speak both to the fact that the model is flawed in its capacity to accurately represent religious experiences and traditions and, more pressingly as Richard King recently observed, that it serves to reify political and cultural assumptions which marginalize those who fall within the historic category of "other" (usually denoted by gender, sex, race, ethnicity, or colonial identifiers) (King 2017: 3). Calls abound to reimagine the discipline in a way that does not rely on the overtly Western categories and essentializing tactics (e.g. Asad 1993; Dubuisson 2003; Fitzgerald 2003; Masuzawa 2005).

In response, many of us have done the hard work of incorporating this critique into both our research and teaching and to a certain degree into our representation of religious studies to colleagues in other departments and administrators at our academic institutions.[6] Our project has been one that has emphasized method and theory over and against topical or content based expertise. We have shifted from the *what* to the *how* when addressing the mainstay of religious studies.

In the context of program and curriculum design over the past four years, I have come to the conclusion that a further step is necessary to complete the dialectic. In certain circles, method and theory have replaced the world religions model in terms of content without actually replacing it in terms of consequences. We have witnessed a shift from learning the "big 5" (or 6, or 7, or 15.76) religions to variant methods and theories. Over the last fifteen years or so, descriptions of the discipline have shifted to a derivative of "religious studies involve textual, anthropological, sociological, historical, philological, philosophical, critical, feminist, etc. etc. approaches to the study of religion." Certainly the shift from *what* we study to *how* we study is necessary, but it might be argued that it has resulted in a new paradigm which merely recasts old assumptions concerning the means by which we populate and deliver our programs. As Leslie Dorrough Smith observes, religious studies undermines itself when it treats "method and theory like accessories to scholarship," a practice which she sees as emerging from "the field's longstanding reverence for certain types of *sui generis* discourse" (Smith 2017: 180; cf. Hughes 2013: 1–2). By focusing on method and theory we have replicated the notion that as long as our students have some sort of broad exposure to difference we are doing our job.[7] Returning to my student whose coursework is restricted to classes about Jesus and Christianity, the method and theory paradigm presupposes that his course of study is acceptable as long as he learns a historical, anthropological, and feminist critique along the way.

Program Design: A New Set of Blueprints

At Middle Tennessee State University, the study of religion reflected the field's roots in theology with a cursory nod toward the world religions paradigm. Originally, housed in the Department of Philosophy, the religious studies minor had existed for thirty plus years staffed by adjuncts who were often local clergy (quite literally, prior to my arrival, it was a priest and a rabbi). They taught the five courses on the curriculum that covered biblical studies, Christian history, and comparative religions. For all intents and purposes, these courses posited the assumption that religious studies and theology were interchangeable in both their content and pedagogy. For example, our course of the Bible had the following description: "How the Bible came into being, including the origin of manuscripts, principles of textual criticism, inspiration, inerrancy, history, and translations." Our Western religions course purported to explore the "Historical development of the idea of one God through Judaism, Christianity, and Islam; their relation to other religions of the world."[8] One of my first tasks was to rewrite the course descriptions for these courses, a process which opened up conversations with administrators regarding the nature of religious studies and its possible contributions to research and teaching at a state institution.

Certainly, the aforementioned course descriptions were cringe-worthy, however, they afforded Jenna Gray-Hildenbrand and myself the opportunity to start from scratch. Unlike most new faculty, our positions were new positions which meant that we were able to avoid the specter of tradition. The idea that professor so-and-so had always taught Course A in a particular fashion was more or less absent. Instead, we were met with enthusiastic leadership in the Office of the Dean and the Provost and supportive colleagues in the Department of Philosophy who listened closely to our descriptions of the state the field and helped us articulate possibilities for application in the context of our institution.[9]

We were directed to design a new religious studies curriculum that would serve as the first of its kind at a public institution in the Middle Tennessee region. Both our training in the discipline and the context of our program within an undergraduate-only department with (at the time) only two tenure-track lines meant that we could not feasibly even consider a world religions model. Furthermore, our commitment to doing something that departed from the world religions paradigm was reinforced as we began the process of making application to various levels of state bureaucracy to establish the major. Over and over again, we had to provide evidence supporting our argument that the world religions model is outdated and ethnocentric. Through that process we learned to speak the administrative language that many faculty disparage. To a certain extent, I have come to appreciate such language and think that religious studies scholars are perhaps distinctively equipped to this task as we are used to deciphering esoteric language, iniquitous hierarchies, and multiple renderings of proof-texts.

We knew we wanted to build a major that departed from the world religions paradigm and the related epistemological problems it generates. We also knew we wanted an approach that speaks to the importance of method and theory in the study of religion. We needed to be able to do that in a way that would reflect to our context and the needs of our institution, department, and most importantly our students. Obviously both University of Toronto and University of California Santa Barbara (where we completed our graduate work) have strong method and theory curricula (in ways that are very different), but neither of those models would fly in middle Tennessee with two tenure-track faculty teaching a 4/4 course load.

A popular theme in pedagogical research and writing is the notion of backwards design. This process advocates that faculty "start at the end" by thinking about what skills or knowledge with which they want their students to walk away. From this point of departure, backwards design advocates breaking the course content and learning activities down into increasingly simplified steps aimed towards a bigger picture (see Biggs and Tang 2011). There is an element of backward design in building curriculum and scaffolding a program of study. Although it might better be conceived of as multi-directional—involving backward, forward, mired in the center, and dropping unexpectedly from the ether, design. Very early on in our self-study it became clear to us that a program in religious studies (or indeed any program) at Middle Tennessee State University would need to articulate that studying religion would *do* something. Like Jonathan Z. Smith famously asserted in his essay on teaching, we would need to "show our work" and teach our students to do likewise as they spoke to the relevance of their degrees to their families, employers, and the larger community (Smith 2007). The pragmatic element was important to getting both administrators and other faculty on board, as well as our students. Forty percent of Middle Tennessee State University's student population are first generation college students; many come with expectations—either their own or their family's—that college should be practical and career oriented. Middle Tennessee State University is the largest university in Tennessee and offers degrees in a variety of fields. We are well known for programs in concrete management, business and aerospace design, and recording industry. The College of Liberal Arts plays an important role in providing the general education curriculum, but it is one of the smaller colleges at the institution. As a result, much of the emphasis of the administration focuses on skills, or more accurately put, incorporates what educators call competency-based learning wherein students gain transferable skills in a flexible format directed by the student's interests and educational needs.

Our program shifts from a content-based model wherein, crudely put, students generate a basic collection of facts and then further refine their expertise on a given topic to a competency-based model wherein skills germane to our discipline are developed and then applied to certain subsets of data that reflects the work we do within the discipline of religious studies. In thinking about the discipline-specific skills we wanted our students to gain, we pinpointed description, analysis, and critique as core areas or competencies. All of the courses in our curriculum are slotted into one of these areas and students are required to take courses in each. Rather than focusing on content or approach, we anticipate that this focus on competencies will move beyond replicating a world religions or disciplinary-based model. According to this logic, I no longer need to be worried about my Jesus-loving student only taking courses about Jesus because I can be confident that even if he were to do so, he is gaining specific tools and transferable skills with which he can do several things with all that information about Jesus and apply the same skillsets to other data—religious or otherwise.

Courses that fit within our description area look at different case studies through a particular lens or category in the field (such as myth, ritual, etc.). Here the training is in learning relevant terms and concepts and identifying their roles in and their impact on different religious phenomena. For example, in that section I teach a film course and a course on ritual and rites of passage. These courses remained focused on their topic while considering different theories, methods, and case studies. In our second competency area, we focus on the task of analysis. These course are intended to provide training in the study of a particular figure, tradition, movement, or text with a clearly stated intention to interrogate the category and problematize the scholarship surround it. In this section, for example, Gray-Hildenbrand teaches a course titled, Cults and New Religious Movements, which takes up the problems of classification and stratification. Students should walk away with a clear understanding of the theoretical and methodological approaches and relevant scholarly debates *apropos* to a given subject.

While all of our courses are intended to provide training in materials that are relevant to the academic study of religion, it is the critique section where we see our students gaining insight into the work of being a scholar of religion. Here we try to encourage our students to think of religion as a verb, something that they themselves as student-scholars can do. Drawing on the particular expertise of our faculty, we emphasize "how to religion." The courses that we offer in this competency area are particular to our own training and work in the field. In this section, I teach a course called "Mapping Religious Diversity" that introduces students to ethnographic methods and theories within religious studies. My aforementioned Jesus course, is also placed within this competency area. While a different course about Jesus could easily be placed in either the analysis or description core areas, this Jesus course focuses on the social impact of discourse more so than biblical criticism or the quest for the historical Jesus.[10] While the course was not explicitly what my Jesus-loving student had anticipated, he surprisingly enjoyed the course. I guess miracles do happen.

Concluding Remarks

One of the most popular programs of study at Middle Tennessee State University is "Concrete Industry Management" (we offer both undergraduate and graduate degrees in this field). Concrete is strong when compressed, but lacks what is known as tensile strength, the ability to withstand elongating or stretching loads. Thus, a reinforcing bar, or rebar, is used in major construction projects prior to pouring concrete to ensure the durability of a given structure. The rebar keeps the foundation in place and as such is essential for structuring and supporting a building even though it is not necessarily visible. Thinking about the architecture of religious studies at the level of the department allows us to think about the way the discipline is reflected in how we scaffold skills, approaches, and content at the levels of program design, course objectives, and individual classroom activities. While not everyone would immediately equate curriculum with department, I see the curriculum doing the work of structuring and supporting the department in multiple ways.

While my focus in this chapter is on curriculum, some of its considerations could be used to assess pedagogical practices, extra-curricular department activities, faculty service projects, and thinking about the position of one's program or department in the context of its larger institution. As I write this chapter, the religious studies major at Middle Tennessee State University is a few months away from completing its first year. It is a new program, so time will tell how it all comes together. In the coming years, I expect we may find flaws and weaknesses, natural cracks in the foundation, which will need to be addressed. But as we prepare to add a third tenure-track faculty person next year and a fourth in a few years' time, our hope is that this model has potential to grow and shift as needed alongside and in response to the state of the study of religion.

Rebekka King, PhD, is an Associate Professor and Director of Religious Studies at Middle Tennessee State University. Her research focuses on the negotiation of boundaries within North American Christianity. Her first book (under contract with NYU Press) charts the development of progressive Christianity in North America as a movement that spurned Christian orthodoxy in pursuit of a resolutely skeptical faith. She teaches courses on method and theory, anthropology of religion, and contemporary Christianity.

Notes

1. The University of Alabama's Department of Religious Studies has done an exceptional job capitalizing on this sentiment in their use of their building, Manly Hall, in their promotional materials and *esprit de corps*—think for example of their social media accounts, the coffee mugs that new majors and visiting scholars receive as gifts, advertisements for their new MA program, or their high-stakes annual faculty-student competition for the Manly Cup (see McCutcheon 2015).
2. In an interactive, multi-format article published on the Religious Studies Project website, Knut Melvær and Michael Stausberg suggest that attending to the interdisciplinary aspects of religious studies might be a by-product of attempts to distances the field from theology (Melvær and Stausberg 2013).

3 "Academic Policies: New Academic Units (Policy Number: A 1.3)," Tennessee Higher Education Commission, www.tn.gov/assets/entities/thec/attachments/THEC_A1.3_New_Academic_Units_Policy_Jan_26_2017.pdf.
4 At many institutions, however, the ur-alignment of the study of religion with theology was inferred (and in some cases remains so) by the placement of Religious Studies programs within already established departments of Philosophy, Classics, and History. The assumption here is that an obvious overlap exists between these disciplines in terms of content, theory, and methodologies. Particularly, telling is the implied connection between Religious Studies and Philosophy as two sides of the same coin addressing concepts of ethics, morality, and truth.
5 At MTSU a minor in Religious Studies consists of fifteen credits (the equivalent of five semester-long courses) and has no required courses or prerequisites, although most students commence with the introductory Religion and Society course of which we offer multiple sections each semester.
6 Indeed, the importance of this task is found in the description of this volume which speaks to the "ongoing political contests that shape the nature of our scholarship" and addresses "the politics of the institutions that make our work possible."
7 A point which is often coded apologetically and recasts the field as delineating which forms of particular traditions are deemed acceptable and authentic and which are not (see Hughes 2015).
8 "2012-2013 Undergraduate Catalog—Archived," Middle Tennessee State University.
9 Elsewhere, Gray-Hildenbrand and I emphasize the importance of program design that attends to and takes seriously one's own institution (Gray-Hildenbrand and King under review). It is essential that anyone tasked with establishing a new program does not place too much trust in the adage "if you build it, they will come." Instead, we adopted the adage suggested to us by Eugene Gallagher, "love the one you're with" (cf. Gallagher 2009: 9).
10 The course's mantra is that we are interested in what people say about Jesus and what people say about what people say about Jesus, rather than the person of Jesus himself.

References

Asad, Talal. 1993. *Genealogies of Religion: Discipline and Reasons of Power in Christianity and Islam*. Baltimore, MD: John Hopkins University Press.
Biggs, John, and Catherine Tang. 2011. *Teaching for Quality Learning at University: What the Student Does*. Maidenhead: Open University Press.
Bourdieu, Pierre. 1990. *The Logic of Practice*. Stanford, CA: Stanford University Press.
Carroll, James B., and Mimi Wolverton. 2004. "Who Becomes a Chair?" In Walter H. Gmelch and John H. Schuh (eds.), *The Life Cycle of a Department Chair*, 3-10. San Francisco, CA: Jossey-Bass. https://doi.org/10.1002/he.144
Cotter, Christopher R., and David G. Robertson (ed.). 2016. *After World Religions: Reconstructing Religious Studies*. New York: Routledge. https://doi.org/10.4324/9781315688046
Dubuisson, Daniel. 2003. *The Western Construction of Religion: Myths, Knowledge, and Ideology*. Baltimore, MD: John Hopkins University Press.
Engler, Steven. 2006. "Religious Studies in Canada and Brazil: Pro-pluralism and Anti-theology in Context." *Studies in Religion/Sciences Religieuses* 35(3-4): 445-471. https://doi.org/10.1177/000842980603500306
Engler, Steven, and Michael Stausberg. 2011. "Introductory Essay. Crisis and Creativity: Opportunities and Threats in the Global Study of Religion\s." *Religion* 41(2): 127-143. https://doi.org/10.1080/0048721X.2011.591209

Fitzgerald, Timothy. 2003. *The Ideology of Religious Studies*. New York: Oxford University Press.
Gallagher, Eugene V. 2009. "Teaching for Religious Literacy." *Teaching Theology and Religion* 12(3): 208–221. https://doi.org/10.1111/j.1467-9647.2009.00523.x
Gray-Hildenbrand, Jenna, and Rebekka King. 2019. "Teaching in Contexts: Designing a Competency-Based Religious Studies Program." *Teaching Theology and Religion* 22(3): 191–204. https://doi.org/10.1111/teth.12495
Hughes, Aaron. 2013. *Theory and Method in the Study of Religion: Twenty Five Years On*. Leiden: Brill.
Hughes, Aaron. 2015. *Islam and the Tyranny of Authenticity: An Inquiry into Disciplinary Apologetics and Self-Deception*. Sheffield: Equinox.
King, Richard. 2017. *Religion, Theory, Critique: Classical and Contemporary Approaches and Methodologies*. New York: Columbia University Press. https://doi.org/10.7312/king14542
Masuzawa, Tomoko. 2005. *The Invention of World Religions: Or, How European Universalism was Preserved in the Language of Pluralism*. Chicago, IL: University of Chicago Press. https://doi.org/10.7208/chicago/9780226922621.001.0001
McCutcheon, Russell T. 2003. *The Discipline of Religion: Structure, Meaning, Rhetoric*. New York: Routledge.
McCutcheon, Russell T. 2015. "Reinventing the Study of Religion in Alabama." In Steven W. Ramey (ed.), *Writing Religion: The Case for the Critical Study of Religion*, 208–222. Tuscaloosa, AL: University of Alabama Press.
Melvær, Knut, and Michael Stausberg. 2013. "What is the Study of Religion\s? Self-Presentations of the Discipline on University Web Pages." Retrieved from www.religiousstudiesproject.com/2013/12/06/what-is-the-study-of-religionsself-presentations-of-the-discipline-on-university-web-pages/#foreword.
Owen, Suzanne. 2011. "The World Religions Paradigm: Time for a Change." *Arts and Humanities in Higher Education* 10(3): 253–268. https://doi.org/10.1177/1474022211408038
Smith, Jonathan Z. 2007. "Afterword: The Necessary Lie: Duplicity in the Disciplines." In Russell T. McCutcheon, *Studying Religion: An Introduction*, 73–80. London: Equinox.
Smith, Leslie Dorrough. 2017. "Theory is the Best Accessory: Branding and the Power of Scholarly Compartmentalization." In Aaron Hughes (ed.), *Theory in a Time of Excess: Beyond Reflection and Explanation in Religious Studies Scholarship*, 179–189. Sheffield: Equinox.
Tolstoy, Leo. 1899. *Anna Karenina*. New York: Thomas Y. Cromwell and Company.

Chapter 19

Religious Studies Research in an Era of Neoliberalization

Gregory D. Alles

In these remarks about the state of research in the study of religions, I want to address two basic topics. The first is my location within the study of religions and its impact on my assessment of the field. The second comprises various changes that have taken place in higher education, conveniently brought together under the label "neoliberalization." These changes are virtually universal, and they form a major influence on the state of the study of religions today, including research.

I want to address my location, because in several ways it diverges from what a reader would typically associate with someone commenting on this topic. To start with, I do not work at a Research 1 university; I work at a national liberal arts college. Before my time our college did manage to produce two graduates who went on to become prominent figures in the study of religions with two rather different theoretical commitments: Luther Martin, one of the founders of NAASR and best known now for his connections to the cognitive science of religion, and Davíd Carrasco, a leading scholar of Mesoamerican religions theoretically opposed to many of the positions that have defined NAASR. Despite having produced these leading scholars, our college sees itself primarily as a teaching institution. Although I have heard it stated that at some elite liberal arts colleges the requirements for promotion and tenure are pretty much the same as at Research 1 universities, we are not such an institution. Indeed, although a certain amount of "professional activity" is expected of colleagues coming up for tenure and promotion, and despite my best efforts for now over thirty years, we still have no stated publication requirements.

I draw attention to this point for two reasons. First, some critics of the neoliberalization of higher education lament the emphasis placed upon quantifiable research results, apparently at the expense of teaching, in the assessment of faculty (Busch 2017: 65–74; cf. Giroux 2014: 30, 34, 56, 191; Ordine 2017: 78–81). I do recognize the problem of expecting people to produce too much too fast, with the result that some of what they produce does not make the contribution that it might have made if they had taken more time and let their scholarship mature. At the same time, I want to acknowledge that I am and always have been in the camp of those about whom the critics are complaining. I think it is important for anyone working in an institution of higher learning to be able to demonstrate their abilities through at least a minimal number of publications before an institution enters into what, given tenure, amounts to a commitment to spend a couple of million dollars or more. In other words, I am not, and do not wish to be seen as, a doctrinaire critic of neoliberalization. As in anything dealing with higher education, assessing the state of research in the study of religions involves hacking one's way through an entangled thicket.

Second, and more positively, I want to draw attention to the amount of research in religious studies that gets done by people who do *not* teach in Research 1 institutions. Compared to many other fields, the number of quality graduate programs in the study of religions is limited—setting to one side graduate programs in theology, such as those offered by denominational seminaries. Given the job market, this is probably as it should be. One implication is that a lot of quality research in the study of religions gets done, almost by default, by people teaching in undergraduate institutions. This is a point that I think Mark Taylor noted many years ago, but it is one that still merits attention—and praise.

There is another way in which my location is oddly suited to someone commenting on the state of research in the study of religions. Much of my recent work has been presented to audiences outside of that study: audiences in anthropology, philosophy, and *dharmik* studies. The last is close to the study of religions, but it is not quite the same thing. At least prima facie my contribution to the *Handbook of Indigenous Religion(s)* (Johnson and Kraft 2017) is within the study of religions, but as I read through the other chapters, I quickly realized that they discussed religion much more than my own chapter did. The closest I came to religion was to say that for *adivasis* ("tribal people" in India today) the notion that they are indigenous functions the way some scholars of religions in the past thought myth functioned. This is just using the study of religions as an analogy.

Some of my current interests—I am thinking specifically of celebrations of the UN's "International Day of the World's Indigenous Peoples"—*could* be given a religious studies slant. I could say that what I am studying discusses what has not been recognized as religious but might usefully be considered to be such—that it is secular religion or religion that flies under the radar or implicit religion. Religious studies scholars have employed all sorts of ways to extend their categories to areas where they do not seem immediately to fit. I, however, generally find such usages forced, distracting, and unnecessary. The language of religion is, after all, not exactly the least controversial category in the academic conceptual arsenal. To my mind introducing it in such a way results in obfuscating objects and dynamics that could be more clearly and straightforwardly identified without mentioning the words "religion" or "religious" at all, such as (to take an example inspired by Durkheim) the power of emotionally powerful symbols to create a sense of communal identity. But let me give this point a more positive spin. In general, since religious studies is a multi-disciplinary field, most scholars of religions possess a wide variety of skills and perspectives. As a result, as researchers they can be quite versatile.

The last point about my location has to do with horizons. Much of my thinking about research results from my experiences co-editing *Numen*, the journal of the International Association for the History of Religion, of which NAASR is an affiliate. In reviewing submissions, I am always attentive when an author uses first-person plural pronouns: we, us, our. Sometimes these pronouns refer to a religious community with which a scholar self-identifies, and this presents issues of its own. Often, however, the first-person plural pronoun refers to the community of scholars to which the author imagines herself or himself belonging; to paraphrase a famous quote from Jonathan Z. Smith by way of example, religion is "our" category, a category that "we" scholars have invented.

Ideally, since *Numen* is an international journal, such pronouns refer to a community of scholars that is global. Too often, however, North American and European scholars use them to refer to scholars in Europe and North America, or perhaps just to English-speaking scholars in those areas. (What scholars in particular did Smith have in mind?) One would be tempted to call this attitude parochial or provincial, but to do so would be to ignore the methodological and theoretical hegemony that North American and European scholarship exercises over the rest of the world, and not just because of the quality of its insights (cf., e.g., Gingras and Mosbah-Natanson 2010).

To be sure, all research takes place within a context, and it is important to acknowledge that context and the way it affects what a scholar does. Furthermore, local and regional discursive communities have their own distinct benefits, whether those communities happen to be in North America, Japan, South Asia, or elsewhere. They are important ways in which scholars encourage, stimulate, and inform one another. Nevertheless, acknowledging contextual embeddedness becomes insidious when it becomes, whether intentionally or not, an excuse for parochiality. At the least, it is useful to learn that scholars in other parts of the world do not find one's ideas and approaches convincing. In last year's NAASR volume I wrote a little about indigenous methodologies, and although the topic continues to merit attention, I will not revisit it here. Instead, I will just recall an email that I had recently received from a young Estonian scholar and that came to mind several times as I was sitting through the NAASR sessions in Boston. Russell McCutcheon's ideas, this scholar wrote, have no traction is Estonia; they just do not address the context in which Estonian scholars find themselves. Specifically, after several decades of imposed Marxism, they are themselves fascinated by religion and not particularly interested in being its critics. Let me be clear. I do not mean to imply that people in NAASR should not be having the discussions that they are having. I am suggesting that there are also more extensive discussions to be had.

Let me use these observations to make another observation about neoliberalism. In the economic sphere, neoliberals are globalizers; their critics are not. Neoliberalism is generally associated with open borders and free trade: NAFTA, the WTO, the World Bank, and so on. There may be a case to be made for restrictions on trade in the economic domain, but if there is, I do not think it applies to knowledge. Knowledge is not an ordinary commodity. Especially in a time when long-distance transportation is relatively quick and cheap—if one ignores the externalities involved in air travel—and communication around the globe can be instantaneous, scholars of religions can and should talk with each other globally. Such conversations are, however, not as easy as they may sound, for scholars in different regions come to the field with different agendas, methods, and theories, and collaboration can be difficult. One may find one's cherished positions summarily dismissed or encounter scholars working in directions that one considers dead-ends. If the study of religions, however, is not simply to represent the parochial activity of isolated groups somewhat mistaken about the universal applicability of their claims, these are discussions that need to take place. Our field will be richer and more interesting as a result.

In other words, here is another respect in which I am not a doctrinaire critic of neoliberalism. If a part of the neoliberalization of higher education involves globalization, I am all for it, at least when it comes to collaborative research and knowledge creation. Globalization becomes more questionable when universities in richer countries establish branches in poorer countries as a way to extract economic resources from them or, as one might more commonly say, a way of overcoming budget deficits and balancing their books. This is especially the case if, as people sometimes lament, the quality of education provided abroad is not the same as that provided at home.[1]

Perhaps now is an opportune time to pivot to the second of my basic topics, namely, neoliberalism's impact on research in the study of religions. I start with a few words about neoliberalism itself, since in my experience people who think of themselves as liberal, especially in the United States, sometimes find the term "neoliberalism" confusing or annoying. "Neoliberalism" can mean a lot of things—as Lawrence Busch (2017: 11) has put it, it may refer to "a school of thought in ... economics, ... a program of action, ... [or] an ideology"[2]—but whichever of these it refers to, it is rather different from political "liberalism" in the US.

As a term of art in economics, "liberalism" refers to the view that societies flourish best when markets are free, that is, unconstrained by governmental interference such as tariffs and central planning and when Adam Smith's "invisible hand" makes everything right. In the 1930s, in the wake of the Great Depression, the liberal faith in the market was shaken. Governments not only came to evaluate intervention in economic affairs more positively; influenced by the economic theories of John Maynard Keynes, they came to see it as absolutely necessary. The Keynesian position remained dominant until the 1970s, when a general economic malaise led people to look for alternatives. Neoliberalism was the alternative that received the most attention.

The birth of neoliberalism is sometimes dated to the first meeting of the Mont Pelerin Society in 1947, attended by figures such as Friedrich Hayek and Milton Friedman (Harvey 2007: 19–20; Steger and Roy 2010: 15). It is liberal in that, contrary to Keynesianism, it sees everything working better if organized as a free, competitive market in which private interests compete. This conviction gained theoretical purchase from Hayek's argument that prices always contain more information than is available to central planners, so that freely operating markets are preferable to managed ones (Hayek 1945). But neoliberalism is not old-style liberalism. It does not see the proper role of government as simply getting out of the way of economic activity. It has an interventionist bent, although one that is highly suspicious of government intervention in the interests of what Friedrich

Hayek once called *The Mirage of Social Justice* (Hayek 1976). It sees the proper role of government as ensuring that all activities are organized according to free market principles—views most often associated with Margaret Thatcher and Ronald Reagan but also shared in more moderate form by Bill Clinton and Tony Blair (Steger and Roy 2010: 21–75). Convinced that private, unfettered markets will always outperform centrally managed ones, neoliberalism insists on privatization and globalization.

Neoliberalism does not restrict the value of markets to what is traditionally thought of as economic activity. For example, by establishing a market for trading carbon credits, the theory goes, governments can effectively address the "externalities" created by carbon emissions. Similar principles apply, *mutatis mutandis*, to higher education.[3] Governments should not fund higher education; those who benefit from it should pay for it, with loans if they do not have immediate access to the necessary resources. Furthermore, rather than giving faculty guaranteed jobs for life, institutions of higher education should allow faculty to compete in a fully functioning labor market. The result in higher education, as in other "industries," has been an increasing reliance on contract labor, that is, on adjunct or contingent faculty. In addition, universities and colleges need to demonstrate the worth of what they do—the "value" that they "add"—in quantifiable terms, and often in financial ones (cf. David Harvey 2007: 33: "Neoliberalization has meant … the financialization of everything"). Perhaps the most extreme step along this path is one that the Japanese Ministry of Education took in June 2015. It decided more or less to eliminate all of the humanities and social sciences from Japanese universities because they were useless fields—a decision that provoked vociferous opposition and a relatively quick, if not entirely convincing, clarification.[4]

Some critics of the neoliberalization of higher education warn against creating a false dichotomy between the natural sciences on the one hand and the humanities and social sciences on the other (Busch 2017: 124–125; Ordine 2017: 103–105). Colleagues in the STEM fields, they point out, also feel the consequences of reduced government funding and of pressure from private finance to devote their attention to research that will be financially remunerative. In its statements on the Japanese Ministry's directive, the Science Council of Japan noted the need for the sciences, social sciences, and humanities to work together.[5] These are sentiments that I endorse. Nevertheless, there are real differences between research in the natural sciences and research in the humanities and social sciences, including religious studies, and they have real consequences. For example, a few weeks before the NAASR meeting in Boston I received an email from a colleague lamenting that at his university only people in the natural sciences are thought of as doing research; everyone else's activities are classified as scholarship.

When I think about research in religious studies today in contrast to research in the natural sciences, I find it difficult not to think in personal terms of the contrast between the research that I do and that which my daughter does. Our locations are different—she works at a Research 1 institution, I do not—but more to the point here is what she does: she directs a research lab in an area of veterinary pharmacology.

There are some differences between my research and hers that would seem to have little to do with neoliberalization. Take collaboration, for example. I have recently been involved in a collaborative research program, hosted at the University of Tromsø, entitled "Indigenous Religion(s): Local Grounds, Global Networks." It has been a marvelous experience. Not only have I encountered indigenous peoples outside of my personal area of interest—the Sami in Sápmi (northern Norway, Sweden, and Finland), the Bribri in Costa Rica—but I have also confronted a broad range of theoretical questions and methodological resources that I might never have encountered on my own. Nevertheless, although some of us have written some collaborative pieces, they can be difficult to pull off and involve negotiation and compromise about positions, goals, and the analysis of materials. At the end of the day, each of us generally returns to our solitary work, enriched by our encounters with the others.

This is quite different from the necessarily collaborative work that takes place in my daughter's lab. The people there all share the same basic theoretical commitments, the same agenda, the same general conceptions of the problems to be solved, or in tough cases the same sense of the kinds of models that need to be developed and techniques to be employed. Despite these similarities, their work is necessarily collaborative, because it requires skills from various disciplines that no one person could reasonably be expected to master. In other words, this is collaborative research in the form of the division of labor. The final product is a truly joint effort. There are some places in the study of religions where such collaborative work gets done, such as programs in the cognitive science of religion at the University of British Columbia, Aarhus University, or the University of Brno. Most humanistic scholars of religion, however, engage in a different sort of collaboration. They are, to use a loose analogy, more like preindustrial craftspeople, coming together to share skills, swap stories, and gain new ideas, but each tooling her or his own individual products.

The kind of research my daughter does differs from research in religious studies in other ways, too. Consider its public implications. Some scholars of religions find themselves testifying in court or advising legislators about minority religions or new religious movements. Needless to say, their activities are important. At the same time, few if any of them make their livings servicing the needs of the courts or the legislature. My daughter's research, by contrast, is instrumental to regulating a multi-billion dollar industry in the US alone. It identifies potential culprits, and in a legal context it provides crucial evidence that, if it stands up in court, leads to felony convictions. Perhaps as a result of these demands, my daughter only teaches 60 minutes a year; the rest of her time is spent in the lab. So far as I know, even in Research 1 universities there are few scholars in religious studies whose contracts require so little teaching year in and year out. I will return to these observations in a bit, but before I do, I want to contextualize research in the study of religions a little further.

In a neoliberal environment, the value of academic programs is largely assessed in terms of numbers, most obviously in an undergraduate environment, numbers of majors, minors, and students in the classroom. This assessment affects in turn the number of teaching positions available and so the demand for graduate education. Add to this the notion, also fostered by a neoliberal approach, that higher education is primarily about job training, and fields like religious studies have a real problem. This is hardly a novel observation. Here I simply want to remind readers that it does not have to be this way. For example, I recall a meeting of religious studies faculty in Munich in the early 2000s when Michael von Brück, who had a very large following of students, urged us not to play a numbers game; we should refrain from thinking that a field that attracted fewer students—in this case masters and doctoral students—was for that reason any less valuable to the program or the university. There are some topics that deserve to be taught and examined for their intrinsic value to the field, regardless of their appeal to the general public or the personal charisma of the researcher.

Topics with such value for work in the study of religions exist outside as well as inside the field itself. For example, religious studies would be immensely poorer if research by North American scholars were confined simply to the study of religions in English and perhaps Spanish-speaking contexts. Much quality work in the study of religions requires a knowledge of what will appear to the general North American public as rather obscure or arcane languages. Consider, for example, the range of languages that scholars of ancient Near Eastern religions need to master, and then consider how different our understanding of the world would be if scholars had never been able to access sources from ancient Egypt, Mesopotamia, Persia, Turkey, or—given the reduction or elimination of classics programs—even Greek and Latin. Yet a quick Google search for "elimination of university language programs" yields over two million hits, and they do not concern the elimination just of programs in languages such as Syriac and Akkadian. It is true that the US government has programs to encourage the study of what it considers critical languages,[6] but while proficiency in these languages may be sufficient for the purposes of diplomacy or espionage, it is not sufficient for the study of religions, even if the field were transformed merely into the study of religions present.

Another feature of higher education in the neoliberal context also deserves mention: the commodification of knowledge. On the one hand, as noted above, this has led to knowledge being treated as a private rather than a public good: those purchasing the commodity should pay for it, not the state. The decline of public funding for higher education has meant both rising levels of graduate student debt and an increasing reliance on contingent or adjunct faculty, many of whom teach an unfathomable number of courses in a term for very little money. It does not take a doctoral degree in economics to recognize that these pressures will have a dampening effect on both the quantity and the quality of research that gets done in any field, including religious studies. Conversely, from the point of view of many "consumers," knowledge is not something that one works for and engages with but something that one purchases, often at a very high price. One should not romanticize the past; students have always pursued higher education with a variety of motives and various degrees of engagement, and colleges and universities have often provided less than ideal opportunities for learning.[7] Still, as universities and governments adopt neoliberal models in thinking about themselves, Wilhelm von Humboldt's ideal of the mutual implication of research and teaching in universities, an ideal that arguably has underlain the best work in a variety of fields for two centuries, seems a distant memory.

I am tempted to extend my contextualization of research in religious studies even further, for example, to comments on the publishing industry, but since time and space are limited, I will stop here. It is easy for faculty members to blame administrators for whatever difficulties they face. It may in fact be that the widely lamented "crisis of the humanities," from which religious studies is hardly immune, results to some extent from a lack of appreciation for the humanities on the part of some administrators, trustees, students, and educators. In many cases, however, administrators have been forced to respond to very difficult constraints posed by a lack of funding. To a large extent, these difficulties are rooted in a culture that sees higher education as a private, not a public, good and that disvalues pursuits that cannot turn a measurable profit.

In a neoliberal environment the best way to demonstrate the value of one's research is economic: to engage in research that demonstrably leads to the development of products that make money or that brings funding to the institution in the form of grants or that, like my daughter's research, is necessary to the successful functioning of an industry. It is possible to argue that one should not be too short-sighted in assessing economic benefits. As Abraham Flexner of Princeton's Institute for Advanced Studies argued long ago, apparently useless basic research, motivated primarily by intellectual curiosity, may prove to be more useful to product development in the long run than research devoted simply to the development of an individual product (Flexner 1939; cf. Flexner and Dijkgraaf 2017). Flexner's examples all had to do with basic research in the natural sciences, but it is possible to extend this argument to include research in the humanities as well. In a publication released in conjunction with the World Economic Forum meeting in Davos in January 2018, Brad Smith and Harry Shum of Microsoft write:

> At one level, AI [artificial intelligence] will require that even more people specialize in digital skills and data science. But skilling-up for an AI-powered world involves more than science, technology, engineering and math. As computers behave more like humans, the social sciences and humanities will become even more important. Languages, art, history, economics, ethics, philosophy, psychology and human development courses can teach critical, philosophical and ethics-based skills that will be instrumental in the development and management of AI solutions. If AI is to reach its potential in serving humans, then every engineer will need to learn more about the liberal arts and every liberal arts major will need to learn more about engineering. (Microsoft Corporation 2018)

Perhaps it would be possible to argue for the economic usefulness of religious studies, but I do not know any scholars of religious studies who actually do so. Is there an elective affinity between devoting one's life to the study of religions and the conviction that other values are more important than economic ones? In any case, it seems more common for people in religious studies to justify their work in terms of its social and political utility.[8] This is certainly the direction in which I have gone as I have attempted to explain my interest in the indigenous peoples of India both to the people themselves and to outsiders. These are people who are marginalized economically and socially; they were previously stigmatized by such terms as "primitive" and "savage," and I have heard them referred to as monkeys by people who should know better. In the North American academy their cultures and religions are little known and studied, in comparison to the traditions, beliefs, and practices of caste Hindus and Dalits (the former untouchables). In a small way, I hope my work redresses these failings. In a neoliberal world, however, such justifications are less effective than economic ones. Theoretically, one leaves oneself open to Hayek's charge that social justice is a mirage or, perhaps less aggressively, Stanley Fish's argument that academic work is not and should not be about pursuing social justice (Fish 2008). More pragmatically, if funds for higher education require legislative action, and if legislative bodies are controlled by people who are convinced that, in general, the politics of the people teaching at institutions of higher learning are opposed to their own, it should not come as too much of a surprise if higher education budgets are cut.

Are there alternatives to the arguments for economic or social and political utility? As we all know, the claim to be doing neutral research is suspicious. In the past it has obscured unsavory agendas. I have myself pointed to the social, political, and colonialist agendas that propelled Rudolf Otto's work with religions other than Christianity and his fascination with the numinous. At the same time, I have to confess that I have a certain nostalgia for "value-free" research in a very particular sense. If value is reduced to financial value—recall Harvey's statement, "Neoliberalization has meant ... the financialization of everything"—perhaps it is useful to celebrate research that is "value-free." To quote Stanley Fish:

> Make a virtue of the fact that many programs of humanities research (and not only humanities research) have no discernible product, bring no measurable benefits, are not time-sensitive, may never reach fruition and (in some cases) are only understood by 500 people in the entire world. Explain what a university is and how its conventions of inquiry are not answerable to the demands we rightly make of industry. Turn an accusation ... into a banner and hold it aloft. (Fish 2010)

If the term "value-free" seems too problematic or confusing, one could shift to the language of utility, as the Italian scholar Nuccio Ordine has done, and champion "the usefulness of the useless" (Ordine 2017; cf. Flexner and Dijkgraaf 2017). Of course, this rhetoric is playing on contradictions. Value-free research in my sense implies that there are other values that are worth pursuing besides monetary ones, an argument that even a Chicago economist, Deirdre McCloskey, has been making in partial reliance on Adam Smith's *Theory of Moral Sentiments* (McCloskey 2006). Similarly, speaking of the usefulness of the useless aims to undercut the very limited sense of utility in terms of which some people think. This move is not, however, unprecedented. In fact, as the many sources collected by Ordine demonstrate, it has a venerable pedigree. For the full panoply I refer the reader to Ordine's book. Here I will mention only the example that I know the best.

It is too schematic to read the history of late nineteenth- and early twentieth-century Germany as a contest between the educated elite (*Bildungsbürgertum*) and the business elite (*Besitzbürgertum*). For example, by birth Rudolf Otto was a member of the business elite (his father owned F. W. Otto Malzfabrik). As an adult, he became a member of the educated elite, as did some, but not all, of his siblings. Nevertheless, the schema is not entirely misleading. In the Weimar years Otto, like some others among the educated elite, opposed the economic rationality of the business elite and championed research that was "value-free" in the sense in which I have been using the term. The work of the university was not done to make a profit; it had inherent value.

A cynical reading of this position could point to more than its internal contradictions; it could also present it as an argument by a privileged, leisured elite that aims to convince people who actually work for a living to support their private indulgences. Nevertheless, at a time when the heritage of the *Besitzbürgertum*, in the form of neoliberalization, is exercising increasing control over the university, research in religious studies will flourish best if scholars in the field make a convincing case that, regardless of its "uselessness" and lack of economic value, their research is in and of itself a social good, that the knowledge that we produce—and I mean "we" in a global sense—makes human life richer. In the current climate doing so will not be an easy task, but it is well worth the effort.

Gregory D. Alles is professor of religious studies at McDaniel College, Westminster, MD. A past president of NAASR, he serves as co-editor of *Numen* and co-chair of the steering committee of the Indigenous Religious Traditions Unit of the American Academy of Religion. He is the author of *The Iliad, The Ramayana, and the Work of Religion: Failed Persuasion and Religious Mystification* as well as a number of articles. He edited *Religious Studies: A Global View*. His current research interests center on the religion and culture of the Rathvas, a scheduled tribe in the western Indian state of Gujarat.

Notes

1. For example, Altbach (2010).
2. For an alternate triad, see Steger and Roy (2010: 11): "Perhaps the best way to conceptualize neoliberalism is to think of it as three intertwined manifestations: (1) an ideology; (2) a mode of governance; (3) a policy package."
3. Extended discussions include Nussbaum (2010), Giroux (2014), and Busch (2017).
4. The Ministry's statement (for those who can read Japanese; I cannot) is available at www.mext.go.jp/b_menu/shingi/chukyo/chukyo3/002/siryo/attach/1360412.htm. Pertinent sections are available in English in a statement of the executive board of the Science Council of Japan entitled "On the Future Direction of the University: In Relation to the Departments/Graduate Schools of Teacher Training and Humanities and Social Sciences 23rd July 2015" (www.scj.go.jp/en/pdf/kohyo-23-kanji-1e.pdf). Cf. the follow-up statement, "Statement from the Executive Board of Science Council of Japan to Express our Sincere Appreciation for the Support and Approval towards the "Statement on the Future Direction of the University: In Relation to the Departments/Graduate Schools of Teacher Training, and Humanities and Social Sciences" and the "Proposal for Nationwide Consensus towards University Reform 15th October 2015" (www.scj.go.jp/en/pdf/kohyo-23-kanji-2e.pdf), and the editorial (www.japantimes.co.

jp/opinion/2015/08/23/commentary/japan-commentary/humanities-attack/#. WmjaUlNG2Ul). Thanks to Satoko Fujiwara, University of Tokyo, who provided these references.

5 See note 4 above.
6 See https://exchanges.state.gov/us/cls and www.nsep.gov/content/critical-languages (accessed January 26, 2018).
7 For example, Hutchins (1933), written in the midst of the Great Depression, makes for sober reading.
8 In the text I emphasize social rather than political issues. Former US Secretary of State John Kerry attracted attention in religious studies circles for championing the need for a knowledge of religions in conducting diplomacy (see, e.g., Kerry 2015). It would also be possible to make an argument that a knowledge of religions is necessary to an informed citizenry in a democratic society (cf. Nussbaum 2010).

References

Altbach, Philip, G. 2010. "Open Door in Higher Education: Unsustainable and Probably Ill-Advised." *Economic and Political Weekly* 45(13): 13–15.
Busch, Lawrence. 2017. *Knowledge for Sale: The Neoliberal Takeover of Higher Education*. Cambridge, MA: MIT Press. https://doi.org/10.7551/mitpress/10742.001.0001
Fish, Stanley. 2008. *Save the World on Your Own Time*. New York: Oxford University Press.
Fish, Stanley. 2010. "Crisis of the Humanities II." Retrieved from http://opinionator.blogs.nytimes.com/2010/10/18/crisis-of-the-humanities-ii.
Flexner, Abraham. 1939. "Usefulness of Useless Knowledge." *Harpers* 179: 544–552.
Flexner, Abraham, and Robbert Dijkgraaf. 2017. *The Usefulness of Useless Knowledge*. Princeton, NJ: Princeton University Press. https://doi.org/10.1515/9781400884629
Gingras, Yves, and Sébastien Mosbah-Natanson. 2010. "Where are Social Sciences Produced?" In Françoise Caillods and Laurent Jeanpierre (eds.), *World Social Science Survey 2010: Knowledge Divides*, 149–153. Paris: UNESCO.
Giroux, Henry A. 2014. *Neoliberalism's War on Higher Education*. Chicago, IL: Haymarket Books.
Harvey, David. 2007. *A Brief History of Neoliberalism*. Oxford: Oxford University Press.
Hayek, Friedrich A. von. 1945. "The Use of Knowledge in Society." *American Economic Review* 35(4): 519–530.
Hayek, Friedrich A. von. 1976. *The Mirage of Social Justice*. Chicago, IL: University of Chicago Press.
Hutchins, Robert M. 1933. "The Higher Learning in America." *Journal of Higher Education* 4(1): 1–8. https://doi.org/10.2307/1973930
Johnson, Greg, and Siv Ellen Kraft (eds.). 2017. *Handbook of Indigenous Religion(s)*. Leiden: Brill. https://doi.org/10.1163/9789004346710
Kerry, John. 2015. "Religion and Diplomacy: Toward a Better Understanding of Religion and Global Affairs." *America: The Jesuit Review* 216(6): 14–16.
McCloskey, Deirdre N. 2006. *The Bourgeois Virtues: Ethics for an Age of Commerce*. Chicago, IL: University of Chicago Press. https://doi.org/10.7208/chicago/9780226556673.001.0001
Microsoft Corporation. 2018. *The Future Computed: Artificial Intelligence and Its Role in Society*. Redmond, WA: Microsoft Corporation.
Nussbaum, Martha C. 2010. *Nor for Profit: Why Democracy Needs the Humanities*. Princeton, NJ: Princeton University Press.
Ordine, Nuccio. 2017. *The Usefulness of the Useless*. Philadelphia, PA: Paul Dry Books.
Steger, Manfred B., and Ravi K. Roy. 2010. *Neoliberalism: A Very Short Introduction*. Oxford: Oxford University Press. https://doi.org/10.1093/actrade/9780199560516.001.0001

Epilogue

The Gatekeeping Rhetoric of Collegiality in the Study of Religion

Aaron W. Hughes and Russell T. McCutcheon

> Reverence is a religious, and not a scholarly virtue. When good manners and good conscience cannot be reconciled, the demands of the latter ought to prevail. (Lincoln 1996)

Collegiality is a term often invoked in the hallowed halls of academe. Although we often judge children on whether "they get along together" or "play well with others," that we would likely never judge working class occupations in terms of such a thing as collegiality, or call workmates in so-called blue collar jobs "colleagues," is something worth considering—that is, the terms carry undisclosed class connotations of gentility and fine breeding, suggesting, right from the outset, that this seemingly innocuous term is doing some undisclosed heavy lifting. Of course, many regard it as the foundation stone upon which is erected all that we do as professors along with the ethos that governs our intellectual interactions with both our data and with one another. Yet, it is a term that is as opaque as it is imprecise—perhaps the very characteristics that account for its wide use when describing (and thereby assessing) the performance of faculty members.

The term's imprecision, however, provides a convenient site to interrogate some of the undisclosed (and, because of that, unchecked) social, political, economic, and intellectual processes that drive our field—an examination that has taken place in other fields, of course (we think here of the work done by those in other fields, in the past few decades, examining the labor conditions of higher education), but which has yet to focus on our own. For, as many have argued, it is these often hidden standards that comingle to create a status quo and an orthodoxy, the breach of which, by means of actions judged "uncollegial," can lead to disciplinary censure and ostracization—everything from the more mild rejection of a submitted paper to the far more significant loss of a career or reputation. It therefore seems to be one of the major reasons for the inherent conservatism of many disciplines and intellectual fields of study—a significant mechanism used in the reproduction of a status quo. Religious Studies, our own academic home, for example, is ostensibly invested in understanding (i.e., recovering the meaning of) the lives of religious practitioners. If one undermines the latter, for instance by calling attention instead to the meta or non-agential structural processes that make the study of religion possible in the first place—and thereby querying what it takes for granted and what it overlooks, for example—one risks transgressing a set of firmly established boundaries, inasmuch as (or so one might be told) the field's members study religion, not "religion." Such transgression is not uncommonly met with accusations of not being "collegial," or of being its antonym, to wit, "too critical" (a term that we propose as the current inheritor of the once used derogatory term "reductionistic"), leading to portraits of one being "out to destroy the field or a particular subfield therein." Indeed, even an article like the present one, one devoted to the trope and rhetoric of collegiality, may well be met in certain quarters with the charge of being uncollegial.

In religious studies, not unlike other the academic fields, undisclosed standards of collegiality set the tone of the conversation about religion and what it means to study it. It would seem to mean that we, as scholars, ought to appreciate (also known as "take seriously") religion and religious devotees (notably their own understanding of their intentions and meanings) and that we endeavor not to offend the religious subjects we are ostensibly charged to study (via detailing what are now termed their lived experiences or embodied practices). Offend believers, either by offering a counter reading of their understanding of their scriptures or their rituals, or by studying the possibly unarticulated reasons for them representing things as they do, and, so the story goes, we offend one another and thus the profession itself (inasmuch as religion is often defined as a universal core of meaningful human nature—a definition that actively implicates scholars, inasmuch as they are human beings too, in their objects of study). In sum, to improperly engage in the study of religion one is seen as breaking the unwritten code of collegiality by not having sufficient respect for the rules that ostensibly govern our collective guild.[1]

A recent expression for this understanding of collegiality may be found in the work of the well-known scholar of American religion, Robert A. Orsi, someone whose general hermeneutic of understanding "lived" religion has become increasingly influential.[2] His method focuses less on theory, we would argue, than it does on what some might characterize as post-theoretical observations.[3] Orsi, in particular, conceives of the scholar of religion in the following terms:

> Once religion is understood as a web not of meanings but of relationships between heaven and earth, then scholars of religion take their places as participants in these networks too, together with the saints and in the company of practitioners. We get caught up in these bonds, whether we want to or not. (Orsi 2005: 5)

Religious practitioners and scholars of religion, on Orsi's reading, are therefore all involved in what we might aptly term a mutually collegial relationship—with this term, "colleagial" stretching now further the boundary of the educational institution implied by the term's etymology (originally from the Latin collegium, meaning guild, community, or just society, implying people with whom one works in such institutions—i.e., colleagues) Scholars, operating in this vein, respect religious practitioners and the latter, in turn, allow the former into their world of meaning, as colleagues. In studying the religious, inasmuch as it is presumed here to be a transhuman universal, we would then seem to better and more fully understand ourselves (a classically humanistic model once also proposed by Wendy Doniger, inasmuch as we study other people's myths so as to better understand our own; see O'Flaherty 1986). Within such a framework, when scholars overstep their bounds (by studying the religious in terms other than their own) they are judged to have acted in bad faith and are considered poor guests in other people's worlds (and even improper inhabitants of their own).

Collegiality in this guest/host model, then, seems to name the parameters of our field's first principles, it's very conditions of possibility. Here, again, collegiality is used synonymously with terms such as "respect," "empathy," "understanding," "propriety," and "appreciation." One transgresses such virtues at one's peril (risking being called impious, in a long past era, a reductionist, more recently, or, now, a cynic, an imperialist, or even worse). Indeed, the deck would seem to be stacked against those who do not perform work in this manner (thereby limiting it simply to description) or who do not act, to use Orsi's words once again, as "practitioners." Undermine religious belief (by, for instance, querying its conditions of possibility rather than taking it as a given) and one risks being represented as difficult, overly critical, or, more specifically, as "uncollegial." This sense of collegiality in the academic study of religion has therefore led to the formation of an inherently conservative field wherein scholars are expected to conserve a certain sort of folksy relation to the peoples or traditions whom they study, in which they are discouraged from straying too far beyond the path tread by their academic predecessors, and in which a certain gentility of interaction among peers is the norm (our disagreements cannot be too animated and our intellectual convictions must be worn lightly). Yet while many regard collegiality as a virtue, that which permits self-governance and respectful cohabitation within a shared academic pursuit, others (ourselves among them) regard collegiality as the silencing of critique, as a strategic boundary maintenance device, and, thus, as a hindrance to a broader sense of academic freedom. What's more, if our argument is persuasive, then it is worth considering that collegiality, being the product of the status quo and a device used to conserve its hold on power, is an activity that is maintained and patrolled on a variety of seemingly innocuous occasions, such as the venerable institutions as "blind" peer- and tenure-review.[4] In such situations uncollegiality is often pointed out anonymously and often in what we would claim to be the most uncollegial of fashions, all the while paradoxically occurring under the guise of being collegial.

While we certainly place a high value on the necessity of academic self-governance and the value of respect, as one might commonly define it, in carrying out scholarly discourses (along with a variety of other values that we prize, e.g., accuracy, rigor, transparency, etc.), we wish to suggest that lurking behind uses of the word collegiality, a term that drives the professional study of religion along with much work in the academy, are a host of undisclosed and hardly self-evident meta-professional issues. For while scholarship and effectiveness in the classroom can, to whatever extent, be measured and quantified, collegiality cannot. It, thus, functions discursively, defined and used at will to deprive or admit access to the profession. At risk of appearing uncollegial to some, our task in this essay is to explore some of these meta-professional issues, trying to illumine the fault lines that lurk beneath disciplinary collegiality. Our contention is that as long as an undefined notion of collegiality can be used arbitrarily to dismiss or marginalize individuals, then institutions—universities, professional organizations, and so on—of higher education will never truly be collegial (as we will later attempt to redefine the term). For it is our hope that such open and explicit scrutiny of this usually undisclosed gatekeeping devise will strike readers as constituting collegiality in its best sense: that of being a co-inhabitant of our field (i.e., a colleague), and thus one who holds peers to high standards of evidence and argumentation in hopes of them doing likewise (what we think of when we recall Bruce Lincoln's challenge, in the closing chapter to his *Theorizing Myth*, for scholars to "show their work").

Although not written in the colloquial style of each of their book's entries, we therefore see this essay as offering an assessment of the discourse on collegiality's doublespeak in a fashion suited to Nelson and Watt's engaging and frankly written *Academic Keywords: A Devil's Dictionary for Higher Education* (1999). Thus, it is an attempt to examine critically the "vocabulary that reinforces various forms of false consciousness" in our profession (ibid.: vii).

Case Study in Gatekeeping

In order to move the discussion along, and provide a specific example of where these implicit operations can be made more evident, we wish to begin by focusing on an organization that we believe to be exemplary of some of these larger institutional issues. This organization, to be named shortly, is devoted to the academic study of religion; its *raison d'être* is to hold

> meetings on an annual basis, where members present papers on a particular theme. In order to encourage rigorous and substantive engagement, papers tend to be short and discussions tend to be long. In addition to the stated theme of the meeting, discussions also may focus on the challenges of comparative work, the history of the field, and the role of the disciplines in the interdisciplinary field of religion. Occasionally the conversation will also engage the topic of pedagogy in the study of religion within the contemporary American academy.

Yes, you are probably thinking to yourself, we know all about the American Academy of Religion (AAR), the largest national professional association in our field. So what is new here? Well, it turns out that this is not the AAR, but, instead, another US scholarly organization—what some might see as a condensed and rarified AAR, as it were—that meets separately and whose membership is by invitation only. The little known (at least to some) American Society for the Study of Religion (ASSR), is, like its larger counterpart, a society devoted to the study of religion, but unlike the AAR it is restrictive and composed of mid-career and senior scholars who themselves determine those allowed into the organization. Founded in 1959, and thus very much associated with the heyday of the Chicago School in the study of religion, ASSR meets annually at the end of April when members and invited non-members (so-called "guests") discuss a particular theme in the academic study of religion.[5] The organization grew out of the Paul Carus Memorial Symposium of 1957, in commemoration of Carus who had served as the secretary of the World's Parliament of Religions held in Chicago in 1893 (O'Flaherty 1986: 293). The Symposium proved to be so successful that its attendees, most notably the late Joseph Kitagawa, petitioned the American Council of Learned Societies (ACLS) for membership, at which point the latter organization created ASSR and it became the American representative to the International Association for the History of Religions (IAHR)—a group comprised of national and regional member societies, one of which is no longer ASSR.

Membership in ASSR, then as now, was by invitation only and open to scholars who worked in more than one religion (comparison, presumably, thus being a valued method). Agility in comparison was (and presumably still is?) judged according to the primary source and research languages that prospective members must have acquired.[6] To show that potential members could work competently in two traditions, they were to be fluent in (at least) two languages. Despite, or perhaps because of, the cross-cultural, comparative nature of the organization, the organizers significantly argued that final term in its ethnonym was to be "religion" (i.e., in the singular) as opposed to the final term of the IAHR's (to wit, religions in the plural). Some of ASSR's early past presidents include such noteworthy scholars in the history of our field: Erwin Goodenough, Mircea Eliade, Wilfred C. Smith, Joseph Campbell, Joseph Kitagawa, and Ninian Smart. Such names, not surprisingly, signal what we see as still being the guiding hermeneutic of the organization (if not, some might claim, the field as a whole).

For the purposes of this essay, what we find most intriguing about ASSR are the current rules around new membership: According to its website:

> New members of the ASSR are elected on an annual basis by vote of the society. They are nominated by current members of the ASSR, and chosen on the basis of their contributions to the field, their achievements and interest in the comparative study of religion, *and their record of collegial engagement*.[7]

"Contributions to the field" and scholarly "achievements" are, in our estimation, correctly noted as valid criteria for membership in a professional association. Although it might seem that these two criteria are verifiable and relatively transparent, it is not entirely clear how one measures "contributions" or "achievements." Are such criteria based on the number of scholarly monographs? Or, is it to be measured on some other objective set of metrics, for example, the number of citations found in relevant citation indices or their so-called impact? Perhaps the latter is more important because we note, without judgment, that several scholars listed among the society's current members have produced only one book, whereas it would not be difficult to identify scholars with numerous publications and recognized reputations who are not members of this organization.[8] As with all private clubs, gaining admission seems to occur when existing members nominate someone, who must subsequently be ratified by a vote of the membership. So what, one might reasonably ask, accounts for the absence of many seemingly qualified members or, to rephrase, what accounts for members, whether mid-career or senior, who, by some measures, have amassed what at first seems to be minimal publication records? Depending how it is defined, the stated criterion "achievements" surely plays a role—there's more to an academic career than publications, of course, and people preside over national scholarly societies, work on grants committees, chair program units at conferences, edit journals and encyclopedias, and fulfill any number of other crucial professional roles that, though sometimes unsung, surely deserve attention and recognition.

But looking over the list of members and lacking a more specific definition of "achievement" or "contribution" one is left wondering. Is it the case of people inviting their friends or perhaps their own students and advisees, thus indicating that some sort of school of thought has emerged over the decades? Group formation would probably dictate that this is inevitably the case to whatever extent. However, it is nowhere stated if one must share some agreed upon pedigree or methodology in order to be part of the group, and thus it is unclear the degree to which the group's origins dictate where it has ended up. We note that, while interdisciplinary, many members list as their area the once meaningful but, we would argue, now rather ambiguous, even outdated, designator "history of religions" as their area of specialization. As just suggested, perhaps this should not come as a surprise since the organization has had, from its beginning, a distinct University of Chicago connection. That institution is one of the few places in the United States that continues to use the term, implying some sort of genealogical connection to the European model that Eliade, among others, helped to introduce and popularize here. As Jerald C. Brauer, former Dean of the Divinity School at the University of Chicago, writes in his forward to Eliade and Kitagawa's once well-known volume, *History of Religions: Essays in Methodology* (written in 1959, the same year as the inaugural meeting of what would become ASSR): "the study of the history of religions appears to be at a critical point in its development" (Brauer 1959: vii), and that the field has much to offer because "the world condition is such that modern man [sic], of the East and West [sic], is struggling to comprehend this revolutionary age, with its sweeping changes and newly emerging patters of life" (ibid.: vii). In his Introduction to that volume, Kitagawa—himself among the largely unsung, or so we would claim, players in the field's mid- twentieth century rise—seeks to define better this field of study:

> There are three essential qualities underlying the discipline of the history of religions; First is a sympathetic understanding of religions other than one's own. Second is an attitude of self-criticism, even skepticism, about one's own religious background. And third is the "scientific" temper. (Kitagawa 1959: 15)

Many members of ASSR, to this day, have some relationship to that institution, and even those that do not, such as Richard Hecht (of the University of California-Santa Barbara) can write,

> I was trained as a historian of religions under the influence of Mircea Eliade through my teacher at UCLA Kees W. Bolle. I have become increasingly interested

in the deep contextualization of religion in its lived environments and most centrally the intersections of religion, politics, and culture. My work is comparative and multidisciplinary, both of which are essential, in my opinion, to the larger study of religion.[9]

It would seem, then, that the spirit of Mircea Eliade, one of the first presidents of the organization, still looms in the background of this organization (despite the claim of many today that the field has left his method far behind).

However, our concern is less with such relative "quantifiable" data used to demote "contributions" and "achievements," though again it is worth repeating that some members seem only to have a handful of publications to their name (suggesting that these seemingly objective measures are just as ideologically loaded terms as any), than it is with the last stated criterion of membership: a "record of collegial engagement." This criterion seemingly has nothing to do with the manner in which we usually assess scholarship (though, come to think of it, the term likely appears on a surprising number of departmental tenure and promotion documents, which, by design, simultaneously disclose—by making standards tangible and public—while also disguising, thereby retaining a degree of ambiguity and thus interpretive "wiggle room" for those in senior positions). Instead, as we've already argued, it has everything to do with "getting along" with others. Case in point, consider Wikipedia, the current go-to source for pretty much everything these days (which, like a dictionary, provides us with the popular or commonsense use of a term), which defines the term in the following manner:

> **Collegiality** is the relationship between colleagues. Colleagues are those explicitly united in a common purpose and respecting each other's abilities to work toward that purpose. A colleague is an associate in a profession or in a civil or ecclesiastical office. Thus, the word *collegiality* can connote respect for another's commitment to the common purpose and ability to work toward it.[10]

Collegiality, as can be seen from this description alone, is a relative term—it names one's place among a group, how one's social interactions are seen *by one's peers*, and thus the extent to which one is understood *by them* to contribute to *what they see as* a common goal. It is therefore a term of boundary maintenance. Key synonyms in the above therefore sensibly include: "relationship," "common purpose," and "respect." Presumably when one violates these or other related virtues (i.e., transgresses the boundaries) one ceases to be collegial. But notice how (usefully) vague these terms are (not unlike "contribution" and "achievement"). What constitutes, for example, an academic relationship? And just what is our common purpose? For in the academic study of religion, not unlike other fields and disciplines in the humanities, there exists numerous ways to study data—longstanding, heated debates over these very issues are the stuff of which undergrad and grad students alike learn in the method and theory courses that now seem to populate most curricula. However, if one studies data in ways that others do not—and the question we must ask is which others get to constitute the others of significance here?—does this make one diverge from a supposedly common purpose and, thus, by implication, uncollegial? Read on one level collegiality would seem to be a key ingredient in the creation of not just a nondescript disciplinary identity but a specific type of disciplinary conformity. For those who explore different explanatory frameworks or who pioneer new methods risk, in the early years of their careers at least, disciplinary censure because they lack sufficient "respect" for pre-existent ones (i.e., those of their social superiors). The question, then, is whether such people would even have the luxury of having careers.

Perhaps it is within this context that we can situate the AAR's recent attempts, from a few summers ago, to formulate a set of "Responsible Research Practices," which we will discuss in greater detail below. Conscious of the fact that scholars of religion occupy various institutional settings and work with "different methods" of analysis, this document seeks to articulate a set of "standards" that govern all of these diverse constituencies. A quick glance at the actual standards, however, reveal less a respect for what we might term the critical study of religion than it does a need to respect those whom we study. Significantly, however, nowhere is the term "respect"—much like its synonym "collegial"—defined in that document. Are we to respect the canons of scholarship—that which has governed the scholarly life from the earliest period—or are we to respect religion and religious actors or are we to respect one another as scholars? If we do not do so, are we being uncollegial? The epigraph we have opted to use in opening this essay should make clear where we stand on the topics and thus the position from which aim to problematize some of our peers' apparent answers to such questions.

If we return to the rules for election to ASSR, as our e.g. for the time being, we might rightly ask, what sort of intellectual work is the phrase "collegial engagement" performing for the current members of this organization? That is a difficult question to answer—we're not just unsure what it means or who gets to decide what it means but also unclear what weight is placed on this one criterion. It may in fact be the case that the very phrase "collegiality"—as vague as it is nontransparent—is what mainly or even exclusively ends up determining membership. This is a reasonable reading given that there are many long-serving non-AASR members in the academic generation beyond our own who have made what at least we see as significant and lasting contributions to the national and international field, at least when compared to many (or at least some) current members; it therefore appears fair to inquire if their lack of inclusion boils down to the fact that "their record of collegial engagement" was somehow found wanting (meaning either that votes did not go in their favor or, as we think likelier, it was apparent that their names were never to be brought forward in the first place).

It deserves to be said at this point that we agree that, as a private organization, it is surely within ASSR's right to limit membership as it sees fit. However, what work this widely used designation "collegiality" is doing in that limitation process is, for us, the curious question. For, as already noted, we find this term used not just in such private scholarly associations but also in tenure and promotion documents all across the field, let alone surely making its fair share of appearances in the undocumented conversations that help to determine our field's membership.

Collegiality, as others before have suggested, is the discourse of the powerful or the status quo. It is the way the majority or the influential protects its interests, its scholarly and related values, and, ultimately, its authority—by finding a peer who "goes along and gets along." Collegiality must, accordingly, be conceived of not as an abstract or substantive concept, but, instead, as a socially formative rhetorical trope whose utility comes from it sounding as if it names something tangible and thus measurable. It is, thus, part of a discourse related to authority, that which Lincoln argues "is best understood in relational terms as the effect of a posited, perceived, or institutionally ascribed asymmetry" between an in-group, the status quo, and those that it deems as marginal or threatening players (Lincoln 1994: 4). As part of the production of authority, to which the charge of collegiality/uncollegiality is therefore related, nonverbal instruments and media are also often invoked—a "whole theatrical array of gestures, demeanors, costumes, props, and stage devices," to again use Lincoln's words (ibid.: 5), come into play when assessing ones collegiality. Peer review, tenure reviews, and reference letters can, as suggested above, count among the more formal elements of these gestures.

Again, as we learn from Lincoln, sometimes the best way to understand a dominant practice and its many interconnected components, is to imagine its failure, allowing us to explore what being collegial entails by, instead, imagining its opposite—a situation in which the normally smooth operations of dominance are called into question. So just what counts as "uncollegial" activity? Rolling one's eyes in a departmental meeting? Interrupting or talking over a colleague? Asking a question of a job candidate out of ranked order? Critiquing in print the writing of someone with whom one works, criticizing one's departmental peers within earshot of your shared students, or perhaps voting publicly against the majority for a decision of some consequence (whom to tenure, or hire, for example)? Maybe using the wrong fork with salad at a banquet? Or perhaps employing a non-phenomenological approach to the study of religion in one's teaching or writing? Of course, we could multiply examples almost endlessly since, given that the value collegiality is necessarily malleable (since it is undefined), there is no limit to what might be included in its membership. Much the same goes for its binary twin, uncollegial behavior or activity (i.e., the economy of collegiality/uncollegiality is utterly and necessarily unregulated). It must be "necessarily" so, we add, if it is to function properly as a coded gatekeeper of the profession. For, were it to be articulated explicitly (i.e., each item defined in a clear and delimited fashion) then the interests that benefit from its ostensibly endless adaptability would be too apparent (and, if apparent, then more easily contested). Rather, eschewing public argumentation or reasoned debate, collegiality functions as a kind of shorthand for those who hold (and seek to extend their hold on) institutional authority—something that, should the discourse on collegiality function "properly," cannot be breached or infiltrated.

Collegiality thus becomes a kind of authoritarianism. To quote Lincoln, once again,

> The exercise of authority depends less upon the "capacity for reasoned elaboration" as on the *presumption* made by those subject to authority that such a capacity exists, or on their calculated and strategic willingness to pretend they so presume. Authorities need not be able to explain themselves so long as others are sufficiently cowed or respectful that they do not ask for explanation. (Lincoln 1994: 5–6)

As a form of double-speak, then, the appeal to collegiality paradoxically works against what some of us might instead understand by this term—e.g., collaborative work with peers who do not always agree but who do so within a publicly disclosed set of conditions that are open to debate and documentation (again: show your work!)—by creating the material and institutional conditions that are defined only by implying that which it is not. The term, thus, strategically conceals what it might otherwise reveal.

Defining an Ill-Defined Term

With the above example in mind, let us return to our initial query: just what is collegiality or what might *we* instead mean by the use of this term? For, as already suggested, everyone seems to know what it is not: A quarrelsome interlocutor; a rogue colleague; an ungenerous hermeneut. But what else might we mean by collegiality (if we're even able to re-purpose the term, that is, and thereby recover it from the dominants' vocabulary and thus social arsenal), and at what point does one transgress its admittedly ill-defined boundaries? Since our main concern is intellectual, professional collegiality, we must necessarily ask whether (or not) collegiality functions as a way to create scholarly consensus? If so, collegiality is less about social posturing than an attempt to marginalize or further marginalize those who seek to move beyond or outside of what appears to be common scholarly paradigms, by portraying them as "beyond the pale," as unprofessional, and thus falling outside the walls of the institution (we think here of dismissing a scholar's work as mere journalism, or characterizing an interlocutor as a dilettante, for example). If so, then as already argued, collegiality implies a status quo, a certain comfort level with received opinion, and a genuine lack of interest (dare we say fear?) in pushing traditional analytical frameworks in new directions. Charges of uncollegiality, then, might have less to do with actual rancor than they do with *perceived* threats or suspected challenges to disciplinary hegemony. The goal of such discourses, then, may not be to deal with the eye rolling but, perhaps, in an entirely preventative measure, *to prevent it from ever happening in the first place.*

It is probably no coincidence, then, that, as already argued, it is precisely the status quo that gets to define both the terms of reference and the various contexts wherein the presupposed virtue of "collegiality" is used. At issue is therefore the very way in which we define scholarship and the purpose and organization of the modern university. Is scholarship, for example, an individual activity (as some might no doubt contend) in which scholars engage in their work independently? Or, do we view the university as a body of, dare we say, colleagues with shared interests, working toward common goals? Regardless, the discourse on collegiality implies a power relationship between potentially competing parties and, as we have seen, an imbalance between the status quo and those that members of the status quo, for whatever reason, deems problematic because they are a threat. It is always this outlier, for example, that is deemed the "uncollegial" one, but never the status quo, regardless how they may act. For idiosyncratic or anti-social behaviors among its members are, often, accepted and managed by being portrayed as "quirky" or "endearing"—a double standard that makes apparent the politics involved in determining what, or who, is tolerated by whom. In fact, as already noted, anyone drawing attention to the often unperceived working of this category will likely gain for themselves the designation of being uncooperative, of not going along—in a word, of being uncollegial.[11] Collegiality then becomes the term by which institutions, such as the one under examination here as our test case, minimize access to those who might otherwise appear to have the proper credentials (when membership is judged by means of seemingly substantive or quantitative criteria). Collegiality, in other words, functions as the undefinable and thus always victorious trump card to deny entry to the otherwise qualified. Somewhat akin to Tillich's rhetorically effective notion of "ultimacy," one can always imagine a scenario in which subjective judgments can use this discourse to pull rank and thereby win the day.

Collegiality thus functions as yet another example of double-speak within the academy.[12] It becomes the term that can be easily invoked by malevolent colleagues to accuse those with whom they have problems of malfeasance. Consider the case of Robert David (KC) Johnson, an American historian at Brooklyn College and the City University of New York Graduate Center. An accomplished historian, Johnson was denied tenure on account of his lack of "collegiality." In what became a national case, that was subsequently overturned on account of the national outcry (see Smallwood 2003), Johnson cites his criticism of a post-September 11 "teach-in" that he believed was weighted too heavily with panelists hostile to US military response and which offered no supporters of US or Israeli policies. He also raised objections to the hiring of what he considered to be an unqualified woman (who was still ABD and with poor teaching evaluations) for a position in the department. Reflecting on the issue of collegiality after he had been initially denied tenure, he writes,

> Academic institutions around the country need to think about how to ensure academic freedom for both tenured and untenured faculty. At Brooklyn, several senior colleagues adopted the same positions that I took regarding both the "teach-in" and the search; tenure afforded them the freedom to speak out. By soliciting feedback from only those tenured colleagues who disagreed with me on these issues and then basing its denial of my promotion and tenure solely on "collegiality," the college, in effect, used tenure as a club to silence a junior faculty member who voiced opinions on controversial issues. (Johnson 2002)

For him, the issue revolved around collegiality. Once again, the concept functions as a fuzzy category that is meant to silence any form of dissent. Johnson continues:

> The wholly subjective standard of "collegiality" tempts faculty members, temporarily blinded by the emotionalism of philosophical disputes or interpersonal squabbles, to abandon the academic ideals that scholars have championed for decades. CUNY Trustee Jeffrey Wiesenfeld articulated the point when asked about my case: "Collegiality is an appropriate criterion if I wanted to join a prestigious country club and play well with the other children, but it is not that which is necessary to determine whether someone is a good professor." As for me, I hope that President Kimmich will soon remedy the error of his previous decision, and that I will be able to continue, without this distraction, the scholarship and teaching that I love—to which even those who have opposed me admit I am deeply committed. (Johnson 2002)

Collegiality ostensibly defines what we are as academics in general and as scholars of religion in particular. We all *seem* to know what a collegial person is: someone who treats colleagues as peers, as equals (even in disagreement), collaborates with others (critique is a form of collaboration, in the classic experimental or conjecture/refutation model of science, no?), engages productively and constructively in larger discourses (that are governed by disclosed and thus debatable rules), and understands one's own interests in relation to the interests of others (Di Leo 2005a: 5). While collegiality would seem to be obvious when approached in this rather more practical way, its opposite—uncollegiality—is perhaps more difficult to define. Is being "uncollegial" a synonym for being "inflexible," "defensive," or "unwilling or unable to cooperate"? Or, as already suggested, is it something much more sinister and insidious? In fact, could it be that the status quo in our field, ironically perhaps, is uncollegial by virtue of the fact that it does not show its work when it comes to the assessment of peers?

We are hardly the first to suggest that collegiality functions as a "weasel clause," that is a hidden or deeply buried clause that denies admittance for whatever intangible reason or reasons (e.g., see Di Leo 2005b). As already indicated, it can often function as the nebulous and always unspoken fourth category (after research, teaching, and service) to deny tenure to the otherwise fully deserving—people who, despite professional competencies, the majority just do not like for some inarticulate reason. Case in point, consider "On Collegiality as a Criterion for Faculty Evaluation," a statement by the American Association of University Professors (AAUP), where we read:

> Relatively little is to be gained by establishing collegiality as a separate criterion of assessment. A fundamental absence of collegiality will no doubt manifest itself in the dimensions of teaching, scholarship, or, most probably, service, though here we would add that we all know colleagues whose distinctive contribution to their institution or their profession may not lie so much in service as in teaching and research. Professional misconduct or malfeasance should constitute an independently relevant matter for faculty evaluation. So, too, should efforts to obstruct the ability of colleagues to carry out their normal functions, to engage in

personal attacks, or to violate ethical standards. The elevation of collegiality into a separate and discrete standard is not only inconsistent with the long-term vigor and health of academic institutions and dangerous to academic freedom, it is also unnecessary.[13]

That the AAUP has taken a position on the nefarious nature of this topic, however, does not mean that collegiality ceases to be invoked in characterizing faculty or evaluating peers. Nor does its continued use mean that it is not uncontested. In fact, some have argued that "collegiality" should in fact be an explicit criterion so that it is at least made transparent to candidates coming up for tenure and promotion and thereby requiring those in power to make clear articulations of its criteria and use (Di Leo 2005b: 101; Connell and Savage 2001a, 2001b). Those who are critical of failing to include collegiality as an explicit criterion often point out that such things as colleagueship, cooperation, and shared stewardship represent the very fabric of the university. While they are aware of the slippery, relative nature of collegiality, they somewhat paradoxically argue that implementing it as an overt criterion will help to reduce that relativity.

And so we return to our above example, the criteria for membership in ASSR. The collegiality clause here functions, presumably, as a way to deprive otherwise qualified potential members as somehow being "unfit" based on perceived undesirable personality or intellectual traits. Despite the fulfillment of relevant "contributions to the field" and "their achievements and interest in the comparative study of religion"—after all, who among us is not interested in our own field and whose work is not comparative?—the collegiality clause enables the institution to decline or prevent admittance to, and thereby withhold certain institutional laurels from, those who are judged, by undisclosed criteria, to represent a threat to the usually-operating power structure or dynamic of the institution (defined in a specific way, to the advantage of a certain few).

Recommendation

We therefore recommend dropping this language entirely, if what we're engaged in is a profession with public standards of argumentation and evidence (i.e., the *public* study of religion). That the term appears in the membership criteria for a private organization is, as we noted above, understandable though still lamentable to us; that the term appears in documents related to the far more public profession at large is, however, another matter entirely. We would argue that it functions there just as it does in the ASSR document. Case in point, consider the already mentioned draft statement on research responsibilities that the American Academy of Religion (AAR) released for member comments in the summer of 2015.[14] The second to the last item on the draft document is the only one that concerns our work with students—odd, if you think about it, since much of our work as scholars concerns preparing a new generation (aka teaching) to be researchers themselves, so you would think that a statement on research responsibilities would give some attention to our role mentoring those who will succeed us. But, instead, the only attention to students reads as follows:

> When working with student research assistants, professors should strive to act with collegiality, providing clear expectations and following institutional guidelines regarding pay equity, workplace safety, and harassment.

Up to this point there had been little to no explicit awareness of the loaded nature of terminology so far used in this draft document, and this undefined use of collegial in its penultimate section is no different. So we have little choice but to accept that the slippery term "collegiality" is used in this earlier draft as if it is self-evidently meaningful, making it yet another example of how the document failed to live up to the standards that (we would hope) many of us routinely work to attain in our own research (e.g., clearly define your terms, recognize which are contested, identify your assumptions and mount a persuasive case for why you use the term as you do, etc.).

Now, this recurring shortcoming suggests to us that this document is merely boilerplate—or, if meant to be substantive, then, in an unintended fashion, it tells us much about what was characterized above as a dominant yet unarticulated consensus (we also termed it a hegemony, of course) that exists within the field (as represented by the committee which drafted these policies) concerning the assumed norms of the profession and their limits. It's for this reason that, in many ways, reading this draft document carefully amounts to a fieldwork experience.

But, returning to that notion of collegiality, what's curious is that amidst the committee's various links to other documents (cited in their footnotes), there's nothing referencing the above-quoted AAUP report on collegiality. Such a citation would be instructive for the committee's casual inclusion of this statement on being collegial toward students/research assistants because near the opening of the AAUP document we read the following:

> In recent years, Committee A has become aware of an increasing tendency on the part not only of administrations and governing boards but also of faculty members serving in such roles as department chairs or as members of promotion and tenure committees to add a fourth criterion in faculty evaluation: "collegiality." For the reasons set forth in this statement, we view this development as highly unfortunate, and we believe that it should be discouraged.

But why is this unfortunate? Our above discussion should make this evident. But if it is not already, the AAUP document argues that collaboration and cooperation—if this is what we mean by collegiality—already inform our activities in the three traditionally- and widely-assessed areas of teaching, research, and service (meaning that its already being tracked and assessed thoroughly), so singling out collegiality as if it is a value that stands apart from these, as some schools and departments do, so as to give it specific attention quite apart from these three areas, suggests that the term is doing unique, non-empirical work.

As phrased by the AAUP document:

> Historically, "collegiality" has not infrequently been associated with ensuring homogeneity, and hence with practices that exclude persons on the basis of their difference from a perceived norm. The invocation of "collegiality" may also

threaten academic freedom. In the heat of important decisions regarding promotion or tenure, as well as other matters involving such traditional areas of faculty responsibility as curriculum or academic hiring, collegiality may be confused with the expectation that a faculty member display "enthusiasm" or "dedication," evince "a constructive attitude" that will "foster harmony," or display an excessive deference to administrative or faculty decisions where these may require reasoned discussion. Such expectations are flatly contrary to elementary principles of academic freedom, which protect a faculty member's right to dissent from the judgments of colleagues and administrators.

A distinct criterion of collegiality also holds the potential of chilling faculty debate and discussion. Criticism and opposition do not necessarily conflict with collegiality. Gadflies, critics of institutional practices or collegial norms, even the occasional malcontent, have all been known to play an invaluable and constructive role in the life of academic departments and institutions. They have sometimes proved collegial in the deepest and truest sense. Certainly a college or university replete with genial Babbitts [a conformist businessperson] is not the place to which society is likely to look for leadership.

Given our view of how unstable this signifier, collegiality, can be, and how its unspecified use can signal possible mischief—especially when used in situations where power relations are askew (in fact, we're not sure when else it would even be used)—we publicized these views when the committee was soliciting input from members of the Academy, asking them to rethink what they intended to say in this item. After all, apart from recommending being collegial and providing clear expectations, all the committee did in that bullet point was provide a list (not unlike their earlier remarks on human subjects research which added nothing not already in place for scholars doing such work) of laws (not just this committee's "guidelines") that already apply to our workplaces. We're not sure, however, that we've gained much by having our main professional association recommend, by means of this document, that, when it comes to research assistants, we should pay attention to issues of pay equity, workplace safety, and harassment.

We are not certain, of course, of the effect of the comments posted online on the shortcomings of the draft statement; neither are we aware of the committee's private discussions and the decision-making that led to the final version of the document.[15] But we do find it significant (and encouraging) that the final version of this document removed any statement on collegiality and, instead, the item on working with research assistants now reads as follows:

> When employing student research assistants, professors should acknowledge their contributions, support their emerging research interests, and, where appropriate, consider possibilities for co-authorship. Professors also should provide clear expectations for their research assistants and follow institutional guidelines regarding pay equity, workplace safety, and sexual harassment.

Despite what we consider to be an important revision, this research responsibility document still reads to us as uncreative boilerplate (evidenced by the inclusion of a series of undefined technical terms, such as the fifth bullet point's unelaborated admonition to treat people "honestly and fairly"), that, at some future point, might provide legal cover for the Academy should someone accuse it of never telling its members, for instance, not to harass people who work with or for them or to tell the truth.

Also, an earlier suggestion that, for whatever reason, seems to have made its way into the final document, advocated for members of the Academy to regularly co-author articles with our grad students—the job market is now so bad that seeing the AAR take a strong stand on what it means in practice to mentor the next generation of researchers would be helpful, we reasoned. For we are continually amazed by the CVs that come in from some early career people who seem to have never been told that they likely need to be writing and publishing despite also working on their dissertations (at least writing book notes, book reviews, abstracts, anything), as an indication to search committees of their wide interests, the degree to which they have already been professionalized, and their ability to juggle a variety of simultaneous projects. While the sort of continually escalating credential inflation that comes with the buyer's market that we've long seen developing in the Humanities is lamentable, it is among the facts that we now live with; so, does graduating doctoral students who have no publications whatsoever (in some cases few if any conference presentations, regardless whether at the national level or not) amount to responsible mentoring of researchers? Is it evidence of collegial behavior toward those whom we train to follow us?

But focusing on this responsibility, which is rather specific, and thus easily witnessed or measured, rather than the grandiose aim to attain an undefined and undocumentable collegial attitude, calls upon faculty to do something empirical and public—a fire to which some may not wish their feet to be held. And thus we return to the ease with which knee-jerk and unelaborated admonitions to be collegial make their way into a field's governance documents. For striving to be collegial, in this un-nuanced and merely rhetorical sense of the term, frees us from, say, co-authoring with our students and writing them into grants, even co-authoring grant applications with them. (Curiously, encouragement to apply for grants to support research, or maybe even to support our students, is mentioned nowhere in the AAR document.) We also no longer need to worry about looking for opportunities to collaborate with other universities in our region, creating informal (or even formal) research networks in order not just to capitalize on resources (given ever-shrinking budgets, at least in many state schools) but for the benefit of our students. Focusing on being collegial removes from consideration the responsibilities a supervisor or member of a supervisory committee has toward a doctoral student—especially when, given our current job market, that dissertation will likely have to be innovative enough to get published so as to give the student as much of a leg up as possible once they graduate and start looking for full-time work. (There was a day, of course, when dissertations were rarely published ...)

While any talk of students might sound to the committee that drafted this research responsibilities statement like we're inappropriately turning their document into a statement on teaching, we think that's a far too compartmentalized, dare we say uncollegial, view of what we do as scholars. Undergraduate research is a catchphrase that's caught on significantly over the past few years in North American higher ed, but the committee seems not to have thought much about undergrads in their document. We also encouraged them to reconsider that, but to no avail. For what might have been an opportunity to make a bold statement about the minimal conditions that we collectively think ought to exist in our efforts to replenish the institution in which we work with innovative and rigorous researchers who will follow us turned into a boilerplate statement that, in the 2015 annual meeting's session on the document, came down to a committee member saying, as we heard it, that other academic associations have such a document so maybe we should as well.

We think that we, as professionals, can do far better than this if we are prepared to get into the weeds, as they say, and entertain the importance of the details and actions. But, like statements on international human rights, the temptation is to limit our expectation to disembodied and undocumented items (e.g., freedom of belief or this ethereal thing we call conscience as opposed to, say, freedom of association or access to potable water), thereby allowing us to feel good about lofty aspirations that may actually have little consequence (after all *access* to clean water doesn't necessarily mean you'll get a drink). And it is in this context that we have tremendous difficulty with the discourse on collegiality—not collegiality itself, we hope to have shown, when defined as, say, practical mentoring of early career scholars so that they successfully move through their careers and contribute to the institutions in which we all work.

Within this context, it might be nice to juxtapose the aforementioned ASSR with another organization devoted to the study of religion. The North American Association for the Study of Religion (NAASR),[16] initially formed in 1985,[17] now regularly sponsors an annual jobs workshop at its national meeting, offered for ABD doctoral students; the workshop, which is free of charge, relies on volunteers from more senior positions in the field, who have served on multiple search committees, and who read participants' cover letters, offer comments on their CVs, and give invaluable practical advice on such topics as soliciting references letters and the job interview itself. It was begun at the suggestion of a graduate student who then became one of its co-organizers and participants. Our point? This strikes us as collegiality in the best sense of the term—if the term has any non-rhetorical senses, that is—for it exemplifies practical labor and beneficial, collaborative relations between social actors at dramatically different positions within the hierarchy of this one field, creating social relationships that outlast the workshop and thereby create the conditions in which participants can imagine themselves into being members of a field and, dare we say, colleagues. The aim of such activities could not be further from the elite gatekeeping of the ASSR's use of the term, as a way to police and thereby delimit membership; for in this one example (we could cite others, of course, such as NAASR's turn toward proactive involvement of early career scholars in its annual program, working in tandem with more experienced presenters) we see an alternative model of collegiality: an effort to bring people aboard, to empower them when they are in a disadvantaged position, and in the process to learn from them (for who reads more avidly and widely than senior doctoral students?), thereby turning collegiality into a duty or obligation to others, an effort to create and nurture new peers, rather than seeing it as an award that signals membership among the privileged who, annually, meet to talk among only themselves.

Our analysis and recommendation are therefore simple: collegiality, though commonly used as a form of ideological double-speak that polices the borders, ought instead to require us to take each other seriously *as scholars*, which means both rigorously testing each other's work, using publicly disclosed criteria and assessments, while also diligently working to increase the number of peers we have and with whom we interact as professionals. That, we argue, will benefit the field far more than creating a two-tier system of the privileged elite, presenting their work to each other alone, and everyone else clamoring to get on the AAR's annual meeting program.

Concluding Anecdotal Postscript

When we originally co-wrote this essay—an essay that, in part, resulted from the shock one of us had upon learning, for the first time, that a private academic society existed in our field—we were mulling over seeing it as part of a larger joint project. Though such a project may still be in our future, we instead decided to submit it to the *Journal of the American Academy of Religion* (*JAAR*), which describes itself (on the AAR website for the journal) as "the premier academic journal in the field of religious studies." While the publisher's webpage offers a more qualified assessment—"is generally considered to be the top academic journal in the field of religious studies"—we'd suggest that given the variety of specialties in the field, many of which are represented by a peer review journal (or more) of their own, such a claim is difficult to maintain. Should the term "generalist" have been added to that description—a term we both value and hardly suggest as any sort of slight—then, perhaps, it could at least be billed more plausibly as the widest circulating generalist journal in the field today. After all, given the population of the U.S. and the AAR's rather broad understanding of the field (thereby allowing it to include members who are openly and unapologetically theological while also being home to humanistic and social scientific scholars) it stands to reason that the *JAAR* (which is part of the membership benefits of the Academy) likely goes to more mailboxes than any other single periodical in the field today. And so, agree or not with self-conception the journal may have, under any given editorial team, it understandably strikes many as a desirable place to publish their work.

At least it did for us.

Although we admit that we were not optimistic for the fate of the submission, on April 27, 2017, we sent it off nonetheless, hoping that an essay examining how our field works—using, but not limited to, one specific case study—might catch the attention of readers and, perhaps, spark a bit of a debate. It was therefore not surprising, though still disappointing, to receive an email back on May 5, 2017 (making evident to us that the submission never made it to the peer review process) saying that the paper "was not suitable for publication" in the journal. The reason that was cited struck us as rather interesting and, though surely in an unintended manner, we read them as providing further evidence to support the paper's thesis on how an academic discipline polices its limits in undisclosed ways—and hence this postscript. For, after citing the journal's mission statement (a statement with which we admit we were completely unfamiliar, not knowing how long it had existed, let alone in the current form)—"This international quarterly journal publishes top scholarly articles that cover the full range of world religious traditions together with provocative studies of the methodologies by which these traditions are explored"—we were informed that because our paper did not discuss a methodology relevant to the study of religions it was not suited to *JAAR*, though, we were told, it might find a home at the more professionally oriented *Religious Studies News* (the AAR's onetime quarterly newspaper, but now online site, devoted to professional issues in the field).

With that mission statement in mind, the stated reason for rejecting the paper outright was therefore that, while obviously not on descriptive information relevant to understanding one or more world religions (such as a paper on, say, ritual in this or that tradition), it didn't even examine broader methodological issues of relevance to studying world religions (e.g., discussing, say, a theory of ritual or way to study rituals) that could then be applied to, as the mission statement phrased it, "the full range of world religious traditions." While the field's still dominant world religions paradigm is prominent in the mission statement and thus the supposed reason for rejection, what we find far more curious is not that the so-called "premier academic journal in the field of religious studies" limits itself to this one conception of the study of religion. For it clearly does not—*but, on this occasion, it did*. To rephrase: a quick look through the table of contents over the years makes evident that while descriptive or comparative articles on items of relevance to one or more of the world's religions dominates the journal's pages, there are plenty of articles and book reviews on things of wider relevance to the field at large. We could, of course, cite many (if not most) of the AAR Presidential addresses themselves, printed annually in the journal, inasmuch as they are often on field-wide or even professional topics that are neither (i) concerned with descriptive items from the world religions nor (ii) concerned with honing a methodology useful in their study,[18] or we could instead cite some of our own past appearances in the journal, such as McCutcheon's early (and perhaps provocative, judging by the published replies it provoked) article on the scholar of religion as a public intellectual (1997)—which was neither descriptive of the world religions nor focused on methodologies useful in their study. Instead, recognizing that allowances may reasonably be made for Presidential addresses (which the journal is presumably required to publish each year, even if that requirement remains unarticulated) and also noting that the journal's self-conception may have changed over the past 20 years, what we'd simply prefer to cite is the then editor's own published statement, included in the second issue produced under her leadership:

> Keep those submissions coming in: *JAAR* publishes in all areas of interest to scholars of religion. (Eller 2016: 285)[19]

So, on the one hand, we have this extremely (and, perhaps, laudably) broad statement concerning the scope of the journal—*in all areas* of interest to scholars of religion (emphasis added)—while on the other we have a rather narrow, traditional understanding of the field, one in which an article on, say, the now much-studied Nones, would likely not find a home, given that they are (at least not yet) not considered a world religion and thus even an article refining how they're studied would also not be ruled in bounds. And, we would imagine, neither would an article on a theory of religion as a human phenomenon nor an article critiquing the world religions paradigm itself, inasmuch as both fail to focus on—in this strict reading of the mission statement—some discrete element among, or approach used to understand, "the full range of world religious traditions."

But it is precisely the strategic wiggle room provided by the oscillation—when needed, that is, *and that's the crucial element here*—between the simultaneously-held narrow and the broad that attracts our attention.

It brings to mind a comment from Burton Mack, sometime ago, concerning this thing that we might just call culture being the creation of a tactical middle space. Our classificatory systems, Mack argued,

> function ... at a certain distance from the actual state of affairs experienced in the daily round. They articulate a displaced system (imaginary, ideal, "sacred," marked off) as a counterpoint to the ways things usually go. The inevitable incongruence between the symbol system and the daily round provides a space for discourse. It is the space within which the negotiations fundamental to social intercourse take place—reflection, critique, rationalization, compromise, play, humor, and so forth. (Mack 1991: 21)

To press this a little further, inasmuch as one might not assume the unproblematic existence of an actual state of affairs that can be juxtaposed to our classification systems, we might instead say that something called an actual state of affairs (i.e., an academic discipline, perhaps), becomes possible for social actors to imagine, to inhabit and then work within, only inasmuch as they employ a nimble classification system that functions as a sliding scale where, in light of some new action or previously unanticipated situation's emplotment in relation to the scheme's opposed, abstract boundaries, the action or situation can be known and understood inasmuch as it is judged to be more or less relevant and closer or further from the truth (or whatever one wish to call the undisclosed ideal or norm for which the one making the judgments aims).

Case in point: an article critical of what is portrayed as the rhetoric (as opposed to, say, the value) of collegiality is submitted to a journal in a field where some members of the private society used, in that essay, as its primary e.g. maybe hold positions of (formal or informal) consequence.

What does one do with this unanticipated development?

There are a number of options, of course, but among them is the choice to exclude it from the authoritative discourse by rejecting it or placing it in a venue of lesser significance.

So it strikes us that our experience with this submission and its quick and outright rejection—conveyed here anecdotally, of course—nicely exemplifies how the rhetoric of collegiality works. For while the journal, seeing itself as broad in scope, regularly publishes articles, review essays, and book reviews on topics far wider than what we assume many would be surprised to learn is its limiting mission statement, that narrow, orthodoxy can be invoked whenever a strict adherence to the letter of the law is seen as advantageous, for whatever reason. (In fact, just a short time after the rejection one of us was invited by this very journal to be an external reader on a paper that was itself not on the world religions or a methodology useful in the study; rest assured that the return comment recommended publication, thereby refusing to flatter the mission statement with continued relevance.) It's a convenient oscillation indicative of any number of social situations, making our experience hardly unique. Consider a traffic cop on the look-out for speeders; this would be a pretty mundane instance of the same strategy, since we all know that not everyone going 70 or 75 mph in a 65 mph zone is pulled over and ticketed. Instead, the sliding scale of more or less lawful comes to play, managed by a variety of factors—one of which is the officer's situated judgment at the time, along with disposition, inclination, intentions, etc.

The rhetoric of collegiality, we have argued, functions in just this manner; it is a handy device, a sliding scale that social actors in a position of authority can invoke to regulate an unanticipated situation, helping them to judge someone as either merely quirky (and thus tolerable) or inappropriate (and thus intolerable). Those not in power have long known of the existence of such tool, of course; although we are both white males, we could easily cite the reports of female colleagues who routinely find that exhibiting anything near the qualities of their male co-workers lands them in characterizations of being bossy and pushy as opposed to being portrayed as (in the case of their male counterparts) born leaders and real go-getters. In fact, just the other day, while working on this postscript, this was made evident in some media representations of a rigorous line of questioning, during a hearing featuring the US Attorney General Jeff Sessions, by a female US Senator (Kamala Harris, Dem., from California) as "hysterical" despite her demeanor being no worse, or perhaps even less robust, than some of her male colleagues on the committee.[20] But this is not a double standard, as it is often popularly understood—for, more accurately, there are an infinite number of standards and gradations, any of which can be operationalized at any given moment; it is therefore best understood as the undisclosed and thus utterly flexible manner in which unanticipated or oppositional situations are policed by interested and authoritative social actors. We see this in a police officer with a radar gun making a judgment call no less than a professor going over a final grade sheet and looking for reasons to be (or not to be) generous with students whose grades are just on the cusp. And we see it when assessing the relevance of submissions to a journal just as we find it present when faculty members try to ascertain the relevance and worth (and thus employability) of those junior to them and with whom they work. Making the criteria by which we, as scholars, navigate these inevitable judgments as public (and thus testable and refutable) as possible is the crux of this chapter's argument.

Russell T. McCutcheon is University Research Professor and Chair of the Department of Religious Studies at the University of Alabama. He has written and published widely on the tools scholars use to study religion as well as the practical implications of their work. His most recent books include *Fabricating Religion* (2018) and the co-edited *Reading J. Z. Smith* (2018).

Aaron W. Hughes is the Philip S. Bernstein Chair of Religion in the Department of Religion and Classics at the University of Rochester. He specializes in Islamic Studies, Jewish Studies and Method and Theory in the Study of Religion. Publications include *Muslim Identities: An Introduction to Islam* (Columbia University Press, 2013); *Jacob Neusner: An American Jewish Iconoclast* (New York University Press, 2016); and *Shared Identities: Medieval and Modern Imaginings of Judeo-Islam* (Oxford University Press, 2017). His work has been supported by the Social Sciences Research Council of Canada (SSHRC) and the National Endowment of the Humanities (NEH).

Notes

1. A suitable example would either be the claim made by Orsi, over a decade ago (2004), concerning McCutcheon's work (2003) being dehumanizing of its subjects; see McCutcheon (2006) for his response or the reception to Hughes's work (e.g., 2012; 2013) that seeks to showcase the identity politics the reside at the heart of Islamic studies and Jewish studies.
2. Witness, for example, the description of a recent book series at the University of Chicago Press (online at http://press.uchicago.edu/ucp/books/series/CLA200.html):

   > The series will publish authors who understand descriptions of religion to be always bound up in explanations for it. It will nurture authorial reflexivity, documentary intensity, and genealogical responsibility. The series presumes no inaugurating definition of religion other than what it is not: it is not reducible to demographics, doctrines, or cognitive mechanics. It is more than a discursive concept or cultural idiom. It is something that can be named only with a precise and poetic wrestling with the nature of its naming.

3. It is now relatively easy to find a generation of scholars who would argue that, having gone through the fires of the 1990s and 2000s in which critical, theoretical issues were emphasized in the study of religion, we now need to return to what might be termed thick descriptive studies, hence this term post-theoretical. For example, consider Kathryn Lofton who, near the opening of part 1 of a three part interview, says as follows: "My generation of Religious Studies ... were just drowning, somewhat productively, in the postcolonial critique; we were all avid readers of Tomoko Masuzawa and Timothy Fitzgerald and Russell McCutcheon, and we felt the words that we'd been handed by our teachers were filled with contradictions, lies and empires that had not been identified ... But it also then, once we all started to be teachers ..., the vocabulary that we were given was so critical we had a hard time making cases for ourselves in that deconstructive idiom ..." The "turn" in the field (away from that deconstructive idiom) that they then go on to discuss could be summed up by the interview's opening allusion to the TV character of Leslie Knope (played by Amy Poehler), from *Parks and Recreation* (2009–2015), whom Lofton characterizes as "piercing through the presumption of

cynicism." Whether cynicism best characterizes the work of Masuzawa, Fitzgerald, or McCutcheon is, of course, highly debatable; in fact, such a characterization may tell us far more about such readers' goals for their own version of the academic study of religion and how they feel impeded by such critical works. For the full interview see https://scholarblogs.emory.edu/sacredmatters/2015/04/30/religion-in-the-post-colonial-humanities-an-interview-with-kathryn-lofton-part-1.

4 Case in point, one of us recently co-authored an unsolicited reply to what they considered to be a very poorly written and argued article published in a leading journals and, upon submission of it to the journal, it was initially rejected by the reviewers for being overly pedantic, too critical and, in the editors' reading, condescending. That the critical reply was rigorous and thoroughgoing is not in doubt; that this was ruled out of bounds is the issue, we contend, in need of examination.

5 For example, "secularization and the sacred" (1967); "new modalities of the sacred" (1971); "sacraments" (1987); "embodied mind" (2012). A full list of topics may be found at www.assr-religion.org/history.asp#programs-anchor. The organization's self-description quoted above is from http://www.assr-religion.org/about.html.

6 Though it is worth noting that there are a number of scholars of American religion on the ASSR's current membership roles, who presumably need only one research language to carry out their work—in many cases, their native tongue.

7 Our italics. See the current full membership list at www.assr-religion.org/membership.html.

8 A list of members may be found at www.assr-religion.org/members.html.

9 See www.religion.ucsb.edu/people/faculty/richard-d-hecht.

10 See https://en.wikipedia.org/wiki/Collegiality.

11 As already noted, in even penning this essay we risk such an assessment ourselves; although we may have overplayed our hand in tackling this topic head-on, it may be the case that our own status in the profession may well protect us from the charge (or from the worst effects of the charge), to whatever extent—something that, if indeed the case, makes our point for us rather elegantly.

12 Another example is the institution of peer review, for inasmuch as the journal editor or acquisition editor privately decides to whom to send the submission, the peer in question may not signify peer of the author under review (as we usually conceive of it) but, instead, a peer of the editor who either disagrees or agrees with the submission. For the assignments are not random but, inevitably, interested.

13 The statement may be found online at www.aaup.org/report/collegiality-criterion-faculty-evaluation.

14 See http://rsn.aarweb.org/responsible-research-practices-statement-standards-professional-conduct-aar-members for the draft posted in the summer of 2015 (accessed November 28, 2016). This portion of the paper is adapted from part 11 of a multi-part blog post on this document; see https://religion.ua.edu/blog/2015/07/a-response-to-responsible-research-practices-index. For background on this AAR document see www.aarweb.org/about/draft-statement-on-responsible-research-practices (accessed November 28, 2016).

15 After a public session on the draft document at the 2015 annual meeting of the Academy (in Atlanta, that year), which we both attended and during which mostly praise was expressed by the session's attendees, a final version of the document was passed by the AAR Board in February 2016 and then posted at www.aarweb.org/node/2541.

16 McCutcheon, who was once its executive secretary/treasurer, has served as the president while Hughes, co-editor for its journal (*MTSR*), served as vice president (2014–2017).

17 See https://naasr.com/about-2.
18 Case in point, consider just the most recent: Thomas Tweed's 2015 address, published in *JAAR* 84(2) (2016)—"Valuing the Study of Religion: Improving Difficult Dialogues Within and Beyond the AAR's 'Big Tent'"—was on the long-standing religious studies versus theology debate and Laurie Zoloth's address, from the prior year but published in 84(1) (2016): 3–24—"Interrupting Your Life: An Ethics for the Coming Storm"—concerned global warming and, or so she argued, the specific moral duty scholars of religion might have in helping to solve it.
19 Our thanks to Matthew Baldwin for reminding us of this statement. Of course, should one narrowly define a scholar of religion as someone solely studying things classified as the world's religions, or approaches useful in their study, then we acknowledge that there's little contradiction between this statement and the rationale for rejecting the preceding essay. But such a narrow definition strikes us not only as extremely odd and difficult to defend but, based on such an restricted understanding, it is unclear if Eller's own work would count as scholarship on religion.
20 For example, see this discussion at www.cnn.com/2017/06/13/politics/powers-miller-kamala-harris-hysterical-sessions-hearing-ac360-cnntv/index.html (accessed June 15, 2017).

References

Brauer, Jerald C. 1959, "Preface." In Mircea Eliade and Joseph M. Kitagawa, eds., *The History of Religions: Essays in Methodology*, vii–x. Chicago, IL: University of Chicago Press.

Connell, Mary Ann, and Frederick G. Savage. 2001a. "Does Collegiality Count?" *Academe* 87(6): 37–40. https://doi.org/10.2307/40252089

Connell, Mary Ann, and Frederick G. Savage. 2001b. "The Role of Collegiality in Higher Education Tenure, Promotion, and Termination Decisions." *Journal of College and University Law* 27(4): 833–858.

Di Leo, Jeffrey R. 2005a. "Editor's Note." *Symplokē* 13(1/2): 5–6. https://doi.org/10.1353/sym.2006.0023

Di Leo, Jeffrey R. 2005b. "Uncollegiality, Tenure and the Weasel Clause." *Symplokē* 13(1/2): 99–107. https://doi.org/10.1353/sym.2006.0024

Eller, Cynthia. 2016. "Editor's Note," *Journal of the American Academy of Religion* 84(2): 285–286.

Hughes, Aaron W. 2012. *Theorizing Islam: Disciplinary Deconstruction and Reconstruction*. Sheffield: Equinox.

Hughes, Aaron W. 2013. *The Study of Judaism: Authenticity, Identity, Scholarship*. Albany, NY: SUNY.

Johnson, Robert David. 2002. "Why I was Denied Tenure." *History News Network* (December 11). Retrieved from http://hnn.us/articles/1115.html.

Kitagawa, Joseph M. 1959. "The History of Religions in America." In Mircea Eliade and Joseph M. Kitagawa (eds.), *The History of Religions: Essays in Methodology*, 1–30. Chicago, IL: University of Chicago Press.

Lincoln, Bruce. 1994. *Authority: Construction and Corrosion*. Chicago, IL: University of Chicago Press.

Lincoln, Bruce. 1996. "Theses on Method." *Method and Theory in the Study of Religion* 8: 225–227. https://doi.org/10.1163/157006896X00323

Mack, Burton. 1991. *A Myth of Innocence: Mark and Christian Origins*. Philadelphia, PA: Fortress Press.

McCutcheon, Russell T. 1997. "A Default of Critical Intelligence? The Scholar of Religion as Public Intellectual," *Journal of the American Academy of Religion* 65(2): 443–468. https://doi.org/10.1093/jaarel/65.2.443
McCutcheon, Russell T. 2003. *The Discipline of Religion: Structure, Meaning, Rhetoric*. New York: Routledge.
McCutcheon, Russell T. 2006. "'It's a Lie. There's No Truth in It! It's a Sin!': The Costs of Savings Others From Themselves." *Journal of the American Academy of Religion* 74(3): 720–750. https://doi.org/10.1093/jaarel/lfj090
Nelson, Cary and Stephen Watt (eds.). 1999. *Academic Keywords: A Devil's Dictionary for Higher Education*. New York: Routledge.
O'Flaherty, Wendy Doniger. 1986. "On the ASSR and Joseph Kitagawa." *History of Religions* 25(4): 293–295. https://doi.org/10.1086/463050
Orsi, Robert A. 2004 "Fair Game." *Bulletin of the Council of Societies for the Study of Religion* 33(3/4): 87–89.
Orsi, Robert A. 2005. *Between Heaven and Earth: The Religious Worlds People Make and the Scholars Who Study Them*. Princeton, NJ: Princeton University Press.
Smallwood, Scott. 2003. "Tenure Madness." *Chronicle of Higher Education* (May 23). Retrieved from http://chronicle.com/article/Tenure-Madness/3373.

Index

9/11, 64, 108–9, 277

Abington v. Schempp, 248
academia (see also "labor" and
    "neoliberalism"), 75, 110, 246, 256,
    258–60, 267, 277
  and curricula, 187, 250–2
  and myth of meritocracy, 232
  and "quit lit", 228ff.
  and tenure, 225, 227, 277
  and Scholarship of Teaching and
    Learning (SoTL), 236–9, 242
  as a type of religion, 187, 231
  as career, 222
  as object of study, 160, 223
  as value-free, 3, 264
  boundaries of, 226, 230, 246
  majors/minors, 186–7, 247–8, 251, 253,
    261, 263
adjunct workers (see "labor, contingent"),
    232, 246, 260, 262, 277
Adorno, Theodor, 137ff.
Alles, Gregory D., 265
Althusser, Louis, 236–7, 239, 241–2
American Academy of Religion (AAR),
    74–5, 127, 238–9, 270, 274, 279,
    282–3
American Association of University
    Professors (AAUP), 278–80
American Council of Learned Societies
    (ACLS), 271
American Society for the Study of Religion
    (ASSR), 270, 272, 274, 279, 283
anachronism (see "religion, as
    anachronism"), 61
as strategic, 42
anthologizing (as scholarly practice), 33–4,
    40
anti-atheism, 105
anti-realism (see also "realism"), 151ff.,
    176, 183, 185–8, 205–7

  reality as mind-dependent, 152, 206–7
  social construction as form of, 152
apocalypticism, 13–14
Appadurai, Arjun, 101
Arnal, William, 52, 131
Arthur Vining Davis Foundation, 239
Asad, Talal, 9, 50–1, 64

Bacon, Christopher M., 195
Bagger, Matthew, 235, 237
Baldwin, Matthew C., 110, 114–7, 120–1,
    123–4, 127–9, 132, 136ff., 206
Barras, Amélie, 63
Barthes, Roland, 224
Barton, Carlin, 9–10, 12, 54, 130, 132
Barylo, William, 63
Bayart, Jean-François, 180
Beaman, Lori G., 63
Beckford, James, 132
Bell, Daniel, 238
Benavides, Pace Gustav, 76
Benjamin, Walter, 139
Bennett, Jane, 85
Berkeley, George, 153
Besky, Sarah, 194
Binary, 136, 139, 208
Biro, Andrew, 230
Bogost, Ian, 229
boundary formation, 10, 51–2, 226, 246,
    249, 284–5
Bourdieu, Pierre, 194, 2747
Boyarin, Daniel, 9–10, 12, 52, 54–5, 130, 132
Boyer, Ernest L., 236–9
Brauer, Jerald C., 272
Braun, Willi, 180
Braver, Lee, 154
Buggeln, Gretchen, 84
Butler, Judith, 151–2, 154

Campbell, Colin, 104
Campbell, Joseph, 271

Canada
	government of, 27-9, 32 131-4
	Indigenous peoples of, 27-8, 30, 32
	Muslims in, 63
capitalism, 118, 122, 194, 222-4, 239
	violence of, 198
Carnegie Foundation, 236, 239
Carrasco, Davíd, 256
Carus, Paul, 271
categorization (see "classification")
	as abstract, 13
	as constitutive, 151, 178
	as constructed, 11-12, 19, 121, 123, 129, 192
	as dichotomy (or simplistic opposition), 45, 55
	as hegemonic, 41, 62
	as self-conscious, 54
	legal uses of (see "law and governance"), 132-3
	method of naturalization, 14
	power and limits of, 10-12, 16, 117, 196, 199
	practice of ordering knowledge, 10-11, 13, 21, 34, 38, 41, 43, 48, 52, 55, 57, 61. 78
Catholicism, 28, 77, 80, 87
Chalmers, Matthew, 42
"Chicago School" (see "history of religions"), 270, 272
Chidester, David, 101
Christianity (see also "Protestantism" and "Catholicism"), 10-11, 54
	and ancient world, 10, 14, 15, 20
	as constructed, 19
	origins of, 12, 17
chronology
	as narrative technique, 11, 15, 17, 33-4, 39, 50ff., 57, 123
	and historical periodization, 40, 42ff.
Cisney, Vernon W., 162-3
classification, 10-13, 47, 79, 140
	as scholarly practice, 10-11, 38, 41, 43, 48, 52, 78, 115, 137-8, 175
	denaturalize systems of (see "anti-realism"), 152
	power of, 11, 13, 27, 117, 196, 199
	systems of, 58, 129, 130, 151
	(see individual terms for specific applications of this topic)

classroom, 2, 185, 221, 227, 238, 242-3, 253, 261, 269
cognitive mapping, 119, 122
Cohen, Shaye, 43
collegiality, 267ff.
	as silencing of critique, 269-70, 275-8, 280, 286
	definitions of, 269, 272-3, 276, 278, 280
colonialism, 33, 53, 114, 129
	as anti-colonial, 56
commodity fetishism (see "Marxism")
continuity, 11, 51, 52ff.
	as constructed, 14
contiguity, 50, 52ff, 117
contrariety, 53
Csikszentmihayli, Mihaly, 223
Culture on the Edge, 180

data 27-8, 38-9, 55, 61, 63, 66, 73ff., 203ff., 222-3
	as an analytical classification, 31-2, 61, 73ff., 114-19, 127-34, 151, 171, 179, 183-4, 198, 203ff., 252, 267, 273
	as flexible, 3, 11, 34
	as gateway to origins, 86
	as incoherent, 3
	as inherently interesting, 1
	as legitimate, 2
	as unwieldy, 61
	criteria for, 2, 128
	domestication of, 5
	exceeds taxonomies, 11, 27, 38, 66
	generated by theory, 73
	mystification of, 88
	production of, 114, 116
	utility of, 28
de Certeau, Michel, 240
definition, 2, 11, 50, 155, 185, 193, 199, 247
	act of, 28-31, 50, 103-4, 130, 167-9, 241, 247
	as boundary construction, 78
	as futile, 2
	as theory, 32-3, 34, 73, 76, 78-9, 205, 268
departments, 185, 240, 246ff.
	and administrative structures, 247
	and relationship to curricula, 250-2
Derrida, Jacques (see also "Language"), 151ff., 176, 202, 204ff.
Dewey, John, 151

difference, 11, 16, 39, 40–1, 44–5, 53, 57, 63, 80–1, 115–6, 119, 124, 163–4, 187, 250
    as antipathy, 44
    as boundary formation, 280
    as synchronic diversity, 50, 57
    as inconvenient, 27, 34
    as irreducible, 159
    categorization of (see "categorization")
    complexifying, 43
    homogenization of, 27, 31–4
    theory of, 19, 21
discipline, 10, 12
    versus field of study, 9–11, 74, 145, 205, 210, 213, 236, 246, 270, 272–3
discourse
    as authoritative, 80, 226, 230, 232, 287
    as constitutive, 151, 171, 179, 183, 189, 197, 275
    as critical, 10, 12, 15, 76, 87–8, 90, 104–5, 110, 116, 131, 143, 151ff., 175–6, 178, 198–9, 204–7, 209–10, 212–3, 269, 270, 275, 277–8, 283, 286
    as methodology, 40, 114, 153, 180, 203
    as process of individuation, 166ff., 176
diversity (see "pluralism"), 50, 57, 105, 188
Doniger, Wendy, 269
Dubuisson, Daniel, 9
Durkheim, Émile, 103, 116, 121–2, 230, 246

Eliade, Mircea, 84, 86, 88–9, 271–3
Ellsworth, Jason W. M., 200
emic and etic perspectives, 11, 78, 102
    and the implicit emic perspective, 89, 103–4
    de-familiarization, 4, 116
empiricism, 53, 101, 156, 158ff., 186, 202–4, 206–9, 212
Engel v. Vitale, 248
Epiphanius, 11, 17–18, 20–21, 39, 61
essentialism, 78, 249
    as core, 5, 50
    family resemblance model, 49–51, 77
    strategic essentialism, 42
ethics, 40, 45
ethnography, 62, 77, 80, 84, 87–8, 252

Fadil, Nadia, 63–4
fair trade (see "food"), 192, 195
    as commodity, 195

Fichte, Johann Gottlieb, 140–1
Fish, Stanley, 264
Fitting, Elizabeth, 196
Fitzgerald, Timothy, 76, 129
Flexner, Abraham, 263
food
    anthropology of, 193
    as commodity, 193–4
    as social, 193
    fair trade, 192, 195
    food labels, 192
    food system, 194
Foucault, Michel, 44, 105, 120, 151–2, 180
Fox, Richard, 55
Friedman, Milton, 259
Fromm, Erich, 223
Furey, Constance, 120

Gaertner, David, 29, 31
Geertz, Clifford, 49
genealogy, 9, 18, 208
Ghosh, Bishnupnya, 122–4
Gill, Parmbir Singh, 56
Glock, Charles, 104
Goldenberg, Naomi, 132
Goodall, Jane, 196
Goodenough, Erwin, 271
Goodman, Nelson, 159, 170
Graeber, David, 230
Gravett, Emily O., 237–8, 240
Gray-Hildenbrand, Jenna, 247, 250, 252
Greece
    Greco-Roman past, 10, 175–7
Grewal, J. S., 55

Hacking, Ian, 154
Hankel, Isiah, 222, 228–9
Harris, Kamala, 287
Harrison, Joel, 213
Hayek, Friedrich, 259, 264
Hayes, Christine, 40, 43
Hecht, Richard, 272
Hefner, Robert, 62
Hegel, G.W.F., 118, 140–1, 151–3, 161
Heidegger, Martin, 151, 153
Hinduism, 52–3, 55
History (capital "H"), 120
"history of religions", 18, 74
Hjelm, Titus, 154–5
Homilies, 11, 15–20, 39, 41, 54, 61

Horkheimer, Max, 139
Hughes, Aaron W., 3, 5, 180
Hughes, Jennifer Scheper, 84–5
Hulsether, Lucia, 188
humanities
    crisis of (see "academia"), 222, 263
    humanistic model, 115, 269
Hume, David, 49–53, 57
Husserl, Edmund, 151, 153, 155ff., 176, 203, 206–7, 210
hybrid
    as hyphenated categories, 11, 39, 52
    as clumsy, 39
    as intersection, 82
    market model, 195
Hypatia, 41–2

icons, 122ff
    as constructed, 123
identity, 10, 21, 41, 49, 55, 129, 140–1, 142, 156, 159, 164, 170, 246, 257
    as category, 10, 16, 19, 41
    as disciplinary, 274
    as non-empirical, 156ff.
India, 257, 264
Indian Residential schools, 27ff.
    and *Indian Residential Schools Settlement Agreement* (IRSSA), 27–30, 32
Indiana Jones, 221ff.
individuation, 166ff.
    as denaturalized, 188
    as discourse-dependent, 168
    matrices of, 169–71, 176, 187
    relativity of, 170
insider versus outsider, 74, 105, 226
International Association for the History of Religions (IAHR), 257, 271
Islam, 54–5, 61–2, 64–5, 108–9, 132–3
    Five Pillars of, 61–4, 66
    and Islamic studies, 62, 66
    "lived religion" and, 63–4, 66

Jacobsen, Douglas, 239
Jacobsen, Rhonda Hustedt, 239
Jaffee, Daniel, 195
Jameson, Frederic, 119–20, 124
Jerry Maguire, 228
"Jewish-Christianity", 11, 39, 41
Johnson, Robert David (KC), 277–8

John Templeton Foundation, 239
Journal of the American Academy of Religion (JAAR), 205, 237, 284, 286
Judaism, 10
    and ancient world, 10–11, 13, 15, 20, 40, 43

Kant, Immanuel, 48–9, 153
Kerry, John, 240–1
Keynes, John Maynard, 259
King, Rebekka, 235, 253
King, Richard, 249
Kitagawa, Joseph, 271–2
Klug, Petra, 111
Knott, Kim, 63
knowledge
    as constructed, 13, 45, 121, 163
    commodification of, 262
    ordering of, 10–11, 13, 21, 34, 38, 41, 43, 48, 52, 55, 57

labor
    academic, 222, 227, 230–1
    and class privilege/prestige, 225, 227
    contingent, 187, 205, 225, 229, 232, 235, 260, 262
language, 153, 162ff.
    and "play", 202, 204, 209, 212
    as constitutive, 164, 204
    as essentialist, 43
    as normative, 136
    as self-referential, 202, 204
    as signification, 209–10
    correspondence theory of, 209
    dependent on categories, 13
    extra-linguistic reality, 154–5, 163, 169
    field of, 211
    ideality of, 160–3
    language games, 49
    linguistic Berkeleyanism, 154–5, 188
    linguistic dualism, 154–5. 188
    linguistic Kantian, 154–5, 170
law and governance, 106–10, 128, 131–3, 241
Lawlor, Leonard, 163
Lease, Gary, 75
Lee, Lois, 110
Lee, Oliver, 230–1

Levi-Strauss, Claude, 208, 209, 212
   and "bricolage", 212
Lily Endowment, 239
Lincoln, Bruce, 74, 180, 232, 241, 275
"lived religion", 63, 81, 76, 138, 268
Lofton, Kathryn, 121-4
Lorde, Audre, 45
LoRusso, James Dennis, 232
Lyon, Sarah, 195

Mack, Burton, 286
Marrati, Paola, 163
Martin, Craig, 172, 175-6, 180-1, 183, 185, 187-9, 192, 196, 202-3, 205ff., 240, 246
Martin, Luther, 256
Marx, Karl, 194, 198, 212
Marxism, 109, 118, 120, 197
   commodity fetishism, 197-9
   discourses of, 120
   neo-Marxism, 117, 242
Masuzawa, Tomoko, 76, 123-4
"material religion" (see also "lived religion"), 50, 80ff., 109, 110, 121, 128, 138
   and objects, 80, 85, 102, 110, 124, 197
   as phenomenology rebranded (see "phenomenology"), 101, 110
   excess of materiality, 116, 138, 143
   material Turn (see "scholarship"), 80, 88, 101-2
   materiality as access to "the real", 86
   "new materialism", 101, 108
Material Religion (journal), 81-2, 101, 110
McCloskey, Dierdre, 264
McCutcheon, Russell T., 5, 9, 52, 73, 76, 101, 109, 131, 178, 180, 187, 205, 227, 232, 258, 285
method and theory (see "method/methodology" and "theory")
method/methodology, 89-91, 137-8
   "native" methodologies, 40
   as category, 73ff., 109-11, 138-9, 151ff., 175, 285, 287
   as curricular focus, 186, 252, 273
Middle Tennessee State University, 247, 250-1, 253
Miller, Patricia Cox, 86
Mindhunter (see "serial killers"), 183, 189

Mintz, Sidney W., 193
Moberg, Mark, 195
Muhammad, Prophet, 62
Müller, Max, 82
Murphy, Anne, 57
Msyterium tremendum et fascinans, 85
   as *mysterium materiae*, 85
mysticism, 13-4
myth, 52, 178, 213, 225, 227-8, 232, 237, 257
   as fabrication, 224
   myth-making, 180

narrativization (as scholarly practice), 15, 17, 33-4, 39-40, 50, 54, 57, 123, 175
   as genealogy (see "genealogy"), 18, 208
natural sciences/STEM, 238, 260
negative dialectics, 137ff.
   as critical approach, 141
Nelson, Cary, 270
neoliberalism, 122, 194, 256, 258-60
Neusner, Jacob, 43
Newton, Richard, 243
Niditch, Susan, 86
Nietzsche, Friedrich, 202, 213
Nongbri, Brent, 9, 11, 14-15, 21, 42, 52, 76, 130
nonreligion, 104, 110
normation, 104-6, 109
   versus normalization, 105
North American Association for the Study of Religion (NAASR), 2-3, 6, 61, 75, 151, 204-6, 235, 241, 243, 256-8, 283

Oberoi, Harjot, 54-5
objection, 74
objects
   as agentive (see "material religion"), 85-6, 101-2
   as analytical classification, 74, 82-3, 89-91, 137-8, 142-3, 154, 176, 197
   as ancient artifacts, 175-7
   as faculty (see "academia"), 160, 207
   as manifestation of the sacred, 80ff., 102
   as "thing-in-itself", 157-8, 164, 166, 176, 196
   comparison of, 116
   excess of, 116, 138, 143, 157
   identity as non-empirical, 156ff.

object-oriented ontology, 86, 139
Omer, Atalia, 33
Ophir, Adi, 20
Oppenheimer, J. Robert, 237
Ordine, Nuccio, 264
origins, 55, 86
    as type of argument, 9ff., 85–6, 89, 179, 184
    word-origin studies, 89, 143
"Origins of Geometry" (Husserl), 158–60, 162–5
Orsi, Robert A., 80, 85, 87, 268–9
Otto, Rudolph, 85–8, 115, 236, 265

Pakistan, 54, 64
Panarion, 11, 39, 61
pattern
    as hermeneutical, 3
    as selective, 17
pedagogy, 114, 235, 243
    and assessment, 235
    and competency-based models, 252
    student–scholar collaboration, 236, 279–81
phenomenology, 154ff.
    as scholarly method, 88–89, 101, 110, 248
    phenomenological consciousness, 155–6, 160–1, 163, 165, 197, 207
    phenomenological experience, 154ff.
    quasi-phenomenological method, 84, 89
    religion as self-evident, 4
Plate, S. Brent, 83–4
pluralism, 105, 131, 188, 241
    as conceptual, 170
politics, 2, 5, 42, 50, 57, 66, 105, 106, 127, 178, 195, 273
postmodernism, 118, 202
poststructuralism, 151, 154, 172, 202, 213
power
    as disciplinary, 105
    structures of, 104, 110, 136, 183, 185, 200, 227, 276–7
Prent, Mieke, 178
private versus public, 50, 104, 107, 118, 129
protention, 156
Protestantism
    as bias in scholarship, 129
    Protestant Reformation, 9

privilege, 227
Putnam, Hilary, 151, 170
Pseudo-Clementine, 11, 15–20, 39, 41, 48, 54, 61

"quit lit" (see "academia"), 228ff.
    religious language of, 231

Raiders of the Lost Ark (see "Indiana Jones")
realism (see also "anti-realism"), 152ff., 176, 183, 187, 206
    discourse of, 185
    philosophical realism, 153
Reed, Annette Yoshiko, 27, 33–4, 38, 40, 42–3, 45, 48–52, 54, 57, 62, 66
religion
    as *a priori*, 48–9
    as anachronism, 9, 11–14, 21, 61
    as category (see also: "classification," "category," "taxonomy"), 9–16, 21, 33, 48–51, 53, 56–7, 66, 76, 102, 119, 129–30, 132, 178, 199, 204
    as discipline, 12, 15, 44, 110–11
    as identity, 56
    as natural, 9
    as opium of scholar, 192, 196ff.
    as politically recognized, 57, 131
    as product of colonialism (see "colonialism"), 53
    as scholarly creation (see "Smith, Jonathan Z."), 4, 16, 52, 76, 79, 132, 183, 186, 198–9, 251, 258
    as self-evident phenomenon (see "phenomenology"), 4, 84
    as subjective experience, 86–8
    as *sui generis*, 102, 250
    as universal, 9, 11, 14, 268
    definition of, 50, 66, 128
    etymology of, 77
    theory of, 2
religious studies, 9, 102, 110–11, 130, 242, 259, 286
    as analytical classification, 75, 78, 274
    as religion, 186
    as social formation, 74–5, 78
    Christo-centric history of, 78
    field versus discipline, 9–11, 74, 145, 205, 210, 213, 236, 246, 267, 270, 272–3

Religionswissenschaft, 82
   scope of, 74
   value of, 260ff.
Religious Studies News, 285
retention, 156
rhetoric (see "Language")
Rives, James, 10
Roberts, Martha Smith, 190
Roman Empire, 10, 12–3
Roseberry, William, 194
Rosen-Zvi, Ishay, 20
Rousseau, Jean-Jacques, 153, 211–3

Saler, Benson, 50, 77
Schiappa, Edward, 167–9, 185
Schleiermacher, Friedrich, 103, 108
scholarship
   act of (as practice), 3, 11, 63, 115, 151ff., 176, 189, 237
   as objective, 1
   as political, 3
   as selective, 19, 63
   as self-conscious, 3, 17, 114, 120, 180–1, 183, 187–9
   as unstable, 3
   material turn (see "material religion"), 81, 101
   linguistic turn (see "language"), 81, 153
   Scholarship of Teaching and Learning (SoTL) (see "academia"; see also "pedagogy"), 236–9, 242
   "Value-free", 3, 264
Schmeiser, Peggy, 134
scholars, 5, 176–9, 221–2
   as practitioners (see "collegiality"), 269
   discursive construction of, 183–4, 246
Schott, Jeremy, 10
Schwartzman, Micah, 132
Scott, Joan W., 120
Searle, John R., 169
Selby, Jennifer, 67
serial killers, 183–4
Sessions, Jeff, 287
Shulman, Lee, 239
Sikhism, 53–4, 55–8
Slingerland, Edward, 76, 154
Smart, Ninian, 104, 271
Smith, Jonathan Z., 4–6, 9, 44, 51, 76, 115–7, 120, 132, 180, 183, 186, 198, 258

Smith, Leslie Dorrough, 250
Smith, Wilfred Cantwell, 9, 11, 15, 76, 271
soap, 121–2
Soboslai, John, 58
social constructionism, 5
Spivak, Gayatri Chakravorty, 42, 110, 153
Stack, Trevor, 131
Stanton, Elizabeth Cady, 108
Stevens, Wallace, 133–4
Stewart, Adam, 259, 264
Stoddard, Brad, 239
subjects, 5, 136ff.
   experiencing subject, 84
subjectivity, 84, 86–8, 122, 137, 141–2
   hegemony of, 140
   subjective reason, 140
substruction, 158–9, 164, 166, 168
Sullivan, Brenton, 76
Sullivan, Winnifred, 131
surprise, as analytical concept, 79ff., 115ff., 120–1, 124

Tafjord, Bjørn Ola, 31
taxonomy (see "classification"), 10–11, 31, 48, 54, 184
   as hybrid (see also "hybrid"), 11
   as "natural", 61
   synchrony of creation and discovery, 183–4, 189
   systems of, 19
Tebbe, Nelson, 132
Templeton Foundation (see "John Templeton Foundation")
Tennessee Higher Education Commission, 247
theology
   as scholarly approach, 4, 10, 40
   theological discourse, 141
   ontotheological, 136, 139
theory
   as analytical classification, 118
   as a type of definition
   as curricular focus
   as "lens", 170, 180
Thomassen, Einar, 43
Tong, M. Adryael, 46
Touna, Vaia, 181
tradition (religious, or academic specialty), 51, 53–5, 58, 64, 86–7, 121, 130–1, 161

discourses of, 175–6
   of scholarship, 66–80, 188
Trigg, Joseph, 43
Truth and Reconciliation Commission of
   Canada (TRC), 27–33
*Truth and Reconciliation Commission of
   Canada: Calls to Action*, 29
   Tuvel, Rebecca, 41
Tweed, Thomas, 74
Tylor, Edward Burnett, 103

unity, 57, 156
   as manufactured, 78

van Beek, Gosewijn, 86
Vásquez, Manuel A., 154
violence, 28
   as religiously motivated, 108
   of homogenization, 34
Voice and Phenomenon, 151, 155
von Stuckrad, Kocku, 151

Walker, Peter W. L., 43
Watt, Stephen, 270
Westerhoff, Jan, 151
wetlands, 167–9, 171, 185
White, Hayden, 3, 179–80, 235
White, Holly, 124
Wiebe, Donald, 50, 205–6
Wittgenstein, Ludwig, 49
witnessing (as Canadian Indigenous term),
   28–31, 33–4
Wolf, Eric, 199
Wolfson, Eliot R., 136, 143
word-origin studies, 89, 143
world religions paradigm, 62, 129, 249
work (see "labor")
Wright, Lucas, 144

Zerubavel, Eviatar, 15
Žižek, Slavoj, 197